RESEARCH IN SOCIAL MOVEMENTS, CONFLICTS AND CHANGE

RESEARCH IN SOCIAL MOVEMENTS, CONFLICTS AND CHANGE

Series Editor: Patrick G. Coy

Recent Volumes:

RESEARCH IN SOCIAL MOVEMENTS, CONFLICTS AND CHANGE   VOLUME 38

RESEARCH IN SOCIAL MOVEMENTS, CONFLICTS AND CHANGE

EDITED BY

PATRICK G. COY

Center for Applied Conflict Management,
Kent State University, Kent, OH, USA

Emerald

United Kingdom – North America – Japan
India – Malaysia – China

Emerald Group Publishing Limited
Howard House, Wagon Lane, Bingley BD16 1WA, UK

First edition 2015

Copyright © 2015 Emerald Group Publishing Limited

Reprints and permissions service
Contact: permissions@emeraldinsight.com

British Library Cataloguing in Publication Data
A catalogue record for this book is available from the British Library

ISBN: 978-1-78560-359-4
ISSN: 0163-786X (Series)

ISOQAR certified
Management System,
awarded to Emerald
for adherence to
Environmental
standard
ISO 14001:2004.

Certificate Number 1985
ISO 14001

INVESTOR IN PEOPLE

CONTENTS

SECTION I
MESO-LEVEL, INTRA-MOVEMENT ANALYSES –
THE DYNAMICS OF MOVEMENT FIELDS

SECTION II
RELIGION AND ATHEISM IN SOCIAL MOVEMENTS

SECTION III
MOVEMENT OUTCOMES AND ABEYANCE

LIST OF CONTRIBUTORS

Soma Chaudhuri	Department of Sociology and School of Criminal Justice, Michigan State University, East Lansing, MI, USA
Patrick G. Coy	Center for Applied Conflict Management, Kent State University, Kent, OH, USA
Carol L. Glasser	Department of Sociology and Corrections, Minnesota State University, Mankato, Mankato, MN, USA
Katja M. Guenther	Department of Gender and Sexuality Studies, University of California, Riverside, Riverside, CA, USA
Howard Lune	Department of Sociology, Hunter College, City University of New York, New York, NY, USA
Kelly Birch Maginot	Department of Sociology, Michigan State University, East Lansing, MI, USA
Kerry Mulligan	Interdisciplinary Studies Department, The Sage Colleges, Albany, NY, USA
Sharon S. Oselin	Department of Sociology, University of California, Riverside, Riverside, CA, USA
Christie L. Parris	Department of Sociology, Oberlin College, Oberlin, OH, USA
Natasha Radojcic	Department of Sociology, University of California, Riverside, Riverside, CA, USA
Belinda Robnett	Department of Sociology, University of California, Irvine, Irvine, CA, USA

Heather L. Scheuerman   Department of Justice Studies, James
                          Madison University, Harrisonburg,
                          VA, USA

Mangala Subramaniam   Department of Sociology, Purdue
                          University, West Lafayette, IN, USA

Elizabeth Tompkins   Department of Peace and Conflict
                          Research, Uppsala University, Uppsala,
                          Sweden

Rebecca Trammell   Department of Criminal Justice and
                          Criminology, Metropolitan State
                          University of Denver, Denver, CO, USA

Celia Valiente   Department of Social Sciences,
                          Universidad Carlos III de Madrid, Getafe,
                          Madrid, Spain

Beth Williford   Department of Sociology and
                          Anthropology, Manhattanville College,
                          Purchase, NY, USA

INTRODUCTION

There are many ways to meaningfully define and describe the work of social movements. Key dimensions of viable definitions include understanding that social movements are collective activities that are organized over time, that use contentious challenges and a repertoire of tactics aimed at bringing about social, political and also cultural changes, and that operate at least partly outside of the traditional institutionalized avenues of politics and policy-making, even while sometimes simply extending those avenues.

While social movements do not aim only at authorities and the various social, political, and cultural structures, practices, and policies associated with them, authority is nonetheless frequently targeted. It is also true that authority must be broadly understood, as was demonstrated so well by the cutting-edge papers included in Volume 25 of this *Research in Social Movements, Conflicts and Change* series, entitled *Authority in Contention* and edited by Daniel J. Myers and Daniel M. Cress in 2004. Such a corrective was necessary due to the fact that in its early decades significant parts of the social movements literature focused on activists who were targeting a state, its leaders, and its policies. While much was profitably learned from this approach, this state-centric orientation has thankfully been challenged in recent years by a plethora of solid research projects that understand the field of social movement action to go far beyond a state or even multiple states.

This welcome refocusing of the research lens is due, in part, to the fact that various globalization forces that social movements were increasingly responded to made it incumbent on researchers to look beyond a state-centric or even authority-based model of analysis. World economic forces that include both people and capital flowing easily across borders, the so-called neoliberal structural adjustment policies, the rise and proliferation of transnational corporations, and the passage of various self-styled free trade pacts have all been part of a trend that has also impacted social movements and how they organize. Revolutions in information technologies have also contributed significantly to these and other shifts in social movement practice (Earl, 2013).

The reality is that social movements come in a variety of shapes and sizes. They are marked by as wide of a range of topics that they focus upon as they are in the tone and the tenor that they take to organizing on their varying issues. They evince diversity in strategies and in the tactics deployed to operationalize their strategies. Some movements and their organizations are exceptionally focused on local issues while others hone in on the regional dimensions of an issue and still others organize primarily nationally. In addition, increasingly more movements now organize trans-nationally, for reasons already mentioned.

As a result of this diversity, context matters analytically. We simply cannot make much headway in developing sophisticated understandings about how and why social movements and their organizations operate as they do unless we pay particular attention to the various contexts within which the movement operates. It is also true that context does not simply refer to the cultural, social, and political conditions surrounding a movement and its organizations. It includes attending in an analytically rich manner to the ways that movements, their organizations, and their actors relate to each other within the broader field of action.

The importance of attending to context and how social movement actors relate to each other within the field of action is magnified further still when dealing with movements that operate transnationally. Thankfully, this volume opens with a section of five papers that help us make headway on the difficult set of problems associated with intra-movement dynamics.

We begin with Howard Lune's analyses of the US-based Fenian Brotherhood that operated transnationally in the middle reaches of the 19th century, laboring for Ireland's independence from Great Britain, including by trying to bring about an armed rebellion. Lune's rich historical research on the rise and fall of the Fenian Brotherhood makes clear that social movements and their organizations operated transnationally in quite significant ways long before some of the recent globalization forces discussed above appeared on the world scene late in the 20th century. This work suggests that historical transnationalism actually shares a goodly number of qualities with cotemporary transnationalism, including not being tied to a state or territory. Lune convincingly demonstrates that transnational movements often involve deterritorialization, and that Irish nationalism even in this early period was deterritorialized, as per the work of the American Fenians in influencing revolutionary actions in an occupied Ireland.

Lune's research is based on content and thematic analysis of wide-ranging primary archival documents, memoirs, conference proceedings, correspondence, and meeting minutes, as well as historical secondary sources. Adopting the analytical framework of strategic action fields, the author focuses in part on meso-level analysis, examining how the Fenian Brotherhood vied for strategic advantage vis-à-vis other national and transnational actors within the field of the Irish independence movement. A strategic action field is a "constructed meso-level social order in which actors (who can be individual or collective) are attuned to and interact with one another on the basis of shared (which is not to say consensual) understandings about the purposes of the field, relationships to others in the field (including who has power and why), and the rules governing legitimate action in the field" (Fligstein & McAdam, 2011, p. 9). Lune suggests that the Fenians were able to significantly influence national discourses and vied for influence and control of the independence movement with other actors based in Ireland, including the closely allied but still competitive Irish Republican Brotherhood. Yet as he also shows, their inability to control the strategic action field was a salient factor in their ultimate demise. This is important research for a number of reasons, including because it takes the relatively new theoretical framework of strategic action fields and shows the analytical utility of applying it to historical movements from the middle 1900s, as well as transnationally.

Continuing with the meso-sociological level of analysis, while also bringing it into the contemporary world, is our second paper by Beth Williford and Mangala Subramaniam. They adopt both a two-sited and a network analysis approach to examine a geo-specific transnational field and the complicated transnational power dynamics that play out on the meso-level within the network when it comes to framing its messages to the public. They ask what frames are deployed transnationally by US-based organizations working with indigenous groups in the Global South? How are these frames alike or different from those originating by the indigenous themselves, and why are they similar or different?

The paper is based on ethnographic research, document analyses, and in-depth interviews with leaders and members from nine Ecuadorian and US organizations that make up a network focused on issues associated with resistance to neoliberal structural adjustment policies and the political economy of oil development in Ecuador. The authors build on past work by Jackie Smith, Margaret Keck, Kathryn Sikkink, and Sydney Tarrow, but go beyond it to describe the power dynamics and circumstances when a particular indigenous-generated frame may be used, adopted as-is, or altered by the transnational network. Significantly, by identifying and analyzing local-level frames originating with the indigenous that were adopted unchanged and deployed at various levels by their US counterparts, this paper suggests that the too common presumption of power flowing from the North to the South in a dominating fashion within a transnational field or network needs to be rethought.

While social movements research has often reduced movements to being either unified or polarized between only radical or moderate factions, Belinda Robnett, Carol L. Glasser, and Rebecca Trammell ask in our third chapter whether the relationships between radical, moderate, and conservative organizations within a movement impact that movement variously during different movement waves or cycles of contention. As part of their ambitious inquiry, they also focus more specifically on the influences that a movement's radical flank may have during waves of contention and the degrees to which those impacts are productive or harmful. In so doing, they extend and contribute to the themes examined in the first two papers, that is, how movement organizations relate to each other across and within a field of action.

These authors offer a set of detailed comparative analyses of the complex and shifting inter-organizational dynamics that played out within three US-based movements: the civil rights movement, the animal rights movement, and the AIDS movement. The data include five civil rights organizations, three AIDS movement organizations, and four animal rights organizations. They rely on primary and secondary data as well as interviews, analyzing the data by coding it thematically.

Applying Downey and Rohlinger's field perspective and their useful conceptual framework of "strategic articulation" or the "overall distribution of actors across a movement and the nature and extent of linkages among them" (2008, p. 1), our authors generate a series of hypotheses about the nature of the relationships between the radical, moderate, and conservative aspects of a movement during differing cycles of protest. Importantly, they first offer a careful and detailed classification schema for characterizing any organization as belonging to the radical, moderate, or conservative factions. It is a schematic that future researchers will find helpful as it includes an assessment of organizational goals, strategic orientations, tactical choices, degrees of state inclusion, and public perceptions. The findings will undoubtedly influence going forward how we conceive of movement flanks and how we think about the relationships among the various flanks of a movement at different moments in the life cycle of that movement.

Only in recent years have researchers begun building bridges between two literatures that have been too long separated and disconnected: social movements research and nonviolent studies (Coy, 2013). Theorizing and researching associated with the roles and impacts of radical flanks in social movements in general, on the one hand, and in nonviolent action campaigns more specifically, on the other, are one manifestation of what has been until recently a long-running problem. The fourth chapter, by Elizabeth Tompkins, is an example of corrective new work that bridges and contributes to both areas of study, even while extending this section's focus on intra-movement dynamics.

There is limited but growing empirical literature on radical flank effects in nonviolent action movements; most of it is tied to cases where the goal of the movement is to topple a government or an occupying power. Conducting a series of large-N regression analyses using the Nonviolent and Violence Campaigns and Outcomes (NAVCO) 2.0 data set, Tompkins builds on and also extends in significant new ways this previous research on radical flank effects in such cases. One of the many novel contributions Tompkins makes is rooted in the fact that she defines radical flanks as intra-movement violent organizations (as opposed to all contemporaneous violent groups associated with a case). Equally important is the fact that she uses campaign years as her unit of analysis instead of the entire campaign period. This allows a more precise operationalization of the impacts that violent radical flanks may have than in previous studies; significantly, this includes their immediate, within-year impacts – both negative and positive. For example, this paper finds surprising – and perhaps disquieting – evidence that intra-movement radical flanks that use violence are often associated with progress toward an otherwise largely nonviolent movement's goals within the same year. This critically important finding builds new theory in nonviolent social movements research – an area of increasingly robust study. Future work in this area will no doubt engage deeply with Tompkins' paper, and she appropriately makes useful suggestions for any subsequent investigations.

The fifth and final paper in this opening section continues the meso-level focus of the section by examining how recent SlutWalk campaigns in three North American cities negotiated the complicated terrain of internal criticisms – from within their larger movement field – of the framing strategies used by the campaigns. SlutWalk emerged in 2011 in response to a spate of instances of high-profile rape and sexual assaults against women that were accompanied by equally high-profile victim blaming, including by politicians. Based on qualitative analysis of online sources including websites, blogs, Facebook postings, Twitter feeds, and 24 interviews, Kelly Birch Maginot and Soma Chaudhuri analyze the evolving use of the word "slut" and a variety of other sexuality-related issues reflected in the campaign's framing. They first situate SlutWalk within the history of anti-rape activism and then extend McCammon's (2012) concept of strategic adaptation by showing how campaign organizers initially responded to internal criticisms from some feminists and women of color about their "slut celebration" frames. The authors carefully demonstrate how the organizers responded to these internal critiques by repeatedly emphasizing their view that slut can indeed be a unifying concept for women. The authors demonstrate how the failure of this approach and the continuing criticism from within aspects of the larger feminist movement eventually led to a strategic adaptation away from the slut celebration frames and toward more "pro-sex, pro-consent" frames that still emphasized women's agency.

This volume's second section contains two papers paired together as opposite sides of the same coin: religiously motivated activism and atheist-motivated activism. We know quite a bit about mobilization issues, that is, the factors that tend to influence why and how individuals become active in social movements and protest activities. However, we know significantly less about the variables that impact whether an activist will sustain the commitment and remain as an engaged participant over time. One piece of that puzzle, the roles of community context in sustained activism, remains particularly under-studied.

The US war in Iraq − now the longest war in US history having begun with the US invasion in 2003 and which continues in 2015 as I write − provides Sharon S. Oselin with an opportunity to shed a data-driven light on this key question. She examines the cultural and social mechanisms in a religious retirement community in California that foster and contribute to very high levels of ongoing participation over a decade-long period of weekly anti-Iraq War protests. Interviewing 14 participants at two different points in time allows Oselin to map both the cultural and social mechanisms that foster long-term, persistent participation in protest events. She argues these include a sense of spiritual and moral duty, shared beliefs in the necessity of service on behalf of others, emotional connections with fellow participants, accountability to the group and to fulfilling tasks, and intersecting personal and social spheres. She additionally finds that a value-based collective identity as opposed to an organizational identity is a key ingredient in what sustains commitment to each other and their shared protest project. An additional reason why Oselin's work merits attention from social movement scholars is that as the post-WWII population boom ages and retires, this demographic will have uncommon degrees of biographical and situational availability for activism, whether motivated by spiritual or religious beliefs, or not.

While we know that it is not only religious beliefs or sensibilities that contribute significantly to mobilization, we have not much studied how the other side of the belief coin, atheism, impacts the complicated dynamics of movement participation. Despite the claims of many Christian conservatives in the country, the United States has strong roots in secularism. But over the past 15 years or more, the New Atheism movement has become a social and cultural force as it broke from even secularism and encouraged non-believers to proudly come out as atheist and promoted overtly atheist activism on a range of social, cultural, and political issues. Nonetheless, atheism remains a hard-sell in the United States and one of the ways that the New Atheist movement has dealt with that is through the use of humor in its activism, according to Katja M. Guenther, Natasha Radojcic, and Kerry Mulligan. They conducted three years of ethnographic field research in the New Atheist movement, interviewed 51 members, and analyzed movement documents. They argue that humor helps build collective identity, assists in the management of stigma too often assigned to atheists, and is central to establishing boundaries for this social movement. Atheists also apparently use humor to mock and deflect the critical claims and frequent attacks upon them. Given the prominence of humor in this and other stigmatized identity movements, this paper creates a foundation for future theory-building.

In our final section we investigate movement policy success in democratic states and the dynamics of abeyance for movements in non-democracies. One of the ongoing areas of critically important inquiry is understanding whether, under what conditions, and how social movements actually impact the passage of policies. Are movements successful in what is often one of their central goals? Despite substantial work having been done on this and related issues, here is a question that continues to haunt activists and researchers alike.

Christie L. Parris and Heather L. Scheuerman zero in on identifying what factors lead to the passage in the 50 US states of hate crime statutes that recognize sexual orientation as a protected status. Constructing a unique and impressive longitudinal data set and using event history analysis, they may be the first to show how social movement organizations (SMOs) and political context affect the state-level adoption of anti-gay hate crime policy longitudinally. Controlling for cultural opportunities and structural conditions, they find that three main factors affect state-level policy passage: political instability, government ideology, and the combination of a strong SMO presence with a strong presence of democrats in the state legislature.

We have known for a long time that some movements have life-cycles of a sort: waxing and waning, peaking and going into abeyance and sometimes rising again. The notion that there are discernible and conceptually meaningful series of waves associated with the women's movement is rooted in these dynamics. However, the abeyance concept as it has been applied to social movements has its origins in democratic and somewhat open political settings. Celia Valiente's case study of the women's movement in Franco's Spain across four decades from the 1930s through 1975 investigates movement abeyance issues in a non-democratic setting. Based on document analysis and 17 interviews, it is an innovative paper that suggests that the transmission of movement-related knowledge between mobilization waves is especially important for movements in abeyance. Since activists from earlier waves are often not present in authoritarian political settings, Valiente's research indicates that the perseveration of the critically important memories and the transmission of knowledge so necessary to nurture and inform subsequent waves are carried out through other cultural activities of movements. An earlier version of this paper won the Best Paper Award from the Women and Politics Research Section of the American Political Science Association.

Although I have served as the overall Series Editor for *Research in Social Movements, Conflicts and Change* since 2000, this is now the 10th volume that I have had the pleasure to personally edit, owing to occasional guest Volume Editors. I remain deeply thankful for the many peer referees who give so selflessly of their time and whose constructive reviews allow us to continue to publish top-level, data-driven research in the areas reflected in the series title. RSMCC was founded in 1977 by Louis Kriesberg of Syracuse University, the Maxwell Professor Emeritus of Social Conflict Studies, Professor Emeritus of Sociology, and founding director of the Program for the Advancement of Research on Conflict and Collaboration (PARCC). Lou presciently envisioned a research series that crossed-over and connected literatures in social movements, conflict resolution, and social and political change. I've tried to maintain that focus over the past 15 years and intend to keep doing so going forward.

This volume was aided immeasurably by the astute editorial assistance of Lana Mobydeen, J.D. Following my initial editorial review of the 53 submissions received for this volume, Lana shepherded the remaining through the RSMCC double-blind review process and assisted in readying the entire volume for submission to Emerald Group Publishing. She did all this with a remarkably careful attention to detail, and the gracious spirit that always marks her personality. Thank you, Lana.

Patrick G. Coy
Editor

REFERENCES

Coy, P. G. (2013). Whither nonviolent studies? *Peace Review*, *25*(2), 257–265.

Downey, D. J., & Rohlinger, D. A. (2008). Linking strategic choice with macro-organizational dynamics: Strategy and social movement articulation. In P. G. Coy (Ed.), *Research in social movements, conflicts and change* (Vol. 28, pp. 3–38). Research in Social Movements, Conflicts and Change. Bingley, UK: Emerald Group Publishing Limited.

Earl, J. (2013). Spreading the word or shaping the conversation: "Prosumption" in protest websites. In P. G. Coy (Ed.), *Research in social movements, conflicts and change* (Vol. 36, pp. 3–38). Research in Social Movements, Conflicts and Change. Bingley, UK: Emerald Group Publishing Limited.

Fligstein, N., & McAdam, D. (2011). Toward a general theory of strategic action fields. *Sociological Theory*, *29*, 1–26.

McCammon, H. (2012). *The U.S. women's Jury movements and strategic adaptation: A more just verdict*. New York, NY: Cambridge University Press.

Myers, D. J., & Cress, D. M. (2004). Introduction. In D. J. Myers & D. M. Cress (Eds.), *Authority in contention* (Vol. 25, pp. XI–XIV). Research in Social Movements, Conflicts and Change. Bingley, UK: Emerald Group Publishing Limited.

SECTION I
MESO-LEVEL, INTRA-MOVEMENT ANALYSES – THE DYNAMICS OF MOVEMENT FIELDS

TRANSNATIONAL NATIONALISM: STRATEGIC ACTION FIELDS AND THE ORGANIZATION OF THE FENIAN MOVEMENT

Howard Lune

ABSTRACT

How do transnational social movements organize? Specifically, this paper asks how an organized community can lead a nationalist movement from outside the nation. Applying the analytic perspective of Strategic Action Fields, this study identifies multiple attributes of transnational organizing through which expatriate communities may go beyond extra-national supporting roles to actually create and direct a national campaign. Reexamining the rise and fall of the Fenian Brotherhood in the mid-nineteenth century, which attempted to organize a transnational revolutionary movement for Ireland's independence from Great Britain, reveals the strengths and limitations of nationalist organizing through the construction of a Transnational Strategic Action Field (TSAF). Deterritorialized organizing allows challenger organizations to propagate an activist agenda and to dominate the nationalist discourse among co-nationals while raising new challenges concerning coordination, control, and relative position among multiple centers of action across national

Research in Social Movements, Conflicts and Change, Volume 38, 3–35
Copyright © 2015 by Emerald Group Publishing Limited
ISSN: 0163-786X/doi:10.1108/S0163-786X20150000038001

borders. Within the challenger field, "incumbent challengers" vie for dominance in agenda setting with other "challenger" challengers.

Keywords: Transnational strategic action field; organizations; social movement; revolution; Irish nationalism; Fenian Brotherhood

INTRODUCTION

Organized collective action requires three defining characteristics: that there is a collective actor; that they act on behalf of the collective; and that the action is organized. Each of these deceptively simple prerequisites, both as individual factors and in combination, has given rise to a wealth of research in studies of social movements (Benford & Snow, 2000; Diani, 2009), revolutions (Goodwin & Skocpol, 1989; Kurzman, 1996), organizations (Davis, McAdam, Scott, & Zald, 2005; Edwards & Marullo, 1995; Ferree & Martin, 1995), networks (Gould, 1995; Lune, 2007; Wang & Soule, 2012), culture (Auyero, 2002; Duany, 2000), and identity (Bernstein, 2005; Meyer, Whittier, & Robnett, 2002). The relatively recent interest in transnational collective action (Basch, Glick Schiller, & Szanton Blanc, 1994; Smith & Johnston, 2002) has added a new level of complexity to these issues, including the problems of defining transnational collective identities (Appadurai, 1996; Djuric, 2003; Tilly, 2007; Werbner, 2005), transnational action (Abdelrahman, 2011; della Porta, Kriesi, & Rucht, 1999; Keck & Sikkink, 1998; Tarrow, 2005), and transnational organizing (Diani, 2009; Smith & Wiest, 2005). In turn, this expansion of our repertoire of study reflects back on our original studies, requiring further consideration of our terms. Can organized collective action that targets a state operate transnationally? And if so, how?

The majority of studies of the origins and trajectories of collective action, social movements, or contentious politics are state-centered: a single state is both the primary target of activism for change and the heart of the political context in which the collective action occurs (McAdam, Tarrow, & Tilly, 2001; Meyer et al., 2002). International movements, on the other hand, seek to transcend specific states both in terms of targets and participants, linking their constituency by class (Hanagan, 2003), religion (Haynes, 2009; Liow, 2011), ethnicity (Hess, 2009), or other shared identity markers (Gamson, 1997). For the purposes of this study and in contrast to both national and international mobilizations, I define transnational collective action as those organized mobilizations that may target states or state-based policies in the traditional sense, but which are deterritorialized in physical and political environments. They have multiple centers of action, but these need not be coterminous with the state or states they target. The key feature of this definition is that the events in question are not national social movements with transnational support (Keck & Sikkink, 1998) but are themselves transnational in origin and action.

Organized transnational collective action implies, at the very least, multiple organizations with a base in each of more than one nation, and active links among them. Such action requires a field of organized actors whose collective purpose is unified is some way that transcends national boundaries. We would not, therefore, be able to analyze and understand the nature of the action without knowledge of the transnational field.

I adopt the concept of Strategic Action Fields (SAF) as a means to organize and analyze the pertinent components of transnational collective action. The SAF model centers on collective strategic action within a recognized field in which "collective actors ... vie for strategic advantage in and through interaction with other groups in what can be seen as meso-level social orders" (Fligstein & McAdam, 2011, p. 2). The social actors in a SAF may be small groups, corporate entities, local networks, or progressively larger collectives of related units, each organized within its own defined environment, and having identifiable constituent parts. These social orders are not determined by fixed criteria, but by a shared perception on the part of their participants, who "interact with knowledge of one another under a set of common understandings about the purposes of the field, the relationships in the field (including who has power and why), and the field's rules" (Fligstein & McAdam, 2011, p. 3).

Collective action within a SAF can take many forms. By intention, the focus of the model is on social order and social change. The model represents strategic action as the application of specific "social skills" that "induce cooperation" from others in the field (Fligstein, 2001). Such skills fall into three broad categories: cognitive, empathetic, and communicative. Social actors apply these skills in their exchanges within a field to construct, propagate, and institutionalize shared meanings and identities (Fligstein & McAdam, 2012, p. 18). Communicative skills in the hands of collective actors, such as organizations or movements, invoke "framing" processes (Benford & Snow, 2000). Collective actors engaged in contentious politics seek to frame their claims and issues in terms that resonate among potential supporters. Among allies and other co-participants, communicative contention more often entails "agenda setting," as various parties compete to define the proper responses to their shared concerns (Fligstein & McAdam, 2012, p. 51).

Skills are highly contextual and their applicability changes as conditions within or surrounding the field shift. In the SAF model, the social movement concept of political opportunities is supplanted by indicators of stability or instability in the field's structures and operating assumptions. Both organized action within a field and "exogenous shocks" in a field's environment can destabilize the relations on which a field depends. Skilled social actors, or social "entrepreneurs," may exploit these shocks as opportunities for strategic action and therefore trigger a realignment of social relations (Fligstein & McAdam, 2012, p. 84).

Strategic action within a field reflects attempts at "position-taking" by participants in order to reorient the flow of power at any given moment (Bourdieu, 1993, p. 30). Dominant "incumbents" struggle with "challengers" who wish to dislodge them, even as peers may struggle for relative advantage in certain exchanges. Many forms of action may indicate position-taking, including rhetorical ones. Contestation within a field may concern the interpretation of the field itself, encompassing questions of structure, action, or language, "social, cultural, or political identity," the nature of privilege or control, or the role of civil society under any given regime type (Touraine, 1985, p. 752). Nonetheless, as institutional theories on fields have suggested, fields develop widely shared "institutional logics" that serve to minimize internal contention and maintain stability (Scott, 2013).

As fields have no natural boundaries, this model suggests that a field structure could emerge that would relate to states and other institutions without being state-centered. This structure may be viewed as a network of groups and associations that share defining elements and have organized to take collective action. The model of incumbents and challengers requires neither incumbents to be states nor challengers to be revolutionaries. Nonetheless, as Goldstone and Useem (2012) point out, the ideal-type of this dynamic is that of a revolutionary movement within a nation. At the same time, the deterritorialization of the space of action in the field model suggests that the impetus for a national movement could come from outside the nation.

I test these implications through an examination of the rise and fall of the collective mobilization organized by the Fenian Brotherhood and its partner association, the Irish Republican Brotherhood, which sought to bring about an armed rebellion against British rule in Ireland in the mid-1800s. The Fenian movement has been extensively studied as part of the long line of Irish uprisings (Brown, 1966; Quinn, 2009), as the inheritor of a developing nationalism (Snay, 2004), as a lower-middle-class revolt

(Steward & McGovern, 2013), and as the basis for a developing transnational collective identity (Hanagan, 1998). Each of these analyses are valid, and along with biographical studies of the leaders of the various organizations, associations, and movements of the period, provide a detailed if sometimes inconsistent representation of the events. In this paper, I situate the organizing work of the focal associations within a transnational SAF. This perspective draws attention to specific factors that demonstrate (1) the transnational origins of the Fenian movement and (2) the unique opportunities and constraints that the movement faced due to these origins.

Transnational Strategic Action Fields

A considerable amount of study on present-day transnational social and economic behavior has shown that transnational links between migrants and their home communities are often defining aspects of their day to day lives (Levitt, 2001; Portes, Guarnizo, & Haller, 2002). Their connections are not incidental; their involvement is active and consequential. These ongoing connections distinguish transnational actors from those who have simply established new lives in a different location.

Relatedly, though less often studied, migrants and exiles engage in "political transnational practices" (Østergaard-Nielsen, 2003, p. 762). Following the definition offered by Portes (1999, p. 464) — wherein transnational activities are "those that take place on a recurrent basis across national borders and that require a regular and significant commitment of time by participants," — research reveals that in addition to easily measurable data such as economic remittances, such activities "include political, cultural and religious initiatives as well." Extra-national actors may act as co-ethnics either with or without the "regular and significant" involvement that characterizes transnational actors.

The conjunction of increasing globalization in all facets of social life with contemporary attempts to measure transnational political activity (Gilson, 2011; O'Neill, 2004) has encouraged a reconsideration of earlier cases of political organizing across state borders (Hanagan, 1998; Smith, 2003; Weber, 1999). Historical transnationalism shares many qualities with contemporary transnationalism, adjusting for differences in the nature of travel and communications. Much of what we know about earlier transnational activity, however, refers to cases of "transnationalism from above" (Guarnizo & Smith, 1998). Like national, ethnic, or religious diasporas, instances of transnationalism from above often involve sending states, churches, or other institutions supporting, encouraging, or at least working with expatriate communities on maintaining ties to the homeland. And while "identities forged 'from below' are not inherently subversive or counter-hegemonic" (Guarnizo & Smith, 1998, p. 23), the independent collective actions of transnational actors in relation to a distant nation have far more freedom to imagine communities differently. Such actors are far less limited by either their original states' hegemonic assumptions or direct application of power.

A politically defined field of action might contain many organized entities competing for power at many levels (Burstein, 1991). Likewise, when we turn our attention to inter-unit relations within policy domains or political fields, we find that "the state" is not a unitary entity. Various divisions, agencies, and/or bureaus have different interests and may work at cross purposes, much as any other stakeholder in the events (Lune, 2007; O'Neill, 2004). Therefore, while forms of strategic action within a SAF can be usefully understood as an interplay between challengers and incumbents, that perspective should not imply that certain participants, or even states, will permanently play either one role or the other, or that, within the same field, incumbents in one set of relations would not simultaneously be challengers, bystanders, or otherwise independent agents in another (Goldstone & Useem, 2012, p. 39).

Within any such fields, certain organizations dominate agenda setting or organizational relations. State agencies tend to be incumbent in political fields, though religious or other organizations may successfully challenge that position. In a social movement field, specific organizations may dominate the agenda setting of the challenger field. We can call such groups "incumbent challengers": who often come to represent the entire challenger field in the public imagination or analysis, though the extent and stability of their incumbency may be open to question. By extension, other movement groups or related associations may operate as challengers within the challenger field.

The SAF model proffers an organizational perspective on collective action that follows from, and builds upon, earlier uses of the term "field" and related concepts, including Bourdieu's (1993) "field of cultural production," the neo-institutionalist "organizational fields" (DiMaggio & Powell, 1983; Fligstein, 2001), social movement sectors (Meyer & Whittier, 1994; Tarrow, 1988), and much of the work on collective strategic action within interorganizational networks (Gould, 1995; Lune, 2007). Thus, we may find interacting social movement organizations acting with or against each other within what some have called a social movement field (Calhoun, 1993).

Each of these fields may be examined as its own SAF, or as a portion of a larger and distinct SAF. Applying this concept to transnational organizing for political change, we may consider the present study a case of a Transnational Strategic Action Field (TSAF). Building on the definitions adopted so far, a TSAF is a linked collection of social actors engaging in strategic — possibly political — action organized over time and across national borders that requires a significant commitment of time and resources. We would expect agents or agencies of at least one state would to participate in such a field, though that is not a definitional requirement.

DATA AND METHODS

This study examines the trajectory of the Fenian movement for Irish independence from 1856 to 1867. Although these events were led by two organizations — the Irish Republican Brotherhood (IRB) in Ireland and the Fenian Brotherhood (FB) in the United States — the two groups were embedded within their two national fields of action concerning Irish national identity. Furthermore, the two national fields joined in a transnational field of action that linked Ireland to America, and encompassed organized action in England, France, Australia, New Zealand, Canada, and parts of South America. The goal of this analysis is to establish the role of this transnational field in the rise and fall of the Fenian organizations. And while the independence movement existed in other forms both prior to and subsequent to the Fenian organization, this study is confined to the organizational endeavor that developed in the United States and Ireland.

As questions of nationalism, national independence, and citizenship were already matters of popular discourse in mid-nineteenth century Europe and the United States, this work uses a fairly straightforward operationalization for these concepts. An organization or association is counted as a nationalist group if: they refer to themselves as such; their founding documents or proclamations refer directly to improving, rescuing, building, or liberating the Irish nation; they define as their purpose opposing British rule in Ireland; or they explicitly act to support an uprising in Ireland against the British. The field of associations organized or reorganized by the Fenians in either the United States or Ireland to address the question of Irish independence is referred to here as the transnational Irish nationalist field. Irish or Irish-American associations that formed for other purposes, but which participated for a sustained period in activities organized by or around the Fenians, are considered part of the Irish nationalist SAF, but are not identified as nationalist associations in and of themselves. Both nationalist associations and non-nationalist groups occupied this field prior to the establishment of the two Fenian organizations.[1]

Data for this study come from the content analysis of archival sources produced by Irish and Irish-American organizations in the nineteenth century. The organizers and organizations of this transnational nationalist field left behind a wealth of archival material, including transatlantic letters, official directives, memoirs, published statements, conference proceedings, and copious accounting documents. Some of these have been edited and published; most are archived in research libraries. A trove of Fenian letters appear as appendices to Joseph Denieffe's Fenian memoir, many of which are referenced here. The primary analysis has entailed archival records pertaining to organizational mobilization and coordination. Sources include FB archives of correspondence, edicts, convention notes, and meeting minutes. Additional primary data come from memoirs and other published accounts written by participants, meeting minutes and related materials from non-movement organizations, and statements written to be published or circulated within the organizations of the field. Further sources include newspaper accounts, books and commentary by non-participants, and historical analyses from the time.

The content analysis of these materials proceeded thematically, first identifying key social actors (individuals, organizations, etc.), goals, and means. Secondly, text was coded for references to Irish identity, nation, nationalism, and their offshoots ("national heroes," "martyrs to the nation," etc.) The contours of the Irish nationalist field were therefore defined by the total set of groups and associations concerned with Irish national identity, who interacted in some manner (cooperatively or not) with others in the field. Subsequent readings identified indicators of relations within the field, including coordination, requests for resources or information, the movement of people, materials or funds, evidence of conflict, questions or discussions pertaining to goals, methods, collective identity, authorities, or other interorganizational or interpersonal relations. Some of the data concerning actual events or actions come from secondary sources, while primary sources addresses the varied perceptions of those events.

This analysis of the Fenian case examines the negotiations and roles among those organized in America and Ireland to challenge the existing power structure in Ireland. It does not give equal attention to the incumbent British administration or its supporters. For the sake of concision, I do not include actions organized outside of the two focal nations.

This paper proceeds in two sections. The first traces the rise of the transnational nationalist field through which the Fenian organizations operated. It attends to the organizational environment and organizing conditions under which the nationalist fields in Ireland and the United States took shape and began to overlap, culminating in the co-creation of two revolutionary associations dedicated to collaboratively bringing about the overthrow of British rule in Ireland.

The second section examines the collapse of these efforts. Much of this discussion recounts the internal organizational failures of the field, the contention among participants, and the inability to come to consensus over the leadership, goals, or strategies of the nationalist endeavor. This period also saw the emergence of a breakaway group that challenged the Fenian organization's leadership and disastrously sought to draw the United States into a war with Great Britain by means of an American Irish invasion of Canada.

FOUNDATIONS OF TWO FIELDS

If strategic action fields are ubiquitous enough to serve as the building blocks of social life, then we need to consider their origins. Prior work that led to the SAF model indicates that new fields generally emerge out of new combinations and offshoots of existing fields. Protest movements, for example, have been shown to emerge from combinations of already existing social change organizations, new associations, and established fields such as churches, colleges, and community groups (McAdam, 1982). Existing organizations in a shared field split off to undertake new efforts and/or combine with groups from nearby fields to establish new subfields. In turn, these subfields may outgrow their organizational origins to form new fields with independent trajectories (Lune, 2007). What, then, of the Irish nationalist field?

While the British governing presence in Ireland dates back to the twelfth century, the period of nineteenth century nationalist organizing had its roots in the failed United Irish uprising of 1798 and the subsequent Act of Union of 1800. This Act abolished the Irish parliament, giving the English parliament at Westminster legislative authority over Ireland's affairs. The British Crown then sought to suppress all collective activity for Irish

independence, suspending *Habeus Corpus*, blocking the rights to free association and free press, enacting ten laws forbidding the right to bear arms
(1831–1848) and four laws forbidding the swearing of oaths to private
societies (Fox, 1890). Moreover, the 1798 uprising suffered enormous
casualties, with its leaders either imprisoned or exiled (Foley, 1996,
pp. 37–38).

Many of those exiles wound up in the United States, then well populated
with Irish associations. There, free of British law and bolstered by
American hostility to British power, the new Irish émigrés memorialized
their recent struggle and shifted the discourse from a mostly charitable or
social focus to a more political one (Byrne, 1907; Emmet, 1915; MacNeven,
1807; Sampson & Taylor, 1832).[2] In David Wilson's summary, "the United
Irishmen … effectively took over Irish America, and remodeled it according to their own revolutionary democratic republican image" (1998, p. 3).

Over the next several decades, organized efforts to improve conditions
in Ireland, most notably those attached to the Catholic Association
(founded by Daniel O'Connell in 1823), were cautiously nationalistic but
did not openly challenge the legitimacy of British rule. O'Connell was an
innovative movement leader, and his association and its offshoots grew
throughout Ireland (McGraw & Wheelan, 2005); affiliate organizations
sprang up in the United States as well. Despite ongoing tensions between
O'Connell and his American supporters (Murphy, 2007), the American
Irish provided considerable support to the cause (Stephens & Ramon,
2008, p. *xvii*). With the passage of Catholic relief measures in Ireland in
1829, Irish Catholics on both sides of the Atlantic celebrated and
O'Connell became known as "the Liberator." The success of this long
national campaign fed calls for a more ambitious one to repeal the Act of
Union, and reinstate an Irish parliament. In response, in 1840 O'Connell
formed a Precursor Association to address the question, and then a
national Repeal Association to lead the charge. Once again, his campaign
looked to the many affiliate societies organized in the United States for
support. While this campaign was less unified, less well fought, more
actively suppressed, and ultimately unsuccessful (Duffy, 1880), O'Connell's
efforts nonetheless attracted dozens of new American Irish associations
into the nationalist field. Although O'Connell was committed to institutional politics, his nationalist mobilization reached adherents of many
forms of action, and thus the repeal movement greatly broadened the organizational foundation of both Irish and U.S. nationalist fields.

Organizational fields grow in numbers by absorbing existing groups,
and in breadth, in part, by dividing into new sites of action (Lune, 2007).

In this regard, both the expansion and the collapse of the repeal movement strengthened the nationalist fields. In its growth, O'Connell's association was the unquestioned incumbent, and the focal point for most action and debate. By the time of O'Connell's death in 1847, repeal efforts in Ireland had splintered; a new, more radical movement (Young Ireland) split from the ranks of the Repeal Association. Without O'Connell, the Repeal Association continued to fade in importance, and the Young Ireland challengers moved to the center. They and their successors maintained four centers of action: Ireland, England, France, and the United States. By 1847, the Young Irelanders further expanded the nationalist field through their Irish Confederation, a decentralized network of Irish clubs and societies officially dedicated to "discussing" the question of national identity. Confederate clubs formed quickly throughout Ireland and spread to England and the United States, where more than two million Irish émigrés now lived; entire associations were recruited into this growing network.

By 1848, the Irish nationalist field in Ireland included all that remained of the repeal movement, an extensive network of Confederate Clubs, several prominent political newspapers, various Catholic organizations, international Chartists, and an assortment of historical and literary societies dedicated to the spirit of 1798. It was a disparate group, with regular membership overlaps, shared histories, and considerable awareness of one another; a stable, if fluid field. But it was not a centralized body. Many repealers remained attached to O'Connell's methods, while the Confederate Clubs and Young Irelanders would not repudiate the potential for a physical force uprising. Some went further, including John Mitchel, who used his position editing *The Nation* and, later, writing for *The United Irishman* to argue that force was the only path to freedom (Jenkins, 2008, p. 12). The predictable lack of unity concerning means and targets reveals the dynamics of the debates within the field but should not hide the degree of consensus among nationalists. Proclaiming that Ireland still was not free, the Young Ireland movement now defined, but did not lead, the nationalist field.

In the United States, a field of more than a dozen charitable associations, principally in Boston, New York, and Philadelphia but also extending west and south, organized alongside of a host of repeal societies, nationalist Catholic associations, emigrant associations, and Irish clubs, such as the Shamrock Friendly Association (New York, 1816) and the Friends of Ireland and of Civil and Religious Liberty (Paterson, New Jersey, 1828). The American Irish were organized, somewhat nationalistic, and ambivalent about the use of physical force. They were also less wedded to O'Connell's leadership, as his powerful attacks on American slavery had alienated many of his supporters (Loyal National Repeal Association, 1843). The American groups followed events in Ireland, organizing branches and support societies for the movement there, but the two fields remained distinct and uncommitted to revolution. Neither was dominated by Catholic interests or participants, though both were already leaning that way. All of that changed quickly beginning in 1848.

Exogenous Shocks and Destabilizing Conditions

From 1845 to 1848, a whirlwind of shocks, both internal and exogenous, beset the Irish nation and its nationalist field. In 1845 Ireland was struck by the devastating Great Famine, which came to a peak in the year known as "Black '47" and lasted seven years. Population dropped by nearly a quarter (Foster, 1989, pp. 323–24), including deaths estimated to exceed one million, and another million emigrating to the United States. Apart from its human and economic toll, the famine threw the established political order into confusion, as a frightened and desperate population searched for relief from an ostensible government that was unable or unwilling to deliver.

The famine ushered in a new chapter in Irish nationalism; sweeping political shifts in Europe gave it focus. Bolstered by the wave of popular revolts that hit Europe in 1848 (Hobsbawm, 1996; Sperber, 1994), Young Ireland political associations aggressively mobilized support for an independent Irish republic. By mid-1848, the Irish Confederation had begun planning for an uprising just after the fall harvest. Their plans were thrown into chaos, however, when the British Crown suspended the Act of Habeas Corpus in July, and issued an arrest warrant for organizer William Smith O'Brien. Leaders of the Confederation, including Smith O'Brien, Michael Doheny, James Stephens, Terence Bellew McManus, Thomas Meagher, and John O'Mahony spread out over the south of Ireland, attempting to rouse the countryside to defend O'Brien and face down the army. Each of these men would later figure prominently in the Fenian organization (one of them posthumously).

Thousands initially responded to the call to unite for Ireland and against Britain, but most withdrew when they realized that they comprised the entirety of the uprising (Doheny & McGee, 1918, p. 173). And, outside of Young Ireland circles, no organized associations rose in support. The one actual skirmish in which the rebels engaged was won by the British army with only two deaths, both among the insurgents. Smith O'Brien was tried for treason and, ironically, acquitted, while many of those who had rallied to his support were convicted for their parts. Meagher and McManus were sentenced to death. O'Mahony, and Doheny, and Stephens escaped to France, the first two with a bounty on their heads; Stephens was reportedly killed (Kee, 1972, p. 286; O'Concubhair, 2011, p. 16). Smith O'Brien referred to the attempted rising as an "escapade," undeserving of the name "insurrection" (Kee, 1972, p. 286).

On the face of it, the events of 1848 appeared to reinforce the stability of British rule in Ireland. In terms of Irish national independence, the Young Ireland "rising" was a hopeless failure. Yet, if Young Ireland's actual goal was to reorient the nationalist field, then they ultimately succeeded. The "men of forty-eight," their various death sentences commuted to exile, became nationalist heroes both at home and abroad. As to the British decision to commute the sentences, if the goal was to weaken the nationalist field by sending the most visible organizers away, then it certainly failed. "Young Ireland's greatest influence may have been on the Irish in America, particularly on the Famine emigrants and their children," Miller observed (2008, p. 74). Their particular organizations may have been suppressed or destroyed, but the wider international fields of Irish nationalists simply absorbed the survivors, reorienting their various discourses of nationalism and identity around them.

Thus, the famine and economic crises at home, combined with sweeping republican uprisings in much of Europe, served to undermine the perceived legitimacy and stability of British control in Ireland, briefly creating opportunities for Irish nationalist leaders to challenge British rule. Despite any immediate failure, they succeeded in rousing, once more, the idea of driving the British out of Ireland through force of arms. These changes in prospects and perspective empowered the nationalists who advocated physical force, elevating them above the rest of the nationalist field. They altered the rules under which the field operated, and established a more ambitious agenda and a realignment that included the prospect of revolution — all they lacked were arms, money, and soldiers. These they would find overseas.

As an army's worth of young Irish men and women were forced off of their land by famine and a collapsing economy, the British sent them military leaders fresh out of prison. Connected by their attachment to the homeland, torn from their families who remained behind, hounded in America by anti-immigrant, anti-Catholic, and anti-Irish assertions that they did not belong and were not welcome, moved by the emerging image of their community as political exiles (Miller, 1985), and deeply disappointed by the defeat of Young Ireland's hopes, the American Irish now organized themselves across an Ireland-centered field of voluntary associations. Many of the participants, particularly the new exiles, had experience with political organizing in Ireland. As an American field of action, their collective sensibility, shared goals, and ethnic pride were tied to the fate of Ireland. The ensuing Fenian organization thus did not invent the transnational field out of which it grew. Rather, in many respects, the existing transnational field invented the organization.

The arrival of the 1848 activists added few resources to the American Irish field. Instead, the self-described martyrs of the movement carried a moral authority, which manifested itself as cognitive and emotive social skills. They elevated the status of the associations that welcomed them as members and leaders, and altered the focus of existing groups toward those associations. The American Irish field had previously been centered on its own communities, showing Irish pride, participating in American civil life, and sending support to the movements in the old country. But after the destabilizing shocks of 1847 and 1848, it shifted. As the more radical nationalists moved to its center, the organized Irish in America began to take up the role of challengers in the Irish political field.

The new social actors and new focus also brought new strategies to the field as a whole. While their distance from Dublin and Westminster allowed some associations to remain outside of Irish politics, it gave others the freedom to openly foment rebellion. As the Confederate Clubs had learned, it was nearly impossible to gather and plan collective action against the state within the bounds of British law and British spies. The Irish nationalist field required a home outside of Ireland.

Field Realignment

The Irish political field seemed to have stabilized after 1850, and the nationalist movement in Ireland appeared to be relatively quiescent, if not actually defeated. Charles Gavan Duffy's Independent Irish Party was nationalist in intent, but directed toward institutional electoral politics more than extra-institutional protest politics (Whyte, 1958). Chartism — the radical British working class movement for universal male suffrage and access to political leadership roles — had numerous followers in Ireland, though its presence was nowhere near the scale of the repeal movement (Reaney, 1984). The secret network of Catholic peasant Ribbon societies still existed but was not then considered a national threat (Garvin, 1982).

Organizing against landlords across much of the country had been consolidated under the leadership of the Irish Tenant League, which also worked through institutional politics (Comerford, 1998, p. 23). Each of these identifiable subfields was nationalist in orientation, each operated as challengers to some other incumbent source of power in the domain in which they organized, and each sought legislative independence for Ireland. Yet each was also oriented around a different center. The Irish Party targeted Parliament; the Chartists and the Tenant League sought specific legislative changes; and the repealers and Ribbonmen supported a vast "restoration" of traditional Irish autonomy, the former seeking legislative redress and the latter reclaiming public land use. Despite their mutual interests, each subfield had its own targets, priorities, and power structures. None held any real power outside their own base of support.

The American Irish nationalist field, however, was growing and radicalizing, as the organized Irish community — confederate clubs and older Irish associations — formed a field of action that was locally controlled but centered on Irish politics. A few groups positioned themselves as outside destabilizing forces, ready to throw Ireland's established order into chaos. In early 1848 American Irish activists in New York connected to the Young Ireland movement formed the militant Irish Republican Union (IRU) to "promote revolutionary movements for the establishment of republican governments all over Europe, especially in Ireland" (quoted in Stephens & Ramon, 2008, p. *xvii*). Following the failed 1848 uprising, Robert Emmet, nephew of the famous Irish martyr of the same name, helped form the American Provisional Committee for Ireland "to aid, support, and encourage the Irish people in the present crisis of their affairs; and to move as the occasion might require" (*New York Herald*, 1848). Emmet introduced the committee at a crowded meeting in New York City attended by the Mayors of New York, Brooklyn, and Jersey City, plus an estimated five thousand participants. His speech called for the American Irish to rally against the British crackdown on Young Ireland. The American Irish groups were in much stronger agreement than their Irish counterparts over the nature of their grievances and the targets of their actions.

While Emmet tied his purpose to that of the nationalist field in Ireland, his actions were organized independently of any organizing body "back home." This new American organization, like the IRU, was created by the Irish abroad on behalf of Ireland, expanding the action field across the sea. Emmet's association shortly thereafter reorganized as the Directory of the Friends of Ireland, recruiting public figures into its membership and soliciting tens of thousands of dollars in support of Irish independence. Despite difficult conditions for the Irish in the United States, coincident with heavy organizing on behalf of the flood of famine refugees, the American Irish created a widespread field of new nationalist associations dedicated to military support for an Irish revolution. Hundreds of Irishmen took up arms for the coming struggle, while many thousands donated funds to the effort.

Increasing immigration, the arrival of the Young Ireland leaders, and the British crackdown all added to the famine-engendered sense that Ireland needed to be saved and that the American Irish were the ones to do it. Operating out of New York, John Mitchel's new paper *The Citizen* faced none of the restrictions that beset challenger publications in Ireland; Mitchel could openly advocate violent revolution at home, backed by arms and money from the United States (Comerford, 1998, p. 33). As a fugitive from the last uprising, Mitchel had the credibility to make such calls. In 1854, he cofounded the Irishmen's Civil and Military Republican Union (ICMRU) for the purpose of raising and arming an American militia to help liberate Ireland. Then in March of 1855, Irish American leaders affiliated with the ICMRU called for a new republican organization to unite the community. The resulting Emmet Monument Association (EMA) was formed under the leadership of Michael Doheny, then a Lieutenant Colonel in New York's 69th (Irish) Regiment — through which many of the militant American Irish nationalists drilled for battle. Doheny was joined by John O'Mahony, who had recently arrived from Paris (Funchion, 1983, p. 102).

Thus, between 1850 and 1855, at least three separate associations of American Irishmen, led by former rebels of 1848, began raising money, collecting arms, and training soldiers. Collectively, the leaders of these new efforts were drawing on their empathetic skills, relying on the symbolic power of their earlier failures, to infuse the field with a new urgency. They drew resources from a dozen or more already existing American Irish associations throughout the nation, and their influence led Irish relief organizations into the nationalist debate and pressed nationalist associations into militarism. Thousands of miles from Ireland's shores, a noncommissioned army was preparing a private invasion in support of an insurrection that wasn't yet being planned in Ireland.

The Merging of Two Nationalist Fields

The next stage in plotting this revolution was to establish a base in Ireland. The Emmet Monument Association took the lead: in June 1855, Joseph Denieffe informed the EMA leaders that he had to return to Ireland to visit his ailing father, and offered to help them if he could. Denieffe, while not an EMA member, had been active in the events of 1848 and in the American Irish nationalist field, and his offer was accepted. In his memoir, Denieffe described how he had asked Doheny who he should report to from his post in Ireland. "'We have no one there as yet,' he replied. 'So we give you carte blanche to do what you can for the organization and yourself'" (Denieffe, 1906, p. 3). A nationalist field existed in Ireland, but the Americans had no part in it.

Immediately upon arrival in Dublin, Denieffe began to arrange meetings with its leading nationalists. One was Thomas Clarke Luby, an organizer of the 1848 rising who had been convicted, imprisoned, and later escaped. While Luby expressed interest, he was hesitant to throw in with people he did not know on behalf of an unknown plot headed by an organization that he had never heard of. This would become a familiar response as Denieffe made the rounds. Eventually he established a network of supporters who "readily promised to assist and co-operate with the American organization" (Denieffe, 1906, p. 11). But no comparable field was prepared for action in Ireland, and the hoped-for American led invasion did not come (Denieffe, 1906, p. 13).

In 1857, O'Mahony and Doheny wrote to their fellow 1848 revolutionary, James Stephens, asking if he would be willing to organize activities in Ireland for the next uprising, with financial and other support to come from them in New York. Stephens enthusiastically accepted, declaring that it could be done quickly and without great expense, and appointed Denieffe to personally carry this response back to the United States on New Year's Day, 1858. "The choice of messenger was tactically inspired," Comerford (1998, p. 47) observed. "By agreeing to undertake this mission Denieffe implicitly surrendered his own commission of 1855 and handed over to Stephens control of what remained of the organizational network he had set up in that year." Echoing a famous phrase of the United Irishman Theobald Wolfe Tone, Stephens warned that "the men of property are not with us." He was counting on American financing to make up the difference. In February, the "Irish Revolutionary Committee" – consisting of Doheny, O'Mahony, and 14 others – appointed Stephens the "Chief Executive of the Irish Revolutionary movement" in Ireland.[3]

Denieffe returned to Ireland with some funding and the letter of appointment for Stephens on St. Patrick's Day, 1858, and he, Stephens, and four others[4] took an oath to the new organization. Shortly after, Stephens named them the Irish Republican Brotherhood (IRB). It was the first Irish nationalist association planned abroad.

The IRB immediately set to work building up their network and positioning themselves as the central agents of the field. They joined with existing organizations within the Irish nationalist field, linked the various Irish
nationalist efforts, and recruited support for their mission from this pre-
existing nationalist base. Promising imminent revolution, they quickly gathered thousands of supporters throughout the southern Ireland. But their
promise was based on money, arms, and coordination from New York,
and the money was not flowing. Months dragged on with no calls to action.
Meanwhile, Irish nationalists of a less revolutionary persuasion were
attempting to establish their own umbrella organizations with which to
guide and shape the field (Comerford, 1998, p. 47).

In December 1858, the committee amended Stephens' appointment to
specify authority over the movement both "at home and abroad."[5] They
went public, announcing the formation of the Fenian Brotherhood (FB), in
early 1859. The fact that the FB declared itself after the formation of the
IRB has created some confusion as to which was the parent organization
(Clark, 1971; O'Concubhair, 2011; O'Leary, 1896, 70n; but see Townshend,
1983). An FB publication from 1865, *Fenian's Progress*, states that the FB
had been in existence as early as 1856, but that its early years were kept a
secret.[6] This is likely to be a reference to the EMA's revolutionary committee, the name under which Doheny and O'Mahony had approached
Stephens. Stephens' formal acceptance of the "job" offer from the EMA
also marks the IRB as the subordinate, though nominally independent,
association. In January 1859, however, just after Stephens' amended
appointment, he replied in a letter appointing O'Mahony "supreme organizer
and Director of the I.R.B. in America,"[7] a position which O'Mahony
formally accepted (Savage, 1868, p. 63). The two lead associations
appeared to be answerable to each other: by arrangement and agreement,
the Fenian efforts were to be organized transnationally, with each lead
organization seeking to mobilize the existing nationalist fields in their
respective countries for the sake of a united and coordinated military
uprising.

The question of organizational lineage is of more than academic interest.
The relationship between the FB and the IRB defined the relationship
between the American and Irish nationalist strategic action fields. As the
leadership of each organization sought to lead the field, and therefore the
other association, the lack of clarity about who was really in charge created
barriers to unified action, and ultimately led to the destabilization of both
sides of the emergent transnational field. At the same time, each association
based its claim of leadership in its national field on its supposed dominance

in the transnational field. The IRB's position relied on what it could deliver from America, while the FB's location in the American field relied on the credibility of its claim to be organizing Ireland. The rest of the American field's failure to concede to this implicit claim to authority left the group in a more peripheral position – one more claimant in a populous field of nationalist aspirants.

Up to this point, the new organizing effort had a transnational foundation. Two (or more) nationally bound fields had intersected to create a transnational field through which strategic action could be coordinated. Implicitly, a foundation of this sort would be necessary to further action, but would still require deliberate action on the part of organizations or organizational entrepreneurs. This was the unique function of the FB/IRB collaboration, without which there could be no transnational movement.

Organized campaigns for social and political change may rely on external support for resources, protection, and global legitimacy. As well, exiles from a land under occupation may form nationalist movements abroad. Neither of those conditions requires the mobilization of transnational identities or organizations, and therefore do not rely on a truly transnational field. But a unified movement for change operating across national borders requires an organizational framework of equal expansiveness, with participants committed to its framing and goals. The Fenian movement almost accomplished this.

INTERNAL CRISIS AND DISSOLUTION

Correspondence between the FB in New York and the IRB in Ireland suggests that organizers in both nations believed that there was a potential army of Irish soldiers in America and a great, unmobilized mass of Irishmen just waiting for the word to rise up and join them. They gave less attention to the issue of who would lead these armies, as that was the role that they had assigned to their own organizations. Such confidence was misplaced. Each of the two lead associations rose quickly to prominence within their respective fields, but neither ever had uncontested control of the larger field's agenda. As much as the IRB was strengthened by promises of backing from New York, it was hampered by contention within the American field over the legitimacy of the FB's leadership.

By the time the Fenian Brotherhood was founded, Doheny's role in it was already fractious. He had entered the American Irish nationalist field via the Irish Republican Union (IRU) in the early 1850s, but the IRU soon after reorganized their brigades into New York State militias. IRU leaders, including Doheny, formed the Irish Brigade of Young Ireland with the explicit goal of drilling soldiers as part of the state militia prior to sending them to Ireland as "force multipliers." IRU organizers (excluding Doheny) also formed a secret society within the brigades known as the "Silent Friends" that was headed by James Huston; in 1851, the Silent Friends organized five New York companies and secretly oversaw their leadership (Sixtyninth.net, n.d.-a, p. 13). Doheny attained the rank of Lt. Colonel in one of those companies, and was often referred to as Colonel Doheny throughout the nationalist field.

From the start, Doheny clashed with Huston over the role of the Silent Friends. The conflict intensified as both Huston and Doheny vied for leadership of the ICMRU military initiative, the Emmet Monument Association (EMA). Most of the regiments supported Doheny, who assumed leadership of the EMA, while Huston withdrew from the New York field entirely (Sixtyninth.net, n.d.-a, p. 27). This new effort represented more of a reorganization of the American Irish nationalist field than an expansion. By this time, the ICMRU had ceased operations (Steward & McGovern, 2013, p. 10), and, apparently, the secretive Silent Friends had also disbanded. The EMA thus emerged as an unplanned successor to both of these associations as well as to the IRU. Doheny's rise was not universally applauded, as other established organizers were supplanted in the process.

The EMA's dominance of the nationalist field was brief and contested. John McClenahan, who had replaced Mitchel as editor of *The Citizen*, joined with Huston to call for a new organization to take over the EMA's role. "Through the pages of his newspaper, McClenahan attacked the plans of the Emmet Monument Association and suggested that some of its leaders were less than sincere" (Funchion, 1983, p. 103). The Boston branch of the EMA sided with McClenahan to form the Massachusetts Emigrant Aid Society, later renamed The Irish Emigrant Aid Society (IEAS), and attempted to redefine the EMA as a subsidiary of this group.[8] Doheny once more denounced Huston, but a number of the New York militia units defected to the IEAS.

By extension, the EMA's problem of its perceived authority in America was the chief obstacle to Denieffe's early mission in Ireland. While there, awaiting word and money from the EMA, he read one of McClenahan's editorials in *The Citizen* urging patriots not to support new organizations that hadn't been properly appointed by the nationalist community, and calling for a congress of Irish societies to choose their representation (Denieffe, 1906, p. 12). The EMA had been planning for a rapid response revolution, or at least an organized uprising in the fall of 1856, then only months away. Implicitly, this would have required the ICMRU, the New York militias, and most of the rest of the American Irish nationalist field to fall in line behind them. With the appearance of the *Citizen* editorial, Denieffe correctly inferred that these plans would not materialize.

In early 1856, the EMA formally ceased operations, and Doheny was forced out of the 69th Regiment (Sixtyninth.net, n.d.-b, p. 7). Rather than yield to the IEAS, which would also fail later that year, Doheny and O'Mahony joined with Emmet's Directory and transferred their resources to it. They also maintained an EMA revolutionary committee, and their military titles, in order to resume the mission if the opportunity arose. The following year, they reemerged with their new Fenian plan with O'Mahony taking the lead role, though he called Doheny "the real founder" (Brotherhood, 1866, p. 8).

Even before they had declared themselves, the Fenians recruited support from Irish nationalist groups throughout America. In 1858, FB leaders joined the Ancient Order of Hibernians, hoping to recruit their membership (Denieffe, 1906, p. 22). Stephens made a visit to New York seeking, unsuccessfully, to convince the Directory of Friends of Ireland to commit their funds to the IRB. The Fenian system spread throughout the American Irish nationalist field, but other associations continued to challenge them. Responding to this ongoing source of contention, leaders of some of the American Centers[9] wrote a declaration of confidence in O'Mahony and Stephens, attacking "the base and unscrupulous men who have been endeavoring ... to asperse the characters and blast the justly earned popularity of ... the most trusted Irish patriots of the present day" (Denieffe, 1906, p. 164). Stephens and Denieffe were enacting the same strategy throughout Ireland, trying to recruit entire societies into their organization while facing down questions regarding legitimacy and intent. "Thus matters went on until the close of 1859, every effort being made to extend and solidify the organization, while frequent communication was held with America where a serious split had taken place in the organization" (Denieffe, 1906, p. 59).

In Ireland, nationalists observed the progress of the IRB, but did not rally to it. Toward the end of 1860 Young Irelanders in Dublin proposed the formation of a National Brotherhood of St. Patrick (NBSP) to bring the nationalist field together for an annual St. Patrick's Day public banquet, as American Irish associations had been doing for some years

(Comerford, 1998, pp. 71–73). While not proposing any action, nor carrying out any program, the NBSP signaled through its mere existence that the leadership question was still unsettled within their field. In fact, Stephens and the Young Irelanders had a deep disdain for one another.

O'Mahony visited Dublin, staying until early 1861, meeting with both IRB organizers and the uncommitted nationalists and seeking to solidify the organizational base in Ireland. But he failed to bring the parties together. Stephens had not been present when O'Mahony arrived, and when the two finally met, second-hand reports indicate that they mostly argued over whether O'Mahony was subordinate to Stephens or his peer (O'Leary, 1896, p. 140). Irish and American efforts coincided, but uneasily.

The start of the American Civil War in 1861 engendered a new shock to the transnational nationalist field, massively disrupting their efforts. In the United States, most of the Irish regiments were called to service on either side of the war. But while the American Irish reaffirmed their commitment to the United States (or the Confederacy) and dreamt of taking the fight to "John Bull," the Irish mobilization languished without them. Irish leaders came to decry the false promises of support by the American Irish. Neither the FB nor the IRB was yet large enough to pose a threat to any government.

The year 1861, however, also saw the Fenian's first publicity triumph and a surge in membership on both sides of the Atlantic (Bisceglia, 1979). Following the death and internment of Terrence Bellew McManus, the San Francisco Fenians proposed the idea of raising funds to ship his body back to Ireland for a homeland funeral. Although retired from nationalist activism, McManus had been a political exile from Ireland due to his role in the 1848 insurgency. The New York Fenians, particularly Doheny, seized upon this proposal. With great fanfare they shipped McManus' coffin to New York, where thousands paid tribute, accompanied by rousing speeches from other 1848 participants now attached to the FB. Local politicians, rival organizers and the Catholic Church all supported the event in a public display of unity (Bisceglia, 1979, p. 57; O'Leary, 1896, p. 155). From there, McManus and a Fenian entourage journeyed to Dublin and an even greater reception. Thomas Luby estimated that at least 50,000 and possibly closer to 200,000 people came out for McManus' final funeral procession (O'Leary, 1896, p. 163). Writing to O'Mahony after the event, Stephens asserted that had they arms, they could have raised a revolution then and there. He marked it a victory for the IRB "for all was done by our body. … Outside our ranks there is no national life in Ireland. And in America, too, may we not claim the work as exclusively ours? … the Irish

Nationalist, who, aware of our action in the McManus funeral, still questions our power and ability is utterly rotten" (Denieffe, 1906, p. 169).

Stephens' use of the words "we" and "our" in this context clearly referred to the IRB and FB together, rather than in opposition. The problem, however, was that the enemies Stephens complained of were other Irish nationalists. Stephens recognized and admitted as much at the end of the letter, though the situation would not change. "Apparently, the government has only to let us alone, and, like the notorious cats, we shall eat each other up to the very tails!" he wrote (Denieffe, 1906, p. 179).

Although triumphant, Stephens' animated 1861 letter to O'Mahony indicates the fractures that ultimately brought an end to the Fenian hopes. Behind the scenes of the McManus funeral in Dublin was a soap opera of internal strife. Nationalists with Young Ireland and NBSP affiliations there attempted to wrest control of the event from the IRB, even to the point of attempting to pressure McManus' sister to sign control of his body over to them the night before the service (Bisceglia, 1979, p. 61; Denieffe, 1906, p. 167).[10] The Church hierarchy refused to allow the Fenians to hold a Catholic service in a church, decrying the intentions of secret societies and forcing the organizers to hold their ceremonies in the Mechanics' Institute. *The Nation* newspaper, a leading nationalist paper, editorialized against Stephens and the Fenian efforts. Stephens subsequently formed a new IRB paper, *The Irish People*, to carry their message and hopefully silence the moderate nationalists. If nothing else, this further alienated the Young Irelanders and their supporters (Quinn, 2009).

Not with a Bang, But a Whimper

The final and most serious split would come in 1864. O'Mahony's efforts at consolidation had failed to satisfy critics both within and outside the organization. "The time is come when I feel called upon to resign my position as H.C F.B. into the hands of my constituents as they are to be represented at the forthcoming general Convention," he wrote to James Kelly in October 1863. His stated conditions for accepting reappointment, aimed at ending the FB's organizational strife, were that he be unanimously elected and the delegates pledge steady and committed support for the IRB. He added that he would "refuse to accept office if subjected to the dictation or control of any person or party outside the F.B. (in America)."[11] O'Mahony explicitly invited representatives from across the American Irish nationalist field to decide on his role in the F.B. while implicitly maneuvering for them to acknowledge the association as the incumbent challenger of the field. He achieved the first, but not the second.

Concurrently, in a separate letter of the same date to Charles Kickham, O'Mahony was far more explicit regarding the transnational dimension and his disputes with Stephens. "As chief officer of the American organization my powers must be put upon an even level with his authority over the Irish. I will no longer consent to be accountable to him for my official conduct. We must treat as equal to equal, when it is necessary for us to treat at all, and as the presiding officers of equal and independent organizations – organizations mutually aiding each other and closely allied through their respective executives but still distinct in their government and internal management."[12]

O'Mahony emerged from the 1864 Congress with an official vote of confidence (Fenian Brotherhood, 1865), but an organized faction took control of the overall agenda of the meeting. At their urging, the secret centers organized under O'Mahony as Head Center were replaced by the more public positions of President and General Congress, with this faction principally making up the Congress (Brown, 1966, p. 39). O'Mahony was unanimously elected as President. This group, "the soon-to-be-called 'Men of Action,' however, carried motions that would dramatically alter executive control of the global movement" (Steward & McGovern, 2013, p. 64). In particular, they officially resolved as a body that the Fenian Brotherhood lead the movement for Ireland's independence, and asserted that the IRB was answerable to them, which only exacerbated the contention between the FB and the IRB. And they introduced a plan to invade Canada as a precursor to action in Ireland. Stephens, meanwhile, wrote a lengthy letter to O'Mahony and the new congress complaining that he was doing all that he could under hopeless circumstances, that the Americans were not keeping up their part and did not show respect for him or his work, and concluded that the Irish were prepared to act if ever the Americans were. "Nothing shall be wanting if our American brothers do their duty."[13] The end of 1864 saw the leaders of each association losing power, unable to maintain dominance within their national contexts, and blaming one another for their difficulties.

On St. Patrick's Day, 1865, O'Mahony issued orders to FB Captain Thomas Kelly to go to Dublin and report on the IRB (Denieffe, 1906, p. 186). Eight years into the movement, the FB was seeking a report on "the state of the I.R.B. ... its constitution, mode of government, the manner of persons whereof said government is composed, its military strength, its financial resources and expenditure, and its general availability for successful action within the present year." In September of that year, the offices of *The Irish People* were raided and Stephens' closest lieutenants were arrested, further weakening the IRB.

Kelly was ordered to only report what he could observe himself, "without submitting it to the approval of any parties living in Ireland." O'Mahony also sent a letter informing Stephens of Kelly's mission, stating that "matters here are not as they were when you and I were as one. An element has been brought into our councils, though by no agency of mine, that must be perfectly satisfied on the points in question."[14] He also mentioned that "under our revised constitution," all of Stephens' official communication to the FB must be cleared by the Head Center. Stephens would no longer be permitted to act as a "provisional dictator," as he had once described his role. These efforts reflected the demands of the challenging Fenian faction, but did not satisfy them.

The Men of Action soon declared O'Mahony to be a tyrant and voted to impeach him. This split the organization permanently. O'Mahony and his supporters – the "O'Mahony wing" – refused to acknowledge the Senate's authority, holding what they called the Fourth Fenian Convention in New York in January 1866 to abolish the Senate and reinstate the Council. The "Senate wing," along with many of the Midwestern centers, held their Fourth National Congress in Pittsburgh in February. Defending his leadership, O'Mahony wrote of "a secret conspiracy which I have since learned to my cost had been for some time covertly corroding the heart of the organization" (Brotherhood, 1866, p. 14). The two versions of the Brotherhood continued on their respective plans to invade either Ireland or Canada, each faction issuing rules that forbade communication with their Irish brethren without the express permission of their President. Both claimed to have Stephens' support, though Stephens actually supported O'Mahony, and came to the United States to try to heal the rift. Since the Senate Wing President would only meet with the O'Mahony wing if they addressed him as the President of the real FB, no meeting occurred.

The Senate wing did undertake their Canadian invasion plans, but to no great effect. O'Mahony's wing tried to get on with the business of revolution in Ireland, but they had lost faith in Stephens' preparedness. The FB removed Stephens from his post and appointed Kelly the new head of the IRB in 1866. The following year, Kelly organized an actual uprising, but spies had reported his plans to the Crown before they could take place, and numerous arrests followed. A few isolated military events occurred, unsuccessfully. The great decade of war planning had come to an end.

CONCLUSION

The Fenian efforts demonstrate that a nationalist movement can be initiated and mobilized by actors outside of the nation. In this case, the events were enabled by the many years of prior organizing and collective action through which a transnational strategic action field of nationalist associations and related groups was constructed. The Fenians successfully operated through this field, achieving a great reach and influence. Ultimately, however, they failed to lead the field, and therefore failed to align the various participant groups into a unified body.

In order to contribute to our understanding of this well-known series of events in Irish history, this paper has considered the Fenian case in the context of a transnational strategic action field. Drawing the greater field into our analysis reveals the contours of the organizational world within which this uprising was planned; emphasizes that the rise and fall of Fenian fortunes depended on interorganizational relations in the field; and demonstrates the usefulness of SAF tools and terms in order to coherently examine organizational actors in the processes of social change dynamics. It also highlights elements of the Fenian case that might otherwise be relegated to the margins.

First, by noting the development of the Fenian ideas and organization throughout the field rather than any one or two associations, we can more clearly trace the American origins of the movement in Ireland. As well, we can distinguish between the movement leaders' considerable mobilization skills and their lesser organizational skills, revealing that while they built on the momentum of an existing nationalist field centered on Ireland's prospects for independence, they were never able to take and hold a dominant position within it. This is not a matter of mere factionalism, though factionalism within the two lead associations was abundant. Rather, it was the inability of the two Fenian associations to control the agenda of their field(s) that brought an end to their efforts. This can be best understood in relation to the shifting orientations of the fields overall. Embedded within a larger Irish political field centered on the British state, the Irish nationalists had to reorient their field around the idea of a future independent government, and around the IRB as the path to its realization. Yet the American Irish nationalist field was embedded in an American political system that encouraged rather than suppressed private associations, and which often found it expedient to allow Irish civil society in general, and the Fenian mobilization in particular, to flourish. They were also working within a larger Irish field that had many social clubs, charitable societies, and volunteer fire brigades. Their challenge was to reorient the American Irish agenda to the nationalist cause, and around the Fenian Brotherhood as its realization. In both national fields, the historical and organizational contexts supported the first goal, but thwarted the second.

Looking only at the FB and the IRB, without consideration of their field locations, one might view the Fenian failure as a framing dispute. Copious research has demonstrated the need to propagate a shared movement frame as a prerequisite to collective action. The many nationalist actors and their supporters were not united, and therefore did not act collectively. Yet, in this case, there was a widespread agreement as to the framing of the Irish condition, the desired solution, and the need for physical force action to bring that solution about. The sticking point was one of leadership, or incumbency in the nationalist fields. The failure was organizational.

The disputes over relative position in the field, or in fields embedded within larger fields, explain the organizational difficulties. Viewing the nationalists within either national field as incumbents and challengers makes sense of their inability to coordinate, even though they were all on the same side – not an uncommon condition. As Irish nationalists, they all shared some version of a challenger location with regard to British rule. As local actors, however, they had their own issues over legitimacy, authority, and trust.

This case also demonstrates that strategic action fields can be transnational, and suggests that a transnational SAF might be a prerequisite to transnational collective action. The growth of the Fenian organization in the United States, specifically during a period of great suppression of organized action in Ireland, highlights that collective action beyond a nation's borders can play much more than a supporting role. The strategic union of the two national fields reveals the potential power of transnational collective action, though the Fenian failure also shows many of the liabilities inherent in such forms.

The Fenian organizations had enough resources in terms of supporters, money, arms, training, leadership, networks, dedicated newspapers, and motivated participants to have posed a much greater challenge to British rule in Ireland in the 1860s. Although the nationalist field in Ireland was heavily suppressed by state power, that same power inadvertently fed the Irish nationalist field in the United States. The transnational nature of the effort greatly strengthened their mobilization and their potential for action. It also created unrealistic expectations within each national field concerning the abilities and intentions of the other. The wealth of letters from Stephens and his inner circle to O'Mahony and other FB leaders demonstrate that the IRB saw themselves as the center of the partnership, with the FB on the periphery. This might not have been such a problem if the American organizers had shared this view. But, seeking to build a true transnational partnership, the FB acted on assumptions that the IRB did not share. This inconsistency fed conflicts between the two and reflected back on the American field itself. Much of the split between the Irish and Canadian factions in the FB came down to the question of what the FB's role should be in the Irish nationalist struggle: O'Mahony's Irish wing was adamant that they were bound to the IRB, while the Senate's Canadian wing declared itself independent of outside associations, and therefore of obligations to other group's plans. The American split, in turn, undermined the IRB's position in the Irish nationalist field — which was otherwise predicated on the transnational partnership.

In these and other respects, a broad network of networks, as any transnational strategic action field must be, faces an uphill battle to form or maintain any sense of unity. Without that, the participants cannot all be in it together. And in revolution, as Ben Franklin observed, "we must all hang together, or assuredly we shall all hang separately."

NOTES

1. The nationalist field in Ireland included many constitutionalist associations, mostly related to Daniel O'Connell's Repeal Association, organizations affiliated with the Catholic Church, and others related to land use and ownership. None of these "joined" the Fenian movement, but all participated in the organization of Irishmen in relation to citizenship and nationalism.

2. Subsequent émigrés were more often economic refugees than political ones. Vast numbers of tenant farmers were evicted from their lands in the years approaching the famine.

3. Davitt Papers, TCD, MS 9659D/207, quoted in Stephens and Ramon (2008, p. 76).

4. Peter Langan, Garrett O'Shaughnessy, Thomas Clark Luby, and Charles Kickham.

5. Davitt Papers, TCD, MS 9659D/208, quoted in Stephens and Ramon (2008, p. 77).

6. There is also a copy of the Constitution of the Fenian Brotherhood, among the George D. Cahill papers, Burns Library, dated 1858.

7. Letter, John O'Mahony, Head Centre and General President of the Fenian Brotherhood, to the C.E. of the I.R.B. (James Stephens), October 18, 1863, from the Fenian Letters collection of the American Catholic History Research Center.

8. The name referred to their plan to train Irish immigrants as soldiers who could then return to Ireland to fight for independence.

9. The FB was organized into regional and local "centers" with O'Mahony acting as Head Centre. The spelling was conventional for the time.

10. Comerford (1998, 75ff) relates these events from the opposite perspective, suggesting that the McManus Funeral Committee was initiated by the National Brotherhood of St. Patrick and that IRB "extremists" had seized control. He further asserts that no great political significance can be attributed to the mass turnout, and no popular endorsement of nationalist ideals should be assumed.

11. To James Kelly from O'Mahony — October 19, 1863.

12. To Charles Kickham from O'Mahony — October 19, 1863.

13. To O'Mahony from J. Hamilton (Stephens) — December 11, 1864.

14. H.C.F.B. to the C.E.I.R.B., March 17, 1865.

ACKNOWLEDGMENTS

Thanks to Michael Benediktsson, Katherine Chen, John Chin, Maureen Cummins, Thomas DeGloma, Mark Halling, Michael Hanagan, Miranda Martinez, Keara O'Dempsey, and the anonymous reviewers at RSMCC for assistance in preparing this work; to the George N. Schuster Faculty Fellowship Fund at Hunter College, the Irish American Cultural Institute, and the Research Fund of PSC-CUNY for research support; and to the American Antiquarian Society, Burns Library at Boston College, The New York Public Library, The Historical Society of Pennsylvania, and the Fenian Brotherhood Collection of the Washington Research Library Consortium for access to archival materials.

REFERENCES

Abdelrahman, M. (2011). The transnational and the local: Egyptian activists and transnational protest networks. *British Journal of Middle Eastern Studies*, *38*(3), 407–424.

Appadurai, A. (1996). *Modernity at large: Cultural dimensions of globalisation*. Minneapolis, MN: University of Minnesota Press.

Auyero, J. (2002). The judge, the cop, and the queen of carnival: Ethnography, storytelling, and the (contested) meaning of protest. *Theory and Society*, *31*(2), 151–187.

Basch, L., Glick Schiller, N., & Szanton Blanc, C. (Eds.). (1994). *Nations unbound: Transnational projects, postcolonial predicaments, and deterritorialized nation-states*. Langhorne, PA: Gordon and Breach.

Benford, R. D., & Snow, D. A. (2000). Framing processes and social movements: An overview and assessment. *Annual Review of Sociology*, *26*, 611–639.

Bernstein, M. (2005). Identity politics. *Annual Review of Sociology*, *31*, 47–74.

Bisceglia, L. (1979). The Fenian funeral of Terence Bellew McManus. *Éire-Ireland, 14*(3), 45–64.

Bourdieu, P. (1993). *The field of cultural production*. New York, NY: Columbia University Press.

Brotherhood, F. (1865). Proceedings of the second national congress of the Fenian Brotherhood. *Cincinnati, OH*. Philadelphia, PA: James Gibbons, Printer.

Brotherhood, F. (1866). *To the state centres, centres, and members of the Fenian Brotherhood of North America*. New York, NY: O'Sullivan & McBride (AAS).

Brown, T. N. (1966). *Irish-American nationalism, 1870–1890*. Philadelphia, PA: J.B. Lippincott & Co.

Burstein, P. (1991). Policy domains: Organization, culture, and policy outcomes. *Annual Review of Sociology, 17*, 327–350.

Byrne, M. (1907). *Memoirs of Miles Byrne*. Dublin: Maunsel.

Calhoun, C. (1993). "New Social Movements" of the early nineteenth century. *Social Science History, 17*(3), 385–427.

Clark, D. (1971). Militants of the 1860's: The Philadelphia Fenians. *The Pennsylvania Magazine of History and Biography, 95*(1), 98–108.

Comerford, R. V. (1998). *The Fenians in context: Irish politics and society; 1848–82*. Dublin: Wolfhound.

Davis, G. F., McAdam, D., Scott, W. R., & Zald, M. (Eds.). (2005). *Social movements and organization theory*. New York, NY: Cambridge University Press.

della Porta, D., Kriesi, H., & Rucht, D. (Eds.). (1999). *Social movements in a globalizing world*. New York, NY: St. Martin's Press.

Denieffe, J. (1906). *A personal narrative of the Irish revolutionary Brotherhood: Giving a faithful report of the principal events from 1855 to 1867*. New York, NY: Gael Pub. Co.

Diani, M. (2009). The structural bases of protest events: Multiple memberships and civil society networks in the 15 February 2003 anti-war demonstrations. *Acta Sociologica, 52*(1), 63–83.

DiMaggio, P., & Powell, W. W. (1983). The Iron cage revisited: Institutional isomorphism and collective rationality in organizational fields. *American Sociological Review, 48*(2), 147–160.

Djuric, I. (2003). The Croatian diaspora in North America: Identity, ethnic solidarity, and the formation of a "Transnational National Community". *International Journal of Politics, Culture, and Society, 17*(1), 113–130.

Doheny, M., & McGee, T. D. (1918). *The felon's track: Or, history of the attempted outbreak in Ireland, embracing the leading events in the Irish struggle from the year 1843 to the close of 1848*. Dublin: M.H. Gill.

Duany, J. (2000). Nation on the move: The construction of cultural identities in Puerto Rico and the Diaspora. *American Ethnologist, 27*(1), 5–30.

Duffy, C. G. (1880). *Young Ireland, A fragment of Irish History, 1840–1850*. London: Cassell, Petter, Galpin, & Co.

Edwards, B., & Marullo, S. (1995). Organizational mortality in a declining social movement: The Demise of peace movement organizations in the end of the cold war era. *American Sociological Review, 60*(6), 908–927.

Emmet, T. A. (1915). *Memoir of Thomas Addis and Robert Emmet, with their ancestors and immediate family*. New York, NY: Emmet Press.

Ferree, M., & Martin, P. Y. (Eds.). (1995). Feminist organizations: Harvest of the new women's movement. Philadelphia, PA: Temple University Press.

Fligstein, N. (2001). Social skill and the theory of fields. *Sociological Theory, 19*(2), 105–125.

Fligstein, N., & McAdam, D. (2011). Toward a general theory of strategic action fields. *Sociological Theory, 29*, 1–26.

Fligstein, N., & McAdam, D. (2012). *A theory of fields*. Oxford: Oxford University Press.

Foley, T. (Ed.). (1996). *Eyewitness to 1798*. Dublin: Mercier Press.

Foster, R. F. (1989). *Modern Ireland, 1600–1972*. New York, NY: Penguin Books.

Fox, J. A. (1890). *A key to the Irish question: Mainly compiled from the speeches and writings of eminent British statesmen and publicists, past and present: With some chapters on the reign of eviction in England and Scotland*. London: K. Paul, Trench, Trübner.

Funchion, M. F. (1983). *Irish American voluntary organizations*. Westport, CT: Greenwood Press.

Gamson, J. (1997). Messages of exclusion: Gender, movements, and symbolic boundaries. *Gender and Society, 11*(2), 178–199.

Garvin, T. (1982). Defenders, ribbonmen and others: Underground political networks in pre-famine Ireland. *Past & Present, 96*, 133–155.

Gilson, J. (2011). Transnational advocacy: New spaces, new voices. *Alternatives: Global, Local, Political, 36*(4), 288–306.

Goldstone, J., & Useem, B. (2012). Putting values and institutions back into the theory of strategic action fields. *Sociological Theory, 30*(1), 37–47.

Goodwin, J., & Skocpol, T. (1989). Explaining revolutions in the contemporary Third World. *Politics and Society, 17*(4), 489–509.

Gould, R. (1995). *Insurgent identities: Class, community and protest in Paris from 1848 to the commune*. Chicago, IL: University of Chicago Press.

Guarnizo, L. E., & Smith, M. P. (1998). The locations of transnationalism. In M. P. Smith & L. E. Guarnizo (Eds.), *Transnationalism from Below* (pp. 3–34). New Brunswick, NJ: Transaction.

Hanagan, M. (1998). Irish transnational social movements, deterritorialized migrants, and the state system: The last one hundred and forty years. *Mobilization: An International Journal, 3*(1), 107–126.

Hanagan, M. (2003). Labor internationalism. *Social Science History, 27*(4), 485–499.

Haynes, J. (2009). Transnational religious actors and international order. *Perspectives, 17*(2), 43–69.

Hess, J. M. (2009). *Immigrant ambassadors citizenship and belonging in the Tibetan diaspora*. Redwood City, CA: Stanford University Press.

Hobsbawm, E. (1996). *The age of revolution: 1789–1848*. New York, NY: Vintage.

Jenkins, B. (2008). *The Fenian problem: Insurgency and terrorism in a liberal state, 1858–1874*. Montreal: McGill-Queen's University Press.

Keck, M. E., & Sikkink, K. (1998). *Activists beyond borders: Advocacy networks in international politics*. Ithaca, NY: Cornell University Press.

Kee, R. (1972). *The green flag: The turbulent history of the Irish national movement*. New York, NY: Delacorte Press.

Kurzman, C. (1996). Structural opportunity and perceived opportunity in social-movement theory: The Iranian revolution of 1979. *American Sociological Review, 61*(1), 153–170.

Levitt, P. (2001). *The transnational villagers*. Berkeley, CA: University of California Press.

Liow, J. C. (2011). Muslim identity, local networks, and transnational Islam in Thailand's Southern border provinces. *Modern Asian Studies, 45*(6), 1383–1421.

Loyal National Repeal Association. (1843). *The following is a copy of the address, which was read by the Liberator,* ... Boston, MA: New England Anti-Slavery Tract Association.

Lune, H. (2007). *Urban action networks: HIV/AIDS and community organizing in New York City.* Boulder, CO: Rowman & Littlefield.

MacNeven, W. J. (1807). *Pieces of the Irish history.* New York, NY: Dermin.

McAdam, D. (1982). *Political process and the development of black insurgency, 1930–1970.* Chicago, IL: University of Chicago Press.

McAdam, D., Tarrow, S., & Tilly, C. (2001). *Dynamics of contention.* Cambridge: Cambridge University Press.

McGraw, S., & Wheelan, K. (2005). Daniel O'Connell in comparative perspective, 1800–50. *Eire-Ireland 40*(1–2), 60–89.

Meyer, D., & Whittier, N. (1994). Social movement spillover. *Social Problems, 41*(2), 277–298.

Meyer, D., Whittier, N., & Robnett, B. (2002). *Social Movements: Identity, culture, and the state.* Oxford: Oxford University Press.

Miller, K. (1985). *Emigrants and exiles: Ireland and the Irish exodus to North America.* New York, NY: Oxford University Press.

Miller, K. (2008). *Ireland and Irish America: Culture, class, and transatlantic migration.* Dublin: Field Day.

Murphy, A. F. (2007). Daniel O'Connell and the "American Eagle" in 1845: Slavery, diplomacy, nativism, and the collapse of America's first Irish nationalist movement. *Journal of American Ethnic History, 26*(2), 3–26.

New York Herald. (1848). Organisation of an American Provisional Committee for Ireland. *New York Herald,* June 7.

O'Concubhair, P. (2011). *The Fenians were dreadful men: The 1867 rising.* Cork: Mercier Press.

O'Leary, J. (1896). *Recollections of Fenians and Fenianism* (Vol. 1). London: Downey & Co.

O'Neill, K. (2004). Transnational protest: States, circuses, and conflict at the frontline of global politics. *International Studies Review, 6*(2), 233–251.

Østergaard-Nielsen, E. (2003). The politics of migrants' transnational political practices. *International Migration Review, 37*(3), 760–786.

Portes, A. (1999). Conclusion: Towards a new world – The origin and effects of transnational activities. *Ethnic and Racial Studies, 22*(2), 463–477.

Portes, A., Guarnizo, L. E., & Haller, W. (2002). Transnational entrepreneurs: An alternative form of immigrant economic adaptation. *American Sociological Review, 67,* 278–298.

Quinn, J. (2009). The IRB and Young Ireland: Varieties of tension. In F. McGarry & J. McConnel (Eds.), *The black hand of republicanism: Fenianism in modern Ireland* (pp. 3–17). Dublin: Irish Academic Press.

Reaney, B. (1984). Irish Chartists in Britain and Ireland: Rescuing the rank and file. *Saothar, 10,* 94–103.

Sampson, W., & Taylor, W. C. (1832). *Memoirs of William Sampson: An Irish exile.* London: Whittaker, Treacher, and Arnot.

Savage, J. (1868). *Fenian Heroes and Martyrs.* Boston, MA: P. Donahoe.

Scott, W. R. (2013). *Institutions and organizations: Ideas, interests, and identities* (4th ed.). Thousand Oaks, CA: Sage.

Sixtyninth.net. (n.d.-a). *History of the sixty-ninth regiment, New York 'Fighting Sixty-Ninth.'* Retrieved from www.sixtyninth.net/downloads/First_Ten_Years.pdf. Accessed on February 7, 2014.

Sixtyninth.net. (n.d.-b). *Michael Doheny: Ever the young Irelander.* Retrieved from www.sixtyninth.net/downloads/Michael__Donheny.pdf. Accessed on February 7, 2014.

Smith, J., & Johnston, H. (Eds.). (2002). *Globalization and resistance: Transnational dimensions of social movements.* Lanham, MD: Rowman & Littlefield.

Smith, J., & Wiest, D. (2005). The Uneven geography of global civil society: National and global influences on transnational association. *Social Forces, 84*(2), 621–652.

Smith, R. C. (2003). Diasporic memberships in historical perspective: Comparative insights from the Mexican, Italian and polish cases. *International Migration Review, 37*(3), 724–759.

Snay, M. (2004). *The imagined republic: The Fenians, Irish American nationalism, and the political culture of reconstruction.* Worcester, MA: American Antiquarian Society.

Sperber, J. (1994). *The European revolutions, 1848–1851.* Cambridge: Cambridge University Press.

Stephens, J., & Ramon, M. É. (2008). *The birth of the Fenian Movement: American diary, Brooklyn 1859.* Dublin: University College Dublin Press.

Steward, P., & McGovern, B. (2013). The Fenians: Irish rebellion in the North Atlantic World 1858–1876. Knoxville, TN: The University of Tennessee Press.

Tarrow, S. (1988). National politics and collective action: Recent theory and research in Western Europe and the United States. *Annual Review of Sociology, 14*, 421–440.

Tarrow, S. (2005). *The new transnational activism.* Cambridge: Cambridge University Press.

Tilly, C. (2007). Trust networks in transnational migration. *Sociological Forum, 22*(1), 3–25.

Touraine, A. (1985). An introduction to the study of social movements. *Social Research, 52*(4), 749–787.

Townshend, C. (1983). *Political violence in Ireland: Government and resistance since 1848.* Oxford: Clarendon Press.

Wang, D. J., & Soule, S. A. (2012). Social movement organizational collaboration: Networks of learning and the diffusion of protest tactics, 1960–1995. *American Journal of Sociology, 117*(6), 1674–1722.

Weber, D. (1999). Historical perspectives on Mexican transnationalism: With notes from Angumacutiro. *Social Justice, 26*(3), 1043–1578.

Werbner, P. (2005). The translocation of culture: 'Community cohesion' and the force of multiculturalism in history. *Sociological Review, 53*(4), 745–768.

Whyte, J. H. (1958). *The independent Irish party, 1850–9.* London: Oxford University Press.

Wilson, D. A. (1998). *United Irish, United States: Immigrant radicals in the early republic.* Dublin: Four Courts Press.

TRANSNATIONAL FIELD AND FRAMES: ORGANIZATIONS IN ECUADOR AND THE US

Beth Williford and Mangala Subramaniam

ABSTRACT

Adopting a two-sited approach, this paper examines frames deployed by a network of organizations by developing the concept of the transnational field. The transnational field is the geo-specific field within which the movement organizations are encompassed which can explain the differential power across ties in a transnational network. It enables analyzing whether frames at the local and transnational level are similar, remain as is or are altered within a field which is mediated by the power dynamics embedded in the political-economic-cultural relationships between countries. Using qualitative data, this study of ties between movement organizations in the Amazonian region of Ecuador (local level) and organizations in the United States (transnational level) provides evidence for empirical and narrative fidelity of frames at both ends of the network. The two-sited approach enriches the understanding of resistance to globalization by prioritizing the perspective of indigenous peoples in the Global South highlighting the North—South power dynamic. Departing from common assumptions about the power of US-based groups in the choice of frames deployed, the analysis show that ties

Research in Social Movements, Conflicts and Change, Volume 38, 37—67
ISSN: 0163-786X/doi:10.1108/S0163-786X20150000038002

between organizations in a transnational network are complex as they rely on each other for resources and information. We discuss the conditions under which local frames are deployed or redefined at the transnational level.

Keywords: Transnational field; transnational network; frames; power; Ecuador

INTRODUCTION

Globalization processes over the past 30 years have been met by contentious protests and involved a range of communities, groups, nongovernmental organizations (NGOs), and social movements cooperating and coordinating their activities and actions transnationally (Hewitt, 2011; Yeates, 2001). Over the same period there has been a growth in the critical academic literature on transnational activism, which has variously conceptualized this new form of opposition as "transnational advocacy networks" (Keck & Sikkink, 1998; Moghadam, 2009), "transnational social movement organizations" (Smith, 1997), "global social movements" (Cohen & Rai, 2001; O'Brien et al., 2000), as well as "solidarities of difference" (Desai, 2005) amongst others (Della Porta et al., 2006). The spread of the antiglobalization movement across countries, in the global North and global South, has been a major impetus to this literature that has provided insights into challenges and consensus in protesting a variety of issues ranging from women's rights to environmental protection (Hewitt, 2011; Lewis, 2011; Smith, 2002).

In this paper, we study the deployment of frames by a network of organizations of the indigenous in Ecuador and the broader environmental movement in the United States which differs from earlier work that analyzes global forums or loosely conceptualized social movements. Following Buroway et al.'s (2000) call to rethink fieldwork as comprising multiple sites, we rely on a two-sited study to consider ties between movement organizations *across* sites and from *both* ends; an approach that allows us to highlight the power relations involved in the North—South dynamic but at the same time have implications for solidarity across borders. It is important to point out here that our reference to the two ends in no way implies that networks are linear. Other factors both internal and external to social movements have been found to facilitate or hinder network ties (cf. Wejnert, 2002).

We adopt Buroway et al.'s (2000) approach to analyze the resistance to oil exploration and its associated adverse impacts. This resistance arose with the discovery of oil in the Ecuadorian Amazon in the mid-1960s. Few indigenous groups had legal title to their lands, and they were almost completely ignored by the state, which hardly considered them citizens. The 1980s brought rising concerns about oil development, alongside community organizing and protests in the Ecuadorian Amazon. Much of the interest in oil was sparked by the government's decision in 1985 to license millions of acres of new Amazon territories to private companies. The impacts of the oil operations were just beginning to reach a national audience, and newly organized indigenous groups joined with environmentalists to oppose further exploration and development, particularly in indigenous territories and national environmental preserves. Sawyer (2004) eloquently chronicles the battle by indigenous organizations against the Ecuadorian government's embracement of neoliberal policies. More than a contest over material resources, these struggles represented an attempt by indigenous peoples to rewrite the national narrative to favor pluralism over transnational corporate capital. Environmental groups with a traditionally conservationist focus began to work more closely with communities in the Amazon to strengthen campaigns for sustainable development. This coming together at the local level was mirrored and supported by an international initiative of some Northern (global North) NGOs. These transnational networks and the frames they employ are at the core of this paper.

Networks across borders exist within a context of complex power dynamics affecting the frames deployed at both ends of the network (Bob, 2005; Merry, 2006; Widener, 2009). A frame functions as a "story line" (Gamson & Wolfsfeld, 1993) by "selectively punctuating and encoding objects, situations, events, experiences, and sequences of actions within one's present or past environment" (Snow & Benford, 1992, p. 137). Movements intentionally frame messages so that people "perceive, identify, and label" the social phenomena as something that deserves their attention and action (Snow et al., 1986, p. 464). By examining frames deployed at the local level and that at the other end (across borders) of the transnational network, we argue that it is possible to account for the variance of power and the language used across the network. In addition, we extend earlier work to consider the field within which cross-currents of frames may alter spaces for claims-making.

The *transnational field for frames*, as we elaborate below, requires specifying the regional field and the sites at which the frames may be deployed to be adopted as is, be redefined, or altered.[1] By field, we mean the geographical region where the movement organizations being studied are encompassed and which is mediated by the power dynamics embedded in the political-economic relationships between countries. Using the concept of the transnational field, we examine anti-globalization protests through transnational ties. We ask: what frames are deployed transnationally by US-based organizations working with the indigenous? And, how are these frames similar or different from those deployed at the local level by indigenous groups in Ecuador? We use data from two vantage points: (1) organizations in the Amazon region of Ecuador, the local level and (2) organizations primarily located within the United States identified by the Ecuadorian organizations, the transnational level. Using qualitative data — ethnographic notes, organizational records, and semi-structured interviews — with leaders and representatives of the nine organizations we analyze the frames deployed at the Ecuador and the US end and explain the variations.

This paper contributes to transnational movement scholarship in three ways. First, the concept of the transnational field facilitates our understanding of the space within which frames are deployed at local and global levels of a network and why particular frames resonate or not at both ends. Second, this study of the adverse effects of globalization originates from the perspective of the Global South, a perspective we argue deserves greater attention in social movement scholarship. By adopting a two-sited perspective of frame deployment across a network, this project recognizes the North–South power dynamic that is often understood as residing in the global North. Third, these analyses of the Ecuadorian indigenous resistance to "development" efforts contribute to the growing scholarship on mobilization against neoliberal globalization in Latin America (cf. Almeida & Walker, 2006; Eckstein, 1989, 2005; Harris, 2002; Postero, 2005; Widener, 2011) but adds a transnational lens to understanding the deployment of frames beyond Ecuador. Furthermore, studying marginalized groups resisting neoliberalism in a specific cultural setting in a developing country contributes to bridging scholarship across borders.

TRANSNATIONAL NETWORKS AND FRAMES

We draw on two conceptual ideas in social movement scholarship — networks and frames — to discuss how the transnational field is critical to explaining the frames deployed at two ends of a network. *Networks* serve as a major enduring resource for transnational interaction

(Keck & Sikkink, 1998; Moghadam, 2005; Smith, 2001). As decentralized and non-hierarchical in form, networks are key to mobilization and have become institutionalized globally as an appropriate and effective means for movement activists to work together despite differences in nationality, ethnicity, and class. Networks facilitate "people (or communities) to interact, to exchange information, to build social capital, and to mobilize for change. They help overcome distances that otherwise might appear insurmountable. And in so doing, they provide the basis for building movements" (Yashar, 2005, p. 73).

Mobilizing to protest issues that are relevant to people across countries through transnational networks entails differential power across countries such as North–South ties (Bob, 2005; Lewis, 2000; Merry, 2006; Piper & Uhlin, 2004; Smith, 2002). Recognizing this shifting power dynamic, we analyze why frames are adopted, altered, or ignored across the two ends of a network. We contend that a different power dynamic, an inequity related to geo-politics, access to power-holders and resources is significant to explaining which frames are adopted or altered in transnational network relations.

In recent years, framing activity in contentious politics has attracted increasing attention from researchers of social movements (Benford & Snow, 2000; Croteau & Hicks, 2003; Johnston & Noakes, 2005; Snow, 2004). The important role of collective action frames in movement emergence, development, and outcomes is now well documented and widely recognized in the field (Benford & Snow, 2000; Cress & Snow, 2000; Gamson, 1992; McCammon, 2009; Zuo & Benford, 1995). Collective action frames are constructed by social movement organizations to name and explain grievances and motivate participation and action (Benford & Snow, 2000; Snow & Benford, 1992). Frames must convey meaning to the participants intended to be mobilized and at the same time be effective to address the targets (state, global financial institutions). This is a challenge for transnational networks where audiences, and understandings, may vary across sites or locations. Thus, movement organizations aim for frame resonance but the choice of frames also involves power.

In order to achieve frame resonance, movement organizations employ existing symbols, language, and themes found in the cultural repertoire of the audience into frames (Snow & Benford, 1988). Frame resonance is related to frame efficacy. Three aspects impacting frame efficacy are: empirical credibility; experiential commensurability; and narrative fidelity (Snow & Benford, 1988). Empirical credibility is explained as the "fit between the framing and events in the world" (p. 208) and experiential commensurability refers to the extent in which frames relate to personal familiarities of potential recruits. Narrative fidelity is the frame's ability to blend with cultural beliefs, ideas, and assumptions within the cultural context (Benford & Snow, 2000; Snow & Benford, 1988). The cultural context is important for framing of injustices at the local level (Cadena-Roa, 2005; Noonan, 1995). Transnational networks thus face real challenges to understand and translate local grievances into issues that target audiences located across cultural and national borders. Our interest in this paper is on the frames deployed in a network comprising organizations in Ecuador and the United States, that is which frames are retained as is, are likely to be modified, or entirely altered to ensure resonance with the target audience. Modification or redefinition may also occur because of the ways organizations encompassed in a network exercise power within a transnational field.

Theorizing the Transnational Field for Frame Diffusion

Earlier work conceptualizes the field as "a structured, unequal, and socially constructed environment within which organizations are embedded and to which organizations and activists constantly respond" (Ray, 1999, p. 6). While this provides a useful starting point for considering the field, it focuses on the immediate environment of movement organizations and the strategies they adopt without much attention to the frames deployed or what that may mean in the increasingly integrated world system (cf. Smith & Wiest, 2012). The more recent work of Fligstein and McAdam (2011) on the strategic action field (SAF) moves theorizing to the level of a general understanding of social actors, institutions, and social change. But as pointed out by Goldstone and Useem (2012, p. 46), the conceptualization of the SAF treats "all organizations as essentially the same" and "discusses social change solely in terms of shifting configurations." The organizations we consider in transnational fields vary in form and are also embedded in different political and cultural contexts. Our concept of the transnational field is distinct from the transnational public sphere because our emphasis is on the context in which transnational ties, between the global North and global South, exist in shaping the exchanges.

In her analysis of transnational social movement organization (TSMO) solidarity, Smith (2002, p. 505) notes that "gaps between Northern and Southern members persist, particularly regarding groups' abilities to relate local concerns to global level campaigns." The differences in perceptions and the cultural biases across the North—South divide have indeed proved to be a key obstacle to transnational cooperation. Activists in Northern countries must often learn new ways of thinking about their own governments' policies and their views of citizenship as they learn about their Southern counterparts' divergent experiences and interpretations of the global economic order. Southern activists often find challenges to their assumptions that citizens from the rich Northern countries necessarily share their governments' views, and that they have substantial influence on the international policies of their governments. Interchanges among activists may also be complicated by class and racial divisions within countries, as many transnational activists are from privileged backgrounds and bring with them cultural biases typical of their class positions and their mostly urban experiences (cf. Brysk, 1996).

We build on prior work (Anner & Evans, 2004; Bob, 2005; Widener, 2011) to characterize the transnational field as a geo-specific field to examine whether and how frames are redefined. Organizations based in countries that wield enormous power within governing bodies and global financial institutions are more likely to have access to global policy-makers, media, and financial resources to participate in and shape the discourse, and therefore can deploy frames, around the issues in which they are involved. Such organizations can exert power at a transnational level. In contrast, organizations, particularly in the Global South, may wield limited influence to shape global policy but they may be able to leverage with transnationally based organizations to deploy the local frame or a modified form of the frame at the global level. The local and global can be specified recognizing that they exist in creative and varying tensions with one end informing the other rather than existing only in opposition to each other.

We posit three scenarios for the deployment of frames in the transnational field. First, local frames and transnational frames may be defined in similar ways. This may occur because of a shared political, economic, and cultural context or explanation of the frame. Second, local frames may be redefined, altered or altogether ignored at the transnational level by the US-based organizations allowing transnational frames to take center stage. This has also been shown by Keck and Sikkink (1998) in their work on transnational advocacy. That is, the content and explanation of frames are altered to fit the transnational context. The third scenario for frames in the transnational field is when a local frame is retained as is and so deployed, and adopted by the transnational-based organization. This "moving up" of a frame is also discussed by Tarrow (2005). That is, the frame deployed by local actors is also used at the transnational level, without the content or meaning of the local frame being altered. The variations across the three scenarios are based in the complexities of global power inequities and the efficacy of frames.

Our analysis shows how the transnational field, a term we use to denote the power differences that organizations wield in resources as well as power inequity in geo-politics, has the ability to influence the frames deployed at the transnational level. In addition, we discuss the circumstances under which we see variations, or not, in the frames employed across the transnational network we examine in this paper. Scholars have argued that structurally equivalent actors can tend to emulate each other (Strang & Soule, 1998) and that structural or institutional equivalence can facilitate the construction of similarity in collective action frames. By focusing on organizations in two different countries the structural differences provide a unique lens to considering the similarity or variations in frames.

DATA AND METHODS

We use qualitative data from ethnographic observations, organizational documents, and in-depth interviews with leaders and members of purposively selected organizations in Ecuador and the United States, which we detail below. We begin with an overview of anti-globalization protests in Ecuador.

Case of Ecuador: An Overview

Resistance to the Ecuadorian state's adoption of neoliberal policies began when the first structural adjustment programs were implemented in 1982. The discontent multiplied quickly leading campesinos and indigenous peoples of the highlands to stage protests (often including roadblocks and boycotting markets), demanding political rights and representation (Becker, 2002; Pacari, 1996). In 1992, the Amazonian indigenous marched from Puyo to Quito (more than 500 kilometers) demanding legalization of ancestral territories and their incorporation into the national dialogue about development. Leaders charged the government with accommodating interests in developing resource extraction on the backs of the indigenous communities (Gerlach, 2003; Sawyer, 2004; Viteri et al., 1992).

Over twenty years since this historic uprising against neoliberal policies and the resistance in indigenous communities continues unabated. Today,

transnational actors work in connection with Amazonian indigenous organizations and have the power to deploy frames that highlight the local
resistance to audiences around the world. Martin (2003, p. 47) notes:
"Although indigenous peoples in Ecuador, and throughout the Andean
region have been organized since the time of the Incas and have a history
of political unrest dating back to the colonial times, recent technological
advancements and influx of transnational actors to the country have changed their mobilization strategies."

The strategies at both the local and transnational ends of the network
we analyze here seek to destabilize the neoliberal project that has displaced
and threatened the Amazonian indigenous way of life. Indigenous leaders
hoped the election of President Correa in 2006 would mark a turning point
in Ecuadorian politics. And in some ways it has. Correa remains publicly
critical of the neoliberal model and his presidency represents the longest
modern period of political stability in Ecuador. Nevertheless, dependency
on natural resources, including oil extraction, continues to play a central
role in the national development plan. Thus, we see the continued efforts of
local indigenous organizations fight against the loss of territory and culture. While the primary audience of the indigenous frames is the
Ecuadorian government in order to pressure it to move away from neoliberal policies, the US-based organizations target transnational oil companies, the Ecuadorian government, and the US public.

Data and Analytic Strategy

Qualitative data were gathered by the first author from two different van-
tage points: organizations within Ecuador and US-based organizations
with ties to the Ecuadorian organizations. Preliminary data collection in
Ecuador in June–July 2006 was followed by additional fieldwork during
June–December 2007. Data from US-based organizations were gathered in
April 2008.

Consistent with qualitative methods, and using a purposive sampling
strategy, six indigenous organizations, representing five nationalities, in the
Ecuadorian Amazon were selected as cases. Puyo served as the base for
data collection as it is home to multiple representative organizations of
Amazonian indigenous organizations. Three criteria were used to select
cases for variation: period of organization's existence, natural resources in
territory, and membership coverage. The three US-based organizations
included in this project were identified by the Ecuadorian organizations as

those groups that have worked or continue to work with the local organizations. Tierra Amazónica was mentioned by four indigenous organizations, three of which were receiving funding for ongoing projects at the time of data collection. Eco-Protection and Green Vida were both mentioned by two different indigenous organizations.[2]

Similar data gathering strategies were adopted at both the local and transnational level. The first author gathered primary data in the form of ethnographic observations of the selected organizations, organizational records, and semi-structured interviews with designated leaders of organizations. Forty-four face-to-face interviews were conducted with leaders and representatives of the organizations. Interviews with indigenous leaders were conducted in Spanish and typically lasted between one and two hours. Interviews with organizational leaders in the United States were conducted in English and also lasted between one and two hours. Interviews focused on organizational history, structure, issues, and messages of the organization. Organizational documents such as newsletters and annual reports were also collected.

The first step in the analysis involved examining the interview data for instances of frames. The first author began by coding interview data from Ecuador, followed by organizational documents and field notes from the local level. But analysis did not begin with a formal list of codes; rather every field note, interview transcript, and organization document was reviewed multiple times to allow codes to emerge from the data (Charmaz, 2006). After identifying consistent themes in the local level (see the "key concepts from coding" column in Table 1), we followed the same steps to analyze the transnational data. The research questions led us to consider similarities and differences in frames at the local and transnational ends and how the frames related to each other.

For example, in interviews with indigenous leaders the first author learned about the significance of land. This was consistent across all interviews with leaders from the six indigenous organizations. Additionally, the indigenous often referred to their relationship with their territory and its significance by relating to it as a family member (a mother for instance), as an entity they know well and depend on for sustenance. During coding, we highlighted the general frequency codes were mentioned, rather than maintain a precise count. Codes such as land/territory, relationship, cultural practices and survival were repeated so often in interview transcripts and field notes that we recognized the frame "land and well-being" was critical to the Ecuadorian indigenous. Moreover, this frame captures the sentiment that it is not merely property to which they refer, but the deep relationship with land and territory that the Amazonian indigenous have.

FRAMES IN THE TRANSNATIONAL FIELD

Utilizing our conceptualization of the three possible scenarios of frames deployed within a transnational field, we discerned six frames deployed by the organizations. First, the "rights" frame is similar at both ends, Ecuador and the United States. It is defined as the "community and collective rights" frame by organizations in Ecuador and "human rights-indigenous rights" by organizations in the United States. Second, the local level frame "land and well-being" is redefined at the transnational level to the frame we call, "environmental devastation and conservation.' This set of frames captures the second scenario which involves a redefinition of a local frame at the transnational level. In the third scenario, we posit a local level frame being deployed unaltered at the transnational level. The Ecuador level frame, "state policy and plunder" is used by the US-based organizations as "holding polluters and state accountable." See Table 1 for a summary of frames, themes encompassed, and dimensions of efficacy met.

We also examine the three dimensions of frame efficacy: empirical credibility, experiential commensurability, and narrative fidelity to explain how power dynamics shape which frames are deployed by organizations in Ecuador and the United States. See Table 2 for a summary of the basis for the three dimensions of frame efficacy. The assessment of the correspondence of frames to real life (empirical credibility) led us to consider whether organizations at both ends use facts, figures or real-life examples to provide credibility to claims made. Our assessments of experiential commensurability and narrative fidelity focus on the efforts of organizations to highlight personal issues and cultural beliefs respectively.

Similar Frames at Local Level and Transnational Level

Ecuadorian indigenous leaders appeal for collective rights in the culturally significant understanding of the collective seeking protection in state documents and which we call the "community and collective rights" frame. The US-based organizations also deploy a "rights" frame by focusing on human rights, a frame we call "human rights-indigenous rights."

Table 1. Frames in the Transnational Field.

Scenario	Frames	Frame Defined as	Dimensions of Efficacy	Key Concepts from Coding
Similar frames at local level and transnational level	Rights frame Ecuador: community and collective rights	Collective rights and desires of indigenous communities as being primary and placed above that of the individual	Empirical credibility Narrative fidelity	Shared experiences of the community; collective rights
	US: human rights-indigenous rights	Rights defined as justice of marginalized and oppressed groups such as the indigenous	Empirical credibility Narrative fidelity	Protecting indigenous rights as human rights
Transnational organizations redefine local level frames	Ecuador: land and well-being	Synergy between indigenous peoples and land; a cultural aspect	Experiential commensurability Narrative fidelity	Territory informs identity, relationship with ancestors
	US: environmental devastation and conservation	Protecting biodiversity and creating a sustainable world	Empirical credibility Narrative fidelity	Conserving biodiversity
Local level frames deployed at the transnational level	Ecuador: state policy and plunder	Indigenous leaders views on neoliberal policies of Ecuadorian government. Includes perceived roles of government, the military, and transnational oil companies, adversely affecting indigenous communities	Empirical credibility Experiential commensurability Narrative fidelity	Impacts of neoliberal policies on communities, lay blame on government and empresa
	US: holding polluters and state accountable	Holding transnational oil companies and government responsible for destruction of indigenous culture and environment. Aim to put pressure on the oil companies	Empirical credibility	Responsibility of government and transnational companies

Table 2. Frame Efficacy.

Dimensions	Definition	Frame Efficacy – Amazonian Region, Ecuador End, and US End
Empirical credibility	Ability of a frame to correspond with real-life events/experiences	Are there attempts to substantiate or verify frames by citing facts, figures, or real-life examples that give credence to claims in protests?
Experiential commensurability	Extent to which frame relates to personal familiarities of potential recruits	Is there effort to illustrate how issues represented in frames affect potential supporters, personally?
Narrative fidelity	Ability of frames to blend with cultural beliefs, ideas, and assumptions	Do content of frames illustrate how their goals conform to cultural beliefs or ideas?

Community and Collective Rights

The local-level frame, "community and collective rights" emphasizes the community. The rights of the collective is a unique characteristic of the indigenous who depend upon each other and respect community solidarity (Fenelon & Hall, 2008; Mander & Tauli-Corpuz, 2002). For example, the prioritizing of the community over the individual is evident in the following example. An Achuar man in Ecuador wanting to work outside of his community is required to come before the community and explain why he wants to do this and what the benefits are for the community. Community leaders and elders then decide if he should go and for how long because his presence is important for *mingas*, the communal work, and to support his wife and family.

Most of the indigenous leaders referred to their "collective rights" in the interviews. These rights are those guaranteed for all indigenous nations in the two most recent Constitutions approved in 1998 and 2008. The collective rights in both Constitutions include "the right to develop and strengthen their identity and spiritual, cultural, linguistic, social, political, and economic traditions; ... to conserve their inalienable communally owned lands; ... to conserve their forms of social organization and authority" (Van Cott, 2000, p. 276). Indigenous leaders, nonetheless, lack confidence in the laws that protect indigenous collective rights and are uncertain of what the government will recognize. Rafael desires:

> a new government that acknowledges all of the nationalities, that protects us all in issues of health, education, economics ... we all look for this acknowledgement. More than anything we as indigenous are marginalized, exploited ... sometimes insulted and

> criticized. It shouldn't be this way because we are a part of the Ecuadorian state and we
> have the right to be recognized.

All the organizations in Ecuador struggle for legal title to their ancestral lands. When an indigenous nation gains a legal land title it means that no one person can buy or sell a portion of property and that the entire nation is the owner. Rafael said:

> We manage our territory in a global form. A [legal] title is for everyone and that is
> respected by everyone ... there are no limits. No one is the owner except all of the
> nation. That is to say if I want to live there, I simply tell everyone and I can go live
> there without problems.

Indigenous nations rely on the collective rights established in the Constitution to be recognized as collective owners of their ancestral lands. This has been a priority since the first indigenous organization was formed in the Pastaza province in 1977. Fausto explained that the organization began with an aim to "defend the territories, the cultural identity and rights of the indigenous peoples." Similarly, Rafael situated the defense of territory as a legal stance through the lens of "rights." He explained that his "organization was created with the end goal being to defend their territorial rights, culture, education, health, justice, liberty, with a vision to live peacefully in [their] territory." This articulation of rights is not entirely distinct from the human rights frame deployed by US-based organizations which holds meaning at global forums (Keck & Sikkink, 1998; Stewart, 2004).

Human Rights-Indigenous Rights
The human rights frame, deployed by the US organizations, encompasses the rights of indigenous peoples who have experienced marginalization and injustice. This frame can mobilize supporters, alluding to both the UN and ILO 169 as a standard for applying a rights-based approach to their work with the Amazonian indigenous.[3] The UN and ILO 169 establishes indigenous rights as a subset of human rights by emphasizing the notion of collective, rather than individual, rights. But the US organizations evoke human rights in conjunction with the environment. For instance, in response to the query of how these important components of Green Vida stack up, Robert said that both components, "environmental protection and so called indigenous rights," are equally important. Robert added, "They are mutually supportive goals, not exclusive."

Similarly, Jeff, a representative at Eco-Protection, characterized their work for indigenous rights and environmental protection as a "partnership with the communities." He added that Eco-Protection wanted to promote the solutions of indigenous communities for "environmental and human rights problems in their area." Emphasizing the need for indigenous communities to have control over their territory, Jeff said:

And that's the best way not only to protect the environment there but to protect it from hydrocarbon expansion and the environmental destruction that ensues. But also that these communities have been the stewards of this territory for thousands of years and they know best how to exist in synergy without destroying the environment.

He noted that they highlight the rights frame in conversations with Ecuadorian indigenous leaders, specifically the need for documenting human rights abuses. Jeff continued: "So the idea is that there's not only violations taking place against the environment but people and they should be protected and documented." Violations of indigenous rights are posted on the organization's website and included in their newsletter serving as a call to action for the organization's members. This we infer as using empirical credibility to substantiate claims made by the organization. Representatives from Green Vida and Tierra Amazónica both explained that they integrate indigenous rights into the goals of protecting the land from oil projects and to protect the land from deforestation.

The claim to "rights" is similar across the local-transnational levels. The indigenous organizations subscribe to the cultural aspect of rights and are also exposed to the notion of human rights advocated by the US-based organizations through their close involvement in UN led forums for indigenous peoples. The language of rights resonates at both ends of the network in spite of differences in political power that may be exercised by the organizations. Rights-based frames embody what Keck and Sikkink (1998) refer to as "languages that cannot be rejected;" these frames offer claims that are difficult for organizations at either end to argue with. Indeed, both ends of the network are basing their frames on the law and as such are acting as a coalition.[4] The rights frames provide a broad tent, enabling many movement actors to join in the use of common language and still feel that their priorities are receiving attention and being validated. The broadly resonant themes in the transnational field between Ecuador and the United States enable organizations to claim heightened legitimacy when working together and with powerful political actors.

Local Level Frames Redefined at Transnational Level

In the second scenario we consider the redefinition of the local level frames by the US organizations. The local frame, "land and well-being" highlights a people-land relationship among the indigenous. It is redefined as "protecting biodiversity and conservation" by the US-based organizations which shifts the meaning from the cultural understanding of livelihood to the rational, scientifically based need for conservation and sustainability.

Land and Well-being
The frame "land and well-being" is defined by the Ecuador-based organizations as the intimate or synergistic relationship the indigenous peoples have with the environment where their ancestral lands are located and the implication this has for their well-being. This relationship is in direct contrast to the neoliberal understanding of land as a commodity with real tangible value. The Ecuadorian organizations emphasize their cultural understandings of land and how the meanings therein fortify their movement. It emerges from inhabiting and depending upon the land for survival.

For instance, the Waorani marched through the streets of Quito on October 31, 2007 to protest the actions of the Ministry of Public Works selling sections of their territory to the highest bidder. Reflecting the tradition of collective land ownership they carried signs, chanting: "El Yasuní no se vende!" ["The Yasuní forest is not for sale!"] Rejecting land commodification, indigenous leaders extol the synergy between people and ancestral lands. A leader of a different indigenous nation explained the synergy as:

> Our life in the jungle is different from the Western world ... our life is the territory. It is a part of my identity, a part of my life. My people in the jungle need money, but without it they can still live for many years because we have everything there. For us the jungle is a market. [In the jungle] what I eat and drink is all free ... In the jungle we have natural medicine, we take care of ourselves, we have our own cosmovisión. We can go to the waterfalls to capture strength to be able to survive in the jungle. This is called "Aruta."

Leaders draw upon myths and stories to frame both the physical and subjective dimension of land that deeply resonates with their communities. Frames rely on the shared experiences of those who inhabit the physical space of the forest and are dependent upon it for daily sustenance. Victor said: "Our territory is important because we were born here. And we have to maintain that. We are talking about our ancestors, our grandparents... those who gave it to us."

Closely tied to the synergy the indigenous experience with the land is "well-being." With increasing extraction of natural resources from the forests, the well-being and health of the indigenous is at stake. Rivers and waterways are the most important source of water in the jungle and, not surprisingly, occupy an important place in indigenous creation stories, cos-movisión, and serve as territory markers. Many indigenous leaders noted the changes in quality of the water since oil companies have entered the area. Felix clarified how the oil companies impact the community:

> The impact, for example, when it rains sometimes crude [oil] particles can collect in the streams and no one notices it because it is raining. When it rains the river grows and the particles enter the rivers as well. They [oil companies] say that the water is safe … It's a lie! And who is controlling 24 hours a day how many drops are passing down the river? No one controls that.

Omar explained that the existence of an exploratory oil well in his community has forever changed life for all in the area: "It started with a strong rain that damaged the well. Afterward the contents of the well spilled into the river. Then the fish were dying, the animals, the boas (snakes) all died there." By drawing on real-life examples of such devastation indigenous leaders create empirical credibility, increasing the likelihood of frame efficacy as it resonates with the experiences of the community they aim to mobilize and also to target the government.

In fact, scholars have documented the effects of oil leakages and toxic chemicals in water resources on the well-being of the indigenous (Kimerling, 2001; San Sebastian & Hurtig, 2004). Oil leakages in the Amazon have resulted from the use of outdated equipment, by the oil companies, as well as a lack of regulatory mechanism. The reckless habit of the empresa of "dumping trash in the rivers" was described as adversely affecting survival of the indigenous. Many indigenous leaders alluded to sicknesses that never existed before the empresa entered the territory. Savana said:

> [All] the people do not know that in the water where the children go to bathe, the water is contaminated. After three months a rash appears and the entire body is covered and contaminated … all over the head. Bumps form on the face.

Thus communities have had to alter their relationship with the water. The issues discussed above are not directly incorporated in the frame deployed by the US-based organizations.

Environmental Devastation and Conservation

The frame, "environmental devastation and conservation," redefines the local (Ecuador) frame to resonate with an audience animated by global calls to "go green" and "save the environment." It is centered on protecting biodiversity and creating a sustainable world. The environmental devastation and conservation frame is about saving the particular physical space which has unique characteristics: biodiversity (plants, animals) and the people (Widener, 2007, 2009). It fails to encompass the cultural meanings the indigenous attach to land and forests.

Highlighting the ecological composition of the Amazon region, by protecting biodiversity, is a central mission of the US-based organizations. Scientific research about the region where the indigenous live is often linked to explanations of biodiversity to make the frame empirically credible. The noteworthy levels of biodiversity in the Ecuadorian Amazon had a resounding impact on several of the transnational actors interviewed. For instance, Michelle explained that she and others were inspired to form Tierra Amazónica because "we started realizing that this rainforest is not just any rainforest. This is one of the most biodiverse and important rainforests on Earth." Working with Ecuadorian activists, Stephan from Green Vida fought the construction of a road by a Brazilian oil company in the Ecuadorian Amazon; "I was struck by the fact that here in one of the most biodiverse parks on the planet and there was no strong movement to stop something as blatant as a road going through it."

For the past three decades the idea of biodiversity has motivated environmental enthusiasts to promote conservation. In fact, trained ecologists at Green Vida have assisted with producing scientific publications about the threats to "wilderness, biodiversity, and indigenous peoples" in the Amazon. The US-based organizations define biodiversity by referring to all of the non-human life that exists in the region. Upwards of one-third of the planet Earth's species are found in the Amazon, making it an unparalleled repository of biodiversity. In fact, the founders of Tierra Amazónica explain that their organization was formed to help the indigenous protect the rainforest by raising awareness in the Global North. The indigenous recognize the power of the US-based organizations in terms of their commitment to conservation across the world.

Interestingly, the US organizations tie in environmental sustainability within the frame related to biodiversity. Global sustainability, a major endeavor of the US organizations, refers to "[sustaining] global life-support systems indefinitely" which includes food, water, air, and energy (Goodland, 1995, p. 6). The concern is that all of these resources can be depleted and therefore these natural sources upon which people are dependent must be maintained. Tierra Amazónica holds regular symposia where the sustainability mission is made explicit, as Simon noted: to bring forth an environmentally sustainable, spiritually fulfilling and socially just human presence on this planet

Tierra Amazónica frames its work in the global North (US primarily) by sharing the story of indigenous leaders requesting the organization's founders to change the modern world's consumption-based lifestyle. Scientists, activists, and indigenous leaders, in an accompanying video indicate that the lifestyle of the North is "threatening to destroy the rainforest, indigenous cultures, and our health." The strategic defining of the frame focused specifically on US audiences ensures empirical credibility. Antonio, an Ecuadorian who works with Tierra Amazónica's efforts in Ecuador, explained that the symposium is "directed exclusively at North Americans." By incorporating messages from indigenous cultures and US experts, the symposium is designed to "help the North American society change its ways of conduct, so that this consumer-driven society will cause less impact on the global resources available." Another representative explained how important it is for the organization's work to be "sold" in a way that its supporters in the United States can recognize and support. When asked about indigenous politics being used to rally US-based audiences, she waved her hand in jest, suggesting that perhaps that topic might not be as palatable in the United States as the topics of sustainability and conservation.

Though both the Ecuadorian and US-based organizations have similar interests in protecting the region, the difference in frames reveals the power exerted by the US organizations to redefine a frame. At first reading it might seem that US-based organizations are co-opting the frames from the local level. We believe the difference at the transnational level reveals the complexity in the relationship within this network. The local and transnational organizations continue to interact despite using distinct frames about land and conservation. Frames in Ecuador urge the protection of indigenous territories by highlighting the cultural meanings of relationships with the land, the connection to ancestral, well-being, and as sources of livelihood for survival.

In contrast the US organizations wield global power to reframe these ideas using a "universal" language of protection of biodiversity and the need for conservation. This increases the likelihood that these organizations can provide more resources and legitimacy for local level actors pressuring for change domestically (Bob, 2005; Lewis, 2000; Rothman & Oliver, 1999; Stewart, 2004; Widener, 2007). However, the ability to raise resources and utilize a language of conservation and sustainability is also because of their location in the transnational field − a position in the geo-political zone which enables articulation of the rational scientific rather than a cultural understanding of the protection of land and forests. Moreover, because many of the US organizations have either organizational branches or links to organizations in countries and regions across the world they can reinforce the universal language. The proximity of these organizations to international institutions such as the UN and the World Bank can make it possible to effective make a case. At the same time, as noted by Smith (2002), organizations in the global North tend to adopt reformist strategies that is "they may accept the view that the World Bank must be severely reduced or abolished, but they may resist adopting such a goal because they believe it would be politically ineffective to do so" (p. 521).

Local Level Frames Deployed at the Transnational Level

Local level organizations are not powerless to define frames that are adopted by the US-based organizations. Local level activists, in this case the indigenous, "provide irreplaceable knowledge of local dimensions of a global issue while also crucially contributing to the legitimacy of transnational campaigns" (Stewart, 2004, p. 262). The local-level frame, "state policy and plunder," refers to the adverse impacts of the neoliberal policies introduced by the Ecuadorian government. It encompasses the indigenous perceptions of the government, military, and the transnational oil companies, believed to be motivated by profit, negatively affecting the lives of the indigenous. This local level frame is adopted by US organizations as "holding polluters and the state accountable."

State Policy and Plunder

Encouraged by global financial institutions and the neoliberal economic trend of the 1980s and 1990s, Ecuador took out massive loans to pay previous debts and propel the country into the ranks of the developed nations. In order to pay these loans, the government subsequently agreed to lease blocks of the Amazon region to transnational oil companies to extract and exploit the subterranean oil reserves. The government's assertions that these policies represent the neoliberal agenda are countered by the indigenous through the frame we call "state policy and plunder." Indigenous leaders assert that the government prioritized the pursuit of profit over protecting lives and the Amazonian ecosystem. Reflecting on the elevated importance of transnational companies to indigenous communities in Ecuador, Delmar noted, "The government is in favor of transnational companies ... the government does not protect us, but we have rights ... we are the owners of the house."

Commenting on the irresponsibility of the previous governments, Felix said: "We live in the Amazon. The government only wants oil and after that they couldn't care less." Two other indigenous leaders from different nationalities made similar assertions. This observation about the government emerges from a community-wide understanding of the government's role in creating policies that are harmful to the indigenous peoples' ways of life (Mander & Tauli-Corpuz, 2002; Stewart-Harawira, 2005). Some indigenous organizations have previously been involved in standoffs with oil companies and have also witnessed the government's involvement in the protection of oil operations through the repression of indigenous communities using the military. The indigenous resist the role of the empresa, the generic name for the oil companies working in the indigenous territories. Ivan, identifies a specific example of military presence, thus helping to explain this event in such a way as to resonate with experiences of his community and government repression. He said:

> The government sends in the military. The military in [to our territory]! In strategic points the military was there, this happened in 2003. Then there was a terrible confrontation. Oh it was terrible, the threats were so strong. One group came out in favor of the oil company and the other group in favor of defending our ancestral territory.

Although the government created a policy to lease blocks of the Amazon for oil extraction, the oil companies often face strong resistance to their entry in the region. Indigenous leaders identify the ways the empresa create divisions within communities, seek profits at the expense of the indigenous lives and ecosystem, and make unfulfilled promises to gain trust and entry into indigenous regions. For instance, Ivan commented that the empresa alters the local cultures and landscapes: "They break the culture. There is impact on the social world and there is environmental impact." Justifying their responses in the interviews, leaders reflected on the experiences of other Ecuadorian indigenous nations whose territories have been destroyed.

Ecuador has not always upheld the standard of free, prior, and informed consent, as described in the Constitution (1998 and 2008), the 1998 ILO Convention (No. 169) and acknowledged by the UN (Perrault, Herbertson, & Lynch, 2007; United Nations, 2005). The government should ensure that indigenous communities are consulted before oil extraction commences. Additionally, the government is responsible for explaining the plan for oil extraction in indigenous territories. The organizations, in accordance with the communities, can either accept or reject the oil company's plans. However, indigenous leaders like Ivan commented on the way in which the empresa consults or convinces some communities to accept their presence. He notes that it usually includes false promises:

> They enter into some of the communities to socialize, to convince the people, saying that the company is going to help them, that the company is going to provide infrastructure (build homes, schools). They are going to give medicine; they are going to give education to their children. They offer a ton of things.

Ivan continued noting that by not going through the organization that legally represents a community, the companies are "entering a house without permission."

Local organization leaders narrated examples of the "dirty tricks" used by the transnational oil companies to weaken indigenous resistance. They draw attention to the ways in which the empresa tries to win over the community by making divisions therein. Lazaro suggested that: "They are going to enter the communities, buying the consciousness of the people." The local organization leaders' description of the empresa as lived experiences demonstrates this frame's empirical credibility and experiential commensurability. Thus, by providing specific examples for their claims and recalling experiences their communities have shared, they frame their messages in a way that resonates with their communities.

Holding Polluters and the State Accountable

The US-based organizations accept the injustice and explanation for who is to blame that their indigenous partners use through the frame we call, "holding polluters and the state accountable." By using the local level frame, the US-based organizations raise awareness about the responsibility of the Ecuadorian government and transnational oil companies for the environmental changes in the Amazon. The US organizations recognize the importance of the export led growth which often means extraction of resources and profit for private transnational oil companies. Holding these parties accountable inspired the founding of one transnational organization, Eco-Protection. Alex from Eco-Protection explained that they "watch, monitor, and do threat assessments of what sorts of operations and development projects were threatening the Amazon rainforest in general and indigenous cultures that inhabit the Amazon." Threats include toxic pollution related to oil operations that have had devastating impacts on the environment. Citing facts and figures, evidence of this frame's empirical credibility, Alex explained:

Texaco discovered oil in the Ecuadorian Amazon in 1967. In 1972 they began to produce and export essentially. They continued to operate there for the next twenty-six
years essentially ... they dumped over 18 billion gallons of toxic waste water into the
Ecuadorian Amazon. This was a deliberate decision that they made ... instead of imple-
menting adequate technology, reinjection systems etc., lining the pools ... which they
were doing and was standard operation procedure in the United States at the time. So
they chose to do this to save money because they could. That resulted in a public health
crisis.

The US-based organizations raise awareness about the above noted
issues by holding public events. They invite indigenous leaders to speak at
fundraising luncheons, participate in shareholder protests, or visit with US
politicians and at the UN to address how transnational oil companies have
polluted indigenous homelands. This extends legitimacy to their frame by
presenting "indigenous partners" to their US-based supporters and provides an opportunity for indigenous leaders to speak directly to their
counterparts.

Alongside calling to task the parties directly involved in the pollution of
the Amazon, US-based organizations work to hold the Ecuadorian government accountable by pressuring it to adopt policies that reflect environmental protections. Two of the US-based organizations in this study influenced
the 2008 Ecuadorian Constitution in this regard. For instance, Jeff details
Eco-Protection's focus on the government's adoption of large-scale
development:

We decided several years ago to focus the niche on hydrocarbons and the effect of drilling mines and natural gas in the Amazon. So not only did we feel that we could be
effective there, but that was also, I think, taken from the guidance of the [indigenous]
communities too, our partners and what they were working on. Where did they think
that we could be most effective?

Another example of pressuring the government comes from Robert at
Green Vida who explained that their work in the North is related to their
direct ties with the indigenous organizations at the local level. He noted the
imperative for the indigenous communities to learn about how "invading
governmental economic interests take advantage of people ... Certainly the
[indigenous] that we know want to protect their lands from being polluted.
So that means less oil, not more." This perspective frames the problem as
the unbridled desire of the Ecuadorian government to exploit the natural
resources of the region and the need to educate the indigenous peoples
about this.

The adoption of the local level frame (state policy and plunder) by the
US-based organizations emphasizes the negative consequences of neoliberal

policies that enable profit by private companies. The frame emphasizes the source of injustice experienced by the Ecuadorian indigenous, in solidarity with the local end of the network. There is commitment by the US-based organizations to allow the indigenous to speak about the injustice and lay blame on the Ecuadorian government and neoliberal policies it has adopted. This perspective is readily identifiable, albeit not experienced directly by US audiences. Thus, the Ecuador-based organizations exert power on the US-based organizations for its use at the transnational level. Moreover, the local frame, when deployed transnationally, draws on a familiar theme of pressuring governments and multinational oil companies to take responsibility for inflicting harm on local populations.

Circumstances under which Frames Are Similar, Different, or Retained

Under what circumstances then are local frames similar, redefined or ignored, or retained as is at the transnational level? The obvious possibility is that organizations based in politically influential countries may rely on their own recognition of a frame and thus choose to deploy it. But that would be a simplistic deduction. The use of the local frame has to be understood in the context of the ties between the organizations within the defined transnational field. The ties between organizations across borders are complex particularly because each end of the network depends on the other for information and resources. In fact, US-based organizations invite the indigenous to speak in forums in the United States and also engage in capacity building initiatives. This, no doubt, legitimizes the advocacy work of the US-based organizations but at the same time compels them to recognize the importance of a local level frame.

Moreover, the shifting power dynamics in the global context may influence the leverage of organizations in different regions of the world. It is important, however, to recognize the tense co-existence of the economic and development policies at the level of the state, mostly guided by the global financial institutions, on the one hand, and the ability of movements to problematize such policies from below and demand for change on the other hand.

Based upon this research we contend that there are certain circumstances that may influence whether a local frame is similar to a transnational frame, redefined, or deployed in a transnational network. Frames that appeal to both local realities and universal legal norms (as in the case of "rights") are likely to be deployed across both ends of a North–South network. In our research the shared "rights" frames were both character-ized with empirical credibility and narrative fidelity. The variations are in the subtleties of the definitions. As noted by Steiner (1991) in his study of human rights organizers, Northern organizers tended to prefer narrow, legalistic definitions of human rights (e.g., civil and political rights) while their Southern counterparts saw in this emphasis a failure to recognize the economic or systemic causes of human rights violations.

Additionally, our data revealed that the transnational organizations redefined the local frames when the local frame would not resonate with their Northern audience who may be unfamiliar with local understandings. Thus we see a discussion of "land and well-being" transformed to a frame we call "environmental devastation and conservation." While the expecta-tion is that the transnational end of a network will have all the power to define and deploy frames, our data challenged us to reconsider this assumption. We found a local frame that laid blame on the government and transnational corporations deployed by the US-based organizations. We argue that the transnational field shifts whereby a local frame is deployed transnationally when it meets all three dimensions of frame effi-cacy and when the target of grievances is shared by both ends of the network.

CONCLUSION

By conceptualizing a transnational field as comprising movement organiza-tions across countries, we draw attention to the power dynamics that influ-ence the frames deployed across the two points of a network. These power dynamics encompass the cultural, political, and economic context that envelope the network. While one may assume that US-based groups, due to the power exerted by the power of the United States in the world, would consistently shape the local frames to their own vision, we find that does not always hold. The transnational field is an analytical tool that captures frame variance across transnational networks. Frames deployed across the local and global level may be similar, be redefined, or be altered depending on frame efficacy in an effort to ensure resonance. The analyses in this paper have three main implications.

First, these analyses draw attention to the importance of understanding the complex relationships of transnational networks existing across the Global North and South. Our two-sited methodology enables examining

network ties across two ends rather than relying on one end and overlook-
ing the power structured between organizations in different regions.
Focusing on frames *at* and *across* the local (Global South) and global (global North) facilitates understanding the mechanisms that influence cross-
currents of frames that, in turn, may alter spaces for claims-making. The
local and global levels exist in creative and varying tensions with the possibility of both ends informing each other rather than existing only in opposition. That is, studying transnational networks as involving only one
location may be limiting in understanding variations in frames across
borders.

Second, the frames deployed within a field that encompasses South and
North America have broader implications for power differences in the
resources that organizations may have access to but more importantly in
the arena of geo-political power. Frames across the local and global levels
vary, are contested, and are deployed strategically. Researchers studying
frame diffusion in other fields may find variations in whether and how
frames may be redefined within a specific local-global field because of the
varying tensions across the levels based on power dynamics. The ever-
changing balance of power at the global level has the potential to alter
frames deployed transnationally.

The local level in Ecuador is composed of organizations mobilizing communities based in large part on their shared indigenous identities and
community-based forms of living. By understanding the local context in
which the organizations work and the connections local level organizations
have to US-based organizations it is possible to understand more clearly
why the frames and their explanations are similar or differ at both ends of
the network. The "rights" frame which is also promoted by the UN transcends borders as it invokes a call for the rights of the marginalized such as
the indigenous. This frame is used by organizations at the local Ecuador
end and the US end and demonstrates both empirical and narrative fidelity.

In contrast, the second set of frames discussed above, Land and
Well-being deployed at the Ecuador level and Environmental Devastation
and Conservation deployed at the US level, differ in their meaning and
content. The local Ecuador frame has experiential commensurability as it
speaks to the cultural aspect of the lives of the indigenous, particularly their
unique relationship with the land. This frame is redefined by the US-based
organizations that exert their power in utilizing universal language of protecting biodiversity and conservation rather than focusing on the lives of
the indigenous. Yet the US-based frames provide authenticity and legitimacy for these organizations (global level). That is to say, explaining "how

the forest is our mother' would not resonate with US-based audiences and mobilize them to support the resistance movement. However, US-based organizations are able to use their position at the global level to adopt entirely different frames from their indigenous partners and to explain the struggle through the lens of rights and environmental protection.

Interestingly, this analysis challenges a presumption of power flowing from the North to the South. We identify a local-level frame deployed by the indigenous that was adopted by their US counterparts unchanged. The frame focuses on the plundering by transnational oil companies the role of the state and the effects of the neoliberal policies. As the Amazonian indigenous have protested the effects of unregulated oil drilling, their grievances have become well-known particularly as marginalized groups around the world recognize the adverse effects of privatization and transnational investments. This frame has empirical credibility at both ends of the network and therefore is adopted as is by the US-based organizations. The overwhelming empirical evidence and resistances to the negative effects of prioritizing export led growth and attraction of transnational investments through state policy in developing countries, we would argue, served as a deterrent to modification or redefinition by the US-based organizations.

Third, these analyses show that there is an inbuilt complexity in frame diffusion in a transnational field. Studies focusing only on one end of a network, typically the global North, assume that the power of the organizations at, for example, the US end dictate the meanings and content of frames. This, we show, does not always hold. But discerning the direction of differential power requires examining a network from multiple ends.

We recognize that frame deployment and adoption is an ongoing and complex endeavor in which organizations constantly engage. Thus, future research involving transnational networks should consider the transnational field that shapes frames in order to account for the power-laden context in which meaning is created and the efficacy of those frames employed.

NOTES

1. There is a complexity in distinguishing between the local and global (Naples, 2009). Indeed, the global originates from *some* location and is influenced by the power and political economy of the Global North (Naples, 2009; Widener, 2011). We classify Ecuadorian organizations as the "local" for three reasons: (1) the grievances of the indigenous are directly felt (2) resistance began first in Ecuador and (3) we prioritize the perspective of the indigenous in this account of transnational activism. The US-based organizations certainly operate in their own local context,

yet we classify them as "transnational" because of their position in relationship with the Ecuadorian organizations and within the Global North.

2. The names of all people and organizations are pseudonyms.

3. The UN has been instrumental in incorporating indigenous rights starting with the 1948 Universal Declaration of Human Rights. In 1982 the UN began a Working Group on Indigenous Peoples to protect indigenous peoples' human rights, their rights as indigenous individuals. In 1989 the ILO Convention no. 169 created the first document to recognize the "self-identification of indigenous and tribal peoples" and specify their rights to "lands, traditions, languages, and to all human rights without discrimination" (Chernela, 2003).

4. We greatly appreciate this insight from a reviewer.

ACKNOWLEDGMENTS

We thank the editor and the anonymous reviewers for their insightful comments and suggestions. We are grateful to the organizations and leaders/ key informants for providing access to their activities and reflections on their work. We also acknowledge Robert Perrucci and Tom Shriver for their comments and suggestions on an earlier draft of this paper. This project was made possible through a 2007 NSF Dissertation Improvement Grant (0727979).

REFERENCES

Almeida, P., & Walker, E. (2006). The pace of neoliberal globalization: A comparison of three popular movement campaigns in Central America. Social Justice, 33(3), 175–190.

Anner, M., & Evans, P. (2004). Building bridges across a double divide: Alliances between the US and Latin American labour and NGOS. Development in Practice, 14(1), 34–47.

Becker, M. (2002). Ecuador. In P. Heenan & M. Lamontagne (Eds.), The South American handbook (pp. 69–79). London: Fitzroy Dearborn Publishers.

Benford, R. D., & Snow, D. A. (2000). Framing processes and social movements: An overview and assessment. Annual Review of Sociology, 26(1), 611–639.

Bob, C. (2005). The marketing of rebellion: Insurgents, media, and international activism. New York, NY: Cambridge University Press.

Brysk, A. (1996). Turning weakness into strength: The internationalization of Indian rights. Latin American Perspectives, 23(2), 38–57.

Buroway, M., Blum, J., George, S., Gille, Z., Gowan, T., Haney, L., … Thaye, M. (2000). Global ethnography: Forces, connections, and imaginations in a postmodern world. Berkeley, CA: University of California Press.

Cadena-Roa, J. (2005). Strategic framing, emotions, and superbarrio, Mexico City's masked crusader. In H. Johnston & J. Noakes (Eds.), Frames of protest (pp. 69–86). Lanham, MD: Rowman and Littlefield.

Charmaz, K. (2006). *Constructing grounded theory*. London: Sage.

Chernela, J. (2003). *The rights of indigenous peoples: International instruments*. AAA Committee for Human Rights website. Retrieved from http://www.aaanet.org/committees/cfhr/chronology.htm. Accessed on July 20, 2009.

Cohen, R., & Rai, S. (2001). *Global social movements*. London: Althone Press.

Cress, D., & Snow, D. (2000). The outcomes of homeless mobilization: The influence of organization, disruption, political mediation, and framing. *American Journal of Sociology*, *105*, 1063–1104.

Croteau, D., & Hicks, L. (2003). Coalition framing and the challenge of a consonant frame pyramid: The case of a collaborative response to homelessness. *Social Problems*, *50*(2), 251–272.

Della Porta, D., Massimiliano, A., Mosca, L., & Reiter, H. (2006). *Globalization from below: Transnational activists and protest networks*. Minneapolis, MN: University of Minnesota Press.

Desai, M. (2005). Transnationalism: The face of feminist politics post-Beijing. *International Social Science Journal*, *57*, 319–330.

Eckstein, S. (Ed.). (1989). *Power and protest: Latin American social movements*. Berkeley, CA: University of California Press.

Eckstein, S. (2005). Globalization and mobilization: Resistance to neoliberalism in Latin America. In M. Guillén, R. Collins, P. England, & M. Meyer, *The new economic sociology: Developments in an emerging field* (pp. 330–368). New York, NY: Russell Sage.

Fenelon, J. V., & Hall, T. D. (2008). Revitalization and indigenous resistance to globalization and neoliberalism. *American Behavioral Scientist*, *51*, 1867–1901.

Fligstein, N., & McAdam, D. (2011). Toward a general theory of strategic action fields. *Sociological Theory*, *29*, 1–26.

Gamson, W. (1992). *Talking politics*. New York, NY: Cambridge University Press.

Gamson, W., & Wolfsfeld, G. (1993). Movements and media as interacting systems. Annals of the American Academy of Political and Social Science *(Citizens, Protest and Democracy)*, *528*, 114–125.

Gerlach, A. (2003). *Indians, oil, and politics: A recent history of Ecuador*. Lanham, MD: Rowman & Littlefield.

Goldstone, J., & Useem, B. (2012). Putting values and institutions back into the theory of strategic action fields. *Sociological Theory*, *30*(1), 37–47.

Goodland, R. (1995). The concept of environmental sustainability. *Annual Review of Ecology and Systematics*, *26*, 1–24.

Harris, R. (2002). Resistance and alternatives to globalization in Latin America and the Caribbean. *Latin American Perspectives*, *29*(6), 136–151.

Hewitt, L. (2011). Framing across differences: Building solidarities: Lessons from women's rights activism in transnational spaces. *Interface: A Journal for and about Social Movements*, *3*(2), 65–99.

Holly, M. (2009). Beyond frame resonance: The argumentative structure and persuasive capacity of twentieth-century U.S. women's jury rights frames. *Mobilization*, *14*, 45–64.

Johnston, H., & Noakes, J. (Eds.). (2005). *Frames of protest: Social movements and the framing perspective*. Lanham, MD: Rowman & Littlefield.

Keck, M., & Sikkink, K. (1998). *Activists beyond Borders: Advocacy networks in international politics*. Ithaca, NY: Cornell University.

Kimerling, J. (2001). International standards in Ecuador's Amazon oil fields: The privatization of environmental law. *Columbia Journal of Environmental Law, 26*, 289–397.

Lewis, T. (2000). Transnational conservation movement organizations: Shaping the protected area systems of less developed countries. *Mobilization, 5*(1), 103–121.

Lewis, T. (2011). The effects of transnational environmentalism on environmental coalitions: Thick conservation networks and thin pollution networks in Ecuador. *Journal of Natural Resources Policy Research, 3*(3), 315–327.

Mander, J., & Tauli-Corpuz, V. (Eds.). (2002). *Paradigm wars: Indigenous peoples' resistance to economic globalization.* San Francisco, CA: International Forum on Globalization & San Francisco: Sierra Club Books.

Martin, P. (2003). *Globalization of contentious politics: The Amazonian indigenous rights movement.* New York, NY: Routledge.

Merry, S. E. (2006). *Human rights and gender violence: Translating international law and local justice.* Chicago, IL: University of Chicago Press.

Moghadam, V. (2005). *Globalizing women. Transnational feminist networks.* Baltimore, MD: The Johns Hopkins University Press.

Moghadam, V. (2009). *Globalization and social movements: Islam, Feminism, and the global justice movement.* Lanham, MD: Rowman and Littlefield.

Naples, N. (2009). Crossing borders: Community activism, globalization, and social justice. *Social Problems, 56*(1), 2–20.

Noonan, R. (1995). Women against the State: Political opportunities and collective action frames in Chile's transition to democracy. *Sociological Forum, 10*, 81–111.

O'Brien, R., Goetz, A., Scholte, J., & Williams, M. (2000). *Contesting global governance.* Cambridge: Cambridge University Press.

Pacari, N. (1996). Ecuador: Taking on the Neoliberal Agenda. *NACLA Report on the Americas, 29*(5), 23–32.

Perrault, A., Herbertson, K., & Lynch, O. (2007). Partnerships for success in protected areas: The public interest and local community rights to Prior Informed Consent (PIC). *Georgetown International Law Review, 19*(3), 475–542.

Piper, N., & Uhlin, A. (2004). New perspectives on transnational activism. In *Transnational activism in Asia.* New York, NY: Routledge.

Postero, N. (2005). Indigenous responses to neoliberalism: A look at the Bolivian uprising of 2003. *PoLAR: Political and Legal Anthropology Review, 28*(1), 73–92.

Ray, R. (1999). *Fields of protest: Women's movements in India.* Minneapolis, MN: University of Minnesota Press.

Rothman, F., & Oliver, P. (1999). From local to global: The anti-dam movement in Southern Brazil, 1979–1992. *Mobilization, 4*(1), 41–57.

San Sebastian, M., & Hurtig, A. K. (2004). Cancer among indigenous people in the Amazon basis of Ecuador 1985–2000. *Revista Panam Salud Publica, 16*, 328–333.

Sawyer, S. (2004). *Crude chronicles: Indigenous politics, multinational oil, and neoliberalism in Ecuador.* Durham, NC: Duke University Press.

Smith, J. (1997). Characteristics of the modern transnational social movement sector. In J. Smith, C. Chatfield, & R. Pagnuco (Eds.), *Transnational social movements and world politics: Solidarity beyond the state* (pp. 42–58). Syracuse, NY: Syracuse University Press.

Smith, J. (2001). Globalizing resistance: The battle of Seattle and the future of social movements. *Mobilization, 6*(1), 1–19.

Smith, J. (2002). Bridging global divides? Strategic framing and solidarity in transnational social movement organizations. *International Sociology, 17*(4), 505–528.

Smith, J., & Wiest, D. (2012). *Social movements in the world-system.* New York, NY: Russell Sage Foundation.

Snow, D. (2004). Framing process, ideology, and discursive fields. In D. Snow, S. Soule, & H. Kriesi (Eds.), *The Blackwell companion to social movements* (pp. 380–412). Oxford: Blackwell Publishing.

Snow, D., & Benford, R. (1988). Ideology, frame resonance and participant mobilization. *International Social Movement Research, 1*, 197–218.

Snow, D., & Benford, R. (1992). Master frames and cycles of protest. In A. Morris & C. Mueller (Eds.), *Frontiers in social movement theory* (pp. 133–155). New Haven, CT: Yale University Press.

Snow, D., Rochford, E. B., Jr., Worden, S., & Benford, R. (1986). Frame alignment processes, micromobilization, and movement participation. *American Sociological Review, 51*(4), 464–481.

Steiner, H. (1991). *Diverse partners: Non-governmental organizations in the human rights movement.* Harvard, MA: Harvard Law School Human Rights Program & Human Rights Internet.

Stewart, J. (2004). When local troubles become transnational: The transformation of a Guatemalan indigenous rights movement. *Mobilization, 9*(3), 259–278.

Stewart-Harawira, M. (2005). *The new imperial order: Indigenous response to globalization.* London: Zed Books.

Strang, D., & Soule, S. (1998). Diffusion in organizations and social movements: From hybrid corn to poison pills. *Annual Review of Sociology, 24*, 265–290.

Tarrow, S. (2005). *The new transnational activism.* Cambridge: Cambridge University Press.

United Nations. (2005). *Report of the international workshop on free, prior, and informed consent and indigenous peoples.* New York, NY: Department of Economic and Social Affairs. Retrieved from http://daccess-dds-ny.un.org/doc/UNDOC/GEN/N05/243/26/PDF/N0524326.pdf. Accessed on January 24, 2008; January 17–19, 2005.

Van Cott, D. (2000). *The friendly liquidation of the past: The politics of diversity in Latin America.* Pittsburgh, PA: University of Pittsburgh Press.

Viteri, C., Gonzales, G. & Veilleux, P. (1992). Press releases April 2, 5, 8. Retrieved from http://abyayala.nativeweb.org/ecuador/quichua_am/apr92_4.html. Accessed on July 2, 2007.

Wejnert, B. (2002). Integrating models of diffusion of innovations: A conceptual framework. *Annual Review of Sociology, 28*, 297–326.

Widener, P. (2007). Benefits and burdens of transnational campaigns: A comparison of four oil struggles in Ecuador. *Mobilization, 12*(1), 21–36.

Widener, P. (2009). Global links and environmental flows: Oil disputes in Ecuador. *Global Environmental Politics, 9*(1), 31–57.

Widener, P. (2011). *Oil injustice: Resisting and conceding a pipeline in Ecuador.* Another World is Necessary series. Lanham, MD: Rowman & Littlefield.

Yashar, D. (2005). *Contesting citizenship in Latin America: The rise of indigenous movements and the postliberal challenge.* New York, NY: Cambridge University Press.

Yeates, N. (2001). *Globalization and social policy.* London: Sage.

Zuo, J., & Benford, R. (1995). Mobilization processes and the 1989 Chinese democracy movement. *The Sociological Quarterly, 36*(1), 131–156.

WAVES OF CONTENTION: RELATIONS AMONG RADICAL, MODERATE, AND CONSERVATIVE MOVEMENT ORGANIZATIONS

Belinda Robnett, Carol L. Glasser and Rebecca Trammell

ABSTRACT

We develop theoretical and conceptual insights into a social movement's strategic articulation, through an examination of the relationships among the conservative, moderate and radical organizations within a movement field before, during and after a wave of contention. Definitions for conservative, moderate and radical organizations that have been lacking in the literature are provided. Three U.S. cases are employed including the Civil Rights Movement, the Animal Rights Movement, and the AIDS Movement to illustrate/apply our concepts and test our theoretical assertions. We find a distinct conservative flank in movements which facilitates linkages to state officials. Moderates have a unique role as the bridge between the radical and conservative flanks. A lack of formal organization among radicals appears to incite state repression. The radical flank, or strong ties between the radial flank and moderates or conservatives, does not have a positive effect prior to or at the peak of a

Research in Social Movements, Conflicts and Change, Volume 38, 69–101
ISSN: 0163-786X/doi:10.1108/S0163-786X20150000038003

wave of contention when there is significant state repression. In the
absence of state repression and after concessions or the peak of activism,
moderates and conservatives benefit by distancing from the radical flank.
Moderate organizations marginally institutionalize except when conser-
vative movement organizations are absent; then full incorporation
occurs.

Keywords: Movements; articulation; flanks; organizations; waves;
repression

INTRODUCTION

Social movements include many organizations that often utilize different
strategies to achieve their goals. Not only must they contend with the state
and bystanders to effect change but they also must work with and react to
one another. These relationships may vary throughout a movement's lifecycle. There is a lack of research on how inter-organizational relationships
shift across movement cycles. Previous research on inter-organizational
relationships typically positioned movements as being polar (e.g.,
McAdam, Tarrow, & Tilly, 2001) — either radical or moderate — but movements are much more dynamic. To fill this gap we grapple with the characteristics of organizations within movement communities, and propose
hypotheses about their relational roles prior to, during, and after movement
peaks.

CONCEPTS, THEORY, AND HYPOTHESES

Studies addressing the influence of radicals on movement moderates and
conservatives raise several issues. First, moderacy and radicalism are rarely
defined. Second, organizations are not systematically classified. For example, in a study of inter-organizational relationships amongst protest, advocacy, and service organizations in women's and minority organizations,
Minkoff (1994) categorizes the National Association for the Advancement
of Colored People (NAACP) as an advocacy organization instead of a protest organization because it did not engage in direct action. Jenkins and
Eckert (1986) classify it as a moderate social movement organization.
Minkoff considers the National Urban League (NUL) a service

organization, but in Haines' (1984) formulation, it and NAACP are moderate civil rights movement organizations. Third, in the social movement literature that focuses primarily on left-leaning organizations, the latter are classified as either moderate or radical, negating the distinctions between the moderate center and conservative flank. Finally, the role of the radical flank in relation to the moderate and conservative organizations throughout a cycle of protest has generally been neglected in the literature. Tarrow (1993, pp. 286–287) operationalized the term "cycles of protest," "as an increasing and then decreasing wave of interrelated collective actions and reactions to them whose aggregate frequency, intensity, and forms increase and then decline in rough chronological proximity." This begs the questions: Do different cycles of protest, or waves of contention, generate particular sets of relationships among movement organizations? To what extent do different organizations need to redefine relationships in different waves of contention? How do these relationships affect movement outcomes?

We offer theoretical and conceptual insights into social movement organizational interactions and consider the processes through which inter-organizational relationships shift throughout the course of a social movement. It is beyond the scope of this paper to examine every possible scenario or context because state formations, political contexts, and the presence or absence of radical, conservative, and moderate organizations varies widely. This paper is best conceived of as a starting point to better understand the "complex pattern[s] of interaction" among the organizations of a particular social movement that, we propose, shift along with a social movement's wave of contention (Wilson, 1995, p. 13).

Focusing on inter-organizational relations, we examine how the relationships among the radical, moderate, and conservative organizations impact social movements variously during different waves of the social movement. First, we grapple with characterizations of organizations within a movement field as radical or moderate that are loosely and variably defined in the literature. (For exceptions regarding the radical flank, see Cross & Snow, 2011; Haines, 1988, 1984.) This is particularly true for the treatment of moderates such that any organization that is not radical is, by default, moderate. We propose that the moderate category is far too broad and that organizations may also represent a conservative flank.

Second, while it is well-known that the radical flank may have positive and negative effects on a social movement, and that it influences the state to make concessions to more moderate organizations, the literature does not systematically address *how* this process occurs or how the process may *shift* at different phases in a wave of contention. We examine a wave of

contention within a social movement to determine if radical flank influences
are more productive or harmful during different phases of a social movement's trajectory. Third, we consider the strength of the relationships
among the radical, moderate, and conservative organizations. Under what
circumstances might the organizations merge or create distance? How does
the strength of the tie with the radical flank affect the moderate center and
conservative flank?

Past research tends to view social movements as cohesive or polarized.
We seek a more nuanced understanding that acknowledges diversity across
a movement and over time. Rather than conceptualizing a movement as
comprised of moderates versus radicals, we conceive of them as having conservative flank, radical flank and moderate center that may converge, overlap, or splinter over time. Our paper focuses, with one exception, on formal
organizations and is further bounded by our consideration of only U.S.
cases. It examines the periods just prior to, during, and after the height of
the wave of social movement contention. While we exclude analyses of
many social movements that may struggle against repressive non-
democratic regimes, we introduce a conceptual framework and pose theoretical considerations through which other social movements in a variety of
contexts may be analyzed.

Defining the Movement Center and Flanks

We analyze movement organization relationships from a macro-
organizational perspective. Downey and Rohlinger (2008) position social
movement organizations according to the depth of the political challenge
sought and the breadth of public and political appeal that may manifest
through an organization's goals and tactical choices. Both are inversely
related. The greater the appeal to the public and relevant state actors, the
weaker the challenge to existing political, economic, or social arrangements. Our concern is with a movement's "strategic articulation" or "overall distribution of actors across a movement and the nature and extent of
linkages among them" (Downey & Rohlinger, 2008, p. 1). This approach
acknowledges that actors/organizations may change their strategic orientation ("theory of social change ....identity and preferred repertoire of tactics") (Downey & Rohlinger, 2008, p. 6) and strategic position or "location
of an actor within a broader movement" (Downey & Rohlinger, 2008, p. 7)
within the social movement field over time. It also positions social movement organizations vis-à-vis cultural norms and attitudes, and each other.

Each social movement occurs within a particular context − for example, what is radical in one country may not be radical in another, and moderacy for one movement may be radical for another. An organization's placement as conservative, moderate, or radical, is relative vis-à-vis the other social movement organizations. By employing a field perspective and elaborating the concept of strategic articulation, we can better classify organizations as representative of or as a part of the conservative flank, radical flank or moderate center and conceptualize how the various dimensions influence the sometimes shifting strategic positions of movement organizations relative to one another.

This approach does not lend itself to a conceptual understanding of just which organizations belong to a particular category − radical, moderate, or conservative. While Downey and Rohlinger (2008) conceive of the radical flank as those organizations that seek the deepest challenge to the status quo, it is but one dimension of the radical flank. Moderate organizations may share the same goals and profess similar deep challenges. Goals can certainly distinguish a radical organization (Gamson, 1975), but that is not always the case and many less radical organizations may hold similar goals at different points in the movement's lifecycle (Tarrow, 1994).

We define the organizations' positions within the field not only according to their goals but also by: (1) the primary strategies and tactics they employ to achieve those goals; (2) how their choice of goals, strategies, and tactics compare to those of other social movement organizations; and (3) the political and cultural context within which the organizations seek change − for goals, strategies, and tactics are only radical if they are perceived as radical. Such considerations have led to our inclusion and conceptualization of a conservative flank.

The four dimensions we consider are not necessarily mutually exclusive. The position of the organization along the dimensions may shift over time for a variety of reasons. The extra-organizational context (political or cultural dynamics) may change; inter-organizational dynamics may be altered to, for example, include or exclude new or contending organizations; or the organization may experience internal crises that stimulate new approaches, strategies, tactics, etc.

We disentangle the organization's *goals* from tactics although we agree with Downey and Rohlinger that the two are correlated. As the goals deepen, tactics are likely to be aggressive, less socially accepted, and/or extralegal. The association is assumed, and there may be exceptions. We separate the two to consider only the relative depth of the goals among the flanks as they seek to challenge existing legal, political, economic, and cultural arrangements. Challenges may concentrate on changing one or more of these arrangements. Seeking inclusion into existing arrangements constitutes significant social change; it nonetheless does not necessarily challenge the foundational or modus operandi of political, economic, or legal systems that sustain and maintain societal norms and expectations. For example, an excluded organization seeking political inclusion through elections does not present the same level of challenge posed by those seeking to supplant democracy with fascism. We conceive of the deepest challenges to mean the pursuit of foundational changes.

Second, we consider the *strategic orientation*. To what extent does the organization embrace a strategy to work within existing institutions or to work outside of them in the pursuit of social change? Organizations may range from engaging in routine political processes (see Meyer, 2007) (work within the system to change it) to a revolutionary orientation (destroy the existing state supported infrastructure). Strategic considerations might reasonably be expected to overlap with a third significant dimension, *tactical choices*. Will the tactics be legal or extralegal? Will they be socially palatable or too radical?

Fourth, is the degree of *state inclusion* of the organization; this can range from *state inclusion-accommodation* (routinized direct contact negotiations with decision-making state targets) to *state exclusion-repression* (no direct contact with decision-making state targets or direct contact through repression). Finally, state inclusion may rest on the extent to which the organization messages resonate with broader *public perceptions*.[1] To what extent are the demands viewed as reasonable or unreasonable? All of these dimensions fall along a continuum, thus organizations may be located anywhere in between the poles on the various lines; and, they may shift positions on any one of the dimensions. At one end, the most conservative organization may share the same goals with the radical organization but have different beliefs about how to obtain those goals, or be perceived in negative ways by the state and the broader public.

In the U.S. context, we view the *most* conservative flank as: seeking the shallowest systemic change; strategically oriented to work within existing institutions; employing only legal tactics; included by the state with a highly routinized role; and as enjoying large support from the general public. A prototypical moderate center is characterized as pursuing deeper systemic changes than those sought by the conservative flank but less than that of the radical flank. They are: strategically oriented to work both within the existing institutions but also outside of them; open to employing both legal and extralegal tactics; cautiously included by the state; and, marginally supported by the general public. At the other extreme end, the most radical flank is: comparatively the most demanding of foundational change; hostile to existing state institutions and works exclusively outside of them; only open to the use of extralegal tactics; excluded or repressed by the state; and disapproved of by a significant majority of the public. Of course, these are prototypes and organizations within the respective flanks may more or less adhere to the far ends, or in the case of moderates, the most center point, that characterize their positions vis-à-vis one another.

Conservative Flank

In the social movement literature focusing primarily on left-leaning organizations, scholars frequently classify organizations as either moderate or radical, and none of these studies identifies a conservative flank (i.e., Haines, 1984; Kriesi, Koopmans, Dyvendak, & Giugni, 1995; Tarrow, 1989). Those that hold strong ties and relationships with political elites and state representatives are included as moderate organizations. Most rely on Blumer's (1946) distinction between reform and revolutionary organizations, thus ignoring more conservative organizations. Yet conservative organizations provide critical linkages to government and political elites. Aveni's (1978) study of the NAACP accounts for its conservatism as a social movement organization by the myriad external linkages to political elites.

Jenkins and Eckert (1986) come close to acknowledging conservative organizations when they separate older professional organizations from protest groups. Moving away from the moderate-radical dichotomy, they distinguish between professional organizations and classical social movement organizations in the civil rights movement, but they lump together direct action organizations including NAACP and SNCC that were quite distinct and held different propensities to employ non-state-sanctioned strategies and tactics. NAACP rarely advocated direct action, preferring legal remedies, while SNCC stood at the forefront of direct action (e.g., Morris, 1984). The conservative flank: embraces shallow rather than foundational goals; implements a strategy of inclusion-accommodation; engages in routine political processes; avoids radical and extralegal tactics; and cultivates support from government officials and political elites.

Hypothesis 1. Social movements may possess a conservative flank that is distinguishable from that of the moderate center as it only sanctions or engages state-approved mechanisms for change.

Moderate Center

The definition of "moderate" is rarely provided in the social movement literature. Conceived of as "not-radical," moderates are a range of organizations lumped indistinguishably together; willing to negotiate, they do not wish to destroy or replace their antagonists (Gamson, 1975). Left undefined, it is not distinguished from the conservatives. We suggest that moderates, like conservatives, engage in legal tactics but are more willing to engage in radical or extralegal tactics and to have deeper challenges. They are more willing than radicals to compromise, negotiate, and make concessions for political inroads. For example, Osa (2001), studying post-Stalinist contention in Poland, found that the moderate center was a powerful connection between radical youth organizations and more conservative organizations. Moderate organizations hold movements together during periods of abeyance, and link radicals to conservatives that provide critical linkages to government and political elites (Taylor, 1989).

> **Hypothesis 2.** Moderate organizations have a unique role as a key link between the radical and conservative flanks — which might otherwise be so strategically disparate as to seem unrelated or to be unable to work together.

Radical Flank

In the U.S. context, radicals utilize movement strategies, tactics, or goals that exist outside the range of socially accepted means of protest and that are not generally approved by a movement's moderate center, conservative flank, the broader culture and/or political elites. In short, they largely rely on extra-institutional actions. However, what is perceived as radical is not stagnant and may shift. The radical flank is typically a minority of a movement but can have a big impact as they are the most likely to incite criticism from bystanders and repression from political elites.[2]

Gamson (1975) studied 30 movement organizations and found the impact of the radical flank to be negligible. The more moderate organizations maintained their standing as representatives of their constituencies, and state concessions and benefits were not impacted by the actions of the radical flank. Conversely, other studies highlight the radical flank effect that serves to enhance political and financial support for moderate organizations (i.e., Haines, 1984; Jenkins & Eckert, 1986; McAdam, 1982; Minkoff, 1994; Kriesi et al., 1995).

Haines' (1984, 1988) work is the best known on the topic. He posited that the "radical flank effect" can be positive or negative. If the actions of the radicals cause movement targets to reject negotiations with the moderates of a movement, the effect is negative. Radicals provide a positive effect if the moderates gain concessions because the radicals make moderates look more tolerable. Gupta (2002) considered additional outcomes in which radicals fare poorly but moderates benefit, moderates do poorly but radicals benefit, or both radicals and moderates suffer. McAdam (1982), Haines (1984, 1988), Jenkins and Eckert (1986), and Minkoff (1994), all found a radical flank effect as precipitating foundation and/or state support for more moderate organizations.

Hypothesis 3. The positive radical flank effect is greatest at or just after the peak of activism.

Studies show that strong linkages between social movement organizations facilitate mobilization and help prevent factionalism (Stoecker, 1993). Rosenthal, Fingrutd, Ethier, Karant, and McDonald (1985) illustrated that strong ties enhance organizational alliances, the sharing of resources, and the exchange of ideas. Such ties can also foster a common community as in the case of the nineteenth century women's rights movement.

Walker's (1963) study of local movement leadership in Atlanta, Georgia suggests that radical, moderate, and conservative organizations work in concert to achieve concessions. He highlighted the role of the moderate organization or leader in brokering deals with white elites: "Those leaders in the middle, who do not identify completely with either the conservative or the protest leaders, have the function of moderating this conflict over tactics" (1963, p. 122). Walker argued that the radical flank lacks the connections to political elites and so they cannot negotiate concessions. It is the relationship among the organizations that leads to successful outcomes. There is a division of labor and character between the protest leaders and bargainers that make it difficult for them to work together (Wilson, 1961). The moderate organization engages in both, and bridges this gap.

The state will be more compelled to deal with a social movement if they are perceived as a threat. Movements are most successful when there is collaboration between radicals and other movement factions and this is most prevalent at the height of a wave of contention. The more collusion between movement conservatives, moderates, and radicals, the more concessions they should experience.

Hypothesis 4. The radical flank effects should vary depending on the strength of the ties between movement conservative, moderate and radical organizations.

Waves of Contention

Waves of contention are phases of intensified conflict that spread across a social sector (i.e., Almeida, 2003; della Porta & Dani, 2006; Koopmans, 1993, 2007; Staggenborg, 1998; Tarrow, 1989, 1993, 1994). Tarrow's (1994, p. 142) definition of a cycle (wave) of contention as "a phase of heightened conflict across the social system" has been widely accepted (della Porta & Dani, 2006; Koopmans, 2007). Theories addressing waves of contention are applied to study an increase in contention across movements (inter-movement dynamics), but the concepts can also be helpful within a specific SM field (intra-movement dynamics) as organizations will interact variably throughout a wave of contention.

We expect the relationships among the flanks and the moderates to vary throughout a wave of contention. Staggenborg (1998) notes that at the height of a protest wave, various movements interact with each other even though they did not prior to the cycle and their connections will loosen after the wave closes. Political elites may renegotiate their stance on an issue, counter-movements might mobilize, or different factions of a movement may develop sharp schisms (Tarrow, 1989). In the post-peak period Tarrow (1993) and Gamson (1975) show that the state facilitates the institutionalization of moderate organizations while increasing repression on radical groups. At the height of or shortly after state concessions, the radical flank becomes more extreme (e.g., della Porta & Dani, 2006, p. 190), and this shift along with greater state repression might reasonably lead to the distancing of moderates and conservatives from this flank as they capitulate to the will of the state (Barkan, 1986).

Hypothesis 5. Since the conservative organizations enjoy stronger ties with political and state elites, they will have little difficulty becoming even more institutionalized and distant from the radical flank.

The moderates balancing between the conservative and radical flanks will struggle to maintain the balance. If the moderates cooperate too extensively with the radicals they risk losing their influence, state, and foundation support and incite government repression as they become undifferentiated from the radical flank. Moderate organizations are often coopted and rewarded with increased funding (Jenkins, 1998; Meyer, 2007; Smith, 2011).

Hypothesis 6. Much like the conservative flank, the moderate organization will become more institutionalized and incorporated.

METHODS AND DATA

This paper compares three cases, the Civil Rights Movement (CRM), the Animal Rights Movement (ARM), and the AIDS movement (AM) to illustrate our concepts and test our theoretical assertions. The cases are not meant to cover all possible social movement contexts or relationship possibilities. The authors have done extensive research on these three movements, thus it is a convenience sample that relies on our previous findings. We include analyses of primary data, secondary data and interviews. The three cases span the peak activist years of the Civil Rights Movement (1954–1968); the AIDS movement (1981–1993); and, one wave (1990–2010) of the Animal Rights Movement.

The three cases present additional points of comparison. After conducting analyses of the organizations in each of the three movements, we were able to assess which organizations fit our descriptions of moderate, conservative, and radical. The CRM included organizations representative of the conservative flank, radical flank, and the moderate center. While the ARM had conservative and moderate organizations, its radical flank did not consist of organizations, but rather loosely representative informal groups or individuals – including coordinated group campaigns, short-lived groups, loners, and small anonymous networks of activists. The AM did not include an autonomous conservative organization; rather, the conservative flank was represented by mainstream political organizations whose goals overlapped with that of the moderate center and radical flank. Finally, while our data for both the CRM and the ARM is at the national level, the data collected for the AIDS movement is state level. This comparative approach provides analytical leverage. Do we see similar patterns when movements stand alone or when they are a part of highly active periods of contention, waves that include multiple social movements? We are able to compare the identity-based CRM with other types of movements; to examine role differences between radical flanks composed of organizations versus loosely tied individuals/groups; and to compare conservative flanks represented by formal political organizations versus movement organizations.

Each study used primary and secondary data sources, archival data, as well as interviews to enhance the validity of the findings through triangulation (Fielding & Fielding, 1986). Data were collected on five national CRM organizations: National Association for the Advancement of Colored People (NAACP), National Urban League (NUL), Southern Christian Leadership Conference (SCLC), Congress of Racial Equality (CORE), and Student Nonviolent Coordinating Committee (SNCC). Three AM organizations were studied: San Francisco AIDS Coalition to Unleash Power (ACT UP); San Diego Democratic Club (SDDC); and Center for San Diego County (CSDC). Four ARM organizations were included: People for the Ethical Treatment of Animals (PETA); The Humane Society of the United States (HSUS); Animal Legal Defense Fund (ALDF); and the Animal Liberation Front (ALF). In addition, the actions of various other radical campaigns and groups in the ARM were tracked.

Though our previous research was not conducted specifically to facilitate a comparison of the movement's moderates and flanks and their relationships prior to during and after the peak of a wave of contention, our detailed accounts of these movements nonetheless allows us to apply our definitions and concepts, and to test our hypotheses. Thus, we employ our previous research for: *How Long? How Long? African-American Women in the Struggle for Civil Rights* (1997), by Belinda Robnett; *Moderates and Radicals Under Repression: The U.S. Animal Rights Movement, 1990–2010* (2011), by Carol L. Glasser; "How Radical Is Too Radical: The Effects of State Concessions on the Radical Flank" (2005), by Rebecca Trammell, as secondary data.[3]

Secondary Sources

Secondary sources provided information on key protest events and inter-organizational interactions. These sources included our own research as well as several autobiographies written by leaders, and additional histories and sociological studies of the AM, the ARM, and the CRM.

Employing the method of qualitative thematic content analyses (Krippendorff, 2013), we first hand coded our previous research to ascertain historically important and significant factors about each movement organization.[4] We analyzed their engagement orientation toward direct action (high-risk vs. low risk sit-ins, protest marches, freedom rides, etc.); inter-organizational interactions; organizational and federal-level interactions (with the President, presidential administration, congressional members); degree of state inclusion; organizational characteristics; organizational decisions regarding goals, strategies, and tactics; and references to public perceptions of the organization (Krippendorff, 2013). We then coded changes in goals, strategies, tactics, and relationships with other organizations. We noted the dates of major state concessions, and examined data documenting changes in state, foundation, corporate, and constituent funding. We then coded our secondary data for the same themes.

Finally, we used our coded information to categorize each organization within the context of each movement, paying attention to the dimensions we outlined above that included: goals, strategic orientations, tactical choices, and degree of state inclusion along with public perceptions. Then, employing our definitions within each movement context, we were able to classify the organizations as a part of the conservative flank, moderate center, or radical flank.

RESULTS

Hypothesis 1. Social movements may possess a conservative flank that is distinguishable from that of the moderate center as it only sanctions or engages state-approved mechanisms for change.

We find mixed support for Hypothesis 1. Two of our movements included conservative social movement organizations. Although the positions of the CRM organizations shifted over time, at the peak, 1964–1965, NAACP and NUL were positioned as conservative organizations in relation to SCLC, SNCC, and CORE (full names of acronyms are listed in appendix). Haines (1984, p. 442) indicates that NUL "was the most conservative of the national black organizations." Like the NAACP, it primarily employed strategies and tactics that utilized state-sanctioned avenues for change (Morris, 1984, p. 216). This was equally true of NUL that, along with NAACP, failed to support the 1963 March on Washington because their tax-exempt status prevented them from direct involvement in legislative lobbying, and they feared damaging their close ties with federal officials (Garrow, 1986). Although NAACP included some radical youth, they were not represented nationally. NUL and NAACP remained compliant with the dictates of the state (Table 1).

Similar to the CRM, the ARM possessed a conservative flank. According to Jasper and Nelkin (1992, p. 37), four organizations were

Table 1. Waves Hypotheses Chart and Results.

	AIDS Movement	Animal Rights Movement	Civil Rights Movement	Overall Support
Hypothesis 1: Social movements may possess a conservative flank that is distinguishable from that of the moderate flank as it only sanctions or engages state-approved mechanisms for change.	−	+	+	+/−
Hypothesis 2: The moderate organization has a unique role as a key link between the radical and conservative flanks − which might otherwise be so strategically disparate as to seem unrelated or to be unable to work together.	+ (Helped political groups, but no conservative flank)	+	+	+
Hypothesis 3: The positive radical flank effect is greatest at or just after the peak of activism.	+	+/−	+	+/−
Hypothesis 4: The radical flank effects should vary depending on the strength of the ties between movement conservative, moderate and radical organizations.	+ Positive flank effect	+ Negative flank effect	+ Positive flank effect	+
Hypothesis 5: Since the conservative organizations enjoy stronger ties with political and state elites, they will have little difficulty becoming even more institutionalized and distant from the radical flank.	N/A (no conservative flank present)	+	+	+
Hypothesis 6: Much like the conservative flank, the moderate organization will become more institutionalized and incorporated.	+	+/−	+/−	+/−

Note: + hypothesis is supported; − hypothesis is not supported; +/− mixed support for the hypothesis.

representative of the ARM coming into the 1990s: ALDF, ALF, PETA, and IDF. These represent the moderate organizations of the movement. What is missing from Jasper and Nelkin's conceptualization is the conservative flank of the movement. HSUS is the largest animal advocacy organization internationally, and represents this conservative flank. Throughout this period, HSUS avoided contentious tactics such as protest, but embraced state-sanctioned forms of advocacy, such as education, legal reform, and building partnerships with corporations and Congress. HSUS openly admonished tactics that stepped outside the boundaries of the law and bounded their advocacy to reform-based, rather than rights-based, changes in the treatment of nonhuman animals.

In the case of the AM in California, there wasn't a conservative *movement* organization. Local political organizations formed the conservative flank of the AM. They networked with state and national political organizations to address the issue of AIDS (Shilts, 1987). SDDC was always a political organization, not a social movement organization. When the AIDS crisis escalated in the mid-1980s, they shifted attention to fundraising and bringing awareness to the disease. Working with state politicians, SDDC pushed for medical research and fought against mandatory HIV screening and quarantines for individuals infected with HIV (Trammell, 2005).

Hypothesis 1 highlights the role of the conservative flank in working with the state on behalf of a social movement cause. Whether operating as a social movement organization or as a political wing for the cause, conservative organizations provide a critical link to state, local and federal politicians. Their tactic and strategy falls well within the boundary of state-sanctioned activities.

Hypothesis 2. Moderate organizations have a unique role as a key link between the radical and conservative flanks — which might otherwise be so strategically disparate as to seem unrelated or to be unable to work together.

Moderate organizations were present in all three movements and played a unique role, moderating between the conservative and radical flanks. In the case of the CRM, just prior to, during and just after the peak of activism, SCLC was positioned squarely between the conservatism of NUL and the NAACP, and the radicalism of SNCC and CORE. Although SCLC supported sit-ins, led marches, and members often went to jail, it also strongly advocated state-sanctioned avenues for change. Much to the dismay of SNCC members, Martin Luther King Jr. and SCLC viewed the federal courts as an ally, and often showed conservatism by refusing to defy court orders in spite of the wishes of the constituents. There is ample evidence to suggest that the state (the Kennedy and Johnson administrations), viewed SCLC as moderate (Branch, 1988, pp. 642–643; also see Garrow, 1986; Morris, 1984). NUL's leaders, Lester B. Granger, and Whitney Young, Jr. were often at odds with SCLC, and hostile to the radical tactics embraced by SNCC that was generally viewed as the odd organization out (Garrow, 1986). That SCLC remained moderate even in 1966, is equally evident by the position Martin Luther King Jr. articulated regarding the rise of Black Power and the use of violence. While the NAACP's leader, Roy Wilkins, and Whitney Young, President of NUL, in a *New York Times* statement, strongly and publicly denounced Black Power and violence, King decided not to sign it. Instead, he issued a press release that "rejected the advocacy of violence and separatism associated with 'black power' and decried 'extremism within the civil rights movement'" while also emphasizing that the "'black power' controversy 'has been exploited by the decision-makers to justify resistance to change'" (quoted in Garrow, 1986, p. 533).

Similarly, PETA was strategically positioned as the moderate organization in the ARM — bridging the conservative HSUS and the radicals of the movement. While PETA's position and their ties to the radicals and conservatives shifted, they remained positioned somewhere between HSUS and the radicals, often supporting the radicals. This included publishing press releases on the radicals' behalf when they engaged in illegal actions and promoting their work. One of their 1990 newsletters, ran a half-page ad encouraging support of ALF, a loosely linked group of anonymous radicals (Glasser, 2011, p. 78). PETA critiqued HSUS' partnerships with corporations that performed experiments on nonhuman animals as well as the organization's reform-based tactics. Even so, they nonetheless bridged the tactics and ideologies of the conservative and radical flanks, tying the two seemingly desperate flanks together. PETA utilized a variety of tactics, many of which overlapped with the conservative flank, including brokering partnerships with corporations and legal reforms. They engaged in civil disobedience, protest, and disruptions. PETA's goals ranged from reform-based to rights-based (Glasser, 2011).

CSDC served as a moderate organization during the AIDS crisis, raising awareness of the problem and promoting safer sex (Trammell, 2005). They publically supported ACT UP's tactics, encouraged their members to protest, and helped mobilize the gay community of San Diego to demand more medical research for AIDS drugs. A key difference between the SDDC and CSDC was their tactics. CSDC took more of an activist role during the height of protest. One CSDC member explained the fusion of moderate and radical organizations: "You have a balance between the radicals and the more mainstream people. We were going to stand up and fight, but that means fighting together and understanding that both sides are needed to work together" (Trammell, 2005, p. 24). National level high profile moderate organizations, such as AmFAR (Foundation for AIDS research), also spoke out in favor of ACT UP. AmFAR was founded in 1983 to support medical research for AIDS. Dr. Mathilde Krim (AmFAR co-founder) wrote "consensus letters" to government officials, to coincide with ACT UP demonstrations against agencies such as the National Institutes on Allergies and Infectious Diseases. Although President Reagan ignored the AIDS crisis in public, he spoke at an AmFAR dinner in 1987. This was considered a great victory by moderate AIDS organizations (Trammell, 2005).

It is clear that when moderate organizations are present, they serve to bridge the conservative and radical flanks whether or not the latter are formal organizations. What we do not know is why some movements develop moderate organizations or whether or not the absence of moderates leads some movements to fail.

Hypothesis 3. The positive radical flank effect is greatest at or just after the peak of activism.

Hypothesis 4. The radical flank effects should vary depending on the strength of the ties between movement organizations.

Hypotheses 3 and 4 are interrelated and partially supported insofar as the radical flank has its greatest effects on moderate and conservative social movement organizations at or just after the peak of activism. Neither these effects nor strong ties among movement flanks and moderates are always positive. As Haines (1984, 1988) and Jenkins and Eckert (1986) previously found with the civil rights movement, Minkoff (1994) found with the women's movement, and Dillard (2002) found with the environmental and animal rights movements, we find that strong ties with the radical flank were positive up until the peak of activism. After this point, movements had divergent experiences. While the CRM and the AM experienced positive radical flank effects in the form of increased state concessions after the activism peak, the ARM experienced negative radical flank effects due to increased state repression aimed at curtailing the radicals.

In the case of the CRM, the 1961 Albany campaign illustrates the necessity of the moderate and radical organizations to maintain strong ties, and the positive effects those ties can have. The Albany movement was initiated by SNCC and emphasized local grassroots leadership. Instead, Martin Luther King Jr. decided to lead the march and negotiate local government concessions. He was arrested and accepted bail by a Kennedy administrator, despite pressure by the radical flank to remain in jail. City officials reneged on their promises, and King complied with a Federal District

Judge's ruling barring continued demonstrations. SNCC members felt that King had failed to support the "will of a black community prepared to generate civil disobedience" (Morris, 1984, p. 247).

Defying the wishes of other civil rights leaders to kick the more radical students of SNCC out of the movement (Branch, 1988, pp. 557–558), King sought to strengthen SCLC's tie to SNCC and hired SNCC leader, James Bevel, in 1962 (Garrow, 1986, pp. 189, 197). By 1963, his wife, Diane Nash Bevel, also a SNCC leader who led the Freedom Rides to Birmingham after violent confrontations in Montgomery, would work for the SCLC (Morris, 1984, p. 253). Birmingham in 1963 marked a turn in King's tactics. Realizing that substantive change would only occur with increased direct action, he did so and tested his relationship with the Kennedy Administration. The result was that the federal agency, the Civil Rights Division of the Department of Justice, negotiated the desegregation of Birmingham. It was the first significant break for the movement. The 1963 campaign success helped protest skyrocket from under 200 movement actions in 1962 to nearly 500 in 1963. They would continue to climb reaching approximately 600 protest actions in 1964 (Jenkins & Eckert, 1986). The Civil Rights Act was passed in 1964.

In the ARM, the conservative organization HSUS actively worked against both the moderate and radical flanks. In the early 2000s they pulled out of the annual National Animal Rights Conference, a conference organized and attended by moderate animal rights organizations, because they claimed some speakers were too radical (Glasser, 2011, p. 136; Oldenberg, 2004), and offered a monetary reward of $2,500 for information leading to the arrest of activists who illegally targeted animal researchers (Glasser, 2011, p. 136; Potter, 2008). With little movement cohesion, the ARM saw few gains. There was only one federal law, the Animal Welfare Act, that protected nonhuman animals at the onset of the wave of contention from 1990 to 2010. At the peak of the ARM wave of contention in the early 2000s, no further federal-level legal concessions had been gained. Moreover, federal authorities targeted radicals engaged in legal and extralegal activities. In six states "ag-gag" laws were passed criminalizing whistle blowers who document animal abuse in "animal enterprises" such as factory farms. The repression culminated with the SHAC 7 case that sent six activists to jail in 2006. Congress passed the Animal Enterprise Terrorism Act (AETA) in 2006, amending an earlier law to include the word "terrorism" and enhance the penalties of illegal actions if they were done in the name of earth or animal activism (Lovitz, 2010). Despite the weak ties with the radical flank, the repression impacted the moderate and conservative organizations.

By the late 1990s PETA was labeled a "terrorist" organization in the mainstream news media and in the early 2000s more moderate and conservative organizations, such as the ALDF, received the terrorist label as well (Glasser, 2011, p. 91, pp. 131–132). The FBI infiltrated national animal rights conferences in 2000 as well as other meetings and events conducted by PETA throughout the early 2000s (Hsu, 2005).

For the AIDS movement, there is support for Hypotheses 3 and 4. As protests grew, state agents addressed the AIDS crisis. The radical flank effect was at its peak in the late 1980s. ACT UP was protesting while receiving public support from moderate and conservative AIDS organizations. Enacted in 1990, the Ryan White Comprehensive AIDS Resources Emergency Act (CARE Bill) was the first bill in U.S. history aimed at a single disease. Millions of dollars in federal funds were sent to AIDS organizations. ACT UP succeeded in doing what other AIDS organizations could not do: they brought this crisis to the national level by keeping it in the headlines, forcing elected officials to answer for their inaction (Trammell, 2005).

That the radical flank had its greatest effect at the peak of activism is clear. However, there were positive effects for only the CRM and the AM. Close ties to the radical flank served to gain significant movement concessions. In contrast, the ARM experienced greater repression, and this served to have a significant negative effect on the movement as a whole as well as on both flanks and the moderates. Thus, there is mixed support for Hypothesis 4. In the case of the CRM and the ARM, when the flanks and the moderates failed to work together, concessions were not granted. In contrast to our other cases, in the ARM strong ties between the conservatives or moderates and the radical flank were damning. Such ties served to undercut the ability of the movement to gain significant concessions from state entities. What we do not know is why this movement was targeted for repression. It is possible that the lack of organizational structure among the radicals led to increased repression and a spillover effect in terms of the overall perception of the movement as radical and threatening to the polity.

Hypothesis 5. Since the conservative organizations enjoy stronger ties with political and state elites, they will have little difficulty becoming even more institutionalized and distant from the radical flank.

When whole movements are reduced to their radical flank by their opponents, conservative and moderate organizations must decide whether to distance themselves from or associate with the radicals. Tensions would play out in in all three of the movements with the moderate center and the radical flank strained after the concessions gained at the height of contention. As stated earlier, the AM did not have a conservative movement organization, so there was little need for the political organization to distance itself from the radicals even though it had previously supported them. However, the conservative flank in both the CRM and the ARM had little difficulty distancing from the radical flank.

Following the passage of the 1964 Civil Rights Act, movement actions climbed to a peak of nearly 700 during 1965 (Jenkins & Eckert, 1986). President Johnson delivered an unprecedented televised speech calling upon Congress to pass the Voting Rights Act. The threat of black militancy was growing. Just one month prior to the "Bloody Sunday" events in Selma, Alabama on March 7, 1965, Malcolm X, invited by SNCC leaders, addressed a Selma audience. He warned, "I think that the people in this part of the world would do well to listen to Dr. Martin Luther King and give him what he's asking for and give it to him fast, before some other factions come along and try to do it another way …" (quoted in Lewis, 1998, p. 313). SNCC was disillusioned by the limited ability of the 1964 Civil Rights Act and the 1965 Voting Rights Act to significantly change the economic and political position of Blacks in the United States. Longtime members felt betrayed by the moderates and conservative flank that had brokered compromises that led to limited change. SNCC members increasingly advocated the use of violence. SNCC minutes dated November 29, 1965 indicate the growing trend, "Stokely has been thinking of taking over Lowdes Co. courthouse – I think he might be thinking of guns, deputizing, etc." (Frank, 1965). Constancia Romilly, a member of SNCC, commented, that "there looked like there might be a real alliance between the Panthers and SNCC – I think the power structure in Washington just totally freaked out" (C. Romilly, interview, June 5, 1992).

As Jenkins and Eckert's research shows, actions related to Black Power peaked in 1965 to 42% of all actions and held steady through the 1970s (1986, p. 821). CORE and SNCC, already the radical arms of the CRM, came under increasing pressure to embrace the Panthers. In 1967, CORE resisted armed insurgency and its members were considered "BLACK AGENTS OF THE WHITE MOTHER COUNTRY" by the Panthers (quoted in Bloom & Martin, 2013, p. 93). Huey Newton and Bobby Seale led the Panthers in armed self-defense, "forcibly contesting the legitimacy of the American political regime" (Bloom & Martin, 2013, p. 13). SNCC leader, Stokely Carmichael, embraced much of the organization's ethos and formed Black Panther organizations in several cities (Bloom & Martin,

2013, p. 113). By 1968, against the backdrop of riots in major U.S. cities, SNCC officially merged with the Black Panther Party, although the alliance would be short-lived (Bloom & Martin, 2013, p. 111).[5]

NAACP and NUL, both conservative arms of the civil rights movement, successfully distanced themselves from the radical arm. Funding for NAACP and NUL soared with NUL enjoying an increase from $1,539,000 in 1964 to $14,542,000 in 1970, and the NAACP's funding rising from $292,579 in 1964 to reach $2,665,373 by 1970. Jenkins and Eckert (1986, p. 822) also document a marked increase in NAACP foundation grants that, in 1965, were significantly less than that of SCLC but far surpassed their funding by the late 1960s.

Similarly, the trajectory of the conservative HSUS of the ARM provides support for Hypothesis 5. The negative radical flank effects experienced at the peak of activism pushed HSUS toward state and corporate partnerships. They openly sought opportunities to work with government bodies and large corporations, and supported government initiatives aimed at curtailing animal rights activism. HSUS president, Wayne Pacelle, openly supported a state bill in California that was similar to the federal Animal Enterprise Terrorism Act, though it did not pass. In 2008, a *New York Times* article described HSUS as "the least radical of the animal rights groups" (Glasser, 2011, p. 161).

Though HSUS was not immune from the negative effects of being associated with radicalism, they were less impacted than others. For example, while PETA offices were infiltrated by undercover agents posing as employees and their offices were wiretapped, HSUS was, as far as is known, not subjected to such tactics. By actively speaking out against radicals, solidifying and displaying the lack of cohesion between their goals and tactics and those of the radicals, HSUS buffered themselves – demonstrating that the weaker the ties, the less the flank effects.

It is clear that the conservative flank distances from the radical flank either after movement concessions are gained, or under conditions of state repression as exhibited in the cases of the CRM and the ARM, respectively. In both contexts, the radical flank increased its radical stance. For the conservative flank, distancing from radicals was far less difficult than it was for the moderate center.

Hypothesis 6. Much like the conservative flank, the moderate organization will become more institutionalized and incorporated.

Overall, our findings for Hypothesis 6 are mixed. For both the CRM and the ARM, instead of institutionalization, moderates struggled to maintain their middling position. Initially, moderate organizations resisted greater institutionalization and conservatism, but as state and funding pressures intensified, they eventually capitulated. Still, they maintained their moderate roles. In contrast, the AM results support Hypothesis 6 without qualification. Following state concessions, the AM moderate organizations immediately distanced from the radicals and became institutionalized.

As the moderate center of the CRM, SCLC struggled to maintain its position between the conservative and radical flank. Dr. King worried about SNCC's growing militancy. Longtime activist Bayard Rustin suggested that SCLC completely distance itself from SNCC. King was not quick to heed Rustin's advice, and in response to media attention that SNCC and SCLC were split because of the former's militancy, he and SNCC leader James Forman issued a joint statement that the civil rights movement was inherently a radical movement that shared the goal of eliminating racism and segregation (Garrow, 1986). As SNCC became increasingly radical, and NAACP and NUL grew satisfied by legislation, King found it difficult to maintain his moderate position. He declared, "Somewhere there has to be a synthesis. I have to be militant enough to satisfy the militants yet I have to keep enough discipline in the movement to satisfy white supporters and moderate Negroes" (quoted in Garrow, 1986, pp. 496–497).

King and SCLC faced two key challenges, Black Power and the Vietnam War. He was forced to take a stand on both, but his tendency to waffle created mistrust on all sides. Initially, he tried to distance SCLC from the Black Power struggle without outright denunciation by condemning violence but empathizing with its cause. He often spoke out against the war, as an advocate of nonviolence, but not as a critic of the Johnson Administration. The more he hedged, the more radicals, news reporters, and conservative black leaders pushed him to take a stand. King began to shift away from radicalism, even if he was conflicted. He refused to endorse the *New York Times* announcement placed by NAACP and NUL denouncing Black Power, though in a news conference, he offhandedly indicated his support for their position. This made headlines and painted an erroneous picture of King as anti-Black Power (Garrow, 1986).

When the SCLC most needed to distance itself from the radical faction, it too, was increasingly professing a radical, vision for change. King's stances increasingly critiqued capitalist principles and embraced social democratic ideology. A redistribution of wealth was at the heart of King's message, as well as that of Black Power leaders. NUL Director, Whitney Young, warned King about the consequences of his increasingly radical stances. King replied that Whitney's position would garner foundation support, but that it avoided the truth (Garrow, 1986). As Lewis (1998, p. 359) noted, "Wilkins' NAACP and Young's Urban League predictably rushed to the side of Lyndon Johnson and Hubert Humphrey, shaking their heads at our 'outrageous' attacks on the Administration. Dr. King refused to join them." These decisions cost the moderate SCLC both financial and political support. As Haines (1984) documented, outside funding for SCLC declined from $1,643,000 in 1965 to $932,000 in 1966 and 1967. By 1970, financial support had tumbled to $400,000. SNCC, in contrast, suffered the most extreme cuts plummeting from a 1964 outside funding base of $631,439 to $25,000 in 1970. Clearly, SCLC's failure to distance itself from the radicalism of SNCC severely hurt its ability to secure outside and government funding.

PETA too attempted to maintain its middling position in the ARM, but as the conservative and radical flanks grew further apart they could no longer maintain their role as a movement bridge and had to choose sides. Much like SCLC, PETA struggled to appeal to the mainstream public and appease conservative organizations, while remaining sympathetic to radicals. They began to be less outwardly radical in the early 2000s, though at times quietly supported the radicals in small ways, such as through small donations to radical activists' legal funds (Glasser, 2011). By 2010 they had settled into a solidly moderate position and pulled back from open support of radical activists and advocating for radical actions (Glasser, 2011, pp. 134–135). This shift allowed PETA to survive as an organization, even if some goals, strategies, and tactics changed in the process.

Moderate AM organizations embraced state concessions and pushed away from ACT UP San Francisco. In doing so, they chose the tactics of their conservative counterpart to work directly with state officials. Moderate and conservative AIDS organizations had benefitted directly from the concessions. When the CARE Act was ratified by Congress in 1990, millions of dollars were funneled into social service and medical organizations creating a financial windfall for these organizations that provided services for AIDS patients. Although the CARE Act was signed into law, President George H. W. Bush immediately began undermining the "education" section of the CARE Act. The Bush Administration did not want to fund programs that would "promote the gay agenda" by educating the public about safer sex. He instead wanted federal funding for medical treatment only. For example, President Bush met with the American Foundation for AIDS Research (AmFAR) Program Officer Terry Beirn to discuss the CARE Act and medical services but refused to discuss any other topic (Trammell, 2005).

Conservative and moderate AIDS organizations were sent into a conservative tailspin. ACT UP members called Bush's actions "blatant homophobia" and decided to focus attention on the President himself (Trammell, 2005). On September 1, 1991, members of ACT UP marched onto the Kennebunkport vacation home of President Bush and conducted a "Die In" (lying down as if dead, while covered in fake blood) on the road around the house. On September 30, 1991, ACT UP members chained themselves to the White House gate and demanded that Bush support AIDS policies; 84 people were arrested. On February 15, 1992, ACT UP protesters smashed the windows of Bush's Campaign offices in New Hampshire. President Bush retaliated by calling ACT UP a "terrorist group" at press conferences (Trammell, 2005). This forced moderate and conservative AIDS organizations to begin separating themselves from the radical flank. In fact, the consensus among AIDS organizations was that the radical flank was no longer necessary (Vaid, 1995).

The moderate organizations became more institutionalized and distant from the radical flank. The fear of losing state concessions and the radical new ideology of ACT UP San Francisco forced these organizations to choose sides, and so they disavowed protesting. For example, in 2001, when California Governor Schwarzenegger announced a $25 million cut in grants to fund the AIDS Drug Assistance Program, that provided medical treatment for indigent AIDS patients, the San Francisco AIDS foundation responded by engaging in letter writing campaigns and fundraising. One member of CSDC discussed the organization's distancing from the radical flank, stating: "We work silently ... we can accomplish more than walking the streets and carrying banners or loudspeakers. We write to the government, we call people, talk to the city council members. That is how we protest." Another commented, "We get some of the ACT UP people at the Center ... HIV causes AIDS, they want me to say otherwise but I won't, it's not true. We have a hard enough time getting funding and they want us to consider their ridiculous position! They should stop putting groups in the middle" (quoted in Trammell, 2005, p. 24). CSDC maintained an amicable relationship with state and federal officials in order to receive any funds at all (Trammell, 2005, p. 21).

Although the moderate organizations in each of the movements distanced from the radical flank, those within the CRM and the ARM found it more difficult to do so. With the absence of a movement conservative flank within the AM, it may have been easier for the moderates to cut ties with the radical flank and fill an undefined position within the movement. In all three cases, the moderates found it difficult to maintain a relationship with the radicals without negative consequences pertinent to their survival.

DISCUSSION

This paper is concerned with a social movement's "strategic articulation" or "overall distribution of actors across a movement and the nature and extent of linkages among them" (Downey & Rohlinger, 2008, p. 1). A conceptual and theoretical framework is introduced through which we may define social movement organizations and understand the importance of the relationships among the flanks and moderates to movement outcomes. The paper explores variations in the structures of social movements – some movements contain a conservative flank while others do not and in some movements the radical flank can lack organizational structure. The contexts varied in which the movements took place with the CRM occurring during a period of heightened activity among an array of causes, while the activism of the ARM and the AM gained momentum during periods of relative inactivity. Finally, the paper pays close attention to the relationships among the conservative flank, the radical flank and the moderate center as the wave of contention grows, peaks, and wanes.

We suggest that social movement organizations may be classified as radical, conservative, or moderate through a consideration of four dimensions that include the organization's goals, strategic orientation, tactical choices, and degree of state inclusion. Our rubric allows for shifts in the classification of movement organizations along one or more of these dimensions over time. Classifications may shift because of internal organization changes or depending upon, for example, how state inclusion is defined, that is, state-level, federal-level, or local-level. In this regard, what may appear to be moderate at one point in time may be considered radical in another, because the dimensions are defined in relation to the specific organizations within the social movement field. Thus, while our findings are specific to the U.S. cases, the application of these dimensions to movements in other times and places should increase understanding of the roles of the radical, moderate and conservative organizations and their relationships to social movement outcomes.

In contrast to models of the social movement field that consist of a radical flank versus a moderate center (i.e., Haines, 1984), we find that in the case of the CRM and the ARM, the social movement field included conservative, moderate, and radical organizations and that the *relationships among these organizations was critical* to social movement outcomes on the road to and after state concessions. Some social movements may lack a conservative organization as we found in our state-level analysis of the AM. Its absence, however, did not appear to negatively impact the movement's outcomes as a political, but independent arm of the movement served a role similar to those conservative movement organizations in the other two movements.

Our study shows that radical flanks can have both negative and positive effects on social movements depending upon the cycle of protest, as well as the strength of ties with the moderate and conservative organizations. In the cases of the CRM and the AM, the radical flank had a positive impact prior to state concessions when ties between the moderate and radical organizations were strong, and a negative impact as the movement declined and the strength of ties were not weakened. Specifically, the radical flank helped the moderates and conservatives to gain state concessions and benefits before and during the peak of activism. Conversely, as concessions were won and the movement's momentum waned, the radical flank began to adversely affect the image of the moderate center while buttressing state support for the conservative flank.

The ARM differed from the CRM and the AM since its radicals were loosely organized. Another significant difference is that the ARM encountered greater initial federal-level repression than the other two movements. It was only when the CRM and the AM began to see the rise of radicalism that followed concessions that federal-level repression began to escalate. The ARM saw few substantive gains. One reason appears to be because the radical flank failed to formally organize, but the movement also faced extensive lobbying efforts by large agricultural conglomerates and corporations that conducted animal testing.

In all three movements, the radical flank served the purpose of escalating the tactics and deepening the goals of the moderate center and the conservative flank. The moderate SCLC, PETA, and CSDC organizations served as negotiators between the conservatives, which rarely pushed for concessions beyond the status quo, and the radicals that were seeking deeper foundational changes. The radicals also served as the "conscience" of the movement. Radicals not only stimulated state concessions, in the case of the CRM and AM, but in all cases held moderates and conservatives accountable to their constituents. The radical flank was vital in the early stages of the movement when it was gaining momentum, and at the peak of protest, which generally occurred right before concessions were made.

The moderate or conservative organizations generally supported the radical flank during the early stages of the movement, occasionally joining them on the front lines of the protest march. Once concessions were gained, or in the case of the ARM, activism peaked, the relationships among the radical, moderate, and conservative organizations changed. Radicals remained active, and in the case of the CRM and the AM, escalated their tactics, while moderate organizations faced strong pressures to institutionalize and to conservatize (Piven & Cloward, 1977).

Following the peak of activism and/or state concessions, in all three cases, the conservatives benefited from pre-existing ties with state officials and distanced themselves from the radical flank. Receiving large amounts of state, corporate, or foundation funding, the conservative flank benefited heavily after concessions. In the case of the ARM, after they successfully conservatized, they evaded the "terrorist" label. The positive relationship with the conservative flank enabled the state to maintain control of the movement's goals and tactics while sustaining an image of support for the cause. The radical flank, on the other hand, lost all credibility with the state and other social movement organizations and became the target of government repression. Ultimately, in all three cases, the radical flank crumbled.

As the conservative and radical flanks pulled apart, the moderate center was in a precarious position. They could no longer serve as negotiators because the flanks had moved too far apart. The moderate organizations must either distance themselves from the radical flank by jumping on the gravy train with the conservatives, or radicalize and destroy their credibility and ties with state officials. Either choice did not bode well for the movement because ultimately the moderate center lost power. When moderate organizations become institutionalized and conservatize, they must prove their allegiance to state officials by relinquishing radical tactics and abandoning many of their goals. Adherence to any of the goals espoused and tactics implemented by the radical flank, mark the moderate center as suspect. While the moderate organizations maintain autonomy, they also lose their power to influence the state. In sum, although the CRM occurred during a period of heightened movement activity in the United States, and the ARM and the AM took place during a period of relative movement inactivity, patterns of interaction among each movement's conservative flank, radical flank and moderate center were strikingly similar.

There are, however, significant outcome differences among the three cases. The radical flank clearly served a vital purpose in the positive outcomes of the CRM and the AM. In the ARM however, the radical flank's failure to organize, coupled with strong opposition from corporations and large agricultural conglomerates that led to state repression, undercut the effectiveness of the ARM. For African-Americans seeking equality, and those seeking remedies to the AIDS crisis, the radical flank was critically important to success. While the ARM moderates played a similar role as those moderates in the other movements, the combination of early state repression and the lack of organization among the radicals served to undercut the ability of PETA to gain concessions. In the CRM and the AM, the success of the radical flank at motivating concessions was dependent on the moderate center that served as a bridge and held the various flanks of the movement together. However, after concessions were won, the effects of the radicals in these two movements became harmful due to a growing distance between the conservative and radical flanks. As the conservatives pushed further and further away, the moderates could no longer bridge the gap and were unable to serve their vital purpose of connecting the movement's goals and tactics; they needed to choose a side or risk collapse.

There is an obvious limitation to our case studies. All three of our movements occur in the United States, a democratic nation-state. We do not know how patterns may vary in other political contexts such as in repressive regimes, although the federal response to the ARM suggests that the early repression of the radical flank may severely undercut the ability of moderates to serve as a bridge between the latter and conservatives. Future research addressing the strategic articulation of social movements in a wider variety of political contexts is clearly needed to better parcel out the conditions under which social movement outcomes are affected by the relationships among the radical flank, conservative flank and moderate center.

NOTES

1. One of our dimensions is public perception, but for the purposes of this paper, we treat state inclusion-exclusion as a reflection of those perceptions. We are aware this might not always be the case, and suggest that future research is required to disentangle the two. Such an exercise was beyond the scope of our data.

2. We are aware that political elites may vary in their perspectives of social movement tactics, strategies, and goals with, for example, local political elites perceiving them as radical while federal political elites view them as moderate. While state elites vary in their perceptions of the demands from and tactics employed by the movements we consider, our references to political elites or state actors are confined

to the U.S. presidential administration and the U.S. Congress. Another consideration regarding classification of organizations is the viewpoint from the field. In our cases, there is no discrepancy between the aforementioned state actors' perceptions and those of social movement organizations within the field regarding the positioning of the CRM, ARM, and AM organizations as conservative, moderate, or radical. This does not imply that perceptions of organizations did not shift over time; only that perceptions were in sync.

3. Please reference these publications for detailed information regarding our methods and treatment of the data.

4. Although our focus is nearly exclusively on social movement organizations, the radical flank of the ARM did not take on an organizational form. Nonetheless, we also employed our methods to this flank to be consistent in our analyses.

5. Although the Black Panther Party was clearly the most radical organization, it was never considered a part of the civil rights movement. Rather, the organization was associated with the Black Power Movement. While Martin Luther King, Jr. had discussions with Malcolm X, whose philosophy inspired the Panthers, the Panthers had no inter-organizational relationships with the core civil rights movement organizations except for SNCC and CORE. SNCC became the most susceptible to the Panther's influences. Thus, our focus is on SNCC and how its increasing radicalization strained its relations with the moderate and conservative civil rights movement organizations.

ACKNOWLEDGMENT

The authors would like to thank the anonymous reviewers and editors for their thoughtful and insightful comments.

REFERENCES

Almeida, P. D. (2003). Opportunity organizations and threat-induced contention: Protest waves in authoritarian settings. *American Journal of Sociology, 109*, 345–400.

Aveni, A. (1978). Organizational linkages and resource mobilization: The significance of linkage strength and breadth. *Sociological Quarterly, 19*(2), 185–202.

Barkan, S. E. (1986). Interorganizational conflict in the southern civil rights movement. *Sociological Inquiry, 56*(2), 190–209.

Bloom, J., & Martin, W. E. (2013). *Black against empire: The history and politics of the Black Panther Party*. Berkeley, CA: University of California Press.

Blumer, H. (1946). Collective behavior. In A. M. Lee (Ed.), *New outline of the principles of sociology* (pp. 167–222). New York, NY: Barnes and Noble Publishing.

Branch, T. (1988). *Parting the water*. New York, NY: Simon and Schuster.

Cross, R., & Snow, D. (2011). Radicalism within the context of social movements: Processes and types. *Journal of Strategic Security, 4*, 115–130.

della Porta, D., & Diani, M. (2006). *Social movements: An introduction*. Oxford: Blackwell Publishing.

Dillard, C. (2002). *The rhetorical dimensions of radical flank effects: Investigations into the influence of emerging radical voices on the rhetoric of long-standing moderate organizations in two social movements*. Ph.D. dissertation, University of Texas, Austin, TX.

Downey, D., & Rohlinger, D. (2008). Linking strategic choice with macro organizational dynamics: Strategy and social movement articulation. *Research on Social Movements, Conflicts and Change, 28*, 3–35.

Fielding, N., & Fielding, J. (1986). *Linking data*. Beverly Hills, CA: Sage.

Frank. (1965). SNCC Papers A 4 7, Martin Luther King Jr. Center for Nonviolent Social Change.

Gamson, W. (1975). *The strategy of social protest*. Homewood, IL: Dorsey.

Garrow, D. (1986). *Bearing the cross: Martin Luther King, Jr. and the Southern Christian Leadership Conference*. New York, NY: Vintage Books.

Glasser, C. L. (2011). *Moderates and radicals under repression: The U.S. animal rights movement, 1990–2010*. Dissertation, University of California, Irvine, CA.

Gupta, D. (2002). *Radical flank effects: The effect of radical-moderate splits in regional nationalist movements*. Conference of Europeanists, Chicago, IL, March 14–16.

Haines, H. (1984). Black radicalization and the funding of civil rights. *Social Problems, 32*, 31–43.

Haines, H. (1988). *Black radicals and the civil rights movement, 1954–1970*. Knoxville, TN: University of Tennessee Press.

Hsu, S. (2005). FBI papers show terror inquiries into PETA. *Washington Post*, December 20. Retrieved from http://www.washingtonpost.com/wp-dyn/content/article/2005/12/19/AR2005121901777.html

Jasper, J., & Nelkin, D. (1992). *The animal rights crusade: The growth of a moral protest*. New York, NY: The Free Press.

Jenkins, J. C. (1998). Channeling social protest: Foundation patronage of contemporary social movements. In W. W. Powell & E. S. Clemens (Eds.), *Private action and the public good* (pp. 206–216). New Haven, CT: Yale University Press.

Jenkins, J. C., & Eckert, C. M. (1986). Channeling black insurgency: Elite patronage and professional social movement organizations in the development of the black movement. *American Sociological Review, 51*, 812–829.

Koopmans, R. (1993). The dynamics of protest waves: West Germany, 1965–1989. *American Sociological Review, 58*(5), 637–658.

Koopmans, R. (2007). Protest in time and space: The evolution of waves of contention. In D. A. Snow, S. A. Soule, & H. Kriesi (Eds.), *The Blackwell companion to social movements* (pp. 19–46). Malden, MA: Blackwell Publishing Ltd.

Kriesi, H., Koopmans, R., Dyvendak, J. W., & Giugni, M. G. (1995). *New social movements in Western Europe: A comparative analysis*. Minneapolis, MN: University of Minnesota Press.

Krippendorff, K. (2013). *Content analysis: An introduction to its methodology*. London, England: Sage Publications.

Lewis, J. (1998). *Walking with the wind*. New York, NY: Simon and Schuster.

Lovitz, D. (2010). *Muzzling a movement: The effects of anti-terrorism law, money and politics on animal activism*. Brooklyn, NY: Lantern Books.

McAdam, D. (1982). *Political process and the development of black insurgency*. Chicago, IL: Chicago University Press.

McAdam, D., Tarrow, S., & Tilly, C. (2001). *Dynamics of contention*. Cambridge: Cambridge University Press.

Meyer, D. S. (2007). *The politics of protest*. New York, NY: Oxford University Press.

Minkoff, D. C. (1994). From service provision to institutional advocacy: The shifting legitimacy of organizational forms. *Social Forces, 72*, 943–969.

Morris, A. (1984). *The origins of the civil rights movement*. New York, NY: Free Press.

Oldenberg, D. (2004). Vegan in the henhouse: Wayne Pacelle, putting animals on (and off) the table. *Washington Post*, August 9. Retrieved from http://www.washingtonpost.com/wp-dyn/articles/A50953-2004Aug8.html

Osa, M. (2001). Mobilizing structure and cycles of protest: Post Stalinist contention in Poland, 1954–1959. *Mobilization, 6*, 211–231.

Piven, F. F., & Cloward, R. (1977). *Poor people's movements: Why they succeed, how they fail*. New York, NY: Vintage Books.

Potter, W. (2008, August 6). Humane society donates money to 'eco-terrorism' witch hunt, but not enough to protect it from the green scare. Green is the new red. Retrieved from http://www.greenisthenewred.com/blog/hsus-green-scare-donation/540/

Robnett, B. (1997). *How long, how long, African-American women in the struggle for civil rights*. New York, NY: Oxford University Press.

Rosenthal, N., Fingrutd, M., Ethier, M., Karant, R., & McDonald, D. (1985). Social movements and network analysis: A case study of nineteenth-century women's reform in New York State. *American Journal of Sociology, 90*, 1022–1054.

Ryan White Comprehensive AIDS Resources Emergency Act. (1990). Pub. L. No. 101–381.

Shilts, R. (1987). *And the band played on: Politics, people, and the AIDS epidemic*. New York, NY: St. Martin's Press.

Smith, A. (2011). The revolution will not be funded: The nonprofit industrial complex. In S. Best, R. Kahn, A. Nocella, & P. McLaren (Eds.), *The global industrial complex: Systems of domination* (pp. 133–154). New York, NY: Lexington Books.

Staggenborg, S. (1998). Social movement communities and cycles of protest: The emergence and maintenance of a local women's movement. *Social Problems, 45*, 180–204.

Stoecker, R. (1993). The federated frontstage structure and localized social movements: A case study of the Cedar-Riverside neighborhood movement. *Social Science Quarterly, 74*, 169–184.

Tarrow, S. (1989). *Struggle, politics, and reform: Collective action, social movements, and cycles of protest*. Monograph. Western Societies Program Occasional Paper No. 21. Center for International Studies Cornell University.

Tarrow, S. (1993). Cycles of collective action: Between movements of madness and the repertoire of contention. *Social Science History, 17*, 281–307.

Tarrow, S. (1994). *Power in movement: Social movements and contentious politics*. New York, NY: Cambridge University Press.

Taylor, V. (1989). Social movement continuity: The women's movement in abeyance. *American Sociological Review, 54*(5), 761–775.

Trammell, R. (2005, August). How radical is too radical: The effects of state concessions on the radical flank. Paper presented at the meeting of the Society for the Study of Social Problems, Philadelphia, PA.

Vaid, U. (1995). *Virtual equality: The mainstreaming of gay and lesbian liberation.* New York, NY: Anchor Books.

Walker, J. L. (1963). Protest and negotiation: A case study of Negro leadership in Atlanta, Georgia. *Midwest Journal of Political Science, 7,* 99–124.

Wilson, J. Q. (1961). The strategy of protest: Problems of Negro civic action. *Journal of Conflict Resolution, 5,* 291–303.

Wilson, J. Q. (1995). *Political organizations.* Princeton, NJ: Princeton University Press.

APPENDIX: ACRONYMS

ACT UP	San Francisco AIDS Coalition to Unleash Power
ALDF	The Animal Legal Defense Fund
AETA	Animal Enterprise Terrorism Act
ALF	Animal Liberation Front
AM	AIDS Movement
ARM	Animal Rights Movement
CORE	Congress of Racial Equality
CRM	Civil Rights Movement
CSDC	Center for San Diego County
HSUS	The Humane Society of the United States
IDA	In Defense of Animals
NAACP	National Association for the Advancement of Colored People
NUL	National Urban League
PETA	People for the Ethical Treatment of Animals
SDDC	The San Diego Democratic Club
SNCC	Student Nonviolent Coordinating Committee

A QUANTITATIVE REEVALUATION OF RADICAL FLANK EFFECTS WITHIN NONVIOLENT CAMPAIGNS

Elizabeth Tompkins

ABSTRACT

Though the coexistence of nonviolent and violent groups within a single movement is a common phenomenon in maximalist campaigns (e.g., regime change, anti-occupation), the effects of this coexistence remain understudied. Focusing on primarily nonviolent movements with a simultaneous "radical flank" pursuing the same goals, this study builds on previous, inconclusive literature which narrowly accounts for limited and often case-specific radical flank effects. After conducting a series of large-N regression analyses using a subset of the NAVCO 2.0 dataset, this study finds that the presence of a radical flank (1) increases both the likelihood and degree of repression by the state and (2) is most significantly linked with decreased mobilization post-repression — yet, (3) is not necessarily detrimental to overall campaign progress.

Keywords: Radical flank; resistance movement; nonviolence; repression; NAVCO

Research in Social Movements, Conflicts and Change, Volume 38, 103–135
ISSN: 0163-786X/doi:10.1108/S0163-786X20150000038004

INTRODUCTION

Past research on nonviolent movements has neglected to address the fact that many nonviolent movements contain some degree of violence, particularly those with so-called maximalist goals (e.g., regime change, anti-occupation). While studies on so-called "radical flanks" – violent subunits within an otherwise-nonviolent movement – do exist, their conclusions are overwhelmingly qualitative and focused on isolated case studies (e.g., Beach, 1977; Braithwaite, 2014; Haines, 1984), falling short on external validity and widely applicable theory. Thus, current literature fails to both construct a theoretical framework for, and test distinct causal mechanisms for, radical flank effects.

A recent study by Schock and Chenoweth (2012) was the first to quantitatively analyze the effect of the presence of a radical flank on the outcome (success vs. failure) of an otherwise-nonviolent campaign, but their results were inconclusive. Their sample identified *all contemporaneous violent groups* as radical flanks (rather than only intra-movement ones), and tested campaign *success or failure* as the outcome variable, without delving into the intermediate variables or mechanisms *between* radical flank presence and ultimate campaign outcome. With this paper, I take on a more micro-level and nuanced analysis of radical flank effects. Examining cases of nonviolent and violent groups acting contemporaneously within a broader resistance movement or "campaign," defining radical flanks as *intra-movement* violent organizations rather than any and all contemporaneous violent groups, and using campaign years rather than entire campaigns as the unit of analysis, I provide a data-driven study of immediate, within-year effects of radical flank presence within otherwise predominantly non-violent movements. I find that the presence of a radical flank within a given campaign year is associated with a higher likelihood that there will be movement repression by the state; higher likelihood that a movement will either gain or lose momentum rather than maintain the status quo; and ultimately, a higher chance that the movement will make some progress or gains in that year.

LITERATURE REVIEW

In the following section, I will synthesize existing literature on resistance movements and clarify past research on nonviolence versus violence as mutually exclusive strategic decisions with unique challenges and implications. Once I have provided an overview of studies which compare nonviolent and violent tactics separately, I provide an overview of the few existing sources on radical flanks, perhaps the most clearly identifiable and common instance of violent and nonviolent tactics overlapping within a single movement. What emerges is a consistent research gap with regard to how the presence of a radical flank alters the internal dynamics of an otherwise primarily nonviolent campaign.

Resistance Movements: Nonviolence versus Violence

Encompassing multiple organizations as varied as civil society, armed insurgencies, NGOs, and even corporations (Hoffman & Bertels, 2010), today's resistance movements aren't necessarily identifiable as a single group, but rather as clusters of organizations united by a common purpose. McCarthy and Zald (1977) were one of the first to define and operationalize resistance movements, focusing on the processes of mobilization by which a social movement becomes an actual force for change via the formation of social movement organizations (SMOs). All resistance movements must first surmount internal divisions in order to mobilize, and then carefully choose their tactics for challenging the political status quo. Scholars usually assume that social movements "have full knowledge of all available options and can freely and objectively choose the most effective ones" (Dudouet, 2013, p. 407); thus, collective action strategies will be selected which provide the most payoffs and lowest costs.

Both nonviolence and violence are coercive strategies which bypass conventional politics and which are employed by organized opposition groups or resistance movements against a regime (Bond, Jenkins, Taylor, & Schock, 1997; Dudouet, 2013), but past studies argue that nonviolence is the more effective of the two. Chenoweth and Cunningham define nonviolent resistance as "the application of unarmed civilian power using nonviolent methods such as protests, strikes, boycotts, and demonstrations, without using or threatening physical harm against the opponent" (2013, p. 271). They use *nonviolent resistance, nonviolent struggle, and strategic nonviolence* interchangeably. Sharp (1973) was the first to systematically identify 198 methods of nonviolent resistance, classifying them into three general types: protest and persuasion, noncooperation, and intervention. Chenoweth and Stephan (2011) provide very staunch support for nonviolent tactics, discovering that nonviolent resistance had a significantly higher likelihood of producing partial or complete success in maximalist campaigns from 1940 to 2006: 78% compared with a success rate of 39% for violent movements. They also found that, from 1900 to 2006, major nonviolent campaigns were successful 53% of the time, compared with only 26% of the time for violent campaigns ($n = 323$). Similarly, Karatnycky and Ackerman (2005) found that nonviolent resistance was a central component of 50 out of 67 democratic transitions from 1973 to 2005. Though nonviolent civil resistance has been shown to be a highly effective strategy, violence also carries its own set of advantages. It is a fast way for lesser-known actors to gain recognition, albeit through notoriety, or even a place at the negotiation table (Cunningham, Bakke, & Seymour, 2012; Lawrence, 2010). When competing for recognition, violent action can create a situation of "escalatory outbidding, in which factions use violence to establish their nationalist credentials, leading other factions to resort to violence" (Cunningham et al., 2012, p. 8). In this manner, violence raises the stakes, also by drawing attention – both domestic and international – to actors and issues that may have otherwise been ignored. Violence is also effective at weakening or, at the most extreme end, eliminating competitors. However, violent movements have also been linked with several negative social and political consequences post-conflict, particularly a higher need for economic recovery and risk reduction (Collier, Hoeffler, & Söderbom, 2008) and a high risk of falling back into violence within a decade (Elbadawi, Hegre, & Milante, 2008).

Whereas civil resistance research tends to draw a very clear line between violence and nonviolence as strategies for political change, social movement and revolution research is a bit more open to the fluidity of social movements, and accepts that nonviolent action and violent action may exist along a continuum (Schock, 2013, p. 280). Taylor and Van Dyke offered a broad definition of protest as "the collective use of unconventional methods of political participation to try to persuade or coerce authorities to support a challenging group's aims," a concept which includes methods within *both* nonviolent and violent spectrums, such as "conventional strategies of political persuasion such as lobbying, voting, and petitioning; confrontational tactics such as marches, strikes, and demonstrations that disrupt the day-to-day life of a community; violent acts that inflict material and economic damage and loss of life; and cultural forms of political expression such as rituals, spectacles, music, art, poetry, film, literature, and cultural practices of everyday life" (2004, p. 263). This is more in line with resistance movements throughout history, which are usually neither purely violent nor purely nonviolent. Many involve multiple organizations employing a variety of tactics: examples include the anti-apartheid struggle in South Africa, in which "most activists over the years viewed violent and nonviolent strategies as more intertwined and complementary than contradictory" (Seidman, 2000, p. 165); or, more recently, the strategy of "an Armalite in one hand and a ballot paper in the other" pursued by Sinn Féin, the political arm of the Irish Republican Army in Northern Ireland (Smithey & Kurtz, 2002, p. 328). Stephan and Chenoweth (2008), after providing the first quantitative comparison of nonviolent and violent resistance campaigns, argued that nonviolent resistance needs to be studied analogously with violent resistance. Chenoweth and Stephan (2011) developed this point, drawing attention to the fact that there are *no episodes of contentious politics* in which nonviolent civil resistance or violent coercion is the sole strategy used. Schock points out that "it would be a grave mistake for social scientists to limit their analysis of nonviolent action to only those rare struggles that were completely nonviolent or to overlook or dismiss the power of nonviolent action in struggles where violence occurred" (2005, xvii).

In conclusion, there have been many studies which conclude that nonviolence is a much better strategic choice than violence. However, while many of these studies express their awareness of the fact that very few conflicts are solely nonviolent or violent, there remains a lack of studies discussing the internal effects of simultaneous, intra-movement violent *and* nonviolent groups. What happens when a campaign is predominantly nonviolent, but contains an active radical flank unit which uses violence? Does such a campaign more closely follow the resulting patterns of a purely nonviolent movement or a purely violent one? In other words, does a limited amount of violence undermine an entire otherwise-nonviolent campaign, or does a cohesive nonviolent movement override the presence of a violent sub-unit? For clues to these questions' answers, we turn to the existing literature on radical flanks.

Radical Flanks

Given the vast spectrum of tactics, it is not surprisingly that internal ideological and strategic disagreements can develop, leading to schisms within groups. Cleavages are common within the high-stakes environment of conflict participation. But while some groups have a minor amount of internal discord, others experience dramatic divides which end in the formation of entirely separate movements. *Radical flank* is the term used to describe a branch-off movement that has more extremist goals or ideologies, or employs more radical tactics. This relational definition means that the term is not always applied consistently. A spinoff group might be called "radical" simply because it seeks more fundamental or extreme changes in the political structure, whether or not it uses violent tactics. For example, Hizb ut-Tahrir in Uzbekistan is considered a radical Islamic movement − its goal is the unification of all Muslim countries into a single Caliphate − yet it has remained fiercely committed to using only nonviolent tactics (Karagiannis & McCauley, 2006). Right-wing extremism in Europe provides its own spectrum of "radical" structures and levels of violence, from "organised political parties that … seek to work within legal frameworks, but may have members who are individually associated with violence" to "smaller groups and networks without formal membership or rigid structures, which tend to adopt more extreme ideological positions" (Goodwin, Ramalingam, & Briggs, 2012, p. 6).

For the purposes of this study, a radical flank will be identified by its use of violence − thus *radical, armed, militant*, and *violent* will be used interchangeably to refer to such groups. More specifically, I will be using Chenoweth and Lewis's (2013a, 2013b) definition, which corresponds with the NAVCO 2.0 dataset: "A radical flank is defined as a group that adopts extremist rhetoric and violent strategies to pursue their goals. They represent a faction within the broader opposition movement. This definition excludes predominantly violent campaigns or other violent groups within the country that are pursuing different political objectives" (see codebook accompanying Chenoweth & Lewis, 2013a, 2013b, p. 10). One of the key elements of this definition is that radical flanks are an *intra-movement* phenomenon rather than an extra-movement one; in other words, while there may be contemporaneous armed actors external to the campaign (with goals differing from those of the campaign), these are not considered radical flanks. Radical flanks share the goals of the other groups within the campaign, but may be employing different strategies (violence rather than nonviolence) to achieve them.

Herbert Haines (1984, 1988) was the first to analyze "radical flank effects," pioneering the construction of a theoretical framework for the role of "radicals" in shaping responses to "moderates." In his intensive studies of the American Civil Rights Movement, Haines (1984) found evidence for positive radical flank effects − "(1) public awareness and recognition; (2) public definition and redefinition; (3) outside resource support; (4) access to decision-makers; and (5) goal attainment" (Haines, 1988, pp. 5−6) − arguing that a radical or violent group increases the leverage of the nonviolent group by making the demands of the nonviolent group comparatively more reasonable. Moreover, radical groups are much better at creating "crisis" situations for the regime to deal with, situations which the moderates can then offer solutions to. Radical flanks can thus change cost structures of participation and can alter the strategic setting of moderate actors in their interplay with the regime. It can be a symbiotic relationship by which militant activities apply pressure to make the regime negotiate with the moderates.

However, this relationship can be negative as well. Haines (1984) also posited a potential negative radical flank effect — essentially a spoiler effect — whereby "the activities of radicals in a social movement can undermine the position of moderates by discrediting movement activities and goals, and by threatening the ability of moderates to take advantage of the resources available from supportive third parties" (32). In such cases, a radical flank's actions are generalized as being representative of the actions of the entire movement. The state may also use this to their advantage, framing an entire movement as violent and thus illegitimate and ultimately undeserving of support or sympathy. This might result in the state deciding to react with indiscriminate repression on all movement organizations and actors. Violent groups thus undermine the entire movement by discrediting all campaign groups and justifying regime repression, which then also reduces popular participation by raising the risk of participation. This negative effect on campaign size was confirmed by Schock and Chenoweth (2012), who found that the presence of a violent campaign (radical flank) is likely to decrease the level of popular participation in the nonviolent campaign by about 50% (within their dataset, purely nonviolent campaigns had 100,000 participants on average, whereas nonviolent campaigns with contemporaneous violent campaigns averaged only 50,000). They offered this as a potential mechanism linking radical flank presence to ultimate campaign failure, since campaign size has a statistically significant relationship with the likelihood of campaign success.

Flanks shape the battle of narratives concerning the identity of the resistance and the values according to which it operates. By virtue of their common goals, a nonviolent movement and a radical flank offshoot are linked, whether they want to be or not. Radical flanks, by changing the costs, symbols, and strategic context of the movement, have a marked impact on the intertemporal dynamics of a movement. It's no great leap to believe that they might subsequently be a key variable in the ultimate outcome of a resistance movement. Haines' (1984, 1988) theory is grounded in subtle sociological processes, and makes it very difficult to derive clearly demarcated, testable hypotheses related to the effects of the presence of a radical flank.

His mechanisms are descriptive rather than explanatory, and his theory is entirely based off of a single case study. Thus, two issues become apparent: (1) the lack of testable theory related to the more direct effects of radical flank emergence, and (2) the lack of large-N studies analyzing such phenomena. Schock and Chenoweth (2012) conducted the only known study addressing the second of these issues. Examining whether the existence of a violent campaign that occurs simultaneously with a nonviolent one increases or decreases the likelihood of *success* of the overall campaign, they conducted a bivariate cross-tabulation using a NAVCO 1.0 subset of 106 nonviolent campaigns with or without simultaneous violent organizations, and found that only 46% of campaigns with a radical flank were successful, compared with 60% of campaigns without the presence of a violent organization ($p < .136$). They concluded that, across a large number of cases, there is no evidence for a positive radical flank effect, because in all models the impact of a simultaneous violent campaign on the outcome of a nonviolent campaign was negative. However, their results were not statistically significant. Furthermore, though offering a general definition of radical flanks as "those with more extreme methods or more extreme demands relative to other opposition groups," they operationalized radical flanks as groups that use methods of violent resistance – including both intra-movement *and inter-movement armed groups*. This means that they were studying armed groups that, while active at the same time, had completely separate objectives from the nonviolent resistance movements they coincided with. Thus, the scope of Schock and Chenoweth (2012) study was too broad to identify significant intermediate mechanisms.

Studies which try to link the presence of a radical flank to ultimate campaign success are a tad overly ambitious at a point where there is still a large lack of clear quantitative studies of the more immediate, within-movement impacts of radical flank emergence. The mechanisms behind the formation of radical flanks have been studied thoroughly (Alimi, 2011; Beach, 1977), and nonviolent tactics have been analyzed in contrast with violent tactics (see section 2.1). Yet, as Sutton, Svensson, and Davidson put it, "the potential of positive radical flank effects to influence the course of unarmed uprisings warrants further investigation" (2012, p. 26). We still lack quantitative studies of the clearly demarcated, immediate results of the presence of a radical flank on the overarching nonviolent campaign within which it emerges. Thus, radical flank effects should not be reduced to the ultimate success or failure of the campaign, a connection which has been shown to be weak and insignificant; rather, intermediate outcome variables should be pinpointed and illuminated. In the following sections, I will undertake such a task, narrowing the unit of analysis from campaign to individual campaign years, in order to relate the presence of a radical flank to other micro-level phenomenon within a resistance movement.

THEORY

In this section, I will construct a theoretical framework for radical flank effects within the broader context of nonviolent resistance movements, synthesizing past research on nonviolent and violent strategies into predictions concerning the effects of violent tactics emerging *within* a nonviolent resistance campaign. Using the presence of a radical flank as my central explanatory variable, I will derive three testable hypotheses.

Research Question and Scope Conditions

When nonviolent and violent groups coexist within a single campaign — thus having the same goals in mind, but using diametrically-opposed means of achieving them — what are the effects of the radical flank on the nonviolent organization and on the campaign as a whole? What intermediate variables might be plausible factors within the relationship between the presence of a radical flank and campaign success or failure? Based on my overarching argument that the effects of radical flanks may not necessarily doom a movement to failure, I will analyze the effects of radical flank presence on: repression likelihood and intensity (H1), campaign backlash (H2), and campaign progress per annum (H3). I will be limiting my focus to primarily nonviolent campaigns, and as per Chenoweth and Lewis's (2013a, 2013b) definition of radical flanks for the NAVCO 2.0 dataset, I will only be examining radical flanks that are intra-movement, meaning which have the same goals as the main nonviolent campaign occurring contemporaneously.

Conceptualizing Radical Flank Effects

Radical Flanks and Repression (H1)

When a state's authority is challenged by a resistance movement, it almost always pursues sanctions to counter or eliminate this threat, what Davenport (2007, p. 7) calls the "Law of Coercive Responsiveness." Stockdill defines repression as "any actions taken by [regime] authorities to impede mobilization, harass and intimidate activists, divide organizations, and physically assault, arrest, imprison, and/or kill movement participants" (1996, p. 146). Repression can consist of a variety of acts ranging from the nonviolent (e.g., passing legislation that counters the resistance movement, censoring the opposition) to the violent (e.g., police brutality, tear gas, military crackdowns); it can also take the form of government support for counter-movements – thus, repressive measures can also be "contracted out" to civil society or other non-state organizations (such as white-power organizations acting against the American Civil Rights Movement). At its most extreme end, the "observable, coercive repression by state agents tightly connected with national political elites" (Earl, 2003, p. 50) that make up a repressive response can escalate to include selective assassinations, disappearances, and political terror – such as was seen in Chile, Uruguay, and Argentina in the 1970s and 1980s (Loveman, 1998).

Given the high stakes of maximalist campaigns – in which goals such as "overthrowing the existing regime, expelling foreign occupations, or achieving self-determination at some point during the campaign" are pursued (Chenoweth & Lewis, 2013a, 2013b, p. 416) – and the assumption that a regime wants to remain in power, the state is likely to use whatever resources it can to suppress an uprising, particularly a movement with maximalist goals and an active radical flank, which poses the most direct threat to regime control. Radical flank presence can have the effect of providing an incentive for the state to equate radicals with the movement as a whole, discredit all regime opponents, and thus justify widespread and indiscriminate repression. This is supported both by Sharp, who warns that "even minor breaks in discipline and very limited violence may be the occasion for quite disproportionate response by the agents of repression" (1973, p. 587), and Zunes (1994), who claims that regimes actually "welcome" violence from resistance groups, as it then makes a violent repression more justifiable, both domestically and internationally. Ackerman and Kruegler put it quite bluntly: "In the context of nonviolent conflict, violent retaliation is not likely to improve one's position and may elicit even harsher reprisals" (1994, p. 38). If a violent radical flank is present within a movement, it may simultaneously elicit more fear from the regime and a perceived justification for harsh repression by the state – not just on the radical flank, but on the movement as a whole. I thus arrive at the following hypothesis:

H1. The presence of a radical flank increases the likelihood and degree of repression by the regime, and the likelihood that such repression will be indiscriminate.

Radical Flanks and Backlash (H2)

The effects of repression depend on several factors. It can decrease participation by increasing the risks connected to involvement in a campaign (Tilly, 1978), can facilitate internal ruptures and the creation of new intra-campaign groups (McAdam, 1983), or provide a rallying point for campaign unity. The variety of outcomes is summed up in the causal model known as "political jiu-jitsu," which is attributed to Sharp (1973), though it was derived from Gregg's original "moral jiu-jitsu" (1966). The term political jiu-jitsu refers to the "paradoxical consequences" which result from a state using violence against an unarmed civilian resistance. "Brutal sanctions expose the regime's viciousness, causing sympathy for the nonviolent resisters to increase and support for the ruler to decrease — both domestically and internationally" (Nepstad, 2011, p. 15). Thus, it is a phenomenon which has in the past been applied solely to nonviolent movement research.

Francisco (2004, 2010) is one of several scholars who found that increased overt, violent repression elicits an *increase* in opposition activities. This increased momentum after regime repression — (1) increasing popular participation, (2) receiving external aid or third party support, (3) prompting international sanctions against the regime, and/or (4) provoking defections from state security forces and bureaucrats (Stephan & Chenoweth, 2008) — is referred to as *backlash* or *backfire*, and is the *coup de grâce* of political jiu-jitsu. In backfire, violent repression results in "the breakdown of obedience among regime supporters, mobilization of the population against the regime, and international condemnation of the regime" (*ibid.*, p. 11). Overall, the regime's grip on power is undermined and it can no longer rely on the forces propping it up, while the nonviolent group gains momentum through increased internal cohesion and external support (Schock, 2005; Sharp, 1973). However, even though repression results in increased momentum for a resistance movement, it has also been linked with decreased likelihood (−35%) of nonviolent campaign success (Chenoweth & Stephan, 2011), leading to the possibility that whether or not an opposition *maintains its commitment to nonviolence in the face of violent repression* is an important factor for eventual success.

One argument concerning the impact of repression on social movements' strategic response is Cunningham and Beaulieu's (2010) "theory of dissent strategy," which is described succinctly by Dudouet: "dissidents analyse past state behaviour with regard to level of repression to a particular tactic, and how consistently it was used, in order to decide which methods of dissent (whether violent or nonviolent) to use" (2013, p. 410). When violent tactics are continuously met with repression, dissidents often shift their main strategy to nonviolence, whereas if the state response is weak or inconsistent, violent tactics will continue. Moore actually finds a link between violent tactics and nonviolent protest prevalence — for every eight acts of "violent dissent," a state experiences one additional nonviolent protest (2012, p. 19). The potential for increased nonviolent measures post-repression is one means of achieving backfire — reframing a movement in more peaceful, reasonable light may be linked with greater international sympathy and even elicit foreign sanctions on the regime.

However, Mason and Krane (1989) found that regime repression actually can further radicalize a group as well. Moore (1998) argues that heightened repression can result in a tactical shift from nonviolence to violence. This happens for several reasons. First of all, moderates and nonviolent protesters might leave the movement due to the increased costs of participation, thus leaving only more radical players in action. On the other hand, when government repression indiscriminately targets both insurgents and civilians, joining with revolutionary forces is no longer the riskier option — in fact, it might even be a strategic decision to gain protection from a state which now identifies *all* demonstrators as the enemy. This provides a potential opportunity for a nonviolent movement *with a radical flank* to effectively mobilize a backlash. One example where increased support was given to a violent insurgency post-repression is Northern Ireland, where the Provisional Irish Republican Army was given a long-term strategic benefit by the British military forces' brutal crackdowns — still, Stephan and Chenoweth (2008, pp. 13—14) stress that this is "rarer," and "despite temporary setbacks, nonviolent campaigns are more likely to gain additional long-term benefits from regime repression than are violent campaigns."

Nonviolent movements are more likely than violent ones to elicit defections by regime security forces and bureaucracy; furthermore, the international community is more likely to denounce and sanction governments when they repress *unarmed* protestors. "Potentially sympathetic publics perceive violent militants as having maximalist or extremist goals beyond accommodation, but they perceive nonviolent resistance groups as less extreme, thereby enhancing their appeal and facilitating the extraction of concessions through bargaining" (Stephan & Chenoweth, 2008, p. 8). Thus, when it comes to violent insurgencies, some foreign states might actually provide counter-insurgency assistance, aiding regimes in crushing such movements (*ibid.*, p. 12). Schock and Chenoweth (2012) mention (but do not test) the assumption that radical flanks cause a decreased likelihood of backfire. Building off of my previous hypothesis — that the presence of a radical flank provides an opportunity for the regime to frame an entire opposition movement as violent — I posit that a movement with a radical flank is less likely to gain the necessary momentum for an effective post-repression backlash.

H2. The presence of a radical flank will decrease the likelihood of a non-violent resistance movement achieving backfire against the regime.

Radical Flanks and Campaign Progress (H3)

Since 1950, so-called "weaker" actors have won 51% of all asymmetric wars (Arreguín-Toft, 2005), so state power is not the sole determinant of conflict outcome. According to nonviolent resistance theory, state power depends on "pillars of support" — predominantly the police, military, civil servants, and media, but also youth, businesses, and NGOs (Helvey, 2004). As a result, the regime's ability to control events is severely weakened if individuals and groups withdraw their support by launching strikes and boycotts, withholding taxes, disobeying orders, and engaging in other acts of civil disobedience and noncooperation. The regime may even collapse altogether if its institutional pillars of support are sufficiently eroded (Gandhi, 1951; Gregg, 1966; Helvey, 2004; Sharp, 1973). As Schock puts it, the key to a nonviolent campaign's success "is not the amount of violence that accompanies it, but rather the ability to remain resilient in a repressive context and to increase its leverage relative to the state, either by directly severing the state's sources of support or by mobilizing the crucial support of third parties that have leverage against the target state" (2005, p. 161). A recent example of this was seen in Egypt, where massive defections by President Hosni Mubarak's military troops to the side of the protesters were a significant factor in Mubarak's regime collapse (Nepstad, 2013).

In general, success is more likely if a resistance campaign has a formalized structure (Gamson, 1975); success is more than four times more likely if a movement garners defections from the state; and progress (not necessarily success) is more likely the longer a campaign endures (Stephan & Chenoweth, 2008). In the face of violent repression, nonviolent movements are more than six times more likely to achieve full success than violent campaigns that also faced violent regime repression, *and* regimes are twelve times more likely to grant concessions to nonviolent organizations (*ibid.*, p. 20). Furthermore, nonviolent campaigns are more likely to succeed with domestic gains, such as eliciting military defections; whereas violent campaigns benefit more from "external pressures" such as foreign sanctions imposed on the state (*ibid.*, p. 24).

Nonviolent action is better qualified to indirectly undermine regime power, and in line with this, previous research has found time and time again that nonviolent resistance has a significantly higher success rate. Meanwhile, radical groups tend not to fare so well when waging purely violent campaigns: in a study of 42 policy objectives of 28 terrorist groups, Abrahms (2006) finds that the groups were successful only 7% of the time. It follows that the presence of *some* violence (in the form of a radical flank) within an otherwise-nonviolent movement will do more to undermine the group than to lead it to success. As previously stated, Schock and Chenoweth (2012) were unable to find a significant causal link between radical flank presence and ultimate campaign success, though there was weak evidence for a negative relationship. Thus, this study posits the following:

H3. The presence of a radical flank decreases the likelihood of a nonviolent resistance movement achieving progress in a given year.

RESEARCH DESIGN

The Nonviolent and Violence Campaigns and Outcomes (NAVCO) project has collected aggregate-level data on resistance campaigns from 1900 to 2006 (NAVCO 1.0) and annual data on campaign behavior from 1945 to 2006 (NAVCO 2.0). In NAVCO 2.0, Chenoweth and Lewis (2013a, 2013b) provide detailed annual data on 250 campaigns (100 nonviolent and 150 violent), which "constitute the full population of known cases between 1945 and 2006 that held 'maximalist' goals of overthrowing the existing regime, expelling foreign occupations, or achieving self-determination at some point during the campaign" (2013a, p. 416). To qualify as a campaign for NAVCO 2.0, a "contentious event with 1,000 or more participants must be followed within a year by another contentious event with 1,000 or more observed participants claiming the same goals *and* there must be evidence of coordination across those events" (*ibid.*, p. 417). Data are consensus-based, from multiple sources. One potential weakness of NAVCO is "an inherent bias in the data towards larger and also often successful campaigns" (Svensson & Lindgren, 2011, p. 224), caused by an underreporting of campaigns which were crushed in their infancy or never established themselves via mobilization or the implementation of a continuous organizational structure.

Using the year as the unit of analysis in NAVCO 2.0, rather than the entire campaign, allows a much more nuanced look at an internal movement factors. Because a single resistance movement is capable of dramatic fluctuations within its lifetime, breaking movements down into annual data allows a consistent, yet adaptable mechanism for taking into consideration variables such as changes in campaign goals or structure from year-to-year, as well as the emergence or disappearance of a radical flank in a given year, the annual extent of state repression, or the amount of progress made toward success in a single year – to name a few. The ability to report on such changes in movement structure, goals, methods, etc. from year-to-year allows a novel opportunity to reevaluate radical flank effects in a graded, sequential manner.

For the purposes of this study, I will be using a subset created from the NAVCO 2.0 dataset. It is made up 119 campaigns further subdivided into 329 data points on campaign behavior per annum. Inclusion was determined by the variable *prim_method*, which denotes whether a campaign used primarily violent or nonviolent tactics in a given year – observations selected for inclusion were all years coded "1 = primarily nonviolent." This means that, in addition to including all 100 of the nonviolent campaigns within NAVCO 2.0, my dataset includes observations from 19 violent campaigns which were "1 = primarily nonviolent" for the particular year of the observation. An example of such an included campaign is the IRA versus British occupation, which NAVCO 1.0/2.0 designates as a primarily violent campaign *overall*, but which contains 11 years in which tactics were actually predominantly *nonviolent* (1968, 1994–5, 1999–2006). Thus, these individual 11 years are included observations within my dataset.

As previously stated, NAVCO 2.0 only includes campaigns that have "maximalist" goals (regime change, secession, self-determination), which are distinguished from "limited" goals, such as institutional reform or greater autonomy. Limited goals are not included in NAVCO 2.0 *except* when a maximalist campaign temporarily slackens its demands for a particular campaign year.

To further illustrate the types of campaigns which are included in my dataset, I offer Table 1 with examples of actual data points included in my sample (please note that this list is not exhaustive by any stretch).

All variables will be operationalized using existing, pre-coded variables within the NAVCO 2.0 dataset. The relevant variables are introduced with some preliminary descriptive statistics in Table 2.

Because data on certain variables was missing in some observations, there are fluctuations in sample size (N) depending on what variables are being used in the analyses which follow.

Table 1. Illustrative Examples of Nonviolent Campaigns in NAVCO 2.0.

Regime change	Carnation Revolution, Portugal, 1973–1974
	Second Defiance Campaign, South Africa, 1990–1994
	Orange Revolution, Ukraine, 2001–2004
	Cedar Revolution, Lebanon, 2005
Policy change	First Defiance Campaign, South Africa, 1952–1959
	Hundred Flowers Movement, China, 1956–1957
	Democracy Movement, China, 1976–1978
	Mongolian Anti-Communist, Mongolia, 1989–1990
Territorial secession	Gamsakhurdia and Abkhazia, Georgia, 1989–1991
	Chechen Separatists, Russia, 1997
	Bougainville Revolt, Papua New Guinea, 1998
	Slovenian Independence, Slovenia, 1990–1991
Anti-occupation	Anti-Colonialist Movement, Cameroon, 1956–1960
	IRA, Northern Ireland, 1968–2006
	Palestinian Liberation, Palestine, 1987–1993
	Singing Revolution, Estonia, 1989–1991

Table 2. Descriptive Statistics for Included Variables.

	Observations	Min	Max	Mean	SD
Explanatory variable					
Radical flank	329	0	1	.43	.50
Outcome variables					
Repression	327	0	3	1.90	1.25
Backlash	322	0	3	1.97	1.33
Progress	329	0	4	1.74	1.61
Control variables					
Campaign size	262	0	5	2.50	1.44
New campaign groups	295	0	11	2.04	3.02
Indiscriminate repression	274	0	1	.56	.50
Hierarchical structure	328	0	1	.30	.46

Explanatory Variable

Radical flank: The central independent variable within this study will be the presence of a radical flank within a primarily nonviolent campaign year. Once the sample was limited to primarily nonviolent campaign years, it was necessary to recode the variable *rad_flank* into a binary variable where 1 signifies the presence of a radical flank. As previously stated, radical flank here refers to "a group that adopts extremist rhetoric and violent strategies to pursue their goals," which must be "a faction within the broader opposition movement" thus excluding any other contemporaneous violent groups or campaigns which are pursuing other objectives (see codebook accompanying Chenoweth & Lewis, 2013a, 2013b, p. 10).

Outcome Variables

Repression: NAVCO 2.0 codes repression as an ordinal scale measuring "the most repressive episode or activity perpetrated by the state in response to campaign activity" (*ibid.*, p. 13), including repression by police or military, economic repression in the form of fines or taxes, and judicial repression. It is coded 0 if the state does not respond, or responds in a conciliatory manner to the opposition, 1 for mild repression (e.g., verbal or threatening action short of physical action, express intent to engage in conflict, use of economic fees and levies to increase costs on opposition, decline to cease ongoing conflict), 2 for moderate repression (e.g., physical or violent action aimed at coercing opponent, harassment and imprisonment of campaign members), and 3 for extreme repression (e.g., physical action exhibiting intent to kill and violently silence opponents, torture, mass violence).

Backlash: Campaign backlash will be measured with the variable *camp_backlash*, which focuses on the ultimate impact state repression has on the campaign's popular mobilization. Coded 0 for no repression (status quo maintenance), this nominal variable offers the following outcomes for backlash: 1 = movement suppressed; 2 = decreased domestic mobilization; and 3 = increased domestic mobilization. "If there is no substantial campaign activity following repressive action, then the movement is considered suppressed. If there are still some opposition activities, but they are fewer and have smaller numbers of participants, then mobilization is considered decreased ... if state repression if followed by larger, more prominent opposition activities, then backlash has occurred in the form of 'increased domestic mobilization'" (*ibid.*, p. 14).

Progress: Progress is an ordinal variable which identifies whether a campaign achieved all or some of its goals within a given year. By goals, it refers to the overarching campaign goals against the regime, rather than micro-level "tactical or operational" goals. The variable is coded as follows: 0 = status quo; 1 = visible gains short of concessions; 2 = limited concession achieved; 3 = significant concessions achieved; and 4 = complete success. "Status quo" means that the state made no concessions; however, if the state "nonetheless changes its behavior to accommodate the opposition, for example by allowing greater protest or political openness than was allowed in the past," it is coded as 1. Limited concessions refer to "verbal statements of conciliation or changes in the stated position of the regime without additional action" and significant concessions refer to "actions short of ultimate capitulation, such as policy changes, the removal of state leaders or the instigation of negotiations with the opposition" (*ibid.*, p. 18).

Control Variables

Campaign size and new campaign groups: Campaign mobilization has been operationalized within NAVCO 2.0 using the variables *camp_size*, which denotes the size of a campaign (coded in incremental ranges: $0 = 1-999$, $1 = 1,000-9,999$, $2 = 10,000-99,999$, $3 = 1,00,000-4,99,999$, $4 = 5,00,000-1$ million, $5 =$ over 1 million); and *camp_orgs*, which denotes the number of "new named organizations" within a campaign for a given year (coded from 0 to 10, with the added variable 11 to denote all numbers above 10). Because this variable is weighted, it does not measure campaign size as a proportion of the population. This coding relies on "peak events," which often indicate the maximum size of the movement. Movement participants include anyone who took any part in any aspect of the campaign, ranging from active organizing to popular participation in large-scale street protests. The addition of new campaign groups illustrates where the campaign fragmented into splinter units (which may include a new radical flank formation).

Indiscriminate repression: In tandem with the variable measuring the degree of state repression, the dummy variable *discrim* will also be used. It denotes whether state repression is discriminate (coded 0) or indiscriminant (coded 1) in targeting key resistance campaign actors, an important distinction to make when there are both nonviolent and violent groups within a campaign.

Hierarchical structure: The dummy variable *camp_structure* provides a simple measure of whether or not a campaign has a hierarchical command structure with centralized, clearly demarcated leadership. 0 refers to a campaign structure where leadership is diffuse and decisions are consensus-based, and 1 refers to a campaign structure with a centralized and hierarchical chain of command. This controls for internal structures within the campaign which might impact the coordination of groups and thus impact a movement's overall effectiveness.

ANALYSIS

Interpretation of Results

Test of H1

H1. The presence of a radical flank increases the likelihood and degree of repression by the regime, and the likelihood that such repression will be indiscriminate.

Dependent variables: Repression, Indiscriminate Repression
Independent variable: Radical flank
Control variables: Campaign size, New campaign groups, Hierarchical structure

Table 3 lists the results of two models – a bivariate regression and a multivariate regression – applied to test the result of radical flank presence on the likelihood and intensity of state repression. H1 is supported by both models. The initial bivariate regression produces a b-coefficient of .61 for radical flank presence, which is statistically significant at the 99% level (t = 4.48). The presence of a radical flank is thus expected to increase repression by .61, which can be interpreted as over "half-a-step" from no repression to mild repression, mild to moderate, or moderate to extreme

Table 3. Bivariate and Multivariate Regressions of Repression.

	(1)	(2)
Radical flank	.61***	.82***
	(.14)	(.14)
Campaign size		−.06
		(.05)
New campaign groups		−.01
		(.02)
Hierarchical structure		−.54***
		(.15)
Constant	1.64***	2.00***
	.09	(.15)
R^2	.0582	.1642
Adj. R^2	.0553	.1508
Root MSE	1.21	1.08
N	327	253

Note: Entries are regression coefficients (standard errors in parentheses).
***$p < 0.01$, **$p < 0.05$, *$p < 0.1$.

repression. However, it should be noted that only 5.82% of the variation in repression is explained by the presence of a radical flank ($R^2 = .0582$). The root MSE of 1.21 is noteworthy, as it corresponds to significant variation in the level of repression faced by campaigns with a radical flank.

The second model includes control variables for campaign size, new campaign organizations, and the presence of a hierarchical structure. The results appear in column 2 of Table 3. In Model 2 the b-coefficient for radical flank presence is .82, significant at the 99% level ($t = 5.86$). This is a very strong relationship, implying that a nonviolent movement with a radical flank will likely be met with a significantly higher degree of repression by the state. Campaign size and the emergence of new intra-campaign organizations show no significant relationship with repression. However, a moderate negative relationship emerges between the presence of a hierarchical structure within the nonviolent movement and repression ($t = -3.60$, $p < .01$). As derived in the previous section, internal campaign structure is closely tied with less internal conflict. Such an organization will be more likely to maintain both consistent demands and tactics, and will be seen as less unpredictable, and perhaps thus less threatening, by a regime. However, regardless, when a radical flank is present, some level of regime repression is highly likely. I now test radical flank presence on the likelihood of repression being indiscriminate. Because the outcome variable (indiscriminate repression) is a binary variable, logistic regression models were used.

The results in the first column of Table 4 show that there is a strong positive relationship between the presence of a radical flank and indiscriminate state repression. For a primarily nonviolent campaign with an active radical flank, the odds of repression being indiscriminate are 3.39 times larger than for a campaign without a radical flank. In this case, the model is highly statistically significant ($z = 4.69$, $\text{Prob} > \text{chi}^2 = .0000$). In the second column (Model 2), where control variables were added for campaign size, new campaign groups, and presence of a hierarchical campaign structure, the relationship between radical flank presence and indiscriminate repression remains. The odds ratio for radical flank in Model 2 is about the same, 3.24 ($z = 4.03$, $\text{Prob} > \text{chi}^2 = .0006$). The same control variables used to analyze repression as the dependent variable are added here as well, but none of them are found to be significantly related to indiscriminate repression. The fact that campaign size shows no significant relationship with either repression or indiscriminate repression is interesting to note, as we would assume that a campaign with massive mobilization would be significantly related to lower repression (showing strength in numbers, a large

Table 4. Logistic Regression of Indiscriminate Repression.

	(1)	(2)
Radical flank	3.39***	3.24***
	(.89)	(.95)
Campaign size		1.16
		(.12)
New campaign groups		1.02
		(.05)
Hierarchical structure		.68
		(.21)
Constant	.78	.60
	(.12)	(.19)
Pseudo R^2	.0610	.0618
LR chi^2 (1)	22.95	19.66
Prob > chi^2	.0000	.0006
N	274	232

Note: Entries are odds ratios (standard errors in parentheses).
***$p < 0.01$, **$p < 0.05$, *$p < 0.1$.

nonviolent movement would be more likely to convince a regime that nego-tiation was a better strategy than attempted repression). Both logistic regression models suggest a very strong relationship between the presence of a radical flank and the significantly increased likelihood for repression to be indiscriminate.

Test of H2.

H2. The presence of a radical flank will decrease the likelihood of a non-violent resistance movement achieving backfire against the regime.

Dependent variables: Backlash
Independent variable: Radical flank
Control variables: Indiscriminate Repression, Campaign size

To estimate the effect of radical flank presence on the likelihood of cam-paign backlash, I employ a multinomial logistic regression (MLR), which compares the probabilities that different independent variables will result in each respective outcome of the dependent variable — in this case (1) movement suppressed, (2) decreased domestic mobilization, and (3) increased domestic mobilization (relative to a base value of no effect, i.e., status quo). Implicit in the definition of backlash is the assumption that repression has already taken place; thus there is no need to incorporate the variable *repression*; however, the distinction between discriminate and indiscriminate repression is not implicit, and I thus include the dummy variable *discrim* as a control variable within both models, to account for the possible differing results when a state cracks down indiscriminately on the entire movement (radical flank and the nonviolent actors) versus solely on the radical offshoot (Sharp, 1973; Zunes, 1994). Furthermore, I also include campaign size as a control variable, as larger groups have been shown to have advantages in resisting repression (Gurr, 2000), building momentum and support (Lichbach, 1995), and ultimately achieving success (Schock & Chenoweth, 2012).

Examining the results in Table 5, we find that campaigns with a radical flank are more likely to lead to movement suppression (1.55, $p < .05$), decreased mobilization (1.67, $p < .01$), or increased mobilization (.91, $p < .1$), relative to the alternative of maintaining the status quo, when controlling for campaign size and whether repression was discriminate or not. The strongest and most significant relationship emerges between radical flank presence and decreased mobilization, which is significant at the 99% confidence level. We can conclude that, while the presence of a radical flank increases the likelihood of all three outcomes relative to status quo maintenance, it *most strongly* increases the likelihood of decreased mobilization.

Table 5. Multinomial Logistic Regression of Campaign Backlash.

	(1) Movement Suppressed	(2) Decreased Mobilization	(3) Increased Mobilization
Radical flank	1.55**	1.67***	.91*
	(.73)	(.59)	(.47)
Indiscriminate repression	.23	.52	.64
	(.69)	(.54)	(.39)
Campaign size	−.48**	−.43**	−.38***
	(.24)	(.19)	(.13)
Constant	−.41	.03	1.88***
	(.78)	(.63)	(.46)
LR chi^2 (9) = 25.67			
Prob > chi^2 = .0023			
Pseudo R^2 = .0555			
N = 233			

Note: Entries are odds ratios (standard errors in parentheses).
***$p < 0.01$, **$p < 0.05$, *$p < 0.1$.

It is perplexing that there is a positive coefficient for the relationship between radical flank presence and *increased* mobilization, as well as a positive coefficient for the relationship between radical flank presence and *decreased* mobilization. Can a radical flank make both of these opposing outcomes more likely? It appears that it can — at least relative to maintaining the status quo. So long as status quo is set as the base value, this model cannot compare *decreased mobilization* with *increased mobilization*. It seems that stasis is hard to maintain when there is a radical flank present. This is a key finding, that radical flanks have catalytic effects on politics for better or for worse. We can more closely examine the relationship between these two outcomes by doing another MLR of campaign backlash, this time setting increased mobilization as the base value (Table 6).

If a movement were to add a radical flank, the multinomial log-odds for decreased mobilization relative to increased mobilization would be expected to increase by 0.76 units while holding all other variables in the model constant. For decreased mobilization relative to increased mobilization, at an alpha level of 0.01, we would conclude that having a radical flank leads to a statistically significant increase in the likelihood that a campaign will be stalled rather than spurred onward. The results suggest that the presence of a radical flank, while increasing the likelihood of a nonviolent resistance movement achieving backfire (increased mobilization) against the regime relative to simply maintaining the status quo, is most

Table 6. Multinomial Logistic Regression of Campaign Backlash.

	(0) Status Quo	(1) Movement Suppressed	(2) Decreased Mobilization
Radical flank	−.91*	.64	.76*
	(.47)	(.60)	(.43)
Indiscriminate repression	.64	−.41	−.12
	(.39)	(.61)	(.44)
Campaign size	.38***	−.10	−.05
	(.13)	(.22)	(.15)
Constant	−1.88***	−2.30***	−1.84***
	(.46)	(.68)	(.50)
LR chi^2 (9) = 25.67			
Prob > chi^2 = .0023			
Pseudo R^2 = .0555			
N = 233			

Note: Entries are odds ratios (standard errors in parentheses).
***$p < 0.01$, **$p < 0.05$, *$p < 0.1$.

significantly associated with strong increase in the likelihood of decreased movement mobilization.

Whether repression was discriminate or not proved not to be a significant predictor of campaign backlash. Campaign size was indeed shown to be a significant variable in all outcomes, with a negative relationship to movement suppression, decreased mobilization, and increased mobilization; but a positive relationship with status quo maintenance. At a 99% confidence level, if a campaign were to increase its size by one point (recall here that campaign size was coded in incremental ranges, so a one point increase is quite significant: $0 = 1 - 999$, $1 = 1,000 - 9,999$, $2 = 10,000 - 99,999$, $3 = 1,00,000 - 4,99,999$, $4 = 5,00,000 - 1$ million, $5 =$ over 1 million), the multinomial log-odds for maintaining the status quo over increased mobilization would be expected to increase by 0.38 units, while holding all other variables in the model constant.

This model could be further specified in future research with a clear-cut time lag variable, which NAVCO 2.0 does not include. For the purposes of this study, there is no differentiation between mobilization which occurs immediately following repression and mobilization which occurs later on in a given year. To more closely examine the impact of a time lag between the onset of repression and subsequent mobilization, this variable must be further specified in future research.

Test of H3.

H3. The presence of a radical flank decreases the likelihood of a nonviolent resistance movement achieving progress in a given year.

Dependent variables: Progress
Independent variable: Radical flank
Control variables: Repression, Backlash, Campaign size

I will first provide a breakdown of my dataset with descriptive cross-tabulations relating level of progress to the presence of a radical flank. The results can be found in Table 7 above. Radical flanks were present in 42% of all campaign years studied − 43% of years in which status quo was maintained, 23% of years in which visible gains short of concessions were gained, 52% of years in which limited concessions were gained, 47% of years in which significant concessions were gained, and 39% of years when complete campaign success was attained. Overall, a high percentage of campaigns included radical flanks, and in years where any level of progress was made (relative to status quo), radical flanks were present 42% of the time (85/201) − suggesting that nonviolent movements aren't necessarily

Table 7. Cross-Tabulation of Progress and Radical Flank Presence in Primarily Nonviolent Campaign Years, with Chi-Square Test.

Progress	No Radical Flank Present	Radical Flank Present	Total (N)
Status quo	73 (˜39%)	55 (˜39%)	128
Visible gains short of concessions	20 (˜11%)	6 (˜4%)	26
Limited concessions	23 (˜12%)	25 (˜18%)	48
Significant concessions	31 (˜16%)	27 (˜19%)	58
Complete success	42 (˜22%)	27 (˜19%)	69
Total (N)	189 (100%)	140 (100%)	329

Chi-Square Test	Chi-Square	df	p-Value
Pearson	6.5369	4	0.162
Likelihood ratio	6.8141	4	0.146

doomed to fail if a violent sub-group emerges. In years of progress, we cannot say whether progress was achieved because of the presence or a radical flank or in spite of it from this data. A Chi-Square Test shows that there is not enough evidence to conclude that the variables are associated. While any existing causal relationships can't be established here, it is certainly worth noting that radical flanks are not a few-and-far-between phenomenon.

I now conduct a series of bivariate and multivariate regression analyses using the above-illuminated ordinal variable progress as the outcome. The results appear in Table 8.

Recalling that Schock and Chenoweth's (2012) results were garnered from NAVCO 1.0, using entire campaigns as the unit of analysis, we can now re-test their findings with the NAVCO 2.0 dataset as well. In contrast to their findings, all of the coefficients for radical flank effect on campaign progress are positive. While Schock and Chenoweth's (2012) findings overwhelmingly supported an overall negative relationship between radical flank presence and campaign success, we now find that when the binary outcome of "success or failure" is broken down into the continuous scale of "progress per year," radical flank presence is positively linked with a semi-successful or successful outcome per annum. Furthermore, this relationship is significant in Models 3, 4, and 5.

In Model 1 (the first column), no significant relationship between radical flank presence and campaign progress is found, though the level of

Table 8. Bivariate and Multivariate Regressions of Annual Nonviolent Campaign Progress.

	(1)	(2)	(3)	(4)	(5)
Radical flank	.14	.32	.36*	.37*	.44**
	(.18)	(.20)	(.20)	(.20)	(.20)
Repression	−.19**	−.21**	−.16*	−.16*	−.34***
	(.07)	(.08)	(.08)	(.09)	(.10)
Backlash					
Movement suppressed			−1.46***		
			(.42)		
Decreased mobilization				−.56*	
				(.30)	
Increased mobilization					.63***
					(.22)
Campaign size		.45***	.42***	.43***	.43***
		(.26)	(.06)	(.07)	(.07)
Constant	2.03***	.93***	.99***	.96***	.83***
	(.17)	(.26)	(.26)	(.26)	(.26)
R^2	.0198	.1884	.2096	.1825	.1967
Adj. R^2	.0137	.1789	.1970	.1694	.1839
Root MSE	1.6011	1.4853	1.4634	1.4883	1.4753
N	327	262	255	255	255

Note: Entries are regression coefficients (standard errors in parentheses).
***$p < 0.01$, **$p < 0.05$, *$p < 0.1$.

repression shows a significant negative relationship with campaign progress ($t = -2.71$, $p < .05$). With the addition of campaign size as a second control variable in Model 2, the b-coefficient for radical flank presence is again not significant, but the negative relationship between repression and campaign progress remains ($t = 2.63$, $p < .05$). Furthermore, campaign size here shows a very strong relationship with campaign progress – the positive b-coefficient of .45 is statistically significant at the 99% confidence level ($t = 1.73$). Campaign size remains a potential confounding variable in the following models, where it consistently shows a strong, statistically significant ($p < .01$) relationship with campaign progress in every model in which it appears. Regardless of backlash and regardless of radical flank presence, campaigns that effectively mobilize greater numbers of participants stand a better chance of gaining concessions from a regime. This is in line with previous research arguing that mass participation is critical for nonviolent campaign success (Chenoweth & Stephan, 2011) – but this study can now conclude that this relationship remains even when a nonviolent campaign has a radical flank.

With the addition of campaign backlash as a control variable in Models 3, 4, and 5, some very interesting new patterns emerge. Backlash was recoded into a series of three dummy variables in order to isolate the three previously studied potential outcomes as separate control variables: movement suppressed, decreased mobilization, and increased mobilization. Three more models were developed, one for each backlash outcome (see columns 3, 4, and 5 in Table 8). Regardless of whether a movement was suppressed, mobilization decreased, or mobilization increased, radical flank presence shows a significant positive relationship with campaign progress per annum.

In Model 3, when movement suppression is controlled for, there is a very strong and significant negative relationship between movement suppression and campaign progress: a suppressed movement will see significantly less progress made in a given year. While it may seem tautological to control for movement suppressed when the dependent variable is progress, the NAVCO dataset allows for campaigns to continue even after being supposedly suppressed. The significant positive relationship between radical flank presence and campaign progress ($t = 1.8$, $p < .1$) here suggests a potential counterbalance to movement suppression. Perhaps a suppressed nonviolent movement is more likely to give way for a violent movement to take over; thus radical flank presence potentially offers a channel for movement continuation through other means. A radical flank may be the only element left completely intact in such cases. Perhaps the radical flank becomes the main face of a movement while the nonviolent branch goes underground and reevaluates its strategy. Perhaps movement suppression leads those who failed nonviolently to radicalize and rally around the radical flank arm of the movement. Not surprisingly, this model accounts for the highest amount of variation in the outcome variable (adj. $R^2 = .1970$).

In Model 4, when decreased mobilization is inserted as a control dummy variable, we see both a significant negative relationship between repression and progress ($t = -1.78$, $p < .1$), and between decreased mobilization and progress ($t = -1.87$, $p < .1$), logical results given that one wouldn't expect a campaign that was repressed and then suffered decreased mobilization to still gain concessions from the regime. Radical flank presence, however, still has a positive, statistically significant relationship with campaign progress, even in cases of decreased mobilization. In Model 5, when increased mobilization is added as a control dummy variable, a strong and highly significant positive relationship appears between increased mobilization and progress ($t = 2.86$, $p < .01$) and a negative relationship between repression and progress remains, though it becomes stronger and more highly significant here ($t = -3.40$, $p < .01$). These two findings are intuitive. The b-coefficient for radical flank presence in Model 5 is positive, stronger than in the previous two models, and more statistically significant ($t = 2.2$, $p < .05$). Together Models 4 and 5 suggest that, regardless of whether a campaign experiences decreased mobilization or increased mobilization (backfire) within a given year, the presence of a radical flank is predicted to result in higher progress made by the campaign that year.

When adding backlash as a variable, radical flank presence becomes significantly associated with increased progress. This alone is sufficient to reject H3. Regardless of whether a movement experiences decreased or increased mobilization post-repression, this positive relationship remains. Of particular note, even when a movement is supposedly suppressed, the presence of a radical flank is still associated with higher gains in a given year. This suggests that a radical flank may be a key vein through which a suppressed movement is able to live on, regain strength, and perhaps even reorganize for a stronger comeback.

CONCLUSION

With this study I have endeavored to craft a statistically based model for the varied and sometimes contradictory effects the presence of a violent group can have within an otherwise-nonviolent movement. Evidence was found in support of several radical flank effects. Within a primarily nonviolent resistance movement or campaign, the presence of a violent radical flank is associated with a higher likelihood and intensity of regime repression and a higher likelihood that such repression will indiscriminately target *all* actors within the campaign. Regarding the effects of radical flank presence on the potential for campaign backlash post-repression, the presence of a radical flank within a movement increases the likelihood of *all studied outcomes* – campaign suppression, decreased mobilization, and increased mobilization – relative to maintenance of the status quo. Radical flank presence strongly increases the likelihood that a campaign will experience decreased mobilization. Thus, backlash failure seems the more probable outcome for nonviolent movements with radical flanks; however, we cannot overlook the data that also link radical flank presence to an *increased* likelihood of further mobilization vis-à-vis no effect at all. Finally, this study draws the conclusion that a radical flank is not necessarily detrimental to overall campaign progress. In fact, this study actually finds evidence that the presence of a radical flank is modestly associated with *increased* campaign progress per annum.

This reframes radical flank theory in a new light: rather than equating radical flanks with purely violent campaigns, radical flanks need to be evaluated as a unique phenomenon within the context of predominantly nonviolent resistance – potentially a tool which, when employed correctly, can advance a resistance movement's chance of success. By redefining radical flanks as *intra-movement* actors (rather than including *all* contemporaneous violent campaigns), this study was able to illuminate several mobilizing effects their presence has on primarily nonviolent campaigns. Also, the radical flank effects identified in this study undermine the black-and-white theoretical framework classifying radical flank effects as either "positive" or "negative," inhabiting a theoretical grey area which begs for further study. Radical flanks are a significant variable in nonviolent resistance campaigns, and should be taken into consideration more frequently in future studies within the field of social movement theory.

Suggestions for Future Research

All of the variables in my models are intrinsic to the campaign and endogenous dynamics. The NAVCO 2.0 dataset could be further supplemented with some additional structural variables in future research. Models in this study may be somewhat underspecified, and the addition of control variables such as degree of democracy, and level of economic development would fine-tune the results to take into consideration contextual factors such as the type and strength of the regime in power. Regarding sequencing of the data, NAVCO 2.0 does allow for sequencing of the campaign years, so that prior outcomes or length of time that the campaign is ongoing could be readily incorporated as variables within future studies.

The definition of radical flank used in this study leaves *degree of affiliation/collaboration with the nonviolent organization(s)* open for development in future research. Future research could attempt to quantify the degree of overt or clandestine orchestration between a nonviolent unit and a radical flank within a common movement, or could compare radical flank effects to the effects of *armed wings*, which are *affiliated* internal subdivisions of an organization, established as an alternative to the official state military. Wings are under the command of the main resistance movement body, whereas a radical flank is a unit which is independent of the central unit which spawned it. Examples of armed wings include the Red Guard in Northern Ireland, which was "charged with the responsibility of protecting People's Democracy speakers from harassment during demonstrations and speeches" (Beach, 1977, p. 309); and the Armed Front of Xanama Gusmao's National Council of Maubere Resistance (CNRM), which was made up of three pillars: an Armed Front, a Diplomatic Front, and a Clandestine Front (Stephan, 2006, p. 61). Armed wings are coded within NAVCO 2.0 as *pi_army* or "parallel institution: army," but future research is needed to clarify how this variable relates to the radical flank variable, and what kind of definitional overlap exists.

What remains to be explored is the clear catalytic effects that radical flanks appear to have on maximalist resistance movements. The year-to-year effects that such an actor may elicit are potentially dynamic enough to alter the outcome of a given year — in what circumstances can this per annum progress lead to ultimate campaign success? Why do concessions in a single year matter if ultimately the movement fails? Out of the 119 campaigns studied, 65 were successful and 36 of those were successful following a year or years of partial progress. It would seem that repression or decreased mobilization in the interim may not fundamentally alter the course of the campaign — gains can still be achieved by a campaign facing both. This study casts new light on the intertemporal dynamics of longer movements, with the finding that radical flanks are associated with progress of particular importance for future exploration. Future research should delve further into how these short-term dynamics impact ultimate campaign success or failure.

ACKNOWLEDGMENT

The author thanks Erika Forsberg, Karen Brounéus, Svenja Wolter, Alja Ladinek, and Katja Oksanen for their valuable guidance and feedback.

REFERENCES

Abrahms, M. (2006). Why terrorism does not work. *International Security*, *31*(2), 42–78.
Ackerman, P., & Kruegler, C. (1994). *Strategic nonviolent conflict*. Westport, CT: Praeger.
Alimi, E. Y. (2011). Relational dynamics in factional adoption of terrorist tactics: A comparative perspective. *Theory and Society*, *40*(1), 95–118.
Arreguín-Toft, I. (2005). *How the weak win wars: A theory of asymmetric conflict*. New York, NY: Cambridge University Press.

Beach, S. W. (1977). Social movement radicalization: The case of the People's Democracy in Northern Ireland. *The Sociological Quarterly, 18*(3), 305−318.

Bond, D., Jenkins, J. C., Taylor, C. L., & Schock, K. (1997). Mapping mass political conflict and civil society: The automated development of event data. *Journal of Conflict Resolution, 41*(4), 553−579.

Braithwaite, J. B. (2014, January). *Rethinking radical flank theory: South Africa.* RegNet Research Paper No. 2014/23. Retrieved from http://ssrn.com/abstract=2377443 or http://dx.doi.org/10.2139/ssrn.2377443. Australian National University − Regulatory Institutions Network, Canberra, Australia.

Chenoweth, E., & Cunningham, K. G. (2013). Understanding nonviolent resistance: An introduction. *Journal of Peace Research, 50*(3), 271−276.

Chenoweth, E., & Lewis, O. A. (2013a). Unpacking nonviolent campaigns: Introducing the NAVCO 2.0 dataset. *Journal of Peace Research, 50*(3), 415−423.

Chenoweth, E., & Lewis, O. A. (2013b). Nonviolent and violent campaigns and outcomes (NAVCO) data project, version 2.0, campaign-year data. [Codebook accompanying Chenoweth and Lewis 2013.].

Chenoweth, E., & Stephan, M. J. (2011). *Why civil resistance works: The strategic logic of nonviolent conflict.* New York, NY: Columbia University Press.

Collier, P., Hoeffler, A., & Söderbom, M. (2008). Post-conflict risks. *Journal of Peace Research, 45*(4), 461−478.

Cunningham, K. G., Bakke, K. M., & Seymour, L. J. M. (2012). Shirts today, skins tomorrow: Dual contests and the effects of fragmentation in self-determination disputes. *Journal of Conflict Resolution, 56*(1), 67−93.

Cunningham, K. G., & Beaulieu, E. (2010). Dissent, repression, and inconsistency. In E. Chenoweth & A. Lawrence (Eds.), *Rethinking violence: States and non-state actors in Conflict.* Cambridge, MA: MIT Press.

Davenport, C. (2007). State repression and political order. *Annual Review of Political Science, 10,* 1−23.

Dudouet, V. (2013). Dynamics and factors of transition from armed struggle to nonviolent resistance. *Journal of Peace Research, 50*(3), 401−413.

Earl, J. (2003). Tanks, tear gas, and taxes: Toward a theory of movement repression. *Sociological Theory, 21*(1), 44−68.

Elbadawi, I., Hegre, H., & Milante, G. J. (2008). The aftermath of civil war. *Journal of Peace Research, 45*(4), 451−459.

Francisco, R. A. (2004). After the massacre: Mobilization in the wake of harsh repression. *Mobilization: An International Journal, 9*(2), 107−126.

Francisco, R. A. (2010). *Collective action theory and empirical evidence.* London: Springer Verlag.

Gamson, W. A. (1975). *The strategy of social protest.* Homewood, IL: Dorsey Press.

Gandhi, M. (1951). *Non-violent resistance (Satyagraha).* New York, NY: Schocken Books.

Goodwin, M., Ramalingam, V., & Briggs, R. (2012). *The new radical right: Violent and nonviolent movements in Europe.* Briefing Paper, Institute for Strategic Dialogue. Retrieved from http://www.strategicdialogue.org/ISD%20Far%20Right%20Feb2012.pdf

Gregg, R. B. (1966). *The power of nonviolence.* New York, NY: Schocken.

Gurr, T. R. (2000). Nonviolence in ethnopolitics: Strategies for the attainment of group rights and autonomy. *PS: Political Science and Politics, 33*(2), 155−160.

Haines, H. (1984). Black radicalization and the funding of civil rights: 1957−1970. *Social Problems, 32*(1), 31−43.

Haines, H. (1988). *Black radicals and the civil rights mainstream, 1954–1970*. Knoxville, TN: University of Tennessee Press.

Helvey, R. L. (2004). *On strategic nonviolent conflict; thinking about the fundamentals*. Boston, MA: The Albert Einstein Institution.

Hoffman, A., & Bertels, S. (2010). Who is part of the environmental movement? Assessing network linkages between NGOs and corporations. In T. Lyon (Ed.), *Good cop bad cop: Environmental NGOs and their strategies toward business* (pp. 48–69). Washington, DC: Resources for the Future Press.

Karagiannis, E., & McCauley, C. (2006). Hizb ut-tahrir al-islami: Evaluating the threat posed by a radical Islamic group that remains nonviolent. *Terrorism and Political Violence, 18*(2), 315–334.

Karatnycky, A., & Ackerman, P. (2005). *How freedom is won: From civic resistance to durable democracy*. Washington, DC: Freedom House.

Lawrence, A. (2010). Triggering nationalist violence: Competition and conflict in uprisings against colonial rule. *International Security, 35*(2), 88–122.

Lichbach, M. I. (1995). *The rebel's dilemma*. Ann Arbor, MI: University of Michigan Press.

Loveman, M. (1998). High-risk collective action: Defending human rights in Chile, Uruguay, and Argentina. *American Journal of Sociology, 104*, 477–525.

Mason, D., & Krane, D. (1989). The political economy of death squads: Toward a theory of the impact of state-sanctioned terror. *International Studies Quarterly, 33*, 175–198.

McAdam, D. (1983). Tactical innovation and the pace of insurgency. *American Sociological Review, 48*, 735–754.

McCarthy, J. D., & Zald, M. N. (1977). Resource mobilization and social movements: A partial theory. *American Journal of Sociology, 82*(6), 1212–1241.

Moore, W. H. (1998). Repression and dissent: Substitution, context, and timing. *American Journal of Political Science, 42*(3), 851–873.

Moore, W. H. (2012). Non-violent v. violent dissent before the Arab Spring: Bahrain, Jordan & Syria, 1990–2004. Presented at "The Repertoire of Tactics in Conflict" Workshop at the annual meeting of the International Studies Association (San Diego, CA) and the Midwest Political Science Association Annual Meeting (Chicago, IL).

Nepstad, S. E. (2011). *Nonviolent revolutions: Civil resistance in the late 20th century*. Oxford Studies in Culture and Politics. New York, NY: Oxford University Press.

Nepstad, S. E. (2013). Mutiny and nonviolence in the Arab Spring: Exploring military defections and loyalty in Egypt, Bahrain, and Syria. *Journal of Peace Research, 50*(3), 337–349.

Schock, K. (2005). *Unarmed insurrections: People power movements in nondemocracies*. Minneapolis, MN: University of Minnesota Press.

Schock, K. (2013). The practice and study of civil resistance. *Journal of Peace Research, 50*(3), 277–290.

Schock, K., & Chenoweth, E. (2012). Radical flank effects and the outcomes of civil resistance movements. Presentation. Fletcher Summer Institute, June 26. Retrieved from http://www.slideshare.net/NonviolentConflict/fsi2012-radical-flank-effects

Seidman, G. W. (2000). Blurred lines: Nonviolence in South Africa. *PS: Political Science and Politics* (June), *33*(2), 161–167.

Sharp, G. (1973). *The politics of nonviolent action*. Boston, MA: Porter Sargent.

Smithey, L. A., & Kurtz, L. R. (2002). Parading persuasion: Nonviolent collective action as discourse in Northern Ireland. *Consensus Decision Making, Northern Ireland and Indigenous Movements, 24*, 319–359.

Stephan, M. J. (2006). Fighting for statehood: The role of civilian-based resistance in the East Timorese, Palestinian, and Kosovo Albanian self-determination movements. *The Fletcher Forum for World Affairs, 30*(2), 57−79.

Stephan, M. J., & Chenoweth, E. (2008). Why civil resistance works: The strategic logic of nonviolent conflict. *International Security, 33*(1), 7−44.

Stockdill, B. C. (1996). *Multiple oppressions and their influence on collective action: The case of the AIDS movement.* Ph.D. dissertation, Department of Sociology, Northwestern University, Evanston, IL.

Sutton, J., Svensson, I., & Davidson, A. (2012). Explaining political jujitsu: The outcomes of severe regime violence against unarmed protests, 1989−2010. Paper presented at the Workshop on Non-Violent Conflicts, Uppsala. October 12−13.

Svensson, I., & Lindgren, M. (2011). From bombs to banners? The decline of wars and the rise of unarmed uprisings in East Asia. *Security Dialogue, 42*(3), 219−237.

Taylor, V., & Van Dyke, N. (2004). 'Get up, stand up': Tactical repertoires of social movements. In D. Snow, S. Soule, & H. Kriesi (Eds.), *The Blackwell companion to social movements* (pp. 262−293). Malden, MA: Blackwell.

Tilly, C. (1978). *From mobilization to revolution.* Reading, MA: Addison-Wesley.

Zunes, S. (1994). Unarmed insurrections against authoritarian governments in the third world: A new kind of revolution. *Third World Quarterly, 15*(3), 403−426.

"NO SHAMING THIS SLUT": [☆] STRATEGIC FRAME ADAPTATION AND NORTH AMERICAN SLUTWALK CAMPAIGNS

Kelly Birch Maginot and Soma Chaudhuri

ABSTRACT

What effect does strategic frame adaptation have on movement continuation and popularity? Using a comprehensive online dataset from three North American cities, we show how SlutWalk's continuous strategic adaptation of frames in response to criticisms and changing political and social climates has influenced its popularity over the past three years. SlutWalk's initial "Shame-Blame" and "Slut Celebration" frames conveyed powerful messages that catalyzed protests and generated outrage mostly from young feminists during its formative phase. However, meanings of the term "slut" varied widely across racial, cultural, and generational contexts, causing the "Slut Celebration" frame to be problematic for some micro-cohorts of feminists and leading to a decline in protest participation after initial enthusiasm waned. The campaign responded to the criticisms by minimizing the use of the word "slut" and emphasizing

[☆] Titular quotation is from a photograph posted online by Black (2011).

Research in Social Movements, Conflicts and Change, Volume 38, 137–170
ISSN: 0163-786X/doi:10.1108/S0163-786X20150000038005

the more transnationally resonant "Shame-Blame" and "Pro-sex, Pro-consent frames," resulting in increased participation and continued prominence of the SlutWalk across North America.

Keywords: Strategic adaptation; strategic framing; SlutWalk; social media

INTRODUCTION

The year 2011 was characterized by transnational youth activism. In December 2010 Tunisian protesters began the first Arab Spring uprising to overthrow the government, triggering protests in other Middle Eastern and North African nations throughout 2011. In September 2011, the Occupy Wall Street protests began in North America, which rapidly expanded to more than 1,500 cities around the world. In April of the same year a group of feminists in Toronto, Canada, held the first SlutWalk, a rally that aimed to end slut shaming and victim blaming as excuses for rape. The Arab Spring uprisings, Occupy, and SlutWalk all quickly escalated from local marches into transnational events that were spearheaded primarily by youth. Employing distinctively twenty-first century tactics such as decentralized leadership and decision making, these movements relied extensively on social media to promote their message, unite participants, and organize action.

Despite the continued popularity of SlutWalk protests, the campaign has received little academic attention (Carr, 2013; Reger, 2014, are exceptions). Today SlutWalk has transitioned from a small, local protest into a resonant, transnational campaign against sexual violence influencing similar protests across the globe. For instance, following the rape of a student in Delhi, India, a nationwide protest against prevailing attitudes toward rape employed slogans that for the first time addressed the victim blaming culture in India. Slogans such as "My voice is higher than my skirt" and "Just because I show my legs does not mean that I will spread them" were influenced by the Delhi *Besharmi morcha* (SlutWalk) (Sen, 2013). In similar cases over the past three years, SlutWalk has influenced global anti-rape activism and discussions of sexual assault, while simultaneously responding to specific incidents of violence (Mitra, 2012; O'Reilly, 2012). Furthermore, the campaign has remained popular through September 2014, the end of our analysis. Summer 2014 witnessed marches in Salt Lake City, Rio de Janeiro, Toronto, Chicago, Munich, and Reykjavik, among others.[1]

Additionally, with the April 2014 White House initiative to launch an anti-sexual assault campaign on American college campuses, we anticipate a renewed interest in SlutWalk protests involving even more university students in the coming years.

In this paper we focus on the evolving usage of the word "slut" in the strategic framing of the campaign. SlutWalk's use of "slut" and specific choice of frames (ones that combine second wave feminist, anti-rape discourse[2] with third wave sex-positivity and playfulness) have directly influenced the sustained popularity of the SlutWalk over the last three years.[3] We situate SlutWalk within the history of anti-rape activism in the United States and examine how the selection of particular frames in response to specific events affects contemporary movements. Specifically we explore how activists' strategic choice of frames in SlutWalks has influenced the development of collective identity, and the resultant increased recruitment and retention of participants. We argue that the SlutWalk's frames have proven their resilience over the past three years; the campaign's success on six continents in over 200 cities is due to the frame's international resonance and dynamism. We further argue that SlutWalk's success depends on its ability to consistently respond to criticisms. As a result, the campaign moved away from the initial "slut celebration/reclaim" frame to the "pro-consent, pro-sex" frame used today. Though the focus of this paper is on North American SlutWalk groups, our findings have implications for how strategic adaptation of frames can influence movement mobilization for future transnational campaigns.

We use data from three North American SlutWalks to examine specific frames employed by the protest. We draw on data from several online sources, including Twitter, campaign websites, blogs, and slogans, resulting in a dataset of 589 slogans selected from marches across the United States and Canada; 653 tweets posted by Lubbock, Chicago, and Toronto-based activists and their followers between April 2011 and September 2014; and website entries and blogs maintained by SlutWalks in Toronto and Chicago. Slogans and Twitter feeds are divided into two periods for analysis: early activity (2011–2012) and recent activism (2013 to present). Together these posts, blogs, websites, and slogans form a comprehensive snapshot of the North American SlutWalk campaign from the perspective of its members. We supplemented the dataset described above with 24 published online interviews with activists and participants. We begin the paper by situating the SlutWalk within the context of previous anti-rape activism, before reviewing the literature on how framing is influenced by discourse, and the relevance of strategic framing for movement success. We extend

McCammon's (2012) concept of *"strategic adaptation"* to include how frame rhetoric is influenced by responses to criticisms and changing social and political environments. We explore choices of frames in SlutWalk and find that, while initial frames were situated around reclaiming and celebrating "slut," campaign activists now prefer to emphasize agency and choice.

THE BEGINNING OF SLUTWALK

Since 2011 sexual assault and rape have gained a prominent place within North American media as government officials and law enforcement representatives have debated the renewal of the Violence Against Women Act (VAWA) and abortion rights for rape survivors, as well as launched an anti-sexual assault campaign in the White House. VAWA lapsed in 2011 and was suspended until March 7, 2013, due to partisan arguments. In August 2012 in Steubenville, Ohio, a female high school student was raped by two athletes who filmed the assault and broadcast it on social media. The assault catalyzed debates about and protests against victim blaming and slut shaming, because the survivor was discredited due to underage drinking. In December 2012 debates continued globally when a New Delhi university student was brutally gang raped causing her death. In April 2014, US President Obama and Vice President Biden launched an anti-sexual assault campaign on college and university campuses across United States, while simultaneously 64 American colleges and universities were investigated for their alleged mishandling of sexual assault cases (Kingkade, 2014).

Concurrently with these highly publicized cases and campaigns, outrage at police officers and politicians' seemingly dismissive attitudes toward sexual violence also were reported in mainstream media and the feminist blogosphere In August 2012, Todd Akin, a Missouri Republican Senate candidate, claimed that victims of "legitimate rape" rarely become pregnant, because their bodies "shut that whole thing down" (McMorris-Santoro, 2012). In the legal sphere, a Florida legislator proposed "stricter dress codes" in response to the rape of an eleven-year-old girl (Thompson, 2011, p. 14). Further, Michael Sanguinetti, a Toronto police officer, told a group of students at Osgoode Hall Law School that women should avoid dressing like "sluts" in order to evade sexual assault (Kwan, 2011). Sanguinetti's comments instigated the first SlutWalk, which protested "sexual profiling" and "slut shaming," focused attention on rape culture, and demanded respect for survivors of assault (Jarvis, Westendorf, & Bhuiyan, n.d.):

> [SlutWalk] began because a few people had had ENOUGH of victim-blaming, of slut-shaming and sexual profiling and policing. We had enough of being angry, of facing violence and harassment, of wanting better education, awareness and treatment and not seeing more about it. Our protective services in Toronto, among many people, had put the responsibility of sexual assault where it didn't belong and were continuing to spread myths and stereotypes about who is sexually assaulted and why, and this was nothing new — it was in a long line of violence, ingrained into institutions and our culture. (Jarvis et al., n.d.)

The agenda was twofold: first, to address sexual violence and victim blaming and, second, to maintain that sexuality can be powerful and empowering. The Osgoode Hall story circulated through Canada within days, and at least 3,000 people attended the march six weeks later. The SlutWalk's founders initially conceived the event as a one-day protest, but it grew rapidly over the next few months, expanding to cities around the globe (O'Reilly, 2012). Six months after the first event, there were sibling marches in at least 45 US cities and 13 other countries (Thompson, 2011). Today SlutWalks have occurred in more than 200 cities, many of which have remained active through local events and social media. As mentioned above, attendance at SlutWalk protests in the United States and Canada declined after the initial marches but has remained relatively steady since.[4] For example, according to SlutWalk Chicago's Facebook page, 8,244 individuals attended the 2011 Chicago March and 684 people attended in 2013. However, 1,626 individuals attended the August 2014 Chicago SlutWalk, according to the organization's Facebook event page (SlutWalk Chicago, n.d.). Similarly, over 1,000 marchers attended the 2014 Toronto SlutWalk (Di Menna, 2014), and Iceland's 2014 march hosted 11,000 participants (Ólafsdóttir Kaaber, 2014). The campaign's popularity has encouraged some feminists to argue that SlutWalk is one of the most successful feminist actions in the past 20 years (O'Reilly, 2012; Tuerkheimer, 2014). Reger (2014) has described SlutWalk as an emerging micro-cohort within contemporary feminism that attracted both supporters and critics. She notes that the SlutWalk followed in the "discursive legacy of tactics" of Take Back the Night (TBtN) and similar marches popularized on college campuses in the 1970s and 80s that pushed to bring attention to sexual violence (Reger, 2014, p. 57). Similarly, we find that SlutWalks have incorporated TBtN frames and messages. For example, slogans at the 2014 Toronto march included "Trans* Folk reclaim our streets!" and "Take back the night." However we emphasize that the SlutWalk differs from previous anti-rape protests in its strategies and explicitly pro-sex approach, specifically its focus on validating sexual empowerment while denouncing sexual violence and rapists via frames such as "celebrate/reclaim slut" and "shame-blame."

FROM EARLY FEMINISM TO THE THIRD WAVE: SLUTWALK'S ORIGINS

SlutWalk continues a contentious history of anti-rape activism within the United States and other countries.[5] As early as 1866, African-American women from the southern United States spoke before Congress about their experiences of rape during slavery, when the rape of slaves by White men had been legally and socially accepted (McGuire, 2004). African-American women continued to protest racialized sexual violence well into the Civil Rights Movement, testifying in court to "[deploy] their voices as weapons in the war against white supremacy" and later marching and demonstrating on college campuses (McGuire, 2004, p. 907). Additionally, when White North American and European women met for the 1915 International Congress of Women to peacefully protest World War I, they emphasized the role of sexual crimes against women in times of war as well as peace (as cited in Rupp & Taylor, 1999, p. 379). Significantly, Rupp and Taylor (1999) note that violence against women "had the potential to unite women across cultures" (p. 379), a role it continued to play with TBtN and SlutWalk.[6]

While earlier women's rights advocates had addressed sexual violence as a symptom of other social problems, such as white supremacy and war, anti-rape activism began in earnest during the 1970s with the contemporary anti-rape movement (Brownmiller, 2007; Maier, 2011; Shaw & Campbell, 2011). The movement emerged out of second wave consciousness-raising (C-R) groups, during which members shared stories and emotions. As women expressed their experiences, it became increasingly apparent that sexual assault and domestic abuse had played a part in many of their lives. Radical feminists began to use C-R groups and "speak outs" as a forum through which they shared personal stories of abuse and violence (Largen, 1985, p. 2). Additionally, early activists advocated their cause using pamphlets, newsletters, and bumper stickers (Brownmiller, 2007); formed "anti-rape squads" to speak out against rape; and provided self-defense classes to women (Largen, 1985, p. 4) (Table 1).

Initially the anti-rape movement had two goals: (1) strengthen laws punishing and preventing rape and (2) transform cultural attitudes surrounding

Table 1. History of Anti-Rape Activism, First Wave to Present.

Time Period	Key Events	Frames and Slogans	Actions	Goals and Outcomes
First wave	Congressional testimonies on racialized sexual assault International women's conference on peace	No specific frames; sexual assault treated as symptom of other social problems	Women spoke about sexual assault privately and at congressional hearings	Plant the seeds for future protest
Second wave	Anti-rape movement	"The personal is political"	Consciousness-raising groups Speak outs Pamphlets, bumper stickers, and newsletters spread awareness	Recognize sexual assault as a social problem Provide space for women to share experiences of sexual assault End women's shame surrounding assault
Third wave TBtN		Rights Frame *"We have the right to take back the night."*	Marches and rallies Speak outs Creation of rape crisis centers to support survivors	Bring awareness to rape as a social problem Change laws associated with violence against women End victim blaming
V Day		Speak the word	Storytelling through monologues and audience participation Documentary film screenings and discussion "One **Billion Rising**" campaign breaks silence through visual and performing arts	End violence against women and girls globally Increase awareness, fundraise, and revitalize anti-rape activism
SlutWalk		Celebrate/reclaim slut and shame-blame: *Blame belongs only to the rapist* ("A dress is not a yes") *Survivors deserve* "support not scrutiny" *"Who you callin' a slut?"*	Speak outs, marches, and provocative costuming Coalitions with International Socialist Organization and others Heightened reliance on social media sites	End victim blaming and slut shaming Place blame on rapists and rape culture rather than victims Introduce the concept of "slut shaming" to popular culture and feminist movement

rape (Largen, 1985; Rose, 1977). The movement was successful in reforming laws that broadened the definitions of rape and sexual assault to include marital rape, the rape of men, and assaults other than vaginal penetration. As the movement developed, it gained a third goal: to provide support and advocacy for victims (Kelly, 1979). This objective motivated the creation of rape crisis centers (RCCs), which offered services to sexual assault survivors through medical advocacy, community support, and counseling.

While the anti-rape movement and second wave feminism were fading away throughout the late 1970s and early 1980s, TBtN marches followed their mission to end sexual violence. TBtN marches and rallies provide an important link between the anti-rape movement and contemporary activism like SlutWalk. Through TBtN women sought to reclaim public spaces and demand safety from sexual violence, rather than be advised to stay off the streets after dark (Mann, 2012). Like SlutWalk activists, TBtN participants argued that rape culture, rather than victims' actions, was responsible for high rates of sexual assault. The first march took place in Pittsburgh, Pennsylvania, in 1977, and these events have continued globally, even after SlutWalk protests began in 2011.

Throughout the 1980s and early 1990s, anti-rape activism was mainly found in RCCs and annual TBtN marches, even as feminism's third wave began. The third wave posited itself as a pro-sex "power feminism," rejected the "victim feminism" of the second wave, and argued in favor of women's agency and desire for sexual satisfaction (Crawford, 2007). Some third wave micro-cohorts centralized and celebrated diversity, a multiplicity of identities, and intersectionality; many third wave feminists[7] rejected the primarily white, heterosexual feminism of the second wave and prioritized the voices of LGBTQ feminists and heterosexual women of color. Moreover, third wavers recognized the roles of culture, technology and the media in forming identities and often reappropriated media as a form of protest or disruption (Crane, 2012; Crawford, 2007).

The third wave's playfulness, diversity and pro-sex attitude are crucial to understanding the SlutWalk campaign and its choices in framing. According to Crawford (2007), the three main tactics used by the third wave are storytelling, coalition-building, and harnessing the media through zines, blogs, and websites. Third-wave goals, distinct from earlier feminist aims, focus primarily on "non-legal (and non-theoretical) aspects of female sexuality" (Crawford, 2007, p. 102). This is true for both of the third wave's anti-rape campaigns, SlutWalk and "V Day," a campaign that developed out of Eve Ensler's *Vagina Monologues* (V Day, 2012). V Day is still active on college campuses, and though the movement does not explicitly address slut shaming, it is similar to the SlutWalk in its transnational character and celebration of women's sexuality and agency. Also like SlutWalk, V Day re-appropriates feminized sexual epithets, for example "cunt," which is chanted by actors and audience members during one of the play's monologues (Ensler, 2008; Reger, 2014).

"Don't Dress Like Sluts:" The SlutWalk Begins

The SlutWalk campaign was born with the same cultural attitude toward sexual agency of TBtN, V Day, and the discursive legacy of feminism (Reger, 2014), particularly that of the third wave. The SlutWalk unifies a pro-sex and anti-rape position, highlighting women's right to sexual agency (Tuerkheimer, 2014, p. 3). The campaign is especially popular with young people, despite criticism from many second wave feminists for its name and tactics (Tillotson, 2011). The protest grew rapidly from the 10 students at Sanguinetti's presentation to thousands of participants and hundreds of satellite marches around the world (Ayuso, 2011; Kapur, 2012; O'Reilly, 2012; Thompson, 2011). Due to rapid online advocacy the campaign expanded too quickly to gain adequate resources, traditional leaders, and elite supporters (O'Reilly, 2012). In fact, SlutWalk may be described as a web of independently run campaigns, all of which plan and execute their own events, often responding to local issues and cultural norms (Hill, 2013). For example, SlutWalks in Britain have protested maltreatment of Muslim women who choose to wear the *hijab*, and SlutWalk South Africa has targeted "corrective rape," a weapon used to "'turn' [lesbians] straight" (Hill, 2013, p. 51). Similarly, activists in India replaced SlutWalk with *Besharmi Morcha* (Shameless Front), a culturally resonant name to reflect their concern with the culture of shame and blame (Mitra, 2012).

Like TBtN, SlutWalk aims to transform the attitudes of police officers and public officials so that women will feel safe and respected if they decide to report a sexual crime (SlutWalk Toronto, 2012). However, despite similarities with some goals of earlier anti-violence activism, SlutWalk's overall objectives are primarily cultural, focusing on the elimination of rape culture, rather than changing laws (Tuerkheimer, 2014). The cultural aim of the SlutWalk aligns with third wave feminism's general stance, which emphasizes the importance of socio-cultural change and consciousness raising, rather than legal or structural revolution (Crawford, 2007).

The SlutWalk's use of storytelling, spontaneous dramas, and dramatic costuming preserves the tactics used by feminists of the second wave (Ayuso, 2011; Hill, 2011; Nussbaum, 2011; Tuerkheimer, 2014). Hill (2011) argues that SlutWalks are the new TBtN, while SlutWalk organizers (Ayuso, 2011) see the marches as part of the anti-rape struggle, similar to other campaigns in many ways. The campaign continues to emphasize solidarity and use disruptive tactics, but it frames victim blaming in a novel way and refashions traditional strategies to align with the youthful playfulness of the third wave. For participants, solidarity initially translated into a communal celebration of their status as "sluts" − "[W]e are all sluts together" − but employed this concept to remind women and girls to support one another instead of attacking each other through slut shaming and competition (Ringrose & Renold, 2012, p. 335). Moreover, participants resignify "slut" and other pejorative terms for women, for example through their choice to wear provocative outfits or "jeans and t-shirts" instead at the marches (Chateauvert, 2013; Ringrose & Renold, 2012).

SlutWalk activists primarily communicate via Internet and online media, maintaining blogs, Twitter pages, and Facebook accounts. The use of blogging provides activists with freedom from traditional forms of writing, allowing them to express themselves in unique ways (Nussbaum, 2011). Members upload and discuss slogans, posters, and photographs that they find powerful or clever (e.g., "Protest sign inspiration: 'Fight the cis-tem'" or "Brainstorming on messaging for a sign for tomorrow's SlutWalk Toronto. Any suggestions?"), and these messages are adopted and filtered through various social, cultural, and political contexts. The campaign's Internet presence also allows the protest to be spontaneous and transcend borders; members communicate with participants in different states and countries, exchanging words of support and solidarity through Twitter and Facebook. Today, though some local groups maintain traditional websites, SlutWalk Lubbock and SlutWalk Chicago have abandoned theirs in favor of Facebook and Twitter feeds.

Criticisms of SlutWalk

Despite its popularity SlutWalk also has been criticized as Western, middle class, and white, which affects its resonance with different audiences. Here we briefly address specific criticisms of SlutWalk[8] to present an overview of the campaign's critiques that have further influenced its choice of frames. First, SlutWalk's celebration of women's sexuality through its reclamation of "slut" is believed to marginalize the experiences of women of color and sex workers, for whom the word has been used to perpetuate a disproportionate level of violence (Reger, 2014; Tuerkheimer, 2014). The campaign's focus on sexuality and sexualization does not differentiate between women's experiences, which discounts the experiences of women for whom race and/or class have compounded threats and experiences of sexual violence (Mitra, 2012; Tuerkheimer, 2014). Moreover, some women of color are conflicted by SlutWalk's use of the word "slut" and provocative imagery, due to the history of racialized sexual oppression and violence in the United States and other nations (Crunk Feminist Collective, 2011; Womanist Musings, 2011). O'Keefe (2014) further argues that SlutWalk privileges thin, Caucasian bodies through the sexuality displayed at SlutWalk marches — fishnet stockings, bras and panties, or miniskirts — and in this way upholds problematic standards of beauty.

Feminists also have criticized SlutWalk for emphasizing "sluttiness" instead of addressing structural change and rape culture in clearer ways (Dines & Murphy, 2011; Murphy, 2011; Pasquale, 2011). These writers have questioned whether SlutWalk is truly feminist movement. For instance, Pasquale argues that reclaiming "slut" has limited SlutWalk's effectiveness "as we have spent more time on semantics than breaking patriarchy" (2011, para. 10). Additionally, Dines and Murphy have argued that SlutWalk is "making life harder for girls" as it does not disaggregate slut reclamation from slut celebration and sexual objectification (2011, para. 9). SlutWalk activists' responses to these criticisms will be addressed in the Findings section.

STRATEGIC ADAPTATION OF FRAMES AND ITS EFFECT ON DISCOURSES AND RHETORIC

The literature on social movements has found that effective frames are crucial for movement success (Noakes & Johnston, 2005, p. 2). Through framing, social movement actors are able to purposely interpret arguments in their favor, which enables them to rationally articulate the problems the movement is facing, transform people's "hearts and minds," inspire potential actors to participate by convincing them that legitimate action is possible, develop solidarity, and rebut rival frames if present (Della Porta & Diani, 2006; Hewitt & McCammon, 2004; McCammon, Newman, Muse, & Terrel, 2007; Snow, 2007, p. 393). Moreover, discourses create the cultural context within which frames are introduced, and it is important to draw on the reciprocal and iterative relationship between discourse and framing. Coy, Woehrle, and Maney (2008) describe discourse as a set of ideas based on assumptions of how the world functions or should function. The authors argue that social movements are always in an attempt to shift or transform dominant discourse (2008, p. 163). For Coy et al., frames and discourses are in a "symbiotic," or mutually beneficial, relationship. While dominant discourses may potentially shape or constrain frames, the authors argue that new frames aim toward shifting, rather than radically changing, the direction of the discourse (2008, pp. 165–66). The distinction between frames and discourse is especially significant for an analysis of SlutWalk's frames: while the campaign employs second and third wave feminism's anti-rape discourses on sexual agency and victim blaming, it frames the arguments differently, thereby shifting the discourse to one focused on slut reclamation and sex-positivity.

Previous studies of frames have commented extensively on the effectiveness of strategic framing particularly when activists' interpretation of the problem aligns with that of the societal (meaning majority's) understanding of a political environment or dominant discourse (Brown, 2014; Diani, 1996; McVeigh, Meyers, & Sikkink, 2004; Snow, Rochford, Worden, & Benford, 1986). For instance, to stop the horrific practice of witchcraft accusations against community women in India, activists strategically framed the accusations as an effect of class conflict and alcohol addiction, instead of directly blaming the accusers which would have been less culturally resonant. This strategic framing proved crucial in mobilizing women against the socially accepted practice of witch hunts. Here the frames tapped into the communities' existing discourse on gender and class conflict to mobilize women against a violent cultural practice (Chakravarty & Chaudhuri, 2012). Similarly, the "reform" frame developed during the US American women's suffrage movement proved to be effective at increasing membership in state suffrage organizations via its ability to provide a perfect balance between "cultural resonance and contestation." Here the movement resonated with the widely held belief that women are naturally superior nurturers compared with men (thereby not challenging the gender equality argument), while simultaneously arguing that women deserve a more active role in the formal political sphere "armed with their female qualities" (Hewitt & McCammon, 2004, p. 162).

To further the argument of how frames may shift discourse, we use the concept of strategic adaptation to examine the dynamic quality of frames. Strategic adaptation in social movements refers to a set of critical steps used to constantly develop and adapt strategies, tactics, and discourses that foster the attainment of social movement goals in response to changing political and social environments and demands (McCammon, 2012). No one tactic or strategy guarantees success; rather tactics, like frames, are dynamic and must be constantly revisited and revised (McCammon, 2012; McCammon et al., 2008). Actors who engage in strategic adaptation are attentive, conscious, and aware of the context in which they operate (McCammon, 2012, p. 17). By strategically pursuing and adapting movement frames, they are more likely to achieve their goals. Research has also pointed out how "rhetorical strategies" between opposing movements can create opportunities for mobilization for one side, thereby furthering the argument that strategic adaptation influences the tone and language of movement claims (Fetner, 2001). In a study on the impact of Christian anti-gay counter movements on lesbian and gay activists, Fetner found that counter movement activism directed toward the elimination of gay rights proved to be strategically useful for lesbian and gay actors, as it provided them with unintended beneficial consequences (giving the movement public prominence). The specific shift in rhetoric and frames of the lesbian and gay activism from before to after the emergence of the anti-gay counter movement demonstrates the ability of conscious, attentive activists with previously few political opportunities to create new opportunities for mobilization via responses to criticism through public debates (Fetner, 2001).

The SlutWalk protest developed at a crucial moment in the history of anti-rape movement. Based on three decades of past activism; reflection on the tactics, goals, and strategic responses to the changing political and social environment and critiques; and widespread Internet access, the SlutWalk has had the unique opportunity to strategically adapt its frames and goals, thereby remaining aligned with second and third wave's anti-rape and sex-positive discourses, respectively. This is especially true considering the campaign's spontaneous conception, "organized by a handful of women ... with no money, little time, and no formal support (O'Reilly, 2012, pp. 246–247).

Thus, the one-day protest originally envisioned by Barnett and Jarvis quickly proved that it would require additional discussion about appropriate slogans and strategies. As it grew, participants strengthened the campaign's resonance by reflecting on and responding to criticisms (strategic rhetoric), all while maintaining the distinctly pro-sex, anti-violence discourse unique to third wave feminism. SlutWalk provides a convincing case for studying the effectiveness of frame change on movement goals, thereby responding to Johnston's call for renewed attention to the study of frame changes in a single movement or "a narrow temporal window" for a deeper analysis (2005, p. 253). Further, given the emergence of framing as one of the three areas dominating social movement research (Noakes & Johnston, 2005, pp. 2–4), it is imperative to pursue new directions within this subfield to avoid repetitive research questions. Recent scholarship on framing sees transnational movements as an important empirical case for pursuing questions related to the effectiveness of framing and movement outcomes. There is "heightened importance of shared frames and collective identities for movements seeking transnational coalitions" (Snow, Benford, McCammon, Hewitt, & Fitzgerald, 2014, pp. 36–37). We respond to the above recommendations for new directions in framing research and argue that SlutWalk's transnational identity coupled with its strategic and adaptive use of framing – which lends it resonance with the third wave feminist discourse as exhibited through the campaign's rapid growth and development of a revived collective identity – makes it an insightful case for understanding frames.

DATA AND METHODS

This paper uses the case of North American SlutWalks to explore how frames are strategically adapted in response to critiques and changing political and social environments, thereby affecting movement popularity in the long run. Three online sources have been compiled to create an original dataset: slogans displayed at SlutWalk events, Twitter posts ("tweets"), and blogs produced by SlutWalk participants. A fourth online source consisting of 24 published online interviews with organizers and participants in the campaign was included as supplementary data wherever necessary. Twitter feeds and slogans were drawn from three North American SlutWalk organizations – Toronto, Canada; Chicago, Illinois; and Lubbock, Texas. These cities were selected for their availability of data, as well as their varied populations, locations, and political climates. Each organization has hosted multiple SlutWalk events and maintained an online presence via Facebook and Twitter since 2011. Together, they represent the campaign's birthplace as well as two cities in the United States; Lubbock is a moderately sized southern city, and Chicago is a vast, global city in the Midwest. Like all SlutWalks, these are organized by local grassroots committees and thus reflect the character of their community, though they share a commitment to ending sexual and domestic violence and rape culture.

To demonstrate how the SlutWalk strategically adapted its frames, we include data points from two moments in SlutWalk history: the campaign's earliest online posts and protests, as well as recent protest activity. The former group includes Twitter feeds from April to September 2011, when SlutWalks were organizing their initial marches, as well as slogans and blog posts from 2011 to 2012, during which SlutWalk gained popularity and media attention. The latter group consists of Twitter posts from June to August 2014, as well as slogans and blogs from 2013 and 2014 marches, after criticisms of SlutWalk as a white, Western, and ineffective campaign had been established. While the debates have subsided, the struggle for the campaign to be more inclusive continues. The two snapshots provide insight as to how the campaign's frames have shifted in response to criticisms and local and global incidents surrounding sexual violence.

Data Compilation

We initially used convenience sampling to gather images of SlutWalk slogans via news articles, official SlutWalk websites, Facebook pages, and blogs written by outsiders and participants.[9] We then narrowed our search to the campaign's Facebook and Twitter pages, which include images uploaded by SlutWalk participants. These slogans are indicative of SlutWalk's chosen frames, whereas mainstream media may oversample images and slogans that are provocative or "newsworthy." This resulted in a dataset of (1) 335 slogans exhibited at SlutWalks around the United States and in Canada from 2011 to 2012 and (2) 254 additional slogans from SlutWalks in Chicago, Lubbock, and Toronto during 2013 and 2014 marches. Twitter feeds[10] from the same cities (SlutWalk Chicago [slutwalkchi], n.d.; SlutWalk Lubbock [SlutwalkLubbock], n.d.; SlutWalk Toronto [SlutWalkTO], n.d.) were then explored to further examine the SlutWalk's frames and tactics. First, all posts on the organizations' Twitter pages were inductively coded by purpose and frame, but 152 posts were deleted because of broken hyperlinks or unrelated content.[11] The subsequent dataset contained 653 posts, 299 from 2011 and 354 from June to August 2014. Additionally, a set of two blogs is included from the websites of SlutWalk Toronto (2012) and SlutWalk Chicago (2011), and relevant blog entries by participants are analyzed for frames. These blogs are included based on availability, as many local SlutWalk protests do not maintain blogs or write often enough to be included in our analysis. Finally, 24 online interviews with campaign organizers and participants were studied by the first author as supplemental data. These interviews were found via targeted Internet searches and social media websites, which often highlight external articles (e.g., a tweet posted by SlutWalk Chicago reads, "A huge honor — Jessica of #SlutWalk Chicago on The Line Campaign's 'Badass Activist Fridays' Feature!") (Table 2).

Data Analysis

All slogans and tweets were initially categorized according to the broad goals of SlutWalk: ending victim blaming, slut shaming, and rape culture (SlutWalk Toronto, n.d.). Messages were categorized according to their usage of key terms such as "slut," "blame," "fault," and "shame," in addition to phrases like "Yes means yes, and no means no," "Clothes are not consent," and, "Blame rapists for rape, not victims." Slogans that drew upon past feminist frames (i.e., "Take back the night" or "Smash the patriarchy") were also noted. Multiple rounds of coding yielded three significant

Table 2. Compiled Dataset, 2011–2014.

Data type	Dates	Number	Source	Purpose
Slogans	• 2011–2012 • 2013–2014	• 335 • 254	Online articles, targeted Internet searches, and social media sites	Illustrate frames that resonate across time with organizers and participants
Tweets	• April–September 2011 • June–August 2014	• 299 • 354	Toronto, Chicago, and Lubbock Twitter accounts	Illustrate frames and demonstrate communication between organizers, participants, potential recruits, and detractors
Blogs	• 2011–2014	• 10 posts (Chicago) • 24 posts (Toronto)[a]	SlutWalk Toronto and SlutWalk Chicago websites	Illustrate the specific frames and foci of SlutWalk satellite organizations
Interviews	• 2011–2014	• 24	Targeted internet searches and social media sites	Emphasize strategic management of frames used by organizers and participants

[a]Only two blogs were included (Chicago and Toronto). Lubbock's website and blog are no longer accessible online and included few posts.

SlutWalk frames, each of which will be addressed below: (1) shame-blame, (2) slut reclamation and celebration versus slut skepticism, and (3) sex-positivity and pro-consent. Slogans, tweets, and blog posts were then examined for changes over the two time periods to demonstrate the adaptive and strategic aspects of SlutWalk's frames, developed in response to socially, politically, and culturally relevant events and criticisms.

FINDINGS AND DISCUSSION

Findings from the dataset indicate three primary frames within the SlutWalk campaign: Shame-Blame; Slut Celebration; and Sex Positive/Pro-consent. All three frames were initially influenced by second and third wave feminism, but the "slut celebration" frame has shifted in nuanced ways over the last three years in response to criticism and the changing social and political climate. Today SlutWalkers continue to rely on the "shame-blame" frame, which wholly rejects victim blaming and slut shaming. However, they have revised the "slut celebration" frame to emphasize their sex-positive position; in this way, they have maintained third wave discourse that calls for enthusiastic, affirmative consent during sexual encounters, while limiting their reliance on "slut pride" and "slut celebration" (Table 3).

Shame-Blame: "Officer Sanguinetti, I'm Very Disappointed"

Approximately 1,200 slogans and tweets were examined to understand SlutWalk's use of the "shame-blame" and "slut celebration/slut skepticism" frames. The shame-blame frame is a direct response to commonly accepted rape myths, which suggest that victims of assault are "asking for it" or dressed in ways that encourage rape, thereby blaming the victim instead of the perpetrator. SlutWalk participants write and speak openly about blame and shame, not only refusing to blame victims but also actively placing blame on rapists and rape culture.[12] Of the slogans examined from 2011 to 2012, 55.2% responded to Constable Sanguinetti's comment that dressing like a "slut" is an implicit signal for sexual consent. This includes slogans such as "My little black dress is not a yes" and "My clothes are not my consent." Also included are slogans that counter the argument that women who drink alcohol or use drugs are responsible for their rape. For example, "Women do not get raped because they were drinking or taking drugs, dressed provocatively, being reckless. Women get raped because someone

Table 3.   SlutWalk Slogans by Word Count.

Frames	Sub Frames	Slogans Used	Usage in 2011–2012	Usage in 2013–2014
Shame-blame	*Shame-blame*	"Real men don't rape." "Shame and blame belong only to the rapist."	24.5% (82)	22.8% (58)
	Lack of consent	"My little black dress does not mean yes." "Not here for you."	26.6% (89)	38.2% (97)
Slut reclamation	*Slut celebration*	"Slut pride" "Slut power"	12.5% (42)	2.8% (7)
	Slut skepticism	"Ending the myth of the slut." "I'm only a slut when I say no to you."	11.9% (40)	9.8% (25)
Sex-positive, pro-consent	*Pro-sex, pro-consent*	"Yes means fuck me, no means fuck you." "Consent is sexy." "I like sex so, so much when it's consensual!"	19.1% (64)	19.3% (49)
References to feminist discourse	*References to feminism or feminist issues*	"Smash the patriarchy." "Take back the night!"	15.2% (51)	11.8% (30)
	References to self-respect, freedom, and control	"I am mine." "Love your body. Respect every body!"	9.6% (32)	12.2% (31)
		Totals	335	254

Note: Columns do not equal 100%, as each slogan potentially fits multiple frames.

raped them." Together these slogans can be classified under the shame-blame frame; they debunk rape myths, removing fault from the victim or survivor and assigning it to the rapist instead. Of the 2011–2012 slogans, 11.9% specifically addressed blame using "blame," "shame," "cause" or "fault." These slogans contain messages such as, "Blame rapists for rape, not women," which echoes the official slogan from SlutWalk Toronto's (2012) march, "Society teaches 'Don't get raped' rather than 'Don't rape.'" In congruence with the blame frame, rape is emasculated and stripped of masculinity, with several slogans that state, "Real men take 'NO' for an answer." Rapists are rejected as adults, as well: "Even toddlers know what *no* means." With the shame-blame frame, slogans at the SlutWalk responded to the trend of slut shaming and victim blaming by reversing the shame toward rapists, police officers and societal attitudes to rape culture. Slogans which label rapists and officers as "disgusting" or tell Sanguinetti, "I'm very disappointed" represent the reversal of blame and shame.

The shame-blame frame has continued to resonate over time. In 2013 and 2014, slogans such as, "Boy, your misogyny is antiquated!" maintained the pattern of shaming and blaming the perpetrators. The 2013 and 2014 slogans echoed their earlier counterparts, often verbatim. Messages like, "We never owe you sex" and "If you can't get consent … Go fuck yourself!" shame rapists, again by addressing them directly. Additionally, like earlier slogans that called out specific individuals − the Toronto Police Department or Sanguinetti, for example − slogans from later marches capitalized upon social, cultural, and political incidences to resonate with their audience. For example, 2013 slogans in Chicago and Lubbock alluded to Akin's comments about "legitimate rape" by asserting, "If it's a legitimate Republican, the female body has ways to try to shut that whole thing down," and, "Every rape is legitimate rape!" Thus, the shame-blame frame did not change, and the tactic of shaming and blaming public officials continued to address current events.

In 2013, Robin Thicke's "Blurred Lines," a popular song that claimed, "I hate these blurred lines/I know you want it/But you're a good girl" (Thicke & Williams, 2013), sparked renewed interest in rape culture and inspired multiple parody videos about consent and sexual objectification (Dunn, Ellwood, & Lubbock, 2013; Hughes, 2013). Like Akin and Sanguinetti, Thicke was publicly shamed via multiple slogans at SlutWalk Chicago. Participants carried posters that asserted, "Fuck Robin Thicke," "There are no blurred lines," and "'No' doesn't mean convince me." Furthermore, these slogans suggest that consent was emerging as a relevant topic throughout 2013, when the sex-positive, pro-consent frame became prominent, as classifying rape as illegitimate had been a primary concern earlier that year.

"Sluts Unite!:" The "Slut Celebration/Slut Skepticism" Frame

Slogans at the SlutWalk protests historically have validated, celebrated, and reclaimed "sluttiness," in addition to shaming perpetrators of violence and rape culture. Of the initial 335 slogans, approximately 80 of them use the terms slut, whore, *puta*, bitch, easy or hot; 42 used these terms with positive connotations such as empowerment or joy, while others expressed skepticism about the meaning and use of the word (e.g., "Ending the *myth* of the slut," emphasis added). Some reappropriated the slut identity as a symbol of pride ("Slut and proud!"; "Don't be a closet slut"), while others carried masks, wore pins or wrote the label "slut" on themselves. Posters that called for "Sluts' rights" or asserted, "Small and loud, this slut is proud," aligned closely with two of SlutWalk Toronto's official 2012 slogans, which stated "Reclaim the word SLUT" and "Sluts and Allies Unite." Reger's (2014) analysis of SlutWalk Toronto organizers' online biographies confirms that the SlutWalk founders aimed to redefine "slut," not merely rendering it acceptable but further illustrating that being a "slut" allows one to be sexually powerful and empowered, an agent who follows his or her own ethical code (see also interviews with Jarvis and Westendorf: Katwiwa, 2013; *Nellie's*, 2012). Additionally, the campaign's emphasis on "slut-positivity" has "[pushed] the boundaries of sexual identity to reveal stereotypes that are 'unnamed' and 'misunderstood', but present in 'everyday life'" (Reger, 2014, p. 57). Thus, "slut" loses its conventional definition and connotation and instead becomes a beacon for sex-positivity and feminist agency.

The initial slogans treated "slut" as a unifying, powerful concept, rather than something derogatory or shameful. While the term was rarely defined within these slogans, the images and statements portrayed a person of any gender and sexual orientation who dressed in whichever clothes suited him or her, whether they were revealing and provocative or a sweatshirt and jeans. The "slut" is self-confident and proud, celebrates his or her sexuality, and cares for other "sluts." Furthermore, the participants celebrated sexual consent with slogans such as "Bringing CONSENSUAL sexy back" and "My consent is my best feature." These slogans can be categorized under a second frame, "Celebrate Slut," through which activists refuse to accept the shame and guilt fostered within rape culture.

Conversely, Twitter posts were primarily used to field critiques about the SlutWalk's reclamation of slut, rather than celebrate it. Lubbock, Chicago, and Toronto all have highlighted the political and cultural need for the word. In 2011, all three groups used Twitter to share articles defending SlutWalk, such as "In Defense of SlutWalk Protests" and "Redeeming the Slut." Additionally, SlutWalk Lubbock posted its own defense of "slut:"

> There are several reasons for keeping the word "slut" in the title of this event. … [T]he word makes people uncomfortable. … [I]t makes *us* uncomfortable, and that, inherently, is the problem. It is not a word that we have created for ourselves. It is a word that we have been labeled with by a culture that blames the victims of sexual assault. (2011, n.p.)

Here, the choice to adopt "slut" is rhetorical, conscious and self-reflective, even if it was difficult for some participants to accept.

Research on the suffrage movement has found that suffragists broadly framed their arguments for women's right to vote around justice (women deserved voting rights in order to equal the rights of their male counterparts) and reform (women's experiences and perspectives lent them a unique lens that would improve society and politics). It was the reform frame that proved to be the mobilizing factor for the movement, leading the authors to suggest that when frames rebut their opponents' arguments, they are more likely to attract more participants (Hewitt & McCammon, 2004, p. 166). Like their suffragist counterparts, members and organizers of SlutWalk have strategically responded to their audience, in this case limiting their use of the "slut celebration" frame and instead attempting to clarify the role of gendered epithets in perpetuating rape culture. However, despite activists' early attempts to defend their use of "slut," the term has remained controversial and its usage has been minimized.

More recently, SlutWalk Toronto has explicitly moved away from celebrating and reclaiming sluttiness: "No matter what you call the [other] woman – slut, whore, skank, tramp, ho – it's simply a way of drawing the line" (SlutWalk Toronto, n.d.). Similarly, SlutWalk Chicago tweeted, "What do you feel about the use of the word slut?" prompting a brief discussion of the word's colloquial and reclaimed meanings (n.d.). These posts have particular relevance when one considers that campaign participants wrote many more posts about victim blaming and shaming than they did about slut celebration; for example, Lubbock started a "Stomp out Shame" campaign that encouraged the participation of celebrities and asserted that "the fight against blame and shame never ends" (SlutWalk Lubbock, n.d.). Similarly, at SlutWalk Chicago's 2014 march, activists beat a piñata labeled "patriarchy" in an effort to "smash the patriarchy." The Lubbock campaign and Chicago action illustrate that SlutWalk has opted to focus not only on the shame-blame frame but also to integrate explicitly second and third wave feminist discourse that rejects sexism, patriarchy, and victim blaming. These choices correspond to past criticisms of the campaign, such as its overemphasis on "slut" and its lack of explicitly feminist language.

Strategic Adaptation: From "Slut Celebration" to "Sex Positive, Pro-consent"

Marches and protests in late 2012 and early 2013 witnessed a rhetoric shift from *celebrating and reclaiming* "sluttiness" to concretely emphasizing agency and choice (see Figs. 1 and 2). Slut celebration and skepticism were still present in the protests ("Sluts pay taxes" and "slut power" were displayed at SlutWalk Toronto and Chicago, respectively) but only 32 slogans (approximately 12.6% of the sample) explicitly addressed "slut" and those that used it primarily did so to debunk rape myths and call for an end to slut shaming. Only seven (2.8%) of the slogans from 2013 and 2014

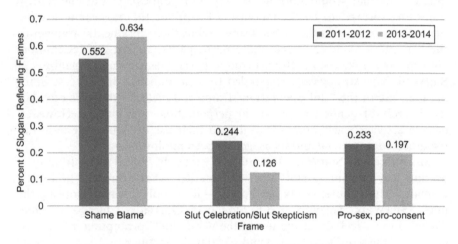

Fig. 1. SlutWalk's Changing Frames, 2011–2014 (*n* = 589).

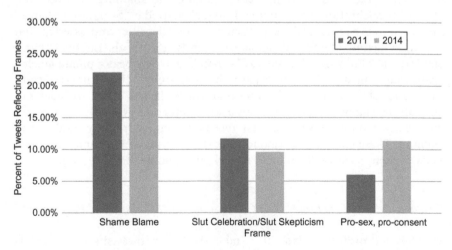

Fig. 2. SlutWalk's Changing Frames by Tweet, 2011 versus 2014 (*n* = 653).

celebrated slut, while 25 (9.8%) sought to problematize the use of sexua-
lized epithets for women and girls (see Fig. 3). For example, a participant
at SlutWalk Chicago's 2013 carried a slogan that asserted, "I'm only a slut
when I say no to you." SlutWalk Toronto's 2014 motto is even more indicative of an intentional shift in framing: "Who are you calling a ___?" with
a blank space. Some participants chose to carry posters that asked, "Who
are you calling a slut?" but others left a blank space or filled their poster
with different epithets, such as "ho," "*puta*," "whore," and "prostitute."
Moreover, SlutWalk Toronto explicitly distanced itself from slut reclamation and celebration before its 2014 march. The organization's website
updated its "About" section to include, "Some of [the] marches [associated
with SlutWalk] have been called SlutWalks, others have taken locally-
driven names; all have been part of international, collective action against
victim-blaming in support of survivors of sexual violence" (SlutWalk
Toronto, n.d.). Similarly, in a 2014 interview SlutWalk Toronto organizer
Natalee Brouse explained that the 2014 march elected not to call itself
SlutWalk, instead using the initials SWTO "[purposefully] to make itself a
little more accessible" (Pinch, 2014). This shift is correlated with an
increase in slogans and tweets adhering to a "slut skepticism" frame alongside a decrease in the "slut celebration" or "slut defense" frame.

Rather than framing their argument around "slut," many SlutWalkers
have begun to privilege the sex positive, pro-consent frame. Some slogans
explicitly addressed lack of consent ("Your curiosity =/= my consent" or

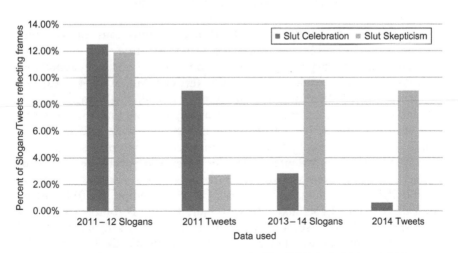

Fig. 3. Changing the Discourse around "Slut," 2011−2014 (*n* = 1,242).

"If you can't get consent ... Go FUCK YOURSELF," at Toronto and Chicago's marches, respectively) while others celebrated individuals' right to consent. For example, classic feminist slogans like "My body, my choice" and "No means no" were coupled with sex-positive, third wave messages such as, "Yes means 'F*ck me!' No means 'F*ck you!'" and "My vagina, my rules." While similar messages also were seen at earlier marches, in the 2011−2012 dataset "slut" was used more frequently than consent and this trend decreased in later marches (see Figs. 1 and 2).

"Shame-blame," "Slut Celebration/Skepticism," and "Sex-positivity, Pro-consent" frames have been significant in contemporary North American feminist movements in their originality as they simultaneously reject rape culture and affirm people's right to safe, consensual and enjoyable sex. However, "Slut Celebration" has proved to be disruptive of the campaign's participation and inclusiveness. Beginning in 2011, debates raged around the use of the term "slut," as stated above. Due in part to these debates, SlutWalk Toronto deliberately chose its initials (SWTO) for its hashtag in 2014, Philadelphia march now calls itself "A March to End Rape Culture," and Northampton adopted the name "Stomp and Holler." However, while celebrating and reclaiming "slut" has faded away, the frame's meaning − that women have the right to be sexual, sexy, and empowered − remains in the "sex-positivity, pro-consent" and "shame-blame" frames.

SlutWalk's Twitter Feeds and Websites

Twitter feeds and websites from SlutWalk organizations in Toronto, Chicago, and Lubbock were analyzed from the first five months of SlutWalk's history, beginning in April and running through September 2011. Posts also were examined from June through August 2014 to explore change over time.[13] In addition to the emphasis on shame-blame, celebrate slut, and sex-positivity, pro-consent, our analysis shows that Twitter pages have been used by activists to provide participants with logistic details, remind followers of upcoming events, announce meeting places and times, and request help from volunteers. Twitter pages also provide resources for members, ranging from support for rape survivors to articles and blogs about bullying, catcalling, and homophobia. For example, a 2014 post by SlutWalk Toronto hyperlinked to Covenant House Toronto, a homeless youth shelter: "Studies show 70 percent of #homelessyouth have suffered some form of physical sexual or emotional abuse" (SlutWalk Toronto, n.d.). Other posts have linked to corollary campaigns such as the Young Muslim

Women's Project or rights for transgender people (i.e., "We need Toby's Law to be in effect, we need trans rights now" posted by SlutWalk Toronto in 2014). These examples demonstrate not only Twitter pages' role as online communities that provide members with advocacy, information, and support; they also illustrate the local grassroots alliances that SlutWalk satellites have formed. For example, SlutWalk Chicago has collaborated with the Sex Workers Outreach Project and Occupy; Lubbock has been supported by PFLAG and Latino Lubbock; and Toronto has worked with LGBT groups, Hollaback, and the Young Muslim Women's Project.

Perhaps most significant, Twitter feeds have served as a forum for addressing criticisms and increasing inclusivity at SlutWalk events. For example, in 2014 Toronto SlutWalkers emphasized the sexual assault and harassment that faces the trans* community: "#SWTO2014: Trans* Contingent, because trans women are real women and all women are affected by victim blaming!!" SlutWalk Toronto also tweeted that "work against sexual violence must include the voices of #trans* people, #sexworkers, #indigenous elders" (SlutWalk Toronto, n.d.). SlutWalk Chicago's organizers have worked toward inclusivity since their first march, according to their Twitter page and interviews with organizers Ashley Bohrer (Jerri, 2014), Jamie Keiles, and Jessica Skolnik (Dries, 2011; White, 2011); the organizers have disseminated materials in Spanish and English and held post-rally forums to discuss race, class, and privilege.

The pages and campaign blogs additionally share articles, personal blogs, and interviews about SlutWalk, from advocates as well as opponents. After each SlutWalk march, members post photographs and stories about their experiences. Toronto has included blog posts by assault survivors in a series of "MyStory" contributions, as well as organizers' biographies, which emphasize their reasons for joining the SlutWalk community and their beliefs in sex-positivity (Reger, 2014). Similarly, SlutWalk Chicago's blog featured a "Sex-Positive Chicagoans" column, which highlighted members of the campaign and their efforts to end sexual violence while celebrating consensual sex and sexuality. The Twitter feeds also serve an important function of solidarity by highlighting satellite marches around the globe and expressing gratitude, love, and support for similar campaigns. Common posts express solidarity, and posts about resources, logistics, and SlutWalk experiences are mixed with statements about victim blaming, slut shaming, rape culture, and slut celebration. Arguably, these posts have become another highly effective tactic, as activists play an active part through sharing with friends and collaborators of the protests. The posts continued to be strategic in their framing through their continued focus on "shame-blame" and "sex-positivity, pro-consent," as they gained new members, encouraged participation, and provided a space for activists to develop a collective identity; share hopes, fears, and frustrations; and respond to critics. Posts such as "Activism starts at home! – Take control of our own stories as opposed to letting others define us" are calls for recruitment based on SlutWalk's pro-consensual sex and anti-victim blaming, slut shaming frames. The conciseness of Twitter posts and their wide accessibility make them a strategic choice for movement activists with few funds and resources.

CONCLUSION

Does strategic adaptation of frames influence movement participation and popularity? Our findings show that the early shame-blame and "slut celebration" frames were influenced by second and third wave feminist discourse, and while the campaign was initially very popular, the bold usage of "slut" in its framing did attract criticism from some feminists, especially women of color who felt marginalized and alienated by the campaign's apparent focus on a certain kind of sexuality. These criticisms affected the popularity of the campaign as evident by the decreasing number of participants after the initial enthusiasm. Despite attempts by the campaign's organizers to respond to the criticisms in their blogs and public posts by repeatedly reaffirming that slut represents a unifying and powerful concept, the campaign moved away from the slut celebration frame in its later period to the more resonant sex-positivity/pro-consent frame. In contrast the shame-blame frame has resonated with participants throughout with its universal message of debunking rape myths and shifting the blame from victims to rapists and society. While in 2012 the campaign witnessed a rhetoric shift in framing from *celebrating and reclaiming* "sluttiness" to concretely emphasizing agency and choice, it is important to note that even in the later periods slut celebration and skepticism were present in the protests via implicit slogans ("Who are you calling a ___?") and the outfits worn by some participants. Alongside the campaign's continuation of the resonant frames and the gradual shift toward a third frame, our findings suggest a growing popularity of the campaign over the last two years.

Since the SlutWalk was a horizontal, leaderless campaign, the impression was that the decision of strategic adaptation of frames lay with the collective decision of members. Our comprehensive analysis of the SlutWalk reveals that while decisions to shift in framing were influenced by responses to criticisms and changing socio-political climates, it is difficult to disaggregate specific individuals behind decisions from other participants.

The spontaneous nature of the SlutWalk, coupled with its strategic use of the Internet, has significant implications for social movement theorizing. The ability to possibly influence change through spontaneous posting of mere 140 characters online, thereby potentially fostering transnational and trans-local relationships, and reaching out to activists thousands of miles away, is powerful for individual participants. Recent research on social movements is now arguing for renewed interest in the implications of "spontaneity" (described as events and action that are not planned or organized prior to their occurrence) in theorizing (Snow & Moss, 2014, p. 1123). Our analysis of North American SlutWalk campaigns revealed both a conscious effort to address criticisms and a spontaneous outpouring of indignation in social media that prompted action. The two may seem incompatible, as strategic action and spontaneity do not seem to go hand in hand in movements. However, spontaneity has always been an important component of collective action, and Snow and Moss argue that some campaigns are "spontaneous and consequential for the larger collective actions in which they are embedded, and sometimes also for subsequent collective action" (p. 1124). Thus, even in the most organized movements there are spontaneous events that have influenced strategic action from time to time.

We concur with Snow and Moss's call for a renewed attention to the relationship between spontaneity and protest events that is fundamental to understanding the character and dynamics in movements. While the focus of our paper was on the strategic decisions of the SlutWalk, future research on the topic may explore the spontaneous nature of the campaign: what impact does spontaneity have on contemporary movements? Moreover, how do participants conceive of their role as agents of change as they spontaneously forge transnational links with 140 characters and the click of a mouse? In today's social media dominated world, where anyone with Internet access could participate in a campaign, we are witnessing the increasing strength and impact of spontaneity in campaigns. Future research on SlutWalk may explore how such spontaneity within the campaign has influenced its popularity and success.

NOTES

1. Though SlutWalks in North America have been attended by fewer participants since 2011, recently membership has remained steady or increased in many cities. SlutWalk protests also continue to occur globally.

2. US feminism typically is categorized by three "waves" (see Mann, 2012). The first wave (19th–20th centuries) focused on women's suffrage. The second wave "women's movement" (1960s–1970s) emphasized women's rights to their bodies and lives. The third wave began in the 1990s as a response to the second wave's weaknesses and sought a more racially and sexually diverse feminism.

3. For instance the word "slut" has been translated into many languages as part of the protests (*Besharmi Morcha* in Hindi, *Marcha das Vadias* in Portuguese, *La Marchas de las Putas* in Spanish). The word *puta* has also been used as an acronym: *Por una Transformación Auténtica y Social* (For an Authentic Social Transformation).

4. McClendon (2014) notes that calculating movement participation is generally done using self-reports of "intent to participate" or reported past participation. Because self-reports were often the most accurate data available, we calculated participation using the number of RSVPs on Facebook event pages. We bolstered these numbers with news articles about specific marches whenever possible. Facebook RSVPs have been previously used to compare intended versus actual participation; McClendon found that people who RSVP'ed to a gay and lesbian pride event did not always attend, and occasionally people who did not RSVP did attend. While this method of estimation is not without challenges, it does indicate continued support and participation in SlutWalks, if not always in person.

5. Though the focus here is on US American anti-rape activism, variations on the anti-rape movement can be found worldwide (see MacMillan, 2007; Kapur, 2012).

6. While SlutWalk has attempted to unite women, the campaign has been criticized for its lack of attention to class and race. As authors, we approach sexual violence from an intersectional standpoint. We do not argue that violence against women is the same across cultures but that it is a social problem faced by women and girls across social positions including race, class, sexual orientation, sexuality, and citizenship.

7. Whittier's (1997) "micro-cohorts" are key here. Micro-cohorts are clusters of social movement participants who develop a unique identity and ideology. "Third wave feminism" is more appropriately described as feminisms; the movement spans over 20 years and includes participants from diverse backgrounds. While some third wavers continue to privilege the voices of white, heterosexual women, others have adopted intersectional approaches.

8. Our discussion is not exhaustive, as Reger (2014) has addressed these criticisms at length (see also Carr, 2013; Feminist Frequency, 2011).

9. Slogans were gathered from images found in Baek (2014), Black (2011), Hamilton (2014), Martin (2014), Misterbuckwheattree (2014), Ratchford & Rodan (2014), Rockit (2013), SlutWalk Chicago Flickr group (2011), Sweet (2014), and Twitchy Staff (2013, 2014), as well as Facebook and Twitter pages.

10. Twitter is a social media site on which individuals or groups can share messages of up to 140 characters with other users and the public. These messages may include links to outside sources or be "retweeted" posts written by other users. Twitter's character limit and public accessibility render it a useful forum on which to explore social movement framing, as posts must be concise and are quickly shared with followers, potential recruits, and antagonists.

11. Many tweets provide logistical information about events (e.g., "We got our official parade permit just now! Stay tuned for an official Facebook event invite and update to our website with route info!," SlutWalk Chicago). These posts were removed if they lacked evidence of framing.

12. "Rape culture" describes a society in which rape is validated and perpetuated by media, laws, myths, and popular values, where victims are asked what they were wearing, drinking, or doing when they were assaulted, thereby blaming the victim instead of the rapist (Brownmiller, 2007).

13. As Twitter accounts post new messages, the oldest ones are deleted. Accounts may show up to 3,200 tweets, and Toronto has made more than 5,400. Thus, we examined tweets from 2011 and 2014 based on limited availability.

ACKNOWLEDGMENTS

An earlier version of this paper was presented at the annual meeting of the American Sociological Association, August 2014, San Francisco, CA. We thank Patrick Coy and five anonymous reviewers for their extensive comments on the manuscript, and Jo Reger for her help with the initial conceptualization of the project.

REFERENCES

Ayuso, S. (2011). SlutWalk: Beyond the right to dress like a "slut". *Tribune Business News*, August 10. Retrieved from http://ezproxy.msu.edu.proxy1.cl.msu.edu/login?url=http://search.proquest.com.proxy1.cl.msu.edu/docview/882237482?accountid=12598/

Baek, C. J. (2014). Photo gallery: SlutWalk Toronto 2014. *Now Toronto*, July 13. Retrieved from http://www.nowtoronto.com/news/story.cfm?content=198856/

Black, N. (2011). 100 awesome signs from SlutWalks worldwide [gallery]. *The Lion's Den University*, June 22. Retrieved from http://www.lionsdenu.com/200-awesome-signs-from-slut-walks-gallery/

Brown, G. (2014). Does framing matter? Institutional constraints on framing in two cases of intrastate violence. *Mobilization, 19*(2), 143–164.

Brownmiller, S. (2007). *Against our will: Men, women and rape* (United States, 1975). In E. B. Freedman (Ed.), *The essential feminist reader* (pp. 311–317). New York, NY: Modern Library.

Carr, J. L. (2013). The SlutWalk movement: A study in transnational feminist activism. *Journal of Feminist Scholarship, 4*, 24–38. Retrieved from http://www.jfsonline.org/issue4/articles/carr/

Chakravarty, A., & Chaudhuri, S. (2012). Strategic framing work(s): How micro-credit loans facilitate anti-witch hunt movements. *Mobilization, 17*(2), 175–194.

Chateauvert, M. (2013). *Sex workers unite: A history of the movement from Stonewall to SlutWalk*. Boston, MA: Beacon Press.

Coy, P., Woehrle, L., & Maney, G. (2008). Discursive legacies: The U.S. peace movement and "Support the Troops. *Social Problems, 55*(2), 161–189.

Crane, C. J. (2012). Social media as a feminist tool. *Herizons, 26*(2), 14–16.

Crawford, B. (2007). Toward a third-wave feminist legal theory: Young women, pornography and the praxis of pleasure. *Michigan Journal of Gender & Law, 14*(1), 99–168.

Crunk Feminist Collective. (2011). *SlutWalks v. Ho Strolls* [Blog post], May 23. Retrieved from http://crunkfeministcollective.wordpress.com/2011/05/23/slutwalks-v-ho-strolls/

Della Porta, D., & Diani, M. (2006). *Social movements: An introduction* (2nd ed.). Malden, MA: Blackwell.

Di Menna, H. (2014). Gender block: SlutWalk Toronto 2014. *This Magazine*, July 14. Retrieved from http://this.org/blog/2014/07/14/gender-block-slutwalk-toronto-2014/

Diani, M. (1996). Linking mobilization and political opportunities: Insights from regional populism in Italy. *American Sociological Review, 61*(6), 1053–1069.

Dines, G., & Murphy, W. (2011). SlutWalk is not sexual liberation. *The Guardian*, May 8. Retrieved from http://www.theguardian.com/commentisfree/2011/may/08/slutwalk-not-sexual-liberation/

Dries, K. (2011). SlutWalk comes to Chicago, motivating a new generation of feminists. *WBEZ*, June 3. Retrieved from http://www.wbez.org/story/slutwalk-comes-chicago-motivating-new-generation-feminists-87357/

Dunn, A., Ellwood, Z., & Lubbock, O. (2013). *Robin Thicke − Blurred lines [Feminist parody] "Defined lines"* [Video file]. Auckland Law Review, August 30. Retrieved from https://www.youtube.com/watch?v=tC1XtnLRLPM/

Ensler, E. (2008). *The vagina monologues*. New York, NY: Villard Books.

Feminist Frequency. (2011). *Link round up: Feminist critiques of SlutWalk* [Blog post], May 16. Retrieved from http://www.feministfrequency.com/2011/05/link-round-up-feminist-critiques-of-slutwalk/

Fetner, T. (2001). Working Anita Bryant: The impact of Christian anti-gay activism on lesbian and gay movement claims. *Social Problems, 48*(3), 411–428.

Hamilton, J. (2014). #Toronto SlutWalk 2014 [Blog post]. *Toronto Grand Prix Tourist: A Toronto Blog*, July 12. Retrieved from http://www.torontograndprixtourist.com/2014/07/toronto-slutwalk-2014.html

Hewitt, L., & McCammon, H. J. (2004). Explaining suffrage mobilization: Balance, neutralization, and range in collective action frames, 1892–1919. *Mobilization, 9*(2), 149–166.

Hill, M. (2011, August 6). At SlutWalk, clothes make the woman − and a point. *Tribune Business News*. Retrieved from http://ezproxy.msu.edu.proxy2.cl.msu.edu/login?url=http://search.proquest.com.proxy2.cl.msu.edu/docview/881402016?accountid=12598/

Hill, S. (2013). *Digital revolutions: Activism in the internet age*. Oxford: New Internationalist.

Hughes, M. (2013). Robin Thicke's "Blurred Lines" gets the feminist response it deserves. *Mic*, July 27. Retrieved from http://mic.com/articles/56585/robin-thicke-s-blurred-lines-gets-the-feminist-response-it-deserves/

Jarvis, H., Westendorf, C., & Bhuiyan, R. (n.d.). How. *SlutWalk Toronto* [Website]. Retrieved from http://www.slutwalktoronto.com/about/how/. Accessed on November 10, 2012.

Jerri, A. (2014, August 23). 814: Shaming the System [Radio broadcast episode]. In T. Humiston, A. Jerri, S. Thayer, and R. Norwood [Producers], *This is Hell!*. Retrieved from http://thisishell.net/shows/814/#.VaaSrvlVhBf

Johnston, H. (2005). Comparative frame analysis. In H. Johnston & J. A. Noakes (Eds.), *Frames of protest: Social movements and the framing perspective* (pp. 237–260). Lanham, MD: Rowman & Littlefield Publishers.

Kapur, R. (2012). Pink chaddis and SlutWalk couture: The postcolonial politics of feminism lite. *Feminist Legal Studies, 20*(1), 1—20.

Katwiwa, M. (2013). Heather Jarvis: Winnovating language appropriation. *Winnovating: Women Innovating* [Website], October 11. Retrieved from http://www.winnovating.com/heather-jarvis-winnovating-language-appropriation-2/

Kelly, J. (1979). Anti-rape coalition. *Off Our Backs,* 9(9), 11.

Kingkade, T. (2014). 64 colleges are now under investigation for their handling of sexual assaults. *Huffington Post,* June 30. Retrieved from http://www.huffingtonpost.com/2014/06/30/colleges-under-investigation-sex-assault_n_5543694.html/

Kwan, R. (2011). Don't dress like a slut: Toronto cop. *Excalibur: York University's Community Newspaper,* February 16. Retrieved from http://www.excal.on.ca/news/dont-dress-like-a-slut-toronto-cop/

Largen, M. A. (1985). The anti-rape movement: Past and present. In A. W. Burgess (Ed.), *Rape and sexual assault: A research handbook* (pp. 1—13). New York, NY: Garland Publishing, Inc.

MacMillan, L. (2007). *Feminists organising against gendered violence.* Hampshire & New York, NY: Palgrave Macmillan.

Maier, S. L. (2011). Rape crisis centers and programs: "Doing amazing, wonderful things on peanuts". *Women and Criminal Justice, 21*(2), 141—169.

Mann, S. A. (2012). *Doing feminist theory: From modernity to postmodernity.* New York, NY: Oxford University Press, Inc.

Martin, R. J. (2014). SlutWalk marches in the streets of Toronto against sexual assault bias. *Demotix,* July 12. Retrieved from http://www.demotix.com/news/5247571/slutwalk-marches-streets-toronto-against-sexual-assault-bias#media-5246944/

McCammon, H. (2012). *The U.S. women's jury movements and strategic adaptation: A more just verdict.* New York, NY: Cambridge University Press.

McCammon, H., Chaudhuri, S., Hewitt, L., Muse, C. S., Newman, H., Smith, C. L., & Terrel, T. (2008). Becoming full citizens: The U.S. women's jury rights campaigns, the pace of reform, and strategic adaptation. *American Journal of Sociology, 113*(4), 1104—1147.

McCammon, H., Newman, H., Muse, C. S., & Terrel, T. (2007). Movement framing and discursive opportunity structures: The political successes of the U.S. women's jury movements. *American Sociological Review, 72*(5), 725—749.

McClendon, G. H. (2014). Social esteem and participation in contentious politics: A field experiment at an LGBT pride rally. *American Journal of Political Science, 58*(2), 279—290.

McGuire, D. L. (2004). "It was like all of us had been raped": Sexual violence, community mobilization, and the African American freedom struggle. *The Journal of American History, 91*(3), 906—931.

McMorris-Santoro, E. (2012). Republican Senate nominee: Victims of "legitimate rape" don't get pregnant. *Talking Points Memo,* August 19. Retrieved from http://2012.talkingpointsmemo.com/2012/08/todd-akin-legitimate-rape.php/

McVeigh, R., Meyers, D. J., & Sikkink, D. (2004). Corn, Klansmen, and Coolidge: Structure and framing in social movements. *Social Forces, 83*(2), 653—690.

Misterbuckwheattree. (2014). *SlutWalk Chicago 2014* [Images]. Retrieved from https://www.flickr.com/photos/misterbuckwheattree/14829060710/. Accessed on August 28, 2014.

Mitra, D. (2012). Critical perspectives on SlutWalks in India. *Feminist Studies, 38*(1), 254–261.

Murphy, M. (2011). We're sluts, not feminists. Wherein my relationship with SlutWalk gets rocky. *Feminist Current* [Blog post], May 7. Retrieved from http://feministcurrent.com/2585/were-sluts-not-feminists-wherein-my-relationship-with-slut-walk-gets-rocky/

Nellie's. (2012). Interview with SlutWalk organizer Colleen Westendorf. *Nellie's: Shelter, Education & Advocacy for all women and children* [Website], May 24. Retrieved from http://www.nellies.org/2012/05/24/interview-with-slutwalk-organizer-colleen-westendorf/

Noakes, J. A., & Johnston, H. (2005). Frames of protest: A road map to a perspective. In H. Johnston & J. A. Noakes (Eds.), *Frames of protest: Social movements and the framing perspective* (pp. 1–29). Lanham, MD: Rowman & Littlefield Publishers.

Nussbaum, E. (2011). The rebirth of the feminist manifesto. *New York Magazine*, October 30. Retrieved from http://nymag.com/news/features/feminist-blogs-2011-11/

O'Keefe, T. (2014). My body is my manifesto! SlutWalk, FEMEN and femmenist protest. *Feminist Review, 107*, 1–19.

Ólafsdóttir Kaaber, E. S. (2014). Eleven thousand attend fourth annual SlutWalk. *Iceland Review Online*, July 28. Retrieved from http://icelandreview.com/news/2014/07/28/eleven-thousand-attend-fourth-annual-slutwalk/

O'Reilly, A. (2012). Slut pride: A tribute to SlutWalk Toronto. *Feminist Studies, 38*(1), 245–250.

Pasquale, B. (2011). SlutWalk: Not radical, not helpful? [Blog post]. *Bobi Pasquale*, May 12. Retrieved from http://bobipasquale.wordpress.com/2011/05/12/slutwalk-not-radical-not-helpful/

Pinch, S. (2014). SlutWalk three years later: Where has the movement taken us? *Rabble.ca*, July 11. Retrieved from http://rabble.ca/news/2014/07/slutwalk-three-years-later-where-has-movement-taken-us/

Ratchford, S., & Rodan, G. (2014). We visited Toronto's SlutWalk. *Vice*, July 14. Retrieved from http://www.vice.com/en_ca/read/we-went-visited-torontos-slutwalk-2014-349/

Reger, J. (2014). Micro-cohorts, feminist discourse, and the emergence of the Toronto SlutWalk. *Feminist Formations, 26*(1), 49–69.

Ringrose, J., & Renold, E. (2012). Slut-shaming, girl power and "sexualisation": Thinking through the politics of the international SlutWalks with teen girls. *Gender and Education, 24*(3), 333–343.

Rockit, R. (2013). SlutWalk Chicago 2013: Third annual march protests rape culture, victim-blaming [Photos]. *Huffington Post*, September 10. Retrieved from http://www.huffingtonpost.com/2013/09/10/slutwalk-chicago-2013_n_3901085.html

Rose, V. M. (1977). Rape as a social problem: A byproduct of the feminist movement. *Social Problems, 25*(1), 75–89.

Rupp, L. J., & Taylor, V. (1999). Forging feminist identity in an international movement: A collective identity approach to twentieth century feminism. *Signs, 24*(2), 363–386.

Sen, R. (2013). *Rapes, resistances, reforms: Reclaiming Delhi as a site of freedom*. Manuscript submitted for publication.

Shaw, J., & Campbell, R. (2011). Rape crisis centers: Serving survivors and their communities. In T., Bryant-Davis (Ed.), *Surviving sexual violence: A guide to recovery and empowerment* (pp. 112–128). New York, NY: Roman and Littlefield.

SlutWalk Chicago. (2011). *SlutWalk Chicago blog* [Blog]. Retrieved from http://www.slutwalk-chicago.org/blog.html/. Accessed on December 9, 2012.

SlutWalk Chicago. (n.d.). *Timeline* [Facebook page]. Retrieved from https://www.facebook. com/slutwalkchicago/. Accessed on August 28, 2014.

SlutWalk Chicago [slutwalkchi]. (n.d.). *Tweets* [Twitter page]. Retrieved from https://twitter. com/slutwalkchicago/. Accessed on December 3, 2011.

SlutWalk Chicago Flickr group. (2011). *Pictures from SlutWalk Chicago at Daley Plaza* [Images], June 4. Retrieved from http://www.flickr.com/groups/1680203@N20/pool/ with/5797858483/

SlutWalk Lubbock. (2011). *Why slut?* [Facebook note], August 2. Retrieved from https://www. facebook.com/notes/slutwalk-lubbock/why-slut/218520484860979/. Accessed on August 28, 2014.

SlutWalk Lubbock [SlutwalkLubbock]. (n.d.). *Tweets* [Twitter page]. Retrieved from https:// twitter.com/SlutwalkLubbock/. Accessed on December 8, 2012.

SlutWalk Toronto. (2012). *SlutWalk Toronto blog* [Blog]. Retrieved from http://www.slutwalk-toronto.com/category/blog/. Accessed on December 9, 2012.

SlutWalk Toronto [SlutWalkTO]. (n.d.). *Tweets* [Twitter page]. Retrieved from https://twitter. com/SlutWalkTO/. Accessed on December 4, 2012.

Snow, D. A. (2007). Framing processes, ideology, and discursive fields. In D. A. Snow, S. A. Soule, & H. Kriesi (Eds.), *The Blackwell companion to social movements* (pp. 380−412). Malden, MA: Blackwell.

Snow, D. A., Benford, R., McCammon, H. J., Hewitt, L., & Fitzgerald, S. (2014). The emergence, development, and future of the framing perspective: 25+ years since "frame alignment". *Mobilization, 19*(1), 23−45.

Snow, D. A., & Moss, D. M. (2014). Protests on the fly: Toward a theory of spontaneity in the dynamics of protest and social movements. *American Sociological Review, 76*(6), 1122−1143.

Snow, D. A., Rochford, E. B., Jr., Worden, S. K., & Benford, R. D. (1986). Frame alignment processes, micromobilization, and movement participation. *American Sociological Review, 51*(4), 464−481.

Sweet, S. (2014). Scene: SlutWalk 2014. *Torontoist*, July 14. Retrieved from http://torontoist. com/2014/07/scene-slutwalk-2014/

Thicke, R., & Williams, P. (2013). *Blurred lines*. Blurred Lines *[CD]*. Santa Monica, CA: Star Trak Entertainment & Interscope Records.

Thompson, C. (2011). Taking *slut* for a walk: Young feminists give an old slur new meaning. *Ms, 21*(3), 14.

Tillotson, K. (2011). "SlutWalk" march divides feminists. *Tribune Business News*, September 29. Retrieved from http://ezproxy.msu.edu proxy1.cl.msu.edu/login?url=http://search. proquest.com.proxy1.cl.msu.edu/docview/894734772?accountid=12598/

Tuerkheimer, D. (2014). SlutWalking in the shadow of the law. *Minnesota Law Review, 98*(March), 1453−1511). Retrieved from http://dx.doi.org/10.2139/ssrn.2009541/

Twitchy Staff. (2013). "Robin Thicke hate is heavy here" at #SlutWalk 2013 [photos]. *Twitchy*, September 7. Retrieved from http://twitchy.com/2013/09/07/robin-thicke-hate-is-heavy-here-at-slutwalk-2013-photos/

Twitchy Staff. (2014). Patriarchy isn't gonna smash itself!" SlutWalk Chicago brings out feminism's best [photos, video]. *Twitchy*, August 23. Retrieved from http://twitchy.com/ 2014/08/23/patriarchy-isnt-gonna-smash-itself-slutwalk-chicago-brings-out-feminisms-best-photos-video/

V Day. (2012). About V-day. *V-Day* [Website]. Retrieved from http://www.vday.org/about.html/. Accessed on November 11, 2012.

White, R. R. (2011). From Riot Grrrl to the streets of Chicago: The SlutWalk Chicago interview. *TimeOut Chicago*, June 1. Retrieved from http://www.timeout.com/chicago/things-to-do/from-riot-grrrl-to-the-streets-of-chicago-the-slutwalk-chicago-interview/

Whittier, N. (1997). Political generations, micro-cohorts, and the transformation of social movements. *American Sociological Review, 62*(5), 760–778.

Womanist Musings. (2011). An open letter from black women to the SlutWalk [Blog post]. *Womanist Musings*, September 23. Retrieved from http://www.womanist-musings.com/2011/09/open-letter-from-black-women-to.html/. Accessed on November 10, 2012.

SECTION II
RELIGION AND ATHEISM IN
SOCIAL MOVEMENTS

HOME IS WHERE ACTIVISM THRIVES: COMMUNITY SETTING AND PERSISTENT PROTEST PARTICIPATION

Sharon S. Oselin

ABSTRACT

Despite the abundant research on social movements, there is sparse scholarly investigation of the link between community settings and how they contribute to persistent protest participation. This paper illuminates the cultural and social mechanisms within a religious retirement community that engender members' sustained commitment to a ten-year long peace protest. A shared religious-based collective identity also deepens activists' commitment to this cause. This study draws on semi-structured interviews with 14 peace protesters who reside in this community at two points in time: 2010 and 2013.

Keywords: Persistent protest participation; community; peace activists; commitment; identity

Research in Social Movements, Conflicts and Change, Volume 38, 173–202
ISSN: 0163-786X/doi:10.1108/S0163-786X20150000038006

INTRODUCTION

It was pushing 100 degrees on a late Friday afternoon in August 2008. While driving, I slowed my car to a stop at a busy intersection in a small, affluent city approximately 30 miles east of Los Angeles, CA. I was intrigued to notice over a dozen elderly protesters holding signs, waving to drivers, and smiling so broadly it was evident they enjoyed this public demonstration, despite the sweltering heat. Their signs and other symbolic props made their grievance clear: they were opposed to the ongoing war in Iraq. As a social movement scholar, I made a mental note of this protest and carried on with my day. After that initial sighting, I observed the same group of individuals on these corners every Friday around the same time over the course of the next few years. This ongoing event made me speculate about the forces that sustained such a strong adherence to this cause. After mentioning this group to a friend, she just so happened to know one of the protesters and introduced me to her. I learned the anti-war protesters all resided within the same religious retirement community and comprised the core participants.

Despite the abundant research on initial entrance into movements, far fewer studies examine the factors that lead to sustained, long-term engagement among activists. Scholars who conduct research in this area attribute this practice to various causes, including personal commitment, effectiveness of leadership, collective identity, a long history with a movement, and organizational structures (Barkan, Cohn, & Whitaker, 1995; Corrigall-Brown, 2012; Klandermans, 1997; Rogne, 1999). What remains to be a focal point within this work, however, is the relationship between community context and prolonged participation.

Some tie specific community settings to recruitment and mobilization (Evans & Boyte, 1986), and even reveal how environments facilitate movement-related actions, such as strategy and tactical development (Zhao, 2001). But we are left wondering if communities function to retain members as well, and if so, how this occurs.[1] Certain scholars have begun to address this query by uncovering particular community features that engender individual commitment to the movement (Downton & Wehr, 1997; Rogne, 2010). Nepstad's (2008) work, for instance, finds rituals and retreats, social interactions, and close ties between participants and leaders cement bonds, heighten commitment, and ultimately produce sustained movement engagement. Summers Effler (2010) stresses the importance of emotions within communities as they generate commitment. Her analysis illustrates these group feelings fluctuate over time and accordingly impact both movement and individual trajectories of persistence and disengagement. This paper extends this line of research by examining the cultural and social mechanisms within a residential retirement community that foster and maintain very high levels of commitment among anti-war activists, leading to over a decade of routine weekly protest. I am reluctant to refer to these protesters as a social movement given they do not exhibit many features that characterize a social movement organization (Rohlinger, 2002) and have virtually no contact with the broader peace movement. While I build upon theories of social movement persistence, this study aims to shed light on long-time activism among participants in this re-occurring protest event.

In order to analyze how a community setting perpetuates prolonged protest participation, I draw on a case study of fourteen anti-war activists who reside within a religious retirement setting, which I call Sojourner Circle (SC). I interviewed 14 SC protesters at two points in time – 2010 and 2013 – to better assess persistence and gain insight into desistance from this public protest. I argue that specific community-based mechanisms, cultural and social, prompt continued engagement at the protest (and the completion of other related tasks). Additionally, my analysis also indicates that collective identity acted as a linchpin of this group, fortified by these mechanisms, and linked to heightened commitment to this cause.

I begin the paper by reviewing research that focuses on persistent social movement participation, and present my methodology and data collection. I then discuss the broader Christian culture of Sojourner Circle and the shared interpretation of faith among those who protest that operates as a cultural mechanism connected to commitment. In the subsequent sections, I explore multiple social mechanisms which transpire on the grounds that engender commitment to protest, including overlapping personal and political spheres, emotional connections between residents, and accountability to the group and its tasks. Finally, I note factors that prompt disengagement among a few protesters and conclude with broader implications of the study.

COMMITMENT, IDENTITY, AND ENDURING ACTIVISM

Scholars connect initial participation in social movements to social psychological factors (e.g., conceptualization of grievances), biographical factors (e.g., time constraints), and social ties and networks (Buechler, 2004; Coy, 2001; Dixon & Roscigno, 2003; Stryker, Owens, & White, 2000). Individuals with biographical availability − those who have time and energy to dedicate to movement activities − are the most likely to engage. This availability varies according to the life cycle, demarcating young adults and advanced middle-agers as optimal targets for mobilization. Turning points in life can facilitate participation because they represent periods when individuals are not only biographically available but are also cognitively and emotionally open to consider new ideas and actions (Munson, 2002). Social networks are perhaps one of the biggest predictive factors that prompt movement participation. The interpersonal relationships participants have with others outside the movement can serve as conduits to recruit new members.

The above literature overwhelmingly focuses on the initial engagement of movement activists but does not address the factors that account for their persistent participation. Researchers in this area highlight commitment as a force that undergirds activist retention within movements (Corrigall-Brown, 2012; Downton & Wehr, 1997; Klandermans, 1997; Nepstad, 2004, 2008). It generally follows that routine activists possess higher levels of commitment compared to those who fall out (Klandermans, 1997), and one's commitment is strengthened when his or her values align with the social movement organization (SMO) (Barkan et al., 1995).

Social movement scholars illuminate the multi-faceted nature of commitment − such as affective and normative forms − as it is linked to persistent activism (Corrigall-Brown, 2012; Klandermans, 1997). *Affective commitment* reflects an emotional attachment to a movement, sustained through affective interactions with fellow participants and rewards derived from such engagement (Taylor, 1989). *Normative commitment* stems from socialization processes and moral obligations that compel individuals to continue to work to accomplish movement goals. Nepstad (2008) cautions this form can fluctuate and therefore needs to be routinely reinforced among members. To that end, there is some evidence that the organizational structure of movements can increase or decrease member commitment to a cause (Corrigall-Brown, 2012).

Various factors deepen activist commitment to a particular movement. One such factor includes early onset of initial activism (during youth) that ultimately leads to lifelong participation in a movement (see Andrews, 1991; McAdam, 1988; Rogne, 2010). Similarly, Schussman and Soule (2005) conclude individuals with a history of political engagement are likely protest candidates throughout life, in part because they have developed a deeply ingrained "culture of responding" (Andrews, 1991) that persists over the life course.

Affiliations with politically oriented organizations can also contribute to longstanding commitment to activism (Andrews, 1991; Rogne, 2013, 2010). Passy and Giugni (2000) note such interconnectedness between individual and political spheres (including social networks) buttresses long-term movement engagement. Morris (1992) attributes the root of this motivation to the development of a "political consciousness" that can result in the formation of a collective identity with other activists.

Collective identity reflects a sense of "we-ness" or "one-ness" based on shared attributes or experiences among group members (Melucci, 1989), and can serve as the foundation that facilitates collective action (Klandermans & de Weerd, 2000). This identity can take three forms: (1) *activist*, those with previous social movement experience, (2) *organizational*, oriented around a particular SMO, or (3) *value*, derived from one's own value system and morals (Gamson, 1991; Gecas, 2000). The type of collective identity may even inform one's longevity in a movement (Corrigall-Brown, 2012). Andrews explains how continued commitment and activism form a sense of continuity over time intricately tied to identity: "Such actions are a constant and fundamental expression by their respondents of who they are, have been, and will be ..." (1991, p. 172).

COMMUNITY SETTING AND SUSTAINED ACTIVISM

Certain environments are known as "free spaces" (Evans & Boyte, 1986), or areas within a community where individuals are removed from the dominant culture, can voice their grievances, and connect to like-minded others. Snow and Soule (2010) argue such a baseline affinity makes it more likely that ties can be activated for protest. These relationships occur within a micromobilization context, or the "small group setting in which processes of collective attribution are combined with rudimentary forms of organization to produce mobilization for collective action" (McAdam, McCarthy, & Zald, 1988, p. 709). Once involved in a movement, members spend copious time carrying out routine activities that become integral to the persistence of such spaces (Glass, 2010).

Zhao (2001) also draws attention to the importance of ecology in his study of the Chinese student democratic movement at Beijing University.

His work reveals that the university setting served as a hub for social movement action: it enabled the spread of information, fostered recruitment and networks, generated frequent interactions among the student body, and influenced the formation of movement strategies. It is well documented that such spaces can operate as catalysts for mobilization, but it is unclear if, and to what extent, they actually help retain those immersed within the movement for long durations.

Moving beyond initial mobilization, a few scholars focus more directly on the ways in which community context produces commitment that leads to sustained activism (for instance, see Downton & Wehr, 1997; Nepstad, 2008; Summers Effler, 2010). In their longitudinal study of student activists, Whalen and Flacks (1980) find being immersed within an activist community — composed of a supportive environment and friendship groups — leads to renewed political involvement. Members within a community can grant fellow activists important emotional support. In fact, emotions play a key role in preserving commitment at they generate efficacy and enthusiasm as well as combat feelings of exhaustion and meaninglessness (Summers Effler, 2010).

Other community settings implement rituals and retreats and encourage the development of ties between participants and leaders, which cement bonds and deepen commitment to sustained engagement (Nepstad, 2008). Downton and Wehr (1997) contend the bonds, mutual support and encouragement that unfold within an intimate community of peace activists are key for persistent participation to flourish. These studies illustrate communities can amplify individual dedication to a movement because they provide supportive environments for activists based upon interpersonal relationships. This paper extends prior work by analyzing the particular mechanisms that transpire within a residential retirement community that maintain very high levels of commitment among SC peace activists, leading to 10 years of ongoing protest against war.

The SC protesters were biographically available as they were retirees living within this residential community. Some had a past history of activism fueled by their spiritual beliefs that predisposed them to fight injustice. In this case, the injustice was the death and destruction perpetuated by war. This group of elderly individuals routinely participated in a weekly public protest to oppose the war in Iraq for over ten years. What sustained their dedication to continued protest engagement? This paper examines this topic by addressing the following research question: What mechanisms, conditions, and circumstances within the community setting foster and sustain commitment among elderly peace activists? To address this concern,

I draw on qualitative interviews at two points in time (2010 and 2013) with fourteen anti-war protesters who reside within Sojourner Circle.

METHODOLOGY AND DATA COLLECTION

After an awareness of this protest, I established contact with a regular participant through a mutual friend. I learned the protesters resided in a nearby retirement community, established in 1915, that offers delineated grounds with detached houses available for rent to qualified individuals. It is immersed within a small, affluent city nestled in the foothills of the San Gabriel Mountains approximately 30 miles due east of Los Angeles. It was specifically created for inhabitants who devoted their lives to Christian service (e.g., pastors, missionaries, deacons), spanning a variety of denominations.

In order to examine persistent protest participation, I relied on conversational and semi-structured interviews with 14 SC residents who regularly attend this weekly anti-war protest (7 women, 7 men). I gave both the residential community and protesters pseudonyms in this paper to ensure their anonymity. The first protester I met, Lily, helped me gain access to the rest of the participants through introduction at a party hosted at her house. I used purposive sampling and therefore only interviewed protesters who resided at Sojourner Circle given my interest in the relationship between community and sustained protest engagement. These individuals made up the core of the public demonstration and were the only consistent attendees. Although other unaffiliated individuals sporadically showed up for the event they were not regular participants. Together, the SC protesters averaged 9.4 years of routine attendance at this protest. The protest first began with only a handful of participants in the fall of 2002, when the United States was gearing up for the invasion of Iraq. After the invasion in early 2003, the protest more than doubled in size with the influx of the core group of SC peace activists who still demonstrate today. The average number of protesters at any weekly protest is approximately ten.

The protesters share many demographic similarities, including age, a history of religiosity and service to others, and immersion within the same retirement community. I summarize the sample characteristics in Table 1. The SC protesters, all of whom are retired, have a mean age of 81.2. While they all self-identify as Christians, the 14 protesters represent 5 Christian denominations (and attend 7 local churches): 4 members of the United

Table 1. SC Protester Characteristics and Demographics.

Name	Age	Former Occupation	Protest Attendance (in Years)	Reduced Participation or Disengagement
Tom	85	Minister	11	
Stan	77	Missionary	9	
John	81	Minister	10	
Janine	72	Pastor	7	
Irene	88	Spouse of pastor	10	
Mildred	81	Spouse of minister	9	Other project[a]
Richard	86	Missionary	11	
Betty	78	Worked for Christian organization	10	Poor health[a]
Lily	83	Worked for Christian organization	10	Caretaker[b]
Roberta	77	Missionary	7	
Robert	79	Pastor	9	Other project[b]
Steve	85	Pastor	10	Poor health[b]
Alvin	80	Missionary	9	Poor health, caretaker[a]
Beatrice	84	Worked with Christian organization	9	

[a]Disengaged completely from protest.
[b]Reduced protest participation.

Church of Christ, 5 Catholics, 1 Baptist, 1 Presbyterian, and 3 members of the First Christian Church (also known as Disciplines of Christ). These denominations can be quite diverse in terms of their theology and political leanings, however, respondents all identified as Democrats.

I initially conducted and digitally recorded the interviews in the homes of protesters during the summer of 2010, and each interview lasted between one and two hours. The questions focused on biographical information, personal history of activism, participation in the current protest, activities of the protest, leadership, motivations for participation, commitment, recruitment, how religion influences their activism, history of religiosity, relationships to fellow protesters, descriptions of the residential community, organizational involvements, and tactics and outcomes. I then carried out follow-up phone interviews in spring 2013 in order to assess whether the original interviewees continued to participate or desisted from the protest, and the causes of any alterations. Using a shorter questionnaire, I primarily inquired about changes to an array of topics: continued engagement in the protest, commitment levels, relationships between protesters, participation in community and social events, protest goals and tactics, and success. I made a point to ask about other members' participation or disengagement to double check self-reports, which ultimately increased my internal validity. Like the initial interviews, the follow-up interviews were also digitally recorded and transcribed.

I used the constant comparative method of coding (Glaser, 1965), which consisted of reviewing transcripts and comparing incidents across individuals to develop initial codes. This methodological strategy involves an inductive approach, where the discovery, refinement or extension of theory is driven by data analysis (Lofland, Snow, Anderson, & Lofland, 2006). I first coded the original interviews in 2010 and early 2011, organized the data into broad codes such as recruitment, personal history of activism, participation in protest, activist tasks, community phenomena and events, commitment levels, relationships to other protesters, and success. After recognizing the limitations of this cross-sectional data, I then conducted follow-up interviews in 2013 in order to present a more compelling argument about causes of sustained engagement and withdrawal among this sample. I found that eight of the original members continue to protest regularly but six either reduced participation or ceased altogether. After applying similar codes, this data confirmed my initial speculations about the link between community and persistence, and enabled me to explain causes of disengagement when it did occur.

I use the concept commitment throughout this paper based upon Andrews' (1991) definition: it reflects intention, duration, action and priority, where one's beliefs are expressed through her actions. In categorizing an individual's level of commitment to this protest event, I consider all of these factors, many of which are reflected in the quotes displayed in the paper. To further clarify, the following example illustrates what I consider a high level of commitment. After 10 years of weekly protest Lily remarked, "I will continue to protest ... well, I guess forever and ever because it's a way for me to show others this is where I stand on war." This statement reflects all markers of commitment listed above. All the SC participants reported regular weekly attendance at the protest, with only occasional absences for illness or travel.

STAYING THE COURSE: UNDERSTANDING PERSISTENT PROTEST PARTICIPATION

For most social movements, attaining tangible goals — such as an increase in the numbers of protesters or heightened frame resonance with bystanders — helps retain activists as it bolsters morale. In contrast, this group of elderly anti-war protesters acknowledged very few markers of success after 10 years of weekly demonstration. John echoed the groups' pragmatic perspective regarding their activities: "The protest is not going to change policy, it's not going to get us out of Iraq, but it's something we *can* do." With little hope this public demonstration will effect change, what compels them to stay the course?

This paper reveals that community context and the mechanisms that transpire on these grounds lead to persistent protest participation for the small group of routine attendees because they deepen both normative and affective commitment tied to a particular collective identity. Such mechanisms encompass immersion within a residential culture of altruism, overlapping personal and political spheres, emotional connections between protesters, and group accountability.

CULTURAL MECHANISM: ALTRUISM AS A SPIRITUAL DUTY

Sojourner Circle is a residential retirement community for individuals with past careers in religious service — pastors, ministers, missionaries, laymen, or laywomen working with religious non-profit organizations, or their spouses. Such criterion operates as a screening mechanism ensuring only residents with this background qualify for housing. Given this lifelong orientation, it is not surprising that many protesters had prior engagement in activism bent on eradicating some form of social injustice: racism, sexism, class issues, environmental damage, and war and military actions.

Tom, an octogenarian, was a United Church of Christ (UCC) minister for 40 years before retiring. He recited his history of social justice activism:

> Yes, my wife and I were part of the racial justice movement when we were in Los Angeles in the 60s and 70s. We also participated in the peace movement against Vietnam. The other social movement we were part of was the gay and lesbian movement in D.C. during the 1980s because our church ministry committed to gay and lesbian folk.

Stan, a Baptist missionary for over 30 years in the Congo, likewise devoted much of his life to uplifting those around him who experienced discrimination and hardship. He protested against Vietnam and also participated in the march to the capital building at the University of Madison, Wisconsin after Reverend Martin Luther King Jr.'s assassination. And,

Janine, an ordained pastor for UCC, confirmed, "I was heavily involved with the anti-war movement during Vietnam after my brother was killed there. And then I got interested in other issues of race and women's issues as well." John, a retired Presbyterian Minister, committed acts of civil disobedience commencing in the 1960s:

> I opposed the Vietnam War and stood in support of young men who were resisting the draft. So I participated in draft burning, worship services, vigils at the draft offices. There was a whole group of us, who were called the Friends of the Resistance at that time. Plus, I served as the director of an ecumenical agency that worked with the United Farm Workers called the California Migrant Ministry. I worked with that movement for twenty-seven years as an organizer.

As the above quotes illustrate, many SC protesters initially got involved with the peace movement during the Vietnam War. Contrary to other studies of peace activists (Rogne, 2010, 2013), however, they did not maintain this lifelong connection to the peace movement via affiliation with local peace organizations (e.g., War Resisters League, American Friends Service Committee).[2] Rather their involvement was sporadic over the life course – during the Vietnam era and again, decades later, during the US invasion of Iraq and Afghanistan while in residence at Sojourner Circle. Their retirement at SC, the onset of the war, and the active peace protesters living within this community coalesced to present an ideal opportunity to reengage in peace activism. Thus, the decision to continue the act of service via the local anti-war protest was a logical progression for certain residents, a way to enact deep-seated altruism.[3]

Sojourner Circle protesters' motivation largely emerged from their interpretation of Christianity that compelled them to improve the world around them and uplift the downtrodden. This ideological stance was often acquired in an early age. Janine explained how she internalized this message: "In the Protestant tradition that I grew up in, spirituality was understood in terms of the work for social justice." Eighty-six year old Richard, a lifelong Roman Catholic, derived a similar mandate from Catholicism:

> I grew up in a very traditional, religiously speaking, way – friendly, neighborly, help-others. And then by the time I got into college I was studying some of that in my religion courses. I've also taken instructions from certain popes, like Pope John the 23rd, and those teachings just gave me a whole new orientation to view the world. What I took from all that is it wasn't enough to just be a good person and try to help others; as a Christian one should actually work to transform structures.

Past studies conclude peace activists often invoke moral authority as they oppose war and government actions that incite it (see Downton & Wehr,

1991; Maney, Coy, & Woehrle, 2009). For SC protesters, morality was informed primarily by religious tenets that nonviolence and peace were Christian attributes, and they felt obligated to change the world to adhere to God's standards (McVeigh, 2001). This is a common tenet of liberal Christian movements because "the gospels' prescriptions to serve, protect, and act for justice on behalf of the disadvantaged is one of the more clear and uncontested injunctions in the Christian scriptures" (Coy, 2001, p. 83). The weekly protest against the war offered residents an opportunity to fulfill this moral and spiritual duty.

Stan, a 75-year-old male, displays this conviction and links it to his continued participation: "I feel what I'm doing is right." When asked to elaborate on what specifically motivated him to return to the protest each Friday, he responded: "For me, as a Christian, I look to Christ as leader of what we should be doing in life, and he definitely had a lot to say about ethical issues, you know, peace, and sensitivity to the issues of those who are in poverty."

Janine's statement illustrates a similar propensity to strive for peace through public demonstration because she feels it is her duty as a Christian: "Well, it's the principle of the thing. As long as the war's going, I'm going to be there [at the protest] because the war is wrong." Her sense of morality and social justice clearly emerge from her religious beliefs:

> I see Jesus as a prophet from whom we all have a lot to learn to the extent we have stories of his life and his work. There's my model for social justice, the form of spirituality that is social justice. But to be active on behalf of others, that's spirituality and religious. That's what is commanded of us.

Eighty-one year old Mildred also attributes her activism against the war to her faith:

> My religious beliefs are a big factor. As Jesus said, blessed are the peacemakers. There are so many reasons why the war is anti-Christian: it's brutal, uncompassionate, wasteful, and destructive. If we worship a God who created life then war is just so counterproductive to that mission. I'd say I put a lot of connection between my theology and my anti-war practices.

And John, just over 80, attempts to model the actions of Jesus by repudiating the war: "I guess in a basic sense, all of my social activism has been my faith, my belief that Jesus showed us the way that we should live. He's not the only one who did that, but he's certainly the one I know. I think Jesus would approve of my protesting. Nonviolence, turn the other cheek, right?" A righteous sense of morality permeates the motivational accounts for why these protesters continue to demonstrate week after week.

Beyond a moral and spiritual duty, some of the protesters even discussed their routine participation as a symbolic spiritual practice of atonement, intended to account for the widespread destruction and death of innocent people caused by militaristic action. This incentive and corresponding beliefs are couched in a religious plausibility structure (Nepstad, 2004). Betty explained: "...[t]he devastation of war, the fact that we are really responsible. And so many people were paying as a result of it, not just ourselves, but the Iraqis, the Afghanis. I, as a Christian, just couldn't sit by and *not* do something." Stan, a former Baptist missionary, also perceived public demonstration as a small way to make amends for death and destruction abroad on behalf of the US government: "I feel I'm doing what's right. Millions of Americans are, in a sense, complicit. So, there's a certain amount of responsibility I feel to do something to fix these wrongs." Beatrice, also a long-time member of the Catholic advocacy organization, The Grail, takes personal responsibility for the global violence committed by American soldiers.[4] Although she does not think her protest participation can absolve these atrocities, she perceives it is one small act that moves toward reparation:

> Violence doesn't solve any problems, and every time we take into our hands the death of some individual, we're wrong. Being out here gives me a sense of doing something, however little it is ... Put your body where your mouth goes, and just be physically present with others who are striving to benefit humanity.

The practice of serving others and a sense of duty to alter deplorable conditions within society and the world at large is endemic to the culture at Sojourner Circle, features that compel some to volunteer their time and energy to the local peace protest. One protester, John, noted that while it is only a minority of residents who attend the protest, the community itself approves of this type of public engagement given their leftist political leanings: "This is a community that while only the minority go [to protest] the majority support what we do. I say there's only twelve Republicans in Sojourner Circle, and they're hard to count."

SC protesters shared a normative commitment to fight injustices, sometime referred to as moral imperatives (Meyer, Allen, & Gellatly, 1990), and this dedication results in part from an interpretation of their faith that compels them to denounce war and advocate for peace. Coy (2001) refers to this as a "personalist approach" where activists take personal responsibility for creating change for the greater good based upon the moral superior character of that action. Accordingly, their religious beliefs instruct them to act on behalf of the poor, weak, and suffering, and even attempt to atone for the "sins" of others. The aforementioned statements suggest this group possesses a value-based collective identity, derived from being Christians. Essentially, the combination of religious instruction, spiritual and moral duty, and community ethos coalesce to form SC peace protesters' collective identity, one that lies at the intersection of faith and action.

SOCIAL MECHANISMS INTENSIFY COMMITMENT

Overlapping Personal and Political Spheres

Besides being immersed within an altruistic residential culture, the routine social interactions that transpired among protesters helped maintain commitment to the peace protest. Sojourner Circle requires that each resident pay for lunch throughout the week. As this is included in their monthly rent, it generally ensures that they frequent the dining hall with fellow residents to eat and socialize each day. As one resident summarized, "Since I'm paying for it, I'm going to make sure I eat there every day and get my money's worth." Beatrice lauds this practice, which builds interpersonal ties among community members:

> The basic good of this community in terms of intention is our lunch program where everybody sits with everybody, the seating rotates. It's really a genius of organization. But beyond that the times that you spend together here are more likely to be around some festival oriented work project or some ongoing thing that people do, such as the peace protest. When you come together and see each other repeatedly you get to be friends.

Although the protesters may not sit together at every meal they still gather in the same building daily, and utilize these opportunities to socialize with one another.

Beyond lunch, the protesters also jointly partake in a variety of other activities and events oriented toward peace that in turn strengthen their relationships, further solidify ideological beliefs, and align with their service-oriented mission. These include participating in the weekly flagpole vigil, serving on the peace committee that organizes the protest, attending social gatherings, and joining other political clubs and organizations. Indeed, many of the social happenings for individuals are politically oriented as well, suggesting a merging of personal and political interests (Passy & Giugni, 2000).

The flagpole peace vigil, which most protesters attend, occurs bi-weekly on the residential grounds. This site consists of an open grassy area located near the center of Sojourner Circle and is demarcated by the large American flag flying from a tall flagpole. Numerous protesters discuss this symbolic location as a site to collectively meditate and pray for peace. Eighty-three-year-old Lily described how this activity began: "Actually the protesters began to sponsor a group that meets at the flag pole twice a week ... for twenty minutes of silence just to think about what war is doing and a prayer for peace." And seventy-six year old Robert confirmed, "I keep going to the flagpole vigil and those who attend keep feeling outrage at what's going on in the world and keep wanting to figure out some things that we can do." The protesters started this event after the protest commenced to further advocate for peace. While the protest itself occurred approximately one mile from Sojourner Circle, the flagpole peace vigil transpired on the premises. Nepstad (2004) notes that rituals within communities help sustain beliefs, offer opportunities for interaction and assuage doubts.

Sojourner Circle protesters also formed a peace vigil committee that ensures the protest persists and devises strategies intended to improve resonance with bystanders. Janine, a protester for seven years and a member of this committee, described its purpose: "We meet regularly and strategize about how to change the signs and to think about how to create a memorial [in the honor of those who died], which becomes more important each year when the war is still grinding on. So it's very straight forward participation." Another committee member, John, remarked that the peace vigil committee also attends local community events in order to "voice their concerns" about the war.

There were regular social gatherings at houses of various SC protesters that provided opportunities to disseminate political views, discuss the war, share their feelings, and enrich bonds with one another. Some of these social events were more narrowly focused on addressing how the protest was going. Irene, a Catholic participant in the protest for 10 years, indicated such get-togethers built solidarity and connection among protesters while also carrying out the necessary maintenance for the weekly demonstration:

> [At these house meetings] you become more knowledgeable of their feelings and their points of view, and you share with them more than you have with some of the others as you're participating in this together. And at these occasional meetings – planning meetings – we give our points of view what we should be doing, what should be on the signs, how we should get better organized.

A spouse of a UCC pastor and member of Church Women United, Lily, confirms, "I'm friends with all of them, and more so because of the protest.

We do other social activities together as well, such as watch the presidential election or the results of different political races; we have numerous parties a year.[5]"

Octogenarian Irene points out that the peace protesters are Democrats and a majority is involved in the local Democratic Club, often attending party sponsored events and fundraisers.

> Most of us are part of this other group as well − the Democratic Party − trying to bring up issues like don't attack Iran. And we have a big thing down at the city hall, speeches and all. I was really proud that it came from the Democratic Party but also involved the peace protest group.

Political engagement among these individuals translates to multiple forms of action, including the protest; therefore producing intersections between personal and political spheres, a phenomenon found to foster normative commitment (Passy & Giugni, 2000). The mutual participation of protesters in an array of social and political events (e.g., Democratic Club, peace vigil committee, protest, house parties) ensures frequent contact between them and cements relationships. Moreover, social interactions among this network of individuals provide an established means of communication and evoke a sense of solidarity (Zhao, 2001). Such intensive socialization and shared practices among SC protesters elevates normative commitment to return to the protest each week. Although beliefs and motivations to advocate for peace may initially emerge from within individuals, they become validated and strengthened as a result of the routine social and political engagement with like-minded others.

Emotional Connections between Protesters

Recent research emphasizes the important role emotions play in social movements and finds they can deepen commitment to activism (Goodwin, Jasper, & Polletta, 2001; Jasper, 1997; Summers Effler, 2010). In fact, emotional fluctuations within the group often hinder or boost a movement, its activities, and affect member trajectories (Summers Effler, 2010). Emotional connections lend themselves to intimate relationships that engender affective commitment, which "develops through pleasurable interactions with fellow activists and through material or cultural rewards gained from movement participation" (Nepstad, 2004, p. 46). To that end, those who possess close bonds with other activists are more devoted to the movement and fellow participants (Barkan et al., 1995; Rogne, 2010).

SC protesters commonly referenced the notion of camaraderie and claimed a genuine affection for fellow protesters as a result of their shared experiences and investment in public opposition to the war. They not only felt an emotional connection to other protesters during their 1.5 hours of demonstration each Friday but the communal living offered ample opportunities to strengthen and maintain those bonds throughout the week via frequent social interactions.

Affective commitment is perhaps best captured in the concept *esprit de corps* – feelings of devotion and enthusiasm shared among group members (Blumer, 1939). Tom highlighted the relevance of affective ties and an esprit de corps among SC protesters: "I would say there's the benefit of the experience of working with a team of people on a regular basis and feeling a part of that company. There's camaraderie of the group, which is important ... and a sense of a common purpose." Richard clarified how the peace activists serve to inspire one another day in and out, a dedication perhaps more difficult to maintain when living apart from other activists: "The people that I'm with [fellow SC protesters] are very inspiring people, and we encourage one another. And that's something most don't necessarily find accessible in your normal lives."

Beatrice believed that the affective commitment transcends the protest site and spills over into their residential setting:

> Oh it's just a really warm bonding of being caught in the same thing, and we cross over paths in so many different ways. But there's a special awareness, you know, among the group that's willing to stand down there on Friday afternoons. We see each other over and over again, and it's a reaffirmation of who we are.

Stan likened the protesters to family, and explained their mutual participation generated a unique closeness for the activists: "I think there's a real camaraderie, real brothers and sisters in arms, so to speak. We are very supportive of one another. Well, you become more knowledgeable of their feelings and their points of view, and you share with them more than you have with the others [at Sojourner Circle]."

As a sign of affective commitment and the power of emotional ties, SC protesters frequently engaged in emotional care and support of one another. UCC pastor Robert provided the following poignant story about how he spontaneously attended the flagpole one evening when he was overcome with despair about the war. He recalled how other protesters rallied around him during this trying emotional time:

> There was one night when I watched the Moyer's news program and a marine went off to the war and left his fiancée at home. When he was there he was involved in an

explosion on the road that blew his face away, and when he came back his face looked like a potato, just no features on it at all. And I just was so outraged by that photograph. It summarized what I was watching every night on the news, what we're doing to our young people in this war. I just burst into tears and shouted and didn't know what to do with all of this rage I was feeling. And I went outside and sat at the flagpole at night. It was getting pretty dark, and I was out there for a couple of hours just crying most of the time. And others [from the protest] saw me and came out. They sat nearby and just let me be. They supported me and understood how I felt.

This scenario suggests the salience of emotions as they cultivate and deepen affective commitment among participants, which in turn reifies a Christian collective identity oriented toward peace. Compassion and emotional support for those adversely affected by the war is paramount among these individuals but it also is an operating principle among them, guiding their daily behaviors and interactions with fellow participants and enhancing their devotion to the group.

Accountability to the Protest and Fellow Members

Social ties are pivotal for movement recruitment and the mobilization of new members (Dixon & Roscigno, 2003; McAdam, 1988). SC peace activists utilize networks with other residents to create awareness about their protest and cause, mobilize others to attend the protest, and to garner broad support for their efforts. To achieve these goals they regularly make public speeches and community announcements, circulate petitions, and publish editorials on the subject of war. Activist generated expectations dictate that all protesters should perform such tasks, which helps keep current participants engaged. These normative guidelines therefore operate as informal social controls that uphold momentum and contribute to persistent engagement.

Savvy activists use communal gatherings as opportunities to disseminate information about peace-focused actions and events in order to generate enthusiasm for this cause. For instance, they capitalized on the time reserved for announcements during lunch each day to promote the weekly protest and other anti-war events in an effort to encourage new participants to join them. Stan, a protester for 9 years, recalled how he initially learned of the protest shortly after moving to SC: "Well, those involved in the protest would make announcements about it during lunch, so I just joined in ... it wasn't that hard to find out about it since people from this retirement community were announcing the details and why it was important." Keenly aware of the left-leaning tendencies of most SC residents, peace activists also used that to attempt to advance their group goals. Lily recounted how when the war first began, she and fellow peace protesters distributed petitions and a letter penned to President Bush that denounced war, called for its end, and advocated for alternative, nonviolent solutions. She emphasized, "There were many petitions against the war and this wonderful letter to Bush, you know, and we got many, many, many signatures from other residents."

Another common practice among protesters was to write and publish editorial pieces in newsletters and papers both internal and external to Sojourner Circle. They relied on such outlets to express their views and feelings about war, with the intention to shed light on government practices and rally support for anti-war efforts. Tom admitted it was a strategy to publicize their anti-war agenda in the hopes of generating broad support and to potentially recruit fresh faces: "Yes, we do a lot of soliciting. For our weekly [protest] event, we publicize it in our SC newsletter every week." This newsletter is circulated to all the community residents.

Many protesters regularly contributed editorial pieces to the city's local paper, *The Messenger*.[6] Beatrice, who attended the protest for 9 years, explained, "*The Messenger* is another example, it's the local newspaper that protesters keep getting articles into or getting coverage and things. Protesters are encouraged to write to editors and to do that to educate people about what's really going on [with the war]." Stan relied on numerous press outlets to showcase his views, including the community newsletter, *The Messenger*, and a letter writing campaign to elected officials. He summarized these activities:

> Then I send out these tirades (essays) from time to time to the members of the group via our community newsletter. I write to *The Messenger*, on average every quarter or so. Then I pester the representatives a little bit, not a whole lot. Well, we encourage each other to write letters to the editor, for instance. And the things I mentioned, supporting people in your vote, political system. And also writing your congressman or senator, secretary of state, or president.

Betty, a 79-year old, confirmed these practices:

> Well, we try to encourage our legislatures here by writing letters and so on. When we're preparing for any major event, we actually take fliers at the market nearby and hand out maybe five hundred fliers trying to get people to attend. We have a number of articles that appear in the local newspaper, *The Messenger*.

Protesters are also expected to participate in a big annual event to showcase their intentions — the city's annual Fourth of July parade.

They march as a group, carry signs and wear clothing that displays their stance on the war (e.g., tie-dyed peace shirts). Betty, a ten-year peace protester, described the event: "We had all the regular protesters and other people marching with signs in the parade behind the SC float. It was just amazing to us, from the time we started until we got through the whole mile, people never stopped clapping and standing up or waving flags."

Making announcements, circulating petitions, and publishing editorial pieces in media outlets certainly promoted the anti-war stance yet these efforts produced few new recruits from the community. While the protesters did occasionally enlist a fresh face from the residential grounds, in general the group number remained fairly consistent over time and hovered in the low teens. Instead these actions served an alternative and advantageous purpose that crafted normative commitment to the protest for current members: they enabled informal social controls to prosper within the group. As noted in the above statements, protesters were keenly aware of what fellow activists were doing to advance anti-war efforts. They even carpooled to the protest each Friday, so any absences drew attention and the absentee typically provided an excuse to justify it. One protester, Richard, even volunteered to write up summaries of what transpired at each protest and send it to all the participants after the event, which ultimately recorded who attended and who did not. A fellow protester explained: "He sends out on an email after each Friday, summarizing what happened, what the mood seemed to be, how many people attended ... just to give us all a little report." Betty confirmed that the weekly emails about the state of the protest perpetuate awareness and "keep a real contact and flow going between all of the protestors." These practices informally encouraged accountability among protesters and reminded them their actions were visible and scrutinized.

The public nature of the multitude of tasks (announcements to the community, publishing editorials and commentaries against war, distributing petitions, protesting, etc....), combined with frequent interactions among members, exerted pressure on protesters to follow suit. While service on behalf of others in some fashion was common for most SC community residents, relentlessly working to challenge war and advocate for world peace became normative for this small band of protesters. Protesters admit they are "encouraged" to regularly complete these actions by fellow participants, yet in effect it becomes an obligation fueled by mutual monitoring and accountability to others. In meeting such expectations, their normative commitment to the protest deepened.

PERSISTENCE VERSUS DISENGAGEMENT

My follow-up interviews with SC protesters in 2013 revealed that eight continued to protest each week, three reduced the frequency of their participation, and three completely disengaged. Those who persisted claimed they sustained high levels of commitment to this protest, with no end point in sight. Stan likened the anti-war protest to a sporting event: "Well, I'll stick with it 'til we win. Hopefully, we can put a stop to it. And even if you can't, you enter into a sport match, not with the assurance you're going to win, but you can keep trying even if you're not guaranteed to win." Janine's statement reflects her deep commitment for the long haul: "Until the wars are over. Does that mean the rest of my life? Maybe it will be." And Richard confirmed: "Yup, I'm going to keep showing up until I am unable to do so due to health problems. I think that if you talk to anyone in the group, they'd probably say that."

SC activists discussed their continued engagement as a product of communal relationships that are upheld by frequent interactions, peace-oriented tasks, accountability, and a shared spiritual purpose. For instance, Roberta, remarked: "I think we're a pretty close group. We're standing down there on the corner together every week. It's a nice relationship, one of solidarity ... I'm gonna keep doing it as long as the group keeps doing it." While she believes it is important to do something [to challenge war], Mildred makes it clear the community is responsible for her prolonged commitment: "I keep going to put the body out there. Because I think it's the right thing to do. But I think it's the community here. If it weren't for the community, I'm not sure I would do it. I feel like I'm part of something and I want to be part of it." Lily confirmed: "Well that you are doing something, and there are people ... that just expect us to be there, it's sort of amazing. Sometimes you'd think 'I'd just as soon not go today' and I think of the different ones from SC that are going regardless ... The source of our connection, which is quite a connection, is Sojourner Circle." In these cases, affective and normative forms of commitment buttress persistent participation.

Perceptions of efficacy, or markers of success, can help keep activists involved in a movement over time (Downton & Wehr, 1997). Peace protesters harbor a less concrete notion of success and efficacy, often linked to ideological beliefs (see Eller, 1991; Rogne, 1999). Eller (1991) found conscientious objectors to World War II understood that their efforts might not end the conflict, yet they framed success as a lengthy process, one that may take many years to come to fruition. By living according to a set of moral rules, informed by spiritual beliefs, they believed their actions would ultimately result in good (if unclear) outcomes because God will produce them. Downton and Wehr (1997) contend even when peace activists perceive little or no success, they felt obliged to continue due to ideological beliefs that peace and social justice work "was the right thing to do."

Similarly, while retaining the hope that world peace will someday ensue, the SC protesters measure success by much more modest markers. When asked about the efficacy of the protest, Steve responded: "I hope it has some impact to change people ... because to go down there and have several thousand cars pass in an hour, and sometimes not a single negative [sign] from motorists. And that in itself is a sort of a victory. And sometimes they even smile or wave at us." The group's acceptance of postponed success is reflected in Betty's statement: "Yes, I think what we do makes a difference but we know it [peace] probably isn't going to be accomplished in our lifetime. We keep on moving toward that, we keep on encouraging people to stand up for that, but we have to face the fact that it's not going to happen soon." As noted at the onset of the paper, it is an ethical and religious approach to peace activism that renders tangible markers of success less imperative.

Impediments to persistent movement participation typically encompass negative reactions and criticisms from significant others, lack of commitment, burnout, children in the home, and full-time employment (Downton & Wehr, 1997; Klandermans, 1997). A united outlook among members, evident in a shared ideology, can counter some of the issues that pose a threat to group cohesiveness (Swarts, 2008). These particular obstacles pose little threat of disruption for SC protesters given their biographical availability, shared ideology, and exposure to multiple community mechanisms that fortify commitment. Rather SC protesters face a different set of challenges to their prolonged engagement, typically associated with the life course, which tend to be physical in nature.

Altogether, six protesters altered their regular participation: three lessened the frequency of their attendance and three completely disengaged from the protest and its related activities. The reasons for these changes consisted of one or more of the following occurrences: (1) unavailability due to time constraints (2) decline in personal health, or (3) caretaker for spouse with poor health.

Mildred and Robert were faithful attendees at the protest until 2012 when they both took on new projects that occupied most of their time.

They are shifters, individuals who direct their energy to another project or social movement, a change that prompted either irregular attendance or complete disengagement (Klandermans, 1997). Mildred no longer attends the protest because she is consumed with a long-term writing project (a book) that she works on each afternoon. She expressed remorse for her absence: "It hasn't worked out for me to keep going because of time constraints but I am still supportive and I haven't changed my beliefs about the war. I am fully behind what they do." Robert still occasionally participates in the protest (once a month on average) but is unable to show up weekly like he did in the past because he is now the head volunteer coordinator for his church's annual convention, a very time-consuming position. He confirmed that most of the others SC protesters continue to protest regularly, and while his involvement lessened, his beliefs about the importance of their action have not diminished: "I still support the cause and I'd be in favor of continuing it even when the troops are withdrawn. There are always ways in which there are extensions of US military in places that don't make a lot of sense." Interestingly, they both note that their views and attitudes have not changed regarding this cause even though their participation decreased (see Whalen & Flacks, 1989).

The main reason for reduced participation or disengagement was due to a significant decline in personal health or in one's spouse's health. Beatrice, a persister who still protests weekly, confirms this cause: "We have people who have aged out. It's physical. They can't stand for an hour and a half or something anymore or are ill. I don't know anyone who stopped who got tired of the idea." Betty was one of the individual who completely desisted, a regular weekly attendee up until her health rapidly deteriorated in the final months before she passed away in 2012 due to a prolonged lung illness.

Lily and Steve, a married couple who regularly protested the war since 2003, also exemplify this phenomenon. A few years back Steve was diagnosed with Alzheimer's disease. Over the three-year span since his initial interview, Steve's mental and physical health diminished significantly and Lily became his primary caregiver, which consumed most of her days. Given these circumstances, they reduced their participation and now only attend once or twice a month, depending on Steve's condition. Alvin experienced both personal health problems and became caretaker for his ailing wife: "My knees bother me and standing there for an hour and half was really painful, and lasted even throughout the next day. Now I am a full-time caretaker to my wife, who has trouble getting around due to her illness of Parkinson's. So I have to help her get around and she can't be left alone really." Due to these health ailments, Alvin stopped attending the protest altogether.

CONCLUSION

This paper contributes to scholarly understanding of the relationship between community settings and persistent protest participation. To that end, I reveal an array of cultural and social mechanisms manifested within a community that amplify and sustain commitment to this protest event. The cultural mechanism consists of shared belief in the necessity of service on behalf of others, couched as a spiritual and moral duty. The social mechanisms include intersecting personal and political spheres, emotional connections between residents, and accountability to the group and its tasks. The cultural predilections of this community serve as the broader milieu where the social features unfold.

Past studies highlight certain community phenomena as they encourage sustained activism in social movements, including information dispersal, social networks and interaction among participants, personal bonds, organizational structures and affiliation, and even rituals (Corrigall-Brown, 2012; Downton & Wehr, 1997; Klandermans, 1997; Nepstad, 2008; Rogne, 2013). This study offers an in-depth examination of a religious retirement community to better elucidate the mechanisms that transpire in this context and the importance of collective identity, as both prompt commitment to prolonged protest attendance.

The SC protesters differed from other samples of peace activists as they operated as a self-contained local protest group rather than an SMO. The SC anti-war protesters were not formally organized, lacked clear leadership, did not hire staff members, possessed minimal group resources, and exhibited very loose connections to the broader peace movement. Although they supported the peace movement in principle, they claimed to have very little interaction with other anti-war activists and organizations outside this community. The data indicate their commitment is specific to this local protest and to their fellow participants, thereby creating a contingent form of devotion not necessarily transferable to other acts of civil disobedience or social movements.

Collective identity is also related to sustained engagement in activism. Research notes those with an activist identity are likely to participate much longer in an SMO compared to individuals with a value or organizational identity (Corrigall-Brown, 2012). Indeed, long-term members of a movement may be so thoroughly socialized into the activist role that they can no longer separate themselves from it (Downton & Wehr, 1997). Does this form of identity similarly explain persistence among SC peace protesters? I find a value-based collective identity, rather than an activist or organizational identity, is the essential glue that binds protesters to one another and sustains commitment to this cause. It is formed among certain SC residents invested in peace as an application of their religious ideology. While many SC protesters appeared to develop a generational consciousness during the Civil Rights era (Mannheim, 1952), many very few had "peace careers" that persisted over the life course (Downton & Wehr, 1997). Instead they dabbled in a variety of social justice causes, sometimes with social movement affiliation, that were then followed by periods of inactivity.

These Christian retirees do not form an identity based upon their past activism or from the broader peace movement, but instead derive a sense of "we-ness" from a shared interpretation of their faith that compels them to take action to oppose war. Many even view their participation as a form of atonement for the "sins" of others, an act intricately tied to religious identity. McAdam and Paulsen (1993, p. 659) observe that a movement's core tends to be composed of members who share "a strong subjective identification with a particular identity, reinforced by organizational and individual ties." This is clearly the case for the SC protesters. The community-based mechanisms increase the salience of this Christian pacifist identity while simultaneously enriching their commitment to one another to stay the course.

The residential context of Sojourner Circle enabled this identity to flourish in part because of its indigenous structure of free space — dense associational ties, strong integrated social networks, and lack of ties to groups in power (Polletta, 1999). As described earlier in the paper, protesters engaged in many mundane activities focused on peace advocacy, central for this setting to continue to function as a free space for activism (Glass, 2010). Through an examination of Sojourner Circle, and the mechanisms that transpire within its confines, this study demonstrates the intersection between community, identity and commitment as it engenders long-term protest participation.

Many movement activists tend to express optimism about the likelihood of success over time (Barr & Drury, 2009; McAdam, 1999), thereby creating favorable social psychological perceptions that sustain ongoing commitment to the movement (Barkan et al., 1995). SC protesters lacked such a hopeful outlook and instead acknowledged their efforts were not likely to produce global peace. Instead they embraced minimal markers of efficacy and acknowledged attaining "success," if it came, would be a lengthy process likely to exceed their lifetime (see Eller, 1991; Rogne, 1999). Given this admission, it is perhaps surprising they continued to protest and perform a variety of related peace tasks for 10 years. External markers of success did not serve as a source of motivation for this population, rather this paper asserts the community mechanisms and shared identity buttress commitment to prolonged protest engagement.

Scholars who investigate disengagement provide various explanations for its occurrence, such as time constraints based upon familial and work responsibilities, dissatisfaction with the movement, emotional drain, or a decline in commitment. With the exception of a few individuals, these factors did not generally disrupt SC protesters' persistent participation. The biggest catalyst of disengagement was the deterioration of mental and/or physical health associated with aging that precluded their regular attendance. Their commitment to the protest remained high despite their absence: only a few stopped completely and the rest attended periodically whenever their health or schedules permitted.

I recognize the small sample size and unique characteristics of this community (and its members) may not be easily generalizable to other contexts and activists. Therefore, future research should continue to analyze the ways in which community context influences sustained protest or other forms of movement participation. This paper offers valuable insights into the phenomena that occur among small community-based groups which fortify prolonged peace activism. Such findings can be a springboard for new lines of comparative inquiry about long-term engagement for those outside exclusive community contexts as well. The findings in this study suggest that reasons for disengagement are contingent on the life phase of participants, which others studies document. Yet few have discussed the specific experiences of elderly activists in relation to their persistence. As the American population ages there will be a greater number of those with biographical and situational availability (Downton & Wehr, 1997), who therefore make ideal candidates for initial recruitment *and* as highly committed, persistent participants. This population is one that warrants additional investigation by social movement scholars.

NOTES

1. A sense of community can form among social movement participants who live very disparate lives, even among those whose contact revolves solely around movement activities. The conceptualization of community used in this paper is different in that is refers to a physical place, largely insulated from outsiders, where all the protesters reside and frequently interact due to close proximity.

2. There were a few exceptions to this pattern. Beatrice was involved with the Peace-links throughout the 1980s and The Grail for most of her adult life, Betty was also a member of The Grail for multiple decades, and Roberta was a lay missionary for years in Nicaragua in her affiliation with Maryknoll, a worldwide Catholic missionary organization that advocates for peace.

3. I use the term "altruism" in line with Downton and Wehr's (1997, p. 19) definition: "values of loving and helping others."

4. The description of The Grail is as follows: "We are an international movement and community of women of different cultures, social backgrounds and generations. We trust in the Spirit of God, Mystery, and Source of Life. We are called to create a sustainable world, transforming our planet into a place of peace and justice" (http://www.thegrail.org/).

5. According to their website, Church Women United (CWU) is a Christian ecumenical women's movement that "brings together women of diverse races, cultures and traditions in closer Christian fellowship, prayer, advocacy, and action for peace with justice in the world" (http://www.churchwomen.org/).

6. The name of this local paper was changed to retain the anonymity of the community.

ACKNOWLEDGMENT

I want to thank Steve Boutcher, Catherine Corrigall-Brown, Gretchen Peterson, Molly Talcott, the anonymous reviewers, and RSMCC editor, Patrick Coy, for providing valuable feedback on this paper.

REFERENCES

Andrews, M. (1991). *Lifetimes of commitment: Aging, politics, and psychology*. New York, NY: Cambridge University Press.

Barkan, S. E., Cohn, S. F., & Whitaker, W. H. (1995). Beyond recruitment: Predictors of differential participation in a national antihunger organization. *Sociological Forum, 10*(1), 113–134.

Barr, D., & Drury, J. (2009). Activist identity as a motivational resource: Dynamics of (dis) empowerment at the G8 direct actions, Gleneagles, 2005. *Social Movement Studies, 8*(3), 243–260.

Blumer, H. (1939). Collective behavior. In R. E. Park (Ed.), *An outline of the principles of sociology* (pp. 221–280). New York, NY: Barnes & Noble.

Buechler, S. M. (2004). The strange career of strain and breakdown theories of collective action. In D. A. Snow, S. A. Soule, & H. Kriesi (Eds.), *The Blackwell companion to social movements* (pp. 47–66). Malden, MA: Blackwell.

Corrigall-Brown, C. (2012). *Patterns of protest: Trajectories of participation in social movements*. Stanford, CA: Stanford Press.

Coy, P. (2001). An experiment in personalist politics: The Catholic worker movement and nonviolent direct action, *Peace and Change: A Journal of Peace Research, 26*(1), 78–94.

Dixon, M., & Roscigno, V. (2003). Status, networks, and social movement participation: The case of striking workers. *American Journal of Sociology, 108*(6), 1292–1327.

Downton, J., & Wehr, P. (1991). Peace movements: The role of commitment and community in sustaining member participation. *Research in Social Movements, Conflict and Change, 13*, 113–134.

Downton, J., & Wehr, P. (1997). *The persistent activist: How peace commitment develops and survives*. Boulder, CO: Westview Press.

Eller, C. (1991). *Moral and religious arguments in support of pacifism: Conscientious objectors and the second world war*. New York, NY: Praeger.

Evans, S. M., & Boyte, H. C. (1986). *Free spaces: The sources of democratic change in America*. New York, NY: Harper and Row.

Gamson, W. (1991). Commitment and agency in social movements. *Sociological Forum, 6*(1), 27–50.

Gecas, V. (2000). Value identities, self motives, and social movements. In S. Stryker, T. J. Owens, & R. W. White (Eds.), *Self, identity, and social movements* (pp. 93–109). Minneapolis, MN: University of Minnesota Press.

Glaser, B. (1965). The constant comparative method of qualitative analysis. *Social Problems, 12*(4), 436–445.

Glass, P. (2010). Everyday routines in free spaces: Explaining the persistence of the Zapatistas in Los Angeles. *Mobilization, 15*(2), 199–216.

Goodwin, J., Jasper, J., & Polletta, F. (Eds.). (2001). *Passionate politics: Emotions and social movements*. Chicago, IL: University of Chicago.

Jasper, J. (1997). *The art of moral protest: Culture, biography, and creativity in social movements*. Chicago, IL: University of Chicago Press.

Klandermans, B. (1997). *The social psychology of protest*. Cambridge, MA: Blackwell Publishers.

Klandermans, B., & de Weerd, M. (2000). Group identification and political protest. In S. Stryker, T. J. Owens, & R. W. White (Eds.), *Self, identity, and social movements* (pp. 68–90). Minneapolis, MN: University of Minnesota Press.

Lofland, J., Snow, D., Anderson, L., & Lofland, L. (2006). *Analyzing social settings: A guide to qualitative observation and analysis*. Belmont, CA: Thomson/Wadsworth.

Maney, G. M., Coy, P. G., & Woehrle, L. M. (2009). Pursuing political persuasion: War and peace frames in the United States after September 11th. *Social Movement Studies, 8*(4), 299–322.

Mannheim, K. (1952). *Essays on the sociology of knowledge*. London: Routledge and Kegan Paul Ltd.

McAdam, D. (1988). *Freedom summer*. New York, NY: Oxford University Press.

McAdam, D. (1999). *Political process and the development of Black insurgency, 1930–1970.* Chicago, IL: University of Chicago Press.

McAdam, D., McCarthy, J., & Zald, M. (1988). Social movements. In N. Smelser (Ed.), *Handbook of sociology* (pp. 695–737). Beverly Hills, CA: Sage.

McAdam, D., & Paulsen, R. (1993). Specifying the relationship between social ties and activism. *American Journal of Sociology, 99*(3), 640–667.

McVeigh, R. (2001). God, politics and protest: Religious beliefs and the legitimation of contentious tactics. *Social Forces, 79*(4), 1425–1458.

Melucci, A. (1989). *Nomads of the present: Social movements and individual needs in contemporary society.* Philadelphia, PA: Temple University Press.

Meyer, J. P., Allen, N. J., & Gellatly, I. R. (1990). Affective and continuance commitment to the organization: Evaluation of measures and analysis of concurrent and time-lagged relations. *Journal of Applied Psychology, 75*(6), 710–720.

Morris, A. (1992). Political consciousness and collective action. In A. D. Morris & C. M. Mueller (Eds.), *Frontiers in social movement theory* (pp. 351–373). New Haven, CT: Yale University Press.

Munson, Z. (2002). *The making of pro-life activists: How social movement mobilization works.* Chicago, IL: University of Chicago.

Nepstad, S. E. (2004). Persistent resistance: Commitment and community in the plowshares movement. *Social Problems, 51*(1), 43–60.

Nepstad, S. E. (2008). *Religion and war resistance in the plowshares movement.* New York, NY: Cambridge University Press.

Passy, F., & Giugni, M. (2000). Life-spheres, networks, and sustained participation in social movements: A phenomenological approach to political commitment. *Sociological Forum, 15*(1), 117–144.

Polletta, F. (1999). Free spaces in collective action. *Theory and Society, 28*(1), 1–38.

Rogne, L. (1999). *The social contexts of persistence: Life stories of World War II conscientious objectors and war resisters.* Unpublished Ph.D. dissertation, University of Minnesota, Minneapolis, MN.

Rogne, L. (2010). The greatest generation revisited: Conscientious objectors and the good war. *Humanity and Society, 34*(1), 3–38.

Rogne, L. (2013). Courage is not something you have alone: Social supports and persistent peace activism among World War II conscientious objectors in the Minnesota twin cities. *Peace and Change, 38*(3), 310–329.

Rohlinger, D. A. (2002). Framing the abortion debate: Organizational resources, media strategies, and movement-countermovement dynamics. *The Sociological Quarterly, 43*(4), 479–507.

Schussman, A., & Soule, S. A. (2005). Process and protest: Accounting for individual protest participation. *Social Forces, 84*(2), 1081–1106.

Snow, D. A., & Soule, S. A. (2010). *A primer on social movements.* New York, NY: W.W. Norton and Company.

Stryker, S., Owens, T. J., & White, R. W. (Eds.). (2000). *Self, identity, and social movements.* Minneapolis, MN: University of Minnesota Press.

Summers Effler, E. (2010). *Laughing saints and righteous heroes: Emotional rhythms in social movement groups.* Chicago, IL: University of Chicago Press.

Swarts, H. (2008). *Organizing urban America: Secular and faith-based progressive movements.* Minneapolis, MN: University of Minnesota Press.

Taylor, V. (1989). Social movement continuity: The women's movement in abeyance. *American Sociological Review, 54*(5), 761–775.

Whalen, J., & Flacks, R. (1980). The Isla Vista 'bank burners' ten years later: Notes of the fate of student activists. *Sociological Focus, 13*(3), 215–236.

Whalen, J., & Flacks, R. (1989). *Beyond the barricades: The sixties generation grows up.* Philadelphia, PA: Temple University Press.

Zhao, D. (2001). *The power of Tiananmen: State-society relations and the 1989 Beijing student movement.* Chicago, IL: University of Chicago Press.

HUMOR, COLLECTIVE IDENTITY, AND FRAMING IN THE NEW ATHEIST MOVEMENT

Katja M. Guenther, Natasha Radojcic and Kerry Mulligan

ABSTRACT

In this paper, we demonstrate the linkages between humor and political and cultural opportunities and present an analysis of the importance of humor for collective identity and framing in the New Atheist Movement, a social movement focused on reducing the social stigma of atheism and enforcing the separation of church and state. Drawing on a qualitative analysis of interview, ethnographic, and web-based data, we show why the New Atheist Movement is able to use humor effectively in the political and cultural environment. We further demonstrate that humor is central to the development and maintenance of collective identity and to the framing strategies used by the New Atheist Movement. Through a diverse range of forms, including jokes, mockery, and satire, humor is a form of resistance and also can be harnessed to support the goals of social movements. We use this case study as a basic for advocating for greater attention to humor within

Research in Social Movements, Conflicts and Change, Volume 38, 203–227
Copyright © 2015 by Emerald Group Publishing Limited
All rights of reproduction in any form reserved
ISSN: 0163-786X/doi:10.1108/S0163-786X20150000038007

social movement studies, and greater attention to social movements in humor studies.

Keywords: Humor; social movements; New Atheist Movement; collective identity; framing

INTRODUCTION

The growing literature on emotions in social movements has drawn scholarly attention to how social movements access and amplify specific emotion states to mobilize constituents and garner public support (Goodwin, Jasper, & Polletta, 2000, 2001; Melucci, 1995). When addressing specific emotion states, this scholarship has tended to focus on anger as a mobilizing emotion. Yet more lighthearted feelings and sentiments also play an important role in social movements.

In this paper, we promote increased attention to the use and role of humor in social movements. With the rise of humor studies in other disciplines, including a journal and professional association dedicated to the field of humor studies, it is puzzling that humor remains at the sidelines of most sociological research in general and of sociological research on social movements in particular. Sociologists have a great deal to offer the field of humor studies, as the nascent sociological literature on humor shows, and we believe that humor as a site for analysis also has a great deal to offer sociology, including the sociology of social movements (see also Kutz-Flamenbaum, 2014). We use the case of the New Atheist Movement to demonstrate how humor is utilized in a specific social movement. Our goal is less to analyze humor in the New Atheist Movement and more to show how deeply embedded humor can be in social movements and what attention to humor can yield analytically. We hope this paper will move social scientists focused on social movements to consider humor as a more central component of their analyses.

Drawing on data from three years of fieldwork within the New Atheist Movement, we show how this particular movement uses humor to mobilize participants. This case study evidences how humor is especially involved in collective identity formation and maintenance and framing work, as well as how humor is shaped by political and cultural opportunities. Attention to humor thus enhances multiple areas of inquiry within the study of social movements. The paper makes an important contribution to scholarship on social movements by mapping a line of inquiry that considers the importance of humor for social movements and that seeks to understand when and why humor is possible and/or effective. A secondary contribution is our focus on a large and rapidly growing mobilization by a segment of the population — atheists and other religious non-believers — that has been significantly understudied in social science.

We begin by briefly introducing the field of humor studies and reviewing extant analyses of humor in social movements. After a discussion of our case and the methods used to examine it, we detail how opportunities for the deployment of humor by social movements are shaped by political and cultural context. We then show how humor is involved in some of the core areas of theoretical interest to scholars of social movements, namely collective identity formation and maintenance and framing. We conclude with suggestions for future directions in analyzing humor in social movements.

HUMOR IN SOCIOLOGICAL PERSPECTIVE

Humor takes on many forms and serves many functions in social life. Satire, mockery, jokes, and puns/wordplay are common forms of humor in contemporary US culture. Although some humor is mean-spirited, humor is often intended to make people laugh and to help them relax and feel lighthearted, as well as to feel better about themselves. Humor serves important social functions, although the study of humor has primarily remained with linguists, social psychologists, and anthropologists and less with sociologists. The role of humor in social life has been a subject of theorizing for centuries; Plato and Aristotle were among the first known to have examined humor through a philosophical lens. The study of humor considers both the stimuli and the response, and theories of humor have been grouped into numerous categories (Keith-Spiegel, 1972). One widespread system of categorization identifies three schools of theory of humor that focus on specific aspects of humor: (1) superiority theory, which emphasizes how humor involves feelings of superiority over other individuals or groups; (2) relief humor, which focuses on humor as a mechanism for relieving social and individual tension; and (3) incongruity theory, which conceptualizes humor as a response to a perceived incongruity (Kutz-Flamenbaum, 2014; Meyer, 2000). Humor involving superiority, relief, and incongruity all emerge in social movements.

Humor serves numerous functions in social life. Perhaps most obviously, humor is a powerful tool for lifting people's spirits in the face of adversity,

including social movement opposition. Humor can simultaneously enter-
tain and comment about the hardships of daily life (Berger, 1997), while
also providing emotional relief. Humor helps solidify social relations as it
increases social solidarity and contributes to the maintenance of group
cohesion and group boundaries (Cundall, 2012; Fominaya, 2007; Gouin,
2004; Wise, 2007). Marginalized groups utilize humor to manage stigma
and challenge authority (Black, 2012), and members of groups with con-
flicting interests or significantly different social statuses, such as inmates
and guards, use humor to manage tension (Franzén & Aronsson, 2013;
Nielsen, 2011). Humor is also a well-documented form of resistance (Basu,
2007; Davies, 2007; Haugerud, 2013; Lundberg, 2007; Wise, 2007). For
example, subordinates in workplace and educational settings use humor to
resist efforts by their superiors at controlling their behavior and productiv-
ity (Barnes, 2012; Huong, 2007; Korczynski, 2011).

In the context of social movements, humor is a common tool to enhance
mobilization. The small empirical literature on humor in social movements
tends to emphasize the unifying functions of humor. Social movement
actors may use humor as an "ice breaker" to help participants get to know
one another and build trust (Gouin, 2004). Humor can also help reduce
feelings of distrust and/or frustration when social movements struggle with
internal divisions or external challenges. For example, in her analysis of an
anti-capitalist social movement organization, Fominaya (2007) finds that
the organization uses humor to overcome internal divisions. Humor helped
attract and retain members. Humor offset the serious nature of the organization's political work, as members laughed together at situations that
would otherwise be considered depressing. Members also told funny stories
of failed attempts at civil disobedience, which helped them make light of
failures and created identification with movement actors. Humorous incidents become embedded and historicized, part of group lore and collective
memory that reinforces solidary (Fine & de Soucey, 2005).

Humor can also support efforts by leaders or other social movement
actors to appear relatable to supporters. In his analysis of the Zapatista
movement, Olesen (2007) finds that the Zapatistas built global support in
part through their use of humor. The Zapatistas, based in rural Mexico,
sought to connect with educated urbanites in Europe and North
America, and humor proved to be an especially effective tool for doing
so. Being funny made them human and relatable, even to people living in
other countries or under very different life circumstances. Similarly,
Sorensen (2008) found that the Serbian Otpor movement used humor to
attract new members. Their use of humor encouraged a view of the

movement as unique, "cool," and in sharp contrast to the rigid and repressive regime it opposed.

Beyond mobilizing functions, humor can be used strategically and tactically. First and Second Wave feminists used humor to challenge sexism and defy stereotypes of feminists as humorless. Feminists have also employed humor to establish that their intellectual acumen is equal to that of men (Cowman, 2007). Thus, feminists' tactical use of humor met strategic goals of challenging sexism and sexist ideologies. Activists involved in the AIDS Coalition to Unleash Power (ACT UP) also used humor tactically and strategically. Through joyful and humorous protests, ACT UP activists contested conservative claims that sexual freedom would lead to social decline and provided alternative images of what a more just and joyful society may look like (Shepard, 2005).

Political satire − a common form of humor utilized by social movements and other political and social actors because of its inherently critical slant − often serves to ridicule specific targets, thereby undermining their legitimacy and shifting their standing from object of public reverence to object of public ridicule (Anderson & Kincaid, 2013; Cohen, 2007; Haugerud, 2013; Lundberg, 2007; Paletz, 1990; Shepard, 2005; Sorensen, 2008; Teune, 2007). Satire focuses on exposing contradictions and challenging powerholders; it is not typically proscriptive of solutions to social, political, or economic problems. However, while not always proscriptive, satire can usefully help establish the existence of contradictions or other problems, identify particular targets, and may increase the public's interest in an issue as well as their willingness to support future resistance (Sorensen, 2008). Satire and other forms of humor are often ritualized in society, and thus may be politically permissible even when other forms of critical dissent are not. Guenther (2010), for example, recounts how East German *kabarett* performers satirized the socialist leadership, receiving rave reviews from the leaders themselves. Thus, beyond serving organizational and mobilizing purposes, humor can help advance movement goals.

Although the extant literature on humor in other social contexts suggests that the inclusion of humor into social movement studies would be worthwhile, there has been little effort to do so. This paper reiterates, updates, and expands a largely unheeded call to social movement scholars made 30 years ago (Hiller, 1983) to incorporate humor. Our goal is to stimulate deeper engagement with humor among scholars of social movements so that the uses and effects of humor can be better understood. To help achieve this goal, we present an analysis of humor within one contemporary social movement, the New Atheist Movement.

CASE BACKGROUND AND METHODS

The present analysis draws on data from an ethnographically oriented research project of the New Atheist Movement. Since the early 2000s, the New Atheist Movement has sought to activate atheism as a collective identity and basis for mobilization. Although many atheists are not involved in atheist activism, and even many who do not identify with the label "New Atheist," New Atheism dominates atheist organizing in the US. New Atheism is a big tent identity open to atheists and other religious non-believers − including agnostics, freethinkers, and humanists − who want to promote the separation of church and state and to reduce the stigma of being irreligious in the United States. Many of the New Atheists have responded to the call of public intellectuals such as Richard Dawkins, Sam Harris, and Christopher Hitchens, who have collectively authored more than a dozen bestselling books decrying religion and promoting the atheist belief system (e.g., Dawkins, 2006, 2010; Dennett, 2007; Harris, 2004, 2008, 2010; Hitchens, 2007a, 2007b; Stenger, 2007). The internet, including dozens of forums, blogs, chat rooms, and sites where visitors can read essays on atheism or view podcasts of atheist lectures and debates, appears to be important in the formation of these groups. Websites like Meetup.com have facilitated the emergence of face-to-face groups of atheists (Cimino & Smith, 2014). In addition to the growth of informal grassroots groups, formal atheist organizations have grown significantly and atheist organizing has become more politicized. Existing organizations have witnessed significant growth in membership. The Freedom From Religion Foundation (FFRF), for example, nearly tripled its membership between 2005 and 2011, while American Atheists almost doubled theirs in the 18 months after appointing David Silverman, an outspoken, publicity-seeking, and self-described "trouble-making" atheist as its Executive Director in 2010. While membership in these organizations is still small − FFRF and American Atheists combined barely have 20,000 members − their rapid growth points to increased interest in atheist organizing. A number of these major organizations also co-sponsored the Reason Rally, a secular political rally in March of 2012 in Washington, DC, in support of reducing stigma against religious non-believers and advocating the separation of church and state. The event was reported as the largest political rally of atheists and other non-believers in US history.

Thus, while historically atheists and other religious doubters were largely invisible and unorganized in the US, and secular activism either occurred behind closed political doors or under the rubric of other issues

(Jacoby, 2004), non-believers have been making more public statements in defense of their religious faithlessness since 2000. Secularism of course has a long and well-documented history in the United States (Baruma, 2010; Jacoby, 2004), but, as Cimino and Smith (2014) detail, the New Atheism represents a break from secular politics with its emphasis on coming out as atheist, generating atheist pride, and promoting activism by atheists to achieve diverse goals. Although the movement disavows proselytizing, it seeks to promote critical thinking and scientific reasoning, and routinely challenges the tenets of religious faith. The movement is comprised of at least a dozen national-level organizations that differ in many ways, including size, scope, strategy, and ideology, but which are bound by a shared commitment to making atheism an accepted identity and practice in the United States and to ensuring the separation of church and state (Cimino & Smith, 2014).

The research strategy for the broader research project from which this paper draws has two prongs, one of which focuses on local-level atheist organizing in southern California, a hotbed of atheist organizing, and a second which focuses on national-level organizing across the United States. The lead author, with some assistance from graduate and undergraduate assistants, attended organizing meetings, social events, conferences, and rallies organized at the local and national levels between 2010 and 2012. Field notes from these events are an important data source.

Another key source of data are 51 in-depth interviews, 26 with participants who are primarily (albeit not exclusively) involved in local-level atheist organizing in southern California, and 25 with participants involved in atheist organizing in other parts of the United States and/or nationally. Respondents include the directors of the largest and most visible atheist organizations in the United States (e.g., American Atheists, FFRF, Atheists Alliance, Secular Student Alliance), as well as staff members and volunteers within national and local-level organizations. Interviews lasted 60–120 minutes and reviewed both the personal history of the interview subject's relationship to atheism and atheist organizing, as well as their understanding of the goals, accomplishments, and deficits of the organization(s) with which they are involved. Because one goal of the larger research project from which this paper is drawn is to examine issues of diversity in social movements, women and people of color, who are underrepresented among movement leaders and participants, are overrepresented in our sample. Women and people of color together represent over half of the sample, whereas we estimate that together they constitute less than a quarter of participants in the New Atheist Movement.

The educational distribution of our sample reflects the movement's demographics more accurately. Almost all participants held college degrees, and more than a third held a degree beyond the Bachelor's degree. The overwhelming majority of respondents live in major metropolitan areas (albeit often in suburbs rather than urban cores), and a handful live in smaller towns. None resided in rural areas at the time of the interview.

During the course of the interviews, respondents discussed how they came to identify as an atheist or other religious non-believer and how they became involved in atheist organizing. They also responded to questions about their political views, their activism, and the atheist organizations with which they are involved, including questions about organizational ideology and strategy. Interviews were transcribed and coded with the assistance of Atlas.ti to identify themes and inconsistencies. Since humor permeated interviews, we consider the full interviews for this paper.

Finally, our analysis draws on written movement documents. These include the 2013 volume of the monthly newsletter of the FFRF, postings on major atheist websites (including discussion boards) in 2012, and materials handed out to participants at atheist events we attended between 2010 and 2012, including complimentary magazines, bumper stickers, flyers, etc.

Our analysis of all the data focused on identifying instances of humor being used and considering the content and type of humor, the apparent purpose or function of the humorous incident, and, when it was possible to evaluate, the effect of the use of the humor on participants. Because we have different types of data, we were able to triangulate data and seek out patterns and inconsistencies. Regarding humor, our data are quite unequivocal: humor is tremendously important in the New Atheist Movement, where it serves a number of purposes we detail in the following sections.

THE CONTEXT OF HUMOR: POLITICAL AND CULTURAL OPPORTUNITIES

For the New Atheist Movement, humor is a culturally available and appropriate tool that helps further its goals of de-stigmatizing atheism, challenging religious beliefs, and upholding the separation of church and state. Although the New Atheist Movement clearly makes extensive use of humor in working toward its goals, humor may not always be a viable tactic for social movements. Social movements may face particular restrictions on the use of humor in specific political and cultural environments (Hart,

2007). In some politically repressive contexts, mocking leaders can be a basis for punishment or threat of punishment. While extant conceptualizations of formal repression do not typically incorporate it, humor, like other forms of expression, can be subject to repression, and considering the acceptability of humor enhances understanding of repression. The ways in which the New Atheist Movement incorporates humor into its movement culture is made possible by the broader culture and its tolerance for questioning authority, challenging religious leaders, and making "off color" jokes. In other times and places, these humor strategies would not be possible for legal and socio-cultural reasons. In repressive contexts, for example, we might expect allegorical satire to be more widespread than directly confrontational humor styles.

Social movement leaders and participants must also have appropriate cultural knowledge to use humor effectively (Kuipers, 2006). When used inappropriately, humor runs the risk of offending targets and/or potential constituents and driving them away. For instance, Basu (2007) describes how the Levellers, a British anti-monarchy social movement in the mid-1600, typically relied on humor in order to garner support. Although the strategy benefitted the movement in some ways, it also provoked a moral backlash in the Puritan-dominated culture, in which laughter and joking were considered both frivolous and ungodly. Thus, humor may not always be strategically wise, nor may all groups be equally viable targets of humor.

A movement may also need to make a degree of cultural progress prior to engaging in combative humor; the New Atheist Movement, for example, has engaged in extensive public relations campaigns focused on how atheists are everyday people, which may have opened doors for more confrontational humor. In the contemporary US, the humor tactics of the New Atheist Movement may be further reinforced by the presence of celebrity humorists who also deride religion, such as Bill Maher and Julia Sweeney. The New Atheist Movement is thus able to draw on – and seek to further expand – a broader culture in which it is socially acceptable to make jokes about religious beliefs, practices, and believers.

In the contemporary United States, jokes about religion are generally widespread and both political and cultural spaces exist in which atheists can make jokes about religion (Kuipers, 2006). Religiously disparaging jokes have a long history in the United States, told by a wide range of social actors. Today, atheists are most able to make jokes about religious groups who are already joked about in the broader culture. Catholics and Mormons, who have long been derided by other Christians, are fair game for atheist mockery, and humor in the New Atheist Movement overwhelmingly focuses on religious extremists such as the Religious Right, as well as religious leaders. Jews, who have a history of violent persecution, are not a group that atheists ridicule. For atheists, the pedophilia scandal in the Catholic Church, which received a good deal of media attention during our period of fieldwork, opened up opportunities for jokes about Catholics, as it did in the broader culture. A popular atheist bumper sticker slogan makes a play on the adage, "Absence makes the heart grow fonder" by stating that, "Abstinence makes the church grow fondlers." Our research reveals that Islam tends to be treated primarily as a threat and less as a subject of jokes, likely reflecting dominant US cultural beliefs about Islam as frightening and problematic. Buddhism, which is a major world religion, receives almost no attention of any kind, apparently because respondents view it as both irrelevant in the US context and as non-threatening (Guenther, 2014). Who is subject to ridicule thus reflects a set of socio-historical dynamics that establish parameters for acceptable targets of humor.

A political and cultural context in which making jokes at the expense of religious belief is accepted has facilitated the routinization of this humor within the New Atheist Movements. By way of one example, as part of a movement strategy for positioning atheists as good and moral and religious people as morally suspect, the FFRF publishes a monthly newspaper, *Freethought Today*, which features a large spread — typically at least two full pages — under the title, "Black Collar Crime Blotter." The spread itemizes moral transgressions by religious leaders such as priests and pastors, as well as transgressions involving missionaries or that took place in religious buildings or at religious events; most involve police or court actions and the blotter is broken down into sections on Arrested/Charges, Pleaded/Convicted, Sentenced, Civil Lawsuits Filed, Civil Lawsuits Settled, Legal Developments, Allegations, Removed/Resigned, and Other. The blotter details cases of sexual abuse and rape (often involving children), fraud, and drug and alcohol-related crimes, all of which point to the particular immorality of religious leaders. The blotter can be read as quite a sad document as it necessarily reflects a good deal of human pain and suffering, yet it primarily incites chuckles and laughter. This is both because of the outlandishness of the crimes and because the blotter often includes details that seem intended to create mirth, such as quotes in which offenders' justify their actions based on religious grounds atheists will see as ridiculous (i.e., "I assaulted that girl because she had Satan in her"). The blotter thus invites laughter, as well as moral outrage, and effectively positions religious people as deviant and as hypocritical. The blotter is made possible by a broader culture amenable to questioning religious authorities, and where, in fact, such challenges, like the investigations into sexual abuse by priests in the Catholic Church, are widely seen as promoting the social good.

Political and cultural contexts influence the subject of humor, such as which groups can be targeted in jokes, and also the content and mode of delivery of humor. The New Atheist Movement incorporates humor into a range of socially accepted media, including cabaret-style song, lectures and presentations (including on-line podcasts, which are popular in the movement), newsletters, and websites and discussion boards. In contemporary society, where very little is off limits in terms of joking, humor can involve sex, swear words, and social taboos, and the New Atheist Movements uses each of these in its humor. Movement participants seem to use language generally accepted in the broader culture, as well as in comedy more narrowly, in their jokes; for instance, atheist humor often uses the derogatory word "bitch," which is widely used in US culture, including comedic culture. The use of swear words and sexual innuendo in New Atheist humor further establishes distance between atheists and religious people.

HUMOR FOR COLLECTIVE IDENTITY

Humor serves many functions for social movements. A core contribution humor can make is to building and maintaining collective identity, or the cognitive, moral, and emotional connections between individuals and a broader community (Polletta & Jasper, 2001). Humor in the New Atheist Movement is important for collective identity in several ways. *First*, humor creates an opportunity to build collective identity among diverse movement participants. Like most movements, the New Atheist Movement involves people with various orientations, such as agnostics, secular humanists, and atheists, as well as individuals with different political ideologies and social locations. Humor breaks the ice, and relaxes people, which may be especially beneficial for newcomers to the movement, who may still be coming to terms with their atheistic identities. At pre-planned atheist gatherings such as conferences and rallies, we found that humor consistently appeared within the first 10 minutes of events, and often within the first few minutes. As one movement leader told the first author while talking informally at an atheist event, scheduling humorous people as speakers is used to "warm" the audience and "bring folks together" by highlighting their "commonalities." To this end, at atheist conferences we attended, which are a key site for New Atheist organizing, humorists and comedians comprised at least 1/6th and sometimes as much as 1/4th of presenters; this figure does not include portions of lectures or presentations by non-humorists and non-comedians that may still have humorous or comedic content.

Second, humor helps individual atheists manage the stigma associated with being an atheist, providing them with a shared strategy for coping with stigma and challenging religious belief. One respondent shares a common view in our sample about the employment of humor:

> Honestly, my favorite way of coping with hostility [against atheists] is probably just humor … I try to use humor a lot. Humor helps me personally in that if someone's being particularly mean to me, it helps be able to laugh it off, and not take it so seriously …

Humor thus enables people to protect themselves from hostility when they "laugh off" religious ideas or negative interactions with people who express bias against them. Experiences "laughing off" religion are widely shared at atheist gatherings, such that humor is an individual and collective strategy in coping with stigma.

Third, being funny is an identity the movement can appeal to, and has become a central feature of what it means to be an atheist among atheists who are part of the New Atheist Movement. That is, individual atheists tend to see themselves as having a good sense of humor, place high social value on humor as a personality characteristic among other atheists, and participate in New Atheist events in part because they are fun and funny. Our respondents, and the presentations of self we encountered at atheist events, consistently emphasize that to be an atheist is to be funny. A number of interview respondents cited the shared laughter and the "good sense of humor" of the group when identifying reasons they participated in atheist organizing. Others described humor as an important part of the atheist media (including books, blogs, videos, and music) they enjoyed. Still other participants used good humor as a criterion for admiring a particular movement leader or movement celebrity; among local-level groups, the funny people in the group were similarly subject to admiration. Analyses of micromobilization reveal that social movements mobilize participants by tapping into multiple, often overlapping, existing identity categories that they already hold (Viterna, 2013); the New Atheist Movement appeals to participants with identities as atheists, humorous people, and, interactively, humorous atheists.

Comedy is deeply embedded in the movement, reflecting the centrality of humor to this movement's identity and the identities of its participants. At atheist conferences and rallies alike, comic elements routinely take center stage, and humorists/comedians are among the most celebrated participants in the movement. The Reason Rally included comedic video presentations by world-renowned satirist Bill Maher and comic Eddie Izzard. Former *Saturday Night Live* star Julia Sweeney is also a regular at large atheist events. Dan Barker, the co-director of the FFRF, is a pianist and singer who always plays music and sings at FFRF events. The overwhelming majority of his songs mock religion and reflect dominant beliefs within the movement. His most recent recorded album, from which he has performed at many atheist events, set previously unpublished lyrics by Yip Harburg, the atheist lyricist of *The Wizard of Oz*, to music, including songs like "Lead Kindly Light":

> Where Bishop Patrick crossed the street
>
> An "X" now marks the spot.
>
> The light of God was with him,
>
> But the traffic light was not.

These lyrics are both funny *and* highlight the atheistic belief in the importance of science and technology (i.e., the traffic light) and the danger of simply "having faith."

Tim Minchin, a comedic singer/songwriter and the writer of the Broadway musical *Matilda*, is a regular headliner at major atheist events, like the Reason Rally, and is a popular recording artist among atheists. Several of his songs comically take on faith, undermining religious belief while simultaneously engaging in comedy. Minchin's song "Thank You God," for example, responds to a news item about a boy named Sam who thanked God for fixing his mother's cataracts after they appeared to vanish when 700 people prayed for her. In the song, in which Minchin sings along to a cheerful piano melody, Minchin humorously and systematically debunks God's involvement in the cataract repair. Through the lyrics of the song, which could not be reprinted here due to permissions issues, Minchin irreverently points out that miracles require praying to specific gods in specific places and sarcastically observes that miracles cannot be better explained by science (in this case, especially surgical advances) or even coincidence. He refers to religious people as experiencing "confirmation bias," "group think," and "mass delusion." Minchin's song thus mocks religious belief while simultaneously challenging the validity of religion. The song iterates beliefs central to movement identity, such as that religious people are deluded and irrational and that benign gods would help all people, not just select grandmothers with cataracts. The song does this by employing humor, which is a key part of how atheists see themselves and which may also help atheists' critiques of religion seem less threatening. Minchin is consistently rewarded with enthusiastic standing ovations at atheist events that suggest crowd approval for his humorous approach to debunking religion, as well as a group identity as people who recognize and appreciate good humor.

Fourth, humor is central to establishing social movement boundaries. Creating an atheistic identity as funny serves to establish and maintain boundaries between atheists and religious believers.[1] Religious people, in the framework of the New Atheist Movement, are droll and humorless. Atheists, in contrast, know how to have fun. Atheists involved in the movement also connect humor and intelligence, such that being clever and witty is a marker of atheist identity.

Some of our respondents expressed finding humor and pleasure simply in the act of experiencing conflicts with religious believers, which serve to create and reinforce boundaries. In reflecting on his path toward participation in an atheist rock band, one interview respondent identified critiquing religion as inherently humorous. Brandon, a male in his mid-twenties, said:

> ... For some reason, it's just really, really funny to me to be offensive about certain subjects .... Like if I hear someone start talking about religion and if I hear something that really bothers me, I'll say something to them. [I will] be like: "Excuse me, do you realize you are really just uninformed? You know you don't know what you're talking about, right?" I get a laugh out of it. (laughs).

This respondent thus reports finding the act critiquing religion fun and pleasurable, and he finds it humorous to critique religious people. The types of interactions he describes allow atheists to reaffirm their atheist identity while also upholding their view of religious believers as inferior/ uninformed.

Ultimately, humor is a major component of collective identity processes in the New Atheist Movement. Movement leaders and participant use humor to welcome new members, reinforce solidarity among existing members, and establish boundaries between movement participants and outsiders, especially religious people and institutions. Being funny and having a sense of humor in this particular movement are even core parts of the primary identity associated with the movement; so prized is humor in the culture of this movement that it would be an insult to accuse another atheist of not having a sense of humor.

HUMOR FOR FRAMING

Frame theory focuses on how shared meanings and ideas influence understandings of issues and events (Benford & Snow, 2000). Social movement frames are often carefully developed self-presentations that social movement actors use to emphasize certain aspects of an issue. Frames provide schema for making sense of issues, and are typically oriented toward promoting a specific form of mobilization.

Humor often manifests in frames. The present analysis suggests that humor is central in depicting opponents in a negative light. *First*, framing strategies represent opponents as ridiculous. By subjecting them to ridicule, atheists undermine attempts by the religious to frame their goals as holy or divine. For instance, a group of religious skeptics who call themselves Pastafarians, or "followers" of the Church of the Flying Spaghetti Monster, purportedly believe that life as we know it was created by a highly intelligent creature made of spaghetti noodles who continues to shape the Earth through "His noodly appendage." Although the Church's website claims that it is *not* satire (Church of the Flying Spaghetti Monster, 2013), the intent is clearly to draw parallels between the ridiculousness of believing in a higher power such as the contemporary understanding of God and the ridiculousness of believing in a higher power such as a pasta-based deity. The flying spaghetti monster is often used as short hand by atheists to reference the ridiculousness of all religious belief. In describing her skepticism toward any non-evidence based beliefs, one respondent said, "The flying spaghetti monster, it's a good joke. It's funny. But it's true. It's exactly as plausible as anything else." This comic tool frames religion as ridiculous and as worthy of ridicule.

At atheist conferences and rallies, speakers routinely also mock specific religious beliefs. At the 2012 Freedom from Religion convention, several speakers jokingly invoked Mitt Romney's Mormon belief in "magic underwear" and "his destiny to have his own planet" (one speaker also much more seriously expressed concern that the American public did not question the suitability of a presidential candidate who held such "unintelligent" beliefs). Being "struck down" is also a repeated joke; at atheists gatherings, when someone either admits to or engages in what they think Evangelical Christians would consider a transgression, such as swearing or being gay, they marvel laughingly that they have not yet been struck down, sometimes making physical motions that mimic how they might try to shield themselves if struck by a divine lightning bolt. Many New Atheist events include presentations from former religious leaders such as ex-ministers. Jerry De

Witt, a former Pentecostal minister cum atheist, usually has the audience yell "Darwin!" at those moments in a sermon when a minister might ask the congregation to yell, "Amen!" This punctuating shout invariably draws laughter from the audience. Shouting back to a minister seems silly to atheists probably in large part because they are neither accustomed to it nor are they accustomed to any call-and-response presentation style.[2] Furthermore, they know that yelling "Darwin!" in place of a religious affirmation is both transgressive and ridiculous, which makes it funny.

Second, framing strategies represent opponents as distant from the mainstream culture. The New Atheist Movement frames opponents – that is, religious people and institutions – as violating core national values. Specifically, atheist humor contributes to framing religious believers as unfair, undemocratic, and irrational because their political and social views are clouded by religion. For example, as a speaker at a 2011 regional freethought conference, Rebecca Watson prompted a great deal of laughter from the audience in her framing of the Alliance Defense Fund, a conservative Christian advocacy organization, as a paranoid and irrational organization that believes SpongeBob Square Pants, a popular children's cartoon character made out of a sponge, was part of the "gay agenda." Watson's invocation of this belief framed religious believers as zealots unable to respond "normally" to a seemingly harmless children's cartoon. Likewise, the New Atheist Movement frames religious believers and the state actors who support their efforts, such as judges who rule in favor of keeping the Ten Commandments posted in public places, as unfair and as violating core US principles like freedom of religion and equal representation. This framing strategy accomplishes several things: (1) it highlights difference between atheists and religious believers; (2) it emphasizes difference between religious believers and mainstream Americans; and (3) it obscures the fact that the majority of religious believers in the United States have weak (if any) ties to religious institutions and/or do not seek to use state policy to maintain their religious beliefs. Humor thus contributes to setting up an "us versus them" dynamic.

Similarly, framing atheists as pro-science and religious believers as antiscience further emphasizes social distance between religious people and atheists, and connects the New Atheist Movement to a host of policy issues, like teaching evolution in schools, reproductive rights, and the role of faith in medicine. Science and reason are central concepts in the New Atheist Movement, and are core framing tools that position religion as *un*scientific and *un*reasonable. Much of this framing work is serious, but humor consistently emerges here, as well. A symbol in the New Atheist

Movement (and among those who support teaching evolution in schools) is an image of the fish, a symbol of Jesus, with feet and sometimes a tool, to suggest evolution. Sometimes the words "Darwin," "Evolution," or "Atheist" are written in the middle of the fish. A more confrontational symbol shows the fish on a barbeque. Additional symbols show dinosaurs eating fish, and slogans state, "My dinosaur ate your Jesus fish." These images are mock religious belief, while also asserting the primacy of science and reason over religious belief.

A deliberately humorous protest likewise functioned to mock religious beliefs and frame religious people and beliefs as irrational and out of touch with mainstream practices and beliefs. Atheist blogger Jennifer McCreight, who was a respondent in this study, used a humorous protest event to counter claims by an Iranian Islamic cleric that women's immodesty causes earthquakes. She recounts:

> When I saw this [claim by the cleric], I'm like, 'That's ridiculous!', and, 'How dare you say that you know women happening to not dress to his standards basically cause earthquakes?' So the way I chose to respond to it was basically I made a blog post and said, 'Hey, on this day, we're gonna test his scientific hypothesis and I'm gonna dress immodestly and show a little cleavage and we'll see if we can cause a boobquake ...' It went viral; it was like five hundred thousand people on Facebook said they were participating and [it] got covered by CNN and every other major news network ... I think the reason why it went viral is because it was funny. It was because we didn't take him seriously. I could have gotten mad and written this post that was very feministy about how he was treating women, or I could have done a scientific post about how earthquakes actually happen, but it was more, it was more effective to be like, 'Alright, we know this guy is wrong, and let's kind of laugh at him' instead.

Boobquake thus differentiated between two groups: the Islamic cleric and other religious people like him, and purportedly rational people who do not believe natural disasters are a punishment from a higher power – a group presumably much larger than atheists alone, who through this virtual protest became participants in an atheist event. Jennifer's comments further hit on a key point about the use of humor: making fun of someone or something can be more effective than attempting to make more sophisticated arguments (such as feminist or scientific arguments, in this instance). She attributes the viral take-off of and media attention to Boobquake to its humorous content. Simultaneously, Boobquake challenged a religiously based view of the world.

A final framing strategy involves using humor to deny the claims of opponents. Atheists employ humor to flip a dominant cultural belief on its head and assert that atheists are moral, patriotic, and intelligent, while religious believers are not (see Edgell, Gerteis, & Hartmann, 2006 for a discussion of the othering of atheists in the United States). Popular slogans on t-shirts and signs at atheist events have pithy messages such as, "Good without God," "Freedom Requires Freethinkers," "Patriotic Atheist," and "One Nation Indivisible."

Danny reported in an interview how a group of atheists responded with humor to people hostile to a small street-corner protest they held aimed at attracting new members and combating stigma. Group members held pro-atheist signs on a Sunday morning at a busy street corner. Several people passing by responded with hostility; the atheist protestors in turn reacted with humor. As Danny recalls:

> One of the funniest [reactions] is, I remember one person actually just flipped us off. And then we waved to him and smiled. Then he flipped us off again and looked at us weird (laughing). And then we did it again! And he got confused.

In this narrative, the atheists hold the moral higher ground; while the hostile passer-by (who the atheists present seemed to assume was religious) used a rude gesture for a swear word — an action of which their religion would presumably not approve — the atheists smiled and waved. Their response ultimately befuddled the hostile passer-by and humorously inverted who is "good" and "bad." This story and similarly humorous narratives about moral transgressions by religious people are often retold at atheist gatherings, as they allow members to challenge conventional views of religious believers as more moral than atheists by framing religious believers as hostile and hypocritical and atheists as more sane, calm, and kind.

The use of framing through humor is especially common in cases of protest and counter-protest, as was apparent at the Reason Rally. During the Rally, protestors from the Westboro Baptist Church ringed parts of the event (the gay son of the founder of the right wing Westboro Baptist Church was among Rally speakers, thus attracting Westboro's attention), waving placards that read "God Hates Atheists," "God Hates Fags," and Biblical excerpts. Atheists responded with signs reading, "Religion: Because Thinking Is Hard," "Dodo [with an image of a Dodo bird, a species now extinct], We're Not In Alabama Anymore," "God Hates Facts," "Fine ... I Evolved You Didn't," and, grabbing especially a lot of attention, a man dressed as Jesus holding a sign reading, "I have 99 Problems; This Bitch Ain't One" with an arrow on the sign pointing to a religious protestor wrapped in the US flag reading, "God Hates Fags."[3] Through such challenges, participants in the New Atheist Movement jockey for the upper hand in the science versus religion debate, using humor to try to demonstrate that they are clever and smart, and thus superior to — and even more evolved than — religious believers.

The New Atheist Movement uses many frames that do not involve humor, but the pervasiveness of humor in the movement's framing strategies suggests that using humor as part of their frames is strategic. The movement seeks to make a mockery of religious believers and religious institutions by highlighting the absurdity of religious belief and the outrageousness of the actions of some religious believers. Humor for this particular social movement may be especially advantageous because, as one interviewee noted, it offers a less overtly threatening challenge to religion, while simultaneously causing people some discomfort and forcing them to rethink their religious views:

> Gentle mockery is also helpful for the people who are being mean or dismissive, or discriminatory, because it's a kind of a more gentle way that [I can convey], 'Hey, I'm not taking you seriously and what you're saying is bad,' instead of just harshly saying that. I think it kind of is a slower way to wake people, or a more gentle way to wake people up to their behavior.

This respondent, like others, views humor as a less confrontational way to challenge religious believers than other available strategies.

Many of our respondents echo the sentiment that humor does not appear as hostile as a direct critique based on science or focused on politics. The humor of the New Atheist Movement also tends to target the most extreme of religious beliefs — such as those held by members of the Westboro Baptist Church — and thus may serve to highlight for more moderate religious people that they have more in common in terms of their values with atheists than with some religious people. Humor, some respondents noted, also has greater mass appeal than the more intellectually complex debates about science and faith that involve philosophy, psychology, biology, and physics, among other academic fields. Humor is thus accessible to a broader public — including adherents, participants, and audiences — in ways that other elements of the movement's discourses and activities are not. However, although none of our respondents specifically discussed this, our observations suggest that humor is also intended to ruffle feathers, particularly of outspoken opponents, such as the Westboro Baptist Church members who engaged in the counter-protest at the Reason Rally. For movement insiders, humor helps manage stigma, builds collective identity, establishes who belongs in the movement, and frames opponents negatively to promote continued mobilization; for movement outsiders, humor may well be seen as hostile and threatening.

CONCLUSION

In the past 50 years, scholarship of collective action and social movements swung away from thinking of social movement actors as irrational crowds incapable of thoughtful, deliberate, or organized action. The critique of the irrationality assumption seems to have slowed engagement with emotions — which are often viewed as irrational, although sociologists and psychologists have both convincingly demonstrated otherwise — and perhaps has likewise retarded scholarly interest in humor. Another contributing factor to the relative neglect of humor in social movements may be that scholars of social movements want movements to be taken seriously; attending to the ways in which movements are fun and funny could appear to undermine that project.

Yet humor is important for social movements. Humor is a communication strategy that may be used to speak to constituents, opponents/targets, and audiences. Humor also fulfills important functions internal to a movement, such as making participation manageable or even fun and exciting. At the micro level, extant scholarship has shown that humor reduces tension when conflicts are present; movements and movement organizations with joking cultures thus may be better managers of dissent and diversity than those that limit humor. While being funny alone is unlikely to cause a movement to achieve its goals, the use of humor can have multiple strategic uses, such as undermining resistance to a movement, building collective identity, and framing movement goals and opposition. Humor may also enhance activist involvement, and make it easier for movements to sustain themselves.

Furthermore, studying humor within social movements stands to enhance knowledge about humor, too. Humor studies has long considered political satire and political humor as important forms of humor that have broader social significance; similarly, studying humor within social movements can illuminate the possibilities of humor for challenging power and contributing to social change. Research on humor in social movements presents a particularly rich opportunity to explore the debate within humor studies on the relationship between power and humor (Speier, 1998). As the present case study suggests, humor does not always function to maintain the dominant order, and in fact can be disruptive to it. How, when, and why this happens requires further investigation. Furthermore, humor studies could integrate perspectives on social movements to illuminate better the deliberate, strategic uses of humor by actors who are outside of the state yet seeking social and/or political change.

As this analysis shows, humor is central to the New Atheist Movement. In the political and cultural context of the contemporary US, in which making jokes about major religions is socially acceptable even for a stigmatized social group like atheists, the New Atheist Movement does not fear repression based on their employment of humor. Making fun of opponents enables the New Atheist Movement to create and maintain collective identity among atheists, emphasizing how atheists and religious believers are different − in part because the first group is allegedly funny while the second is not − while also building a sense of identity and community among atheists as funny people. Because the New Atheist Movement is heavily reliant on scientific discourses that appear to have limited public appeal, humor also offers a more accessible mode of communication among participants and with the public. Humor is delivered through many modes, including on-line, at rallies, conferences, and discussion groups, and through books and other texts.

Studying the "joking culture" (Fine & de Soucey, 2005) of social movements and social movement organizations illuminates their values and norms, and offers additional tools for understanding social movements and their outcomes. Analyzing movement humor helps reveals processes of collective identity and framing, and helps uncover the boundaries of membership and of movement discourse. *How* humor is primarily used − as subversion, a basis for solidarity, etc. − reflects internal humor, or humor that is oriented inside the movement, as well as external humor, or humor that is oriented outside of the movement (Kutz-Flamenbaum, 2014). The presence, absence, and/or degree of humor may be linked to the broader political and cultural context in which a movement operates, as well as to the goals and content of the movement itself.

Although we focus here on only one movement, we anticipate that humor emerges in all movements − albeit in different ways due to differing goals and opportunities. Seeking to understand variation across social movements in if and how humor is deployed would provide a new angle on conceptualizations of opportunity and constraint, and thereby better illuminate the complex relationships between social movements and the societies in which they are embedded. Comparative analyses of humor use across social movement organizations working on the same issues would potentially reveal linkages between humor and organizational outcomes.

Comparative analyses of humor in social movements would also illuminate when and why humor can effectively be used. The prominence of humor in the New Atheist Movement and the Gay Liberation Movement, for example, might suggest that stigmatized identity groups can use humor to appeal to a broader constituency while minimizing how threatening the movements appear.

Our ultimate hope is that the study of humor will be better integrated into the study of social movements because it offers analytic utility in understanding social movements and their relationship to the social world (and an added benefit is that it might lighten the mood!). As demonstrated in the case of the New Atheist Movement, humor can be central to a social movement, informing a movement's collective identity process and framing strategy within contemporary political and cultural constraints. By relegating humor to the sidelines (as was also the case for emotions), social movements scholarship fails to consider a potentially important tool for social movements in their strategic efforts. When, why, how, and to what effect humor is used in social movements warrants further investigation.

NOTES

1. Humor secondarily also occasionally serves to relegate some members of the New Atheist Movement itself — notably women — as devalued members, particularly through the use of sexist jokes and language. For a more detailed discussion of gender in the New Atheist Movement, see Guenther 2012.

2. The growth of Sunday Assemblies and other gathering spaces for atheists that mimic churches may result in shifts about whether this practice is perceived as funny.

3. The Westboro Baptist Church is especially high profile because of their protests at US military funerals. They maintain US soldiers are killed because of the expansion of gay rights in the US. The US Supreme Court upheld Westoboro's right to hold these protests in March, 2011. Most likely, the protestor in question at the Reason Rally was a Westboro member. The protestor in question would not speak with us.

REFERENCES

Anderson, J., & Kincaid, A. D. (2013). Media subservience and satirical subservience: *The Daily Show, The Colbert Report*, the Propaganda model, and the Paradox of parody. *Critical Studies in Media Communication, 30*(3), 171–188.

Barnes, C. (2012). It's no laughing matter … Boys' humor and the performance of defensive masculinities in the classroom. *Journal of Gender Studies, 21*(3), 239–251.

Baruma, I. (2010). *Taming the gods: Religion and democracy on three continents*. Princeton, NJ: Princeton University Press.

Basu, S. (2007). A little discourse Pro and Con: Levelling laughter and its Puritan criticism. *International Review of Social History, 15*(52), 95–113.

Benford, R. D., & Snow, D. A. (2000). Framing processes and social movements: An overview and assessment. *Annual Review of Sociology, 26*, 611–639.

Berger, P. L. (1997). *Redeeming laughter: The comic dimension of human experience*. New York, NY: Walter De Gruyter.

Black, S. P. (2012). Laughing to death: Joking as support among stigma for Zulu-speaking South Africans living with HIV. *Journal of Linguistic Anthropology, 22*(1), 87–108.

Church of the Flying Spaghetti Monster. (2013). Retrieved from http://www.venganza.org/about/. Accessed on December 7, 2013.

Cimino, R., & Smith, C. (2014). *Atheist awakening: Secular activism and community in America*. Oxford: Oxford University Press.

Cohen, M. (2007). Cartooning and American popular radicalism. *International Review of Social History, 15*(52), 35–58.

Cowman, K. (2007). Doing something silly: The uses of humor by the women's social and political union. *International Review of Social History, 15*(52), 259–274.

Cundall, M. (2012). Towards a better understanding of racist and ethnic humor. *Humor, 25*(2), 155–177.

Davies, C. (2007). Humor and protest: Jokes under communism. *International Review of Social History, 52*(Suppl. 15), 291–305.

Dawkins, R. (2006). *The god delusion*. Boston, MA: Mariner.

Dawkins, R. (2010). *The greatest show on earth: The evidence for evolution*. New York, NY: Free Press.

Dennett, D. C. (2007). *Breaking the spell: Religion as a natural phenomenon*. New York, NY: Penguin.

Edgell, P., Gerteis, J., & Hartmann, D. (2006). Atheists as 'Other': Moral boundaries and cultural membership in American society. *American Sociological Review, 71*(2), 211–234.

Fine, G. A., & de Soucey, M. (2005). Joking cultures: Humor themes as social regulation in group life. *Humor, 18*(1), 1–22.

Fominaya, C. F. (2007). Humor and autonomous groups in Madrid. *International Review of Social History, 15*(52), 243–258.

Franzén, A. G., & Aronsson, K. (2013). Teasing, laughing, and disciplinary humor: Staff-youth interaction in detention home treatment. *Discourse Studies, 15*(2), 167–183.

Goodwin, J., Jasper, J., & Polletta, F. (2000). The return of the repressed: The fall and rise of emotions in social movement theory. *Mobilization, 5*(1), 65–83.

Goodwin, J., Jasper, J., & Polletta, F. (2001). Why emotions matter. In *Passionate politics: Emotions and social movements*. Chicago, IL: University of Chicago.

Gouin, R. (2004). Why so funny?: Humor in women's accounts of their involvement in social action. *Qualitative Research, 4*, 25–44.

Guenther, K. M. (2010). *Making their place: Feminism after socialism in Eastern Germany*. Stanford, CA: Stanford University Press.

Guenther, K. M. (2014). Bounded by disbelief: How atheists in the United States differentiate themselves from religious believers. *Journal of Contemporary Religion, 29*(1), 1–16.

Harris, S. (2004). *The end of faith: Religion, terror, and the future of reason*. New York, NY: WW Norton.

Harris, S. (2008). *Letter to a Christian nation.* New York, NY: Vintage.

Harris, S. (2010). *The moral landscape: How science can determine human values.* New York, NY: Free Press.

Hart, M. (2007). Humor and social protest: An introduction. *International Review of Social History, 15*(52), 1–20.

Haugerud, A. (2013). *No billionaire left behind: Satirical activism in America.* Stanford, CA: Stanford University Press.

Hiller, H. (1983). Humor and hostility: A neglected aspect of social movement analysis. *Qualitative Sociology, 6*(3), 255–265.

Hitchens, C. (2007a). *God is not great: How religion poisons everything.* New York, NY: Twelve.

Hitchens, C. (2007b). *The portable atheist: Essential readings for the nonbeliever.* Cambridge, MA: DeCapo Press.

Huong, N. L. (2007). Jokes in a garment workshop in Hanoi. *International Review of Social History, 15*(52), 209–223.

Jacoby, S. (2004). *Freethinkers: A history of American secularism.* New York, NY: Metropolitan Books.

Keith-Spiegel, P. (1972). Early conceptions of humor: Varieties and issues. In J. H. Goldstein & P. E. McGhee (Eds.), *The psychology of humor: Theoretical perspectives and empirical issues.* New York, NY: Academic Press.

Korczynski, M. (2011). The dialectical sense of humour: Routine joking in a Taylorized factory. *Organization Studies, 32*(10), 1421–1439.

Kuipers, G. (2006). *Good taste, bad humor.* Berlin: Walter De Gruyter.

Kutz-Flamenbaum, R. V. (2014). Humor and social movements. *Sociology Compass, 8*(3), 294–304.

Lundberg, A. (2007). Laughter in the Stockholm pride parade. *International Review of Social History, 52*(Suppl. 15), 167–187.

Melucci, A. (1995). The process of collective identity. In H. Johnston & B. Klandermans (Eds.), *Social movements and culture.* Minneapolis, MN: University of Minnesota.

Meyer, J. C. (2000). Humor as a double-edged Sword: Four functions of humor in communication. *Communication Theory, 10*(3), 310–331.

Nielsen, M. (2011). On humour in prison. *European Journal of Criminology, 8*(6), 500–514.

Olesen, T. (2007). The funny side of globalization: Humor and humanity in Zapatista framing. *International Review of Social History, 15*(52), 21–34.

Paletz, D. L. (1990). Political humor and authority: From support to subversion. International Political Science Review., *11*(4), 483–493.

Polletta, F., & Jasper, J. M. (2001). Collective identity and social movements. *Annual Review of Sociology, 27*, 283–305.

Shepard, B. (2005). The use of joyfulness as a community organizing strategy. *Peace & Change, 30*(4), 435–468.

Sorensen, M. J. (2008). Humor as a serious strategy of nonviolent resistance to oppression. *Peace & Change, 33*(2), 167–190.

Speier, H. (1998). Wit and politics: An essay on power and laughter. (R. Jackall, Trans.). *American Journal of Sociology, 103*(5), 1352–1401.

Stenger, V. (2007). *God: The failed hypothesis: How science shows that god does not exist.* Amherst, NY: Prometheus Books.

Teune, S. (2007). Humour as a guerrilla tactic: The west German student movement's mockery of the establishment. *International Review of Social History*, *15*(52), 115–132.

Viterna, J. (2013). *Women in war: The microprocesses of mobilization in El Salvador*. Oxford: Oxford University Press.

Wise, J. (2007). Fighting a different enemy: Social protests against authority in the Australian imperial force during World War I. *International Review of Social History*, *52*(S15), 225–241.

SECTION III
MOVEMENT OUTCOMES AND ABEYANCE

HOW SOCIAL MOVEMENTS MATTER: INCLUDING SEXUAL ORIENTATION IN STATE-LEVEL HATE CRIME LEGISLATION

Christie L. Parris and Heather L. Scheuerman

ABSTRACT

This paper examines the conditions under which states include sexual orientation as a protected status in hate crime policy over the course of 25 years. Previous research in this area has generally focused on the passage of either general hate crime statutes longitudinally or the inclusion of sexual orientation in hate crime legislation via cross-sectional analysis. Moreover, previous work in this area tends to concentrate on two types of factors affecting policy passage: (1) structural factors such as social disorganization and economic vitality, and (2) political characteristics including governor's political party and the makeup of the state legislature. We argue that a strong LGBT social movement organizational presence may also influence LGBT hate crime policy passage. Using an event history analysis, we test how state-level social movement organizational mobilization, as well as the state-level political context, affect policy passage from 1983 to 2008. Our findings indicate that political opportunities, including political instability and government

Research in Social Movements, Conflicts and Change, Volume 38, 231–257
Copyright © 2015 by Emerald Group Publishing Limited
ISSN: 0163-786X/doi:10.1108/S0163-786X20150000038008

ideology, matter for the passage of anti-gay hate crime policy. We also find evidence to support political mediation, as the interaction between social movement organizational presence and Democrats in the state legislature affect policy passage.

Keywords: Social movements; policy; LGBTQ; hate crimes; event history analysis

INTRODUCTION

Do social movements affect policy outcomes? In recent years, social movement scholars have taken up this question (see Amenta, Caren, Chiarello, & Su, 2010 for a review). Here, we investigate what factors lead to states' passage of hate crime statutes that recognize sexual orientation as a protected status. Under federal law, hate crimes occur when a crime is committed due to the victim's actual or perceived race, color, religion, national origin, gender, sexual orientation, or gender identity (United States Department of Justice, 2009). While previous research has investigated several aspects of policy passage, we are the first to examine how social movement organizational mobilization and political context affect the state-level adoption of anti-gay hate crime policy longitudinally. We focus on the inclusion of sexual orientation as a protected status for three reasons.

First, federal hate crime law only recently recognized sexual orientation as a protected class. Historic federal hate crime laws such as the Civil Rights Act of 1964 and the Violent Crime Control and Law Enforcement Act of 1994 included protections based on race, color, religion, national origin, and ethnicity. It was not until 2009 when President Obama signed The Matthew Shepard and James Byrd, Jr. Hate Crimes Prevention Act that sexual orientation, as well as gender, gender identity, and disability, became recognized as protected groups in federal law. Additionally, while 45 states currently have hate crime policies that criminalize bias on the basis of race, ethnicity, and religion, only 30 states and the District of Columbia currently recognize sexual orientation as a protected status. As such, sexual orientation is not recognized as a protected category at the same rate as other demographic groups.

Second, a large number of social movement organizations (SMOs) (many within the LGBT movement) consider policy advocacy to be a central goal of their work (Jenness, 1995; Kane, 2003, 2007; Soule & Earl, 2001). Indeed, on a national level, lesbian and gay communities have participated in an "unprecedented level of organizing against violence"

(National Gay and Lesbian Task Force, 1991, p. 22; also see Jenness, 1995). Due to this focus on policy initiatives and anti-violence within the LGBT community, it is reasonable to expect states to pass statutes regarding these issues.

Third, with the 2013 Supreme Court decisions regarding the unconstitutionality of the Defense of Marriage Act (*U.S. v. Windsor*) and Proposition 8 in California (*Hollingsworth et al. v. Perry et al.*), and with the recent Supreme Court decision to legalize same-sex marriage nationally, gay rights are currently being heralded as the next civil rights struggle (Becker & Scheufele, 2011). Consequently, anti-gay hate crime policy is an optimal case for studying the political consequences of social movements. Thus, our research serves to bolster literature focused on disentangling the many factors possibly affecting state-level policy passage.

Previous research investigating state-level policy passage of hate crime legislation has examined how states' structural conditions and political context influence when states adopt hate crime policy. Many studies include structural measures such as urbanization, unemployment, and the economic vitality of the state in question, as well as state-level political factors, such as voter party affiliations, governor's political party, and the makeup of the state legislature (e.g., Earl & Soule, 2001; Jenness & Grattet, 1996; Soule & Earl, 2001). Others have considered interstate characteristics such as contagion, emphasizing the roles of neighboring states' policy passage (e.g., Grattet, Jenness, & Curry, 1998; Soule & Earl, 2001). While we agree that structural and political conditions affect policy passage, we argue that social movement resources and a favorable political context within a state distinctively shape the adoption of hate crime policies individually, and potentially via an interaction with one another (see Amenta, 2006; Amenta, Caren, & Olasky, 2005; Amenta, Carruthers, & Zylan, 1992; Amenta, Dunleavy, & Bernstein, 1994; Amenta & Young, 1999; Cress & Snow, 2000). As such, we explore the relationship between social movement organizational mobilization, political context, and state-level inclusion of sexual orientation in hate crime policy across all 50 states over time.

In the following section, we discuss previous research on the passage of state-level hate crime policy passage and review the literature regarding the political outcomes of social movements. Next, we use event history analysis to test how the presence of LGBT SMOs and a conducive political environment influence the timing and inclusion of sexual orientation as a protected status within hate crime laws between 1983 and 2008. We conclude with a discussion of the implications our findings have for the political consequences of social movements.

Previous Research on Hate Crimes

The United States is currently witnessing a shift in both public opinion (Pew Research Center, 2013) and policy (e.g., *Hollingsworth et al. v. Perry et al.*; *U.S. v. Windsor*) regarding the rights of the LGBT community. Previous research on the factors affecting the explicit inclusion of sexual orientation in hate crime policy, however, is relatively sparse. The research that does exist focuses on hate crimes in a variety of contexts, including federal-level (Jenness, 1999) and state-level (Grattet et al., 1998; Soule & Earl, 2001) analyses of hate crime policy, as well as state-level policy specifically aimed at the inclusion of sexual orientation as a protected status (Earl & Soule, 2001; Haider-Markel & Kaufman, 2006; Haider-Markel & Meier, 1996). Most of this previous research is longitudinal, as it attempts to understand the processes through which states adopt hate crime policy over time.

For instance, event history analyses of general state-level policy passage find that both internal and external state factors affect the adoption of hate crime legislation (Grattet et al., 1998; Soule & Earl, 2001). Based on the notion of innovation and diffusion, these projects investigate the processes through which internal state policy innovation and interstate policy diffusion impact the passage of state-level hate crime legislation. Specifically, Grattet et al. (1998) conduct an event history analysis from 1977 to 1995, and find that a state's internal political culture and its position within the interstate system both affect policy passage. Their findings indicate that internal state characteristics, such as civil rights policy innovativeness (with regard to housing, public accommodations, and employment) and general policy innovativeness (based on an index of 60 pieces of legislation passed between 1930 and 1970) have a positive effect on the likelihood of a state passing hate crime law. Moreover, external state characteristics measuring policy diffusion are also significant. The authors find that time has a positive impact on the adoption of hate crime policy, indicating that a "learning curve" of sorts operates across states. As more time passes and hate crime policies become institutionalized, states will tend toward homogenization, increasing the likelihood of all states passing similar policies (Grattet et al., 1998).

A more recent event history analysis conducted by Soule and Earl (2001) finds that interstate and intrastate factors affect the adoption of state-level hate crime statutes. Their findings indicate that both internal state characteristics, including per capita income, previous civil redress laws, percentage of democrats in the state legislature, and policy innovativeness and external state characteristics such as regional diffusion, susceptibility of states that repealed sodomy laws, and the infectiousness of states with a divided elite matter for hate crime policy passage. Again, the pattern of internal state innovation and interstate diffusion influencing the adoption of state-level hate crime policy emphasizes the importance of structural factors in policy passage (Grattet et al., 1998; Jenness & Grattet, 1996; Skocpol & Amenta, 1986; Soule & Earl, 2001).

While these research endeavors have been crucial to our understanding of the structural and political factors affecting hate crime policy passage over time, they do not include specific measures of the impact of social movement mobilization (although Grattet et al., 1998; Soule & Earl, 2001 both include a dummy variable for the presence or absence of an Anti-Defamation League office). We argue that, in addition to the Anti-Defamation League, many other organizations advocate for LGBT rights and that acknowledging their influence on policy passage is imperative. We add to these previous studies, then, by not only controlling for structural factors, but also including a measure of LGBT social movement organizational mobilization by state, over time. Moreover, these past studies did not test whether social movement factors influence the passage of *certain provisions* of bias-motivated statutes. As discussed above, there are a variety of protections encompassed in hate crime statutes, ranging from race and ethnicity to gender to disability. Theoretically, then, we could expect a different, though potentially overlapping, set of factors to affect the inclusion of different categories of protected groups within state-level hate crime policies. Building on the general hate crime policy research conducted by Grattet et al. (1998) and Soule and Earl (2001), we limit our examination to one specific type of bias: sexual orientation.

To our knowledge, three other studies have singled out sexual orientation to investigate the circumstances under which states include specific demographic groups as a protected status in hate crime policy. First, Haider-Markel and Kaufman (2006) examine the influence of public opinion on state-level passage of various laws affecting the LGBT community, including hate crime laws that designate sexual orientation as a protected status. The authors consider three measures of public opinion, including public acceptance of gay sex, public acceptance of gays in the workplace, and a general measure of citizen political ideology. Their findings indicate that when accounting for acceptance of gays in the workplace, gay interest group social movement mobilization ceases to affect the likelihood of states adopting anti-gay hate crime legislation. Haider-Markel and Kaufman (2006) argue that this finding reflects the "divided but majority support for including sexual orientation in hate crime laws and for banning sexual orientation discrimination in employment" (p. 173).

Second, Earl and Soule (2001) consider how affecting state-level hate crime policy may differ for different target groups (i.e., sexual orientation, gender, and disability). They find that while issue salience and economic vitality matter for all three groups, their political variables operate differently across the groups. Democratic state legislatures are more likely than Republican state legislatures to include both sexual orientation and disability, but not gender. Interestingly, they also find that states with Republican governors are more likely to include sexual orientation and disability in their hate crime statutes. The authors attribute this unexpected finding to either issues with their time-dependent model or possible efforts on the part of Republican governors to pursue bipartisanship efforts.

Finally, Haider-Markel and Meier (1996) investigate what factors affect antidiscrimination policies based on sexual orientation in a variety of realms (e.g., employment, education, housing, etc.). This study includes two types of models, one focused on interest group, or social movement influence, and the other focused on morality politics. The authors find that the interest group model best predicts the inclusion of sexual orientation in state-level antidiscrimination policy. Specifically, membership in the Gay Task Force, Task Force wealth, and political allies (measured by congressional votes) are significant. Haider-Markel and Meier's (1996) research, however, uses cross-sectional data and therefore cannot speak to how social movement mobilization operates in states to impact policy passage over time. We build on Haider-Markel and Meier's (1996) work, then, by introducing a longitudinal analysis of the social movement factors affecting state-level adoption of hate crime statutes with sexual orientation as a protected status. Again, while we expect that social movements matter, we also expect some of the structural conditions examined in previous research to remain significant features of the policy-passage process. We propose a model that tests the consequences of social movements on the legislative process while also controlling for several structural variables.

In the next section we detail previous research regarding social movement success, outcomes, and consequences. Additionally, we highlight empirical findings that explain how SMOs hinder or help the passage of policy as a result of mobilization and political opportunities.

Theoretical Considerations

How do we know when a social movement has been successful? How do we even define success? These seemingly straightforward questions have been at the center of social movement research over the past decade. Scholars conceptualize social movement success, outcomes, and consequences differently. In his influential typology, Gamson (1990) contends that a successful SMO is one with high levels of both effectiveness and legitimacy. This, Gamson argues, leads to a politically oriented SMO's acceptance in the political sphere.

Drawing on Gamson's work, other scholars have complicated the question of social movement success. For example, an SMO may become defunct, but only after it has met its goal(s). Additionally, some scholars argue that once accepted into the political sphere, SMOs become co-opted and therefore much less able to achieve their stated aims (Piven & Cloward, 1977). Research conducted by Amenta and colleagues (Amenta, Caren, Fetner, & Young, 2002; Amenta & Young, 1999) regarding social movement consequences focuses on the importance of the acquisition of collective benefits, arguing that "It may be possible for a challenger to fail to achieve its stated program – and thus be deemed a failure – but still to win substantial new advantages for its constituents. This is especially likely for challengers with far-reaching goals" (Amenta & Caren, 2004, p. 463).

Here, we define social movement success simply: the inclusion of sexual orientation as a protected status within state-level hate crime statutes. As such, we implicitly enter the current debate regarding social movements' ability to affect political change. While some scholars argue that social movements play an instrumental role in political change (e.g., Baumgartner & Mahoney, 2005; Kane, 2003; Piven, 2006), others claim that political institutions dwarf social movement efficacy (Burstein & Sausner, 2005; Skocpol, 2003). We believe a causal model regarding policy outcomes is best informed by *both* political and social movement factors. As such, we include measures of movement organizational mobilization in addition to that of the state-level political context.

MOBILIZATION

The most straightforward argument regarding social movement outcomes is that the same factors that lead to social movement mobilization will also have an effect on social movement outcomes (Amenta et al., 2010).[1] Amenta and Caren (2004) argue that, "mobilization of various resources is needed to engage in collective action, and collective action, wherever aimed, is designed and expected to bring a certain amount of collective benefits" (p. 469). As such, one crucial component to social movement success is the mobilization of SMOs. SMOs do the work of social movements, including gathering resources, recruiting members, creating claimsmaking frames, providing legitimacy to the broader movement, mapping strategies, and engaging in tactical behaviors. For the LGBT movement, as stated above, this means more activities targeting legislative initiatives. We thus expect that as the number of LGBT organizations increases, so too will the likelihood of the inclusion of sexual orientation as a protected status in hate crime statutes.

While some scholars argue that increasing numbers of SMOs may indicate movement fragmentation (e.g., Minkoff, 1995), we do not believe this to be the case with the LGBT movement. As Kane (2010, p. 263) argues:

> in the case of the lesbian and gay movement ... organizational proliferation is more likely to indicate strength than weakness. Armstrong (2002) argues that the modern gay and lesbian movement is an identity movement where difference is celebrated. A key expression of this diversity was the creation of identity specific organizations, such as the National Coalition of Black Lesbians and Gays and the Lesbian and Gay Teachers' Association, which dramatically increased the number of SMOs.

As past research has shown, organizational capacity and acquisition of resources are necessary conditions for achieving desired policy change (McAdam, 1982). For example, Haider-Markel and Meier (1996) find that Gay Task Force members and Gay Task Force wealth both significantly impact state-level LGBT rights. Greater levels of LGBT SMOs, then, indicate a stronger level of resource mobilization. Therefore, we hypothesize:

Hypothesis 1. States with higher levels of LGBT social movement organizational mobilization will be more likely to pass anti-gay hate crime legislation.

POLITICAL CONTEXT

A second factor that scholars of social movement outcomes have considered is the political opportunities and constraints within which SMOs operate. These scholars argue that the availability of tangible resources is insufficient in explaining social movement activity, since the state is unlikely to engage in activity that would challenge the status quo under normal circumstances (McAdam, 1982; Tarrow, 1998; Tilly, 1978). Tilly's (1978) polity model focuses on the conditions under which collective action occurs, as well as factors affecting social movement success or failure. Regarding social movement outcomes, the model suggests that success depends upon the degree to which the state facilitates or represses contenders, and the availability of political opportunities or threats facing contenders.

Tarrow (1998) builds on Tilly's polity model by examining two additional political context factors. First, he argues the importance of division among political elites. In this case, conflict and disagreement among political actors provides SMOs the opportunity to enter into a fractured political structure. Tarrow (1998) also argues the need for the presence of influential political allies. In the case of sexual orientation inclusion in hate crime laws, such political allies would include a general liberal ideology among state-level policy makers, as well as a Democratic majority in the state legislature. While political ideology does not necessarily map on to party affiliation, historically, members of the Democratic Party and individuals possessing a general liberal ideology have allied with the LGBT community to tackle a number of issues, including domestic partnership rights, adoption rights, and discrimination policy including hate crime legislation (Rayside, 1998). Haider-Markel and Meier (1996), for instance, find that under most circumstances the presence of political allies and the resources of interest groups (measured as monetary contributions) have significantly influenced gay rights policy outcomes. Similarly, Jenness (1999) argues that movement mobilization and structural opportunities paved the way for the inclusion of sexual orientation as a protected class by hate crime policy (see also Grattet et al., 1998). We therefore predict:

> **Hypothesis 2.** States with higher levels of political opportunities, including political instability and political allies, will be more likely to pass anti-gay hate crime legislation.

POLITICAL MEDIATION

Amenta and colleagues (Amenta, 2006; Amenta et al., 1992, 1994, 2005; Amenta & Young, 1999; Cress & Snow, 2000) developed a political mediation model in which they argue that it is the combination of political context and social movement mobilization that leads to political outcomes. Specifically, the political mediation model holds that mobilization and collective action is not sufficient for creating policy change. Instead, SMOs operate within the political context of the state, and challengers are more likely to meet their policy goals when political allies perceive it to be beneficial for themselves for assisting challengers. Amenta et al. (1994) argue that the political mediation model, "holds that political conditions not only influence the mobilization of a protest group, but also the relationship between its mobilization and collective actions taken, on the one hand, and policy outcomes, on the other" (p. 683). Therefore, a favorable political context (e.g., one open to LGBT rights) *and* the presence of policy-oriented LGBT SMOs are needed for policy change. We consider two types of political mediation, one involving political instability and one involving political allies.

Hypothesis 3a. States with higher levels of both LGBT social movement organizational mobilization and political instability will be more likely to pass anti-gay hate crime legislation.

Hypothesis 3b. States with higher levels of both LGBT social movement organizational mobilization and political allies will be more likely to pass anti-gay hate crime legislation.

DATA AND METHODS

Dependent Variable

Our outcome of interest is state-level inclusion of sexual orientation as a protected status in hate crime legislation. To construct our dependent variable, we documented the years during which states passed hate crime legislation in the United States that include sexual orientation as a protected status, focusing on the years 1983–2008.[2] While we relied mainly on Westlaw and the National Gay and Lesbian Task Force for these data, we also drew upon Berrill and Herek (1992), Haider-Markel (2000), and Haider-Markel and Kaufman (2006) to construct this variable.[3] As we are interested in understanding when states decide to pass legislation as a protected status, we coded the year of enactment and not when the law went into effect (see Grattet et al., 1998; Kane, 2007). Although 30 states currently have state hate crime statutes that criminalize acts perpetrated against others on the basis of sexual orientation, our database examines 31 states, as Pennsylvania passed LGBT hate crime legislation in 2002, only to repeal it in 2008 (see the appendix for complete list of the 30 states).

Independent Variables

We use two sets of variables to examine the role that social movement factors play in passing anti-gay hate crime legislation: social movement organizational mobilization and political opportunities. Each variable is measured annually.

LGBT Social Movement Organizational Mobilization

We assume, as others have (Kane, 2003, 2010), that the presence of more SMOs translates into more social movement activities. Our social movement measure is thus operationalized as *social movement organizational mobilization*. We use a variable borrowed from Kane (2010) that measures the number of LGBT SMOs per capita, per state year. We consider the number of SMOs to illustrate the ability of a state's population to mobilize resources and to work collectively toward a common goal. This variable is based upon information collected from the *Gayellow Pages*, a "national guide to the gay and lesbian community that has been published since 1973" (Kane, 2010, p. 262). The publication contains information regarding movement organizations, gay owned and gay friendly businesses, publications, and nonprofit organizations, all categorized by state and over time. The measure includes both explicitly political organizations as well as general pride organizations. Each organization is weighted per 1 million adult state residents. As Kane's (2010) data are available through 1999, we expand on this measure by collecting data through 2008. The copyright year of a specific volume of the *Gayellow Pages* corresponds to a particular year. As consecutive editions of this resource skip copyright years for 2002 and 2004, we interpolate for these two missing years.

Political Opportunities

In addition to the level of social movement organizational mobilization, we examine broader factors in the political environment that potentially facilitate or constrain the LGBT movement. Our first measure is an indicator of *political instability*. We include a dummy variable indicating whether the governor's political party is the same as the majority party of the state legislature. States where the governor's party and the legislature's majority party differ are coded "1," indicating political instability.

In order to evaluate the presence or absence of political allies we draw upon two variables. First, we include a measure of the number of *Democrats in the state legislature*. This variable is comprised of raw counts of Democrats in the upper and lower houses of the state legislature, drawn from the Statistical Abstracts of the United States.[4] Higher levels therefore indicate a greater presence of political allies. Second, we include a measure of *government ideology*, which assesses how liberal or conservative state political leaders are on a scale from 0 to 100 (with higher numbers indicating a higher level of liberalism) (see Berry, Ringquist, Fording, & Hanson, 1998 for a fuller discussion).

Political Mediation
We create several different interaction terms to test for political mediation. First, we multiply LGBT social movement organizational mobilization with our political instability measure. Next, we multiply LGBT social movement organizational mobilization with our variable measuring the Democratic makeup of the state legislature. Finally, we multiply LGBT social movement organizational mobilization with our variable measuring government ideology. These variables are mean centered to prevent issues with multicollinearity (Aiken & West, 1991; Kreft & de Leeuw, 1998).[5]

Controls

In order to assess the impact of social movement factors, net of other variables, we include several controls in our analyses. First, based on burgeoning research regarding cultural opportunities (Borland, 2004; Faupel & Werum, 2011; Ferree, 2002; Frank & McEneaney, 1999; Williams, 2004) we control for the ways in which cultural opportunities may potentially facilitate or constrain LGBT movement outcomes. First, we include a measure of citizen ideology, or the general liberalness and conservativeness of state citizens, drawn from Berry et al. (1998). This measure ranges on a scale from 0 to 100, with higher numbers indicating a higher level of liberalism (see Berry et al., 1998 for a more detailed discussion). In order to control for cultural opposition to gay rights, we include a measure of the proportion of a state's population identifying as evangelical, with higher values indicating greater opposition to anti-gay hate crime legislation. This measure is drawn from the Association of Religion Data Archives.[6]

Moreover, based on previous research (Grattet et al., 1998; Jenness & Grattet, 1996; Soule & Earl, 2001) we also control for structural and regional considerations. First, we control for structural factors, including per capita disposable income, percent nonwhite, unemployment, urbanization, and population density. Additionally, given historical geographic variation with regard to many of our independent variables, we introduce a regional control variable. We include a dummy measure for the south, as southern states tend to be reticent to adopt anti-gay hate crime legislation (Kane, 2003). Last, as states may be influenced by the policy actions of neighboring states (e.g., Grattet et al., 1998; Haider-Markel & Kaufman, 2006; Soule & Earl, 2001), we control for the possibility of interstate diffusion via a dummy variable coded "1" for when adjacent states passed hate crime legislation that include sexual orientation as a protected status and "0" for all other states.[7]

Research Design

We employ an event history analysis to test our hypotheses. Also known as survival time analysis, this type of statistical analysis focuses on the occurrence and timing of an event. Using state-level independent variables for the years between 1983 and 2008, we attempt to explain the presence or absence of sexual orientation as a protected status in hate crime policy in 50 states.[8] Event times are often measured in discrete units of time, for example, months or years, especially when collected retrospectively (Steele, Diamond, & Wang, 1996). In our analysis, we observe changes over the course of one year time intervals to determine whether anti-gay hate crime legislation was adopted, and what factors impacted policy adoption.

Specifically, we run Cox proportional hazards models, as this type of model ensures a flexible duration model (Box-Steffensmeier, Jones, Alvarez, Beck, & Wu, 2004). We present several models that reflect our theoretical focus. The first two models test whether SMO mobilization and the political context separately affect the adoption of anti-gay hate crime policy. Our next model presents an additive model that includes both SMO mobilization and political opportunities to determine whether social movement organizational resources matter above and beyond a favorable political climate. Last, we present models that examine a multiplicative political mediation via the examination of interaction terms between our measures of SMO mobilization and political opportunities. Last, we present an additive model that includes both SMO mobilization and political opportunities. Ultimately, we are concerned with determining how social movement factors affect the passage of anti-gay hate crime legislation and as such do not make any assumptions regarding the distribution of failure times, or in our case, the distribution of when states passed this type of legislation (Cleves et al., 2010). Moreover, in order to properly handle instances of when states passed these statutes at the same time, we use the

Efron method for handling tied values as it is better at approximating risk set changes at each period than the Breslow method (Box-Steffensmeier et al., 2004).

Additionally, in order to account for missing data, linear interpolations of our numerical variables of interest were conducted. Variables were interpolated within each state across time, or by panel. We first logged our variables in order to avoid negative or nonsensical results. After interpolation was conducted, we took the anti-log of our interpolated variables. We present our results in Table 1.

RESULTS

We present the coefficients of our models as the coefficients are parameterized in terms of the hazard rate (Box-Steffensmeier et al., 2004).[9] The hazard rate estimates the rate at which durations end, or in our case, when states pass anti-gay hate crime legislation (Box-Steffensmeier et al., 2004). In contrast, the survival time function refers to the probability that a unit will survive (or fail) longer than time, which in our case is the probability that a state does not adopt legislation that protects against anti-gay hate crime (Box-Steffensmeier et al., 2004; Singer & Willett, 2003).

We present several different models in our analysis. Model 1 reflects a baseline organizational mobilization model, while Model 2 represents a baseline political opportunities model. Model 3 accounts for SMO mobilization and political opportunities. The final set of models (4a–4c) present three political mediation models. The first (4a) includes an interaction term for organizational mobilization and government ideology, the second (4b) an interaction term for organizational mobilization and the number of Democrats in the state legislature, and the final model (4c) includes an interaction term for organizational mobilization and political instability.

The baseline organizational mobilization model (Model 1), indicates that SMO mobilization has a positive, marginally significant effect on the inclusion of sexual orientation as a protected status in state-level hate crime policy ($\beta = .051$, $p \leq .10$). This suggests that the greater the presence of SMOs in states, the higher the hazard rate and lower survival time that states pass anti-gay hate crime legislation. This finding lends support to Hypothesis 1 regarding the positive relationship between SMO mobilization and policy passage in that states with greater social movement presence should be quicker to pass hate crime legislation. Namely, the hazard

Table 1. Cox Regression Coefficients (with Robust Standard Errors) of Factors Influencing the Passage of Anti-Gay Hate Crime Policy 1983-2008.

	Model 1	Model 2	Model 3	Model 4a	Model 4b	Model 4c
Resource Mobilization						
Standardized SMOs	.051$^+$		.043	.022	.062*	.056*
	(.035)		(.036)	(.035)	(.034)	(.029)
Political Opportunities						
Political Instability		.975**	.958**	.939**	.812*	1.068**
		(.404)	(.403)	(.426)	(.422)	(.424)
Democrats in State		.012$^+$	.012$^+$	.013$^+$	.011$^+$	.014$^+$
Legislature		(.008)	(.009)	(.009)	(.008)	(.009)
Government Ideology		.031**	.032**	.033**	.036**	.034**
		(.012)	(.012)	(.013)	(.013)	(.013)
Political Mediation						
SMOs*Instability						−.082
						(.080)
SMOs*Democrats in					.001*	
Legislature					(.001)	
SMOs*Government				.002$^+$		
Ideology				(.001)		
Controls						
Citizen Ideology	.008	−.035	−.034	−.047$^+$	−.054$^+$	−.042$^+$
	(.019)	(.029)	(.029)	(.031)	(.034)	(.030)
Evangelical Population	−.010	−.052$^+$	−.044$^+$	−.046$^+$	−.038	−.051$^+$
	(.027)	(.033)	(.034)	(.035)	(.031)	(.034)
Per Capita Disposable	.029*	.030*	.021	.032$^+$	.026$^+$	.024
Income	(.017)	(.017)	(.020)	(.020)	(.019)	(.020)
Percent Nonwhite	−.022$^+$	−.023$^+$	−.029$^+$	−.027$^+$	−.025	−.029$^+$
	(.016)	(.017)	(.019)	(.020)	(.020)	(.019)
Unemployment	.039	−.026	−.044	.004	−.024	−.013
	(.142)	(.159)	(.162)	(.176)	(.170)	(.158)
Urbanization	.040$^+$	.037$^+$	.050*	.047*	.048*	.051*
	(.026)	(.024)	(.027)	(.028)	(.025)	(.026)
Population Density	−.001	−.002$^+$	−.002$^+$	−.002$^+$	−.002	−.002$^+$
	(.001)	(.001)	(.001)	(.002)	(.001)	(.001)
South	.179	−.443	−.181	−.297	−.138	−.169
	(.512)	(.581)	(.635)	(.638)	(.621)	(.630)
Contagion	−.167	−.326	−.369	−.346	−.327	−.302
	(.466)	(.473)	(.469)	(.486)	(.452)	(.463)
Wald X^2	48.39***	53.58***	66.28***	76.56***	61.74***	61.00***
Number of Observations	843	843	843	843	843	843
Number of failures	31	31	31	31	31	31
Number of subjects	50	50	50	50	50	50

$+p \le .10$; $*p \le .05$; $**p \le .01$; $***p \le .001$; one-tailed tests.

for including sexual orientation as a protected status is 1.05 times greater for states that have a greater presence of LGBT SMOs.

The political opportunities baseline model (Model 2), the mobilization and political opportunities model (Model 3), and certain of the political mediation models (Models 4a and 4b), all indicate support for Hypothesis 2. Political instability is significant in both the baseline ($\beta = .975$, $p \leq .01$) and the mobilization and political opportunities models ($\beta = .958$, $p \leq .01$). This significance persists in two of the political mediation models as well (4a: $\beta = .939$, $p \leq .01$; 4b: $\beta = .812$, $p \leq .05$).[10] This relationship indicates that the more instability within a state government, the quicker states will adopt anti-gay hate crime policy. For instance, the hazard of passing anti-gay hate crime policy increases by 2.65 times in Model 2 and 2.61 times when accounting for SMO mobilization (Model 3) for politically unstable states. Additionally, these models indicate that the number of Democrats in the state legislature has a marginally significant effect on policy passage. Last, government ideology is also positive and significant in Model 2 ($\beta = .031$, $p \leq .01$) and Model 3($\beta = .032$, $p \leq .01$), as well as for the political mediation models that do not test its interaction with SMO mobilization (4b: $\beta = .036$, $p \leq .01$; 4c: $\beta = .034$, $p \leq .01$). That is to say, the more liberal a state government's ideology, the lower the survival time, and the more quickly it will be to adopt anti-gay hate crime policy. On average, the hazard for including sexual orientation in hate crime policy is 1.03 times greater (Models 2 and 3) in states that have more of a liberal ideology. These findings are consistent with previous work on political opportunities (e.g., Haider-Markel & Meier, 1996).

As mentioned above, we ran three models regarding political mediation. First, Model 4a includes a SMO mobilization*government ideology interaction term. A true interaction effect is not detected as the interaction between SMO mobilization and government ideology attained only marginal significance ($\beta = .002$, $p \leq .10$), indicating that the hazard of increasing anti-gay hate crime policy increases by 1.00 times in states that have a more liberal government ideology. In addition, political instability reaches significance in this model ($\beta = .939$, $p < .01$) and the presence of democrats in the state legislature is only marginally significant ($\beta = .013$, $p < .10$).

Our second political mediation model (Model 4b) combines SMO mobilization with our measure of Democrats in the state legislature. In this model, political instability ($\beta = .812$, $p \leq .05$), government ideology ($\beta = .036$, $p \leq .01$), and the interaction ($\beta = .001$, $p \leq .05$) reach significance. The hazard for protecting against hate crimes perpetrated on the basis of sexual orientation is 1.00 times greater when there is a combined presence of SMO mobilization and a greater number of Democrats in the state legislature. This finding suggests that SMOs are better able to affect policy when political allies exist.

Finally, our third political mediation model (Model 4c) includes a SMO*political instability interaction term. Here, government ideology ($\beta = .034$, $p \leq .01$) reaches significance, while Democrats in the state legislature ($\beta = .014$, $p \leq .10$) approaches significance. However, the interaction term between SMO mobilization and political instability is not significant.

Overall, these findings do not support Hypothesis 3a, which predicts a positive effect regarding the interaction between SMO mobilization and political instability. Hypothesis 3b, however, which predicts a positive effect regarding the interaction between SMO mobilization and political allies, is partially supported as one of our measures of political allies does significantly interact with SMO mobilization (Model 4b). This finding lends support to the political mediation argument that social and political change is not brought about via the mere presence of SMOs, but it is the combination of SMOs along with political allies that best achieves SMOs' political goals. Namely, SMO mobilization and political allies, specifically having a majority of Democrats in the state legislature, are important for the passage of anti-gay hate crime legislation.

When accounting for our controls regarding cultural and structural context, with the exception of per capita disposable income and urbanization, we do not find any significant influences on the passage of anti-gay hate crime policy. Regarding per capita disposable income, the hazard of states including sexual orientation as a protected status in hate crime legislation increases by 1.03 times (Models 1 and 2) in states that have greater monetary resources. Moreover, in states that have higher levels of urbanization, the hazard of passing policy that protects against anti-gay hate crimes increases by 1.05 times (Models 3–4c).

The important relationship between SMOs and political allies, in particular the presence of Democrats in the legislature, in influencing the passage of anti-gay hate crime policy can be seen in Fig. 1. This figure provides a graph of the smoothed hazard rate, which displays changes in the hazard rate over the range of observed failure times (or when states passed anti-gay hate crimes) for each state (Cleves et al., 2010). One can see that states with greater social movement organizational presence and Democrats in the state legislature have larger hazard rates than states that do not. Moreover, the figure shows that over time, states are increasingly more likely to adopt sexual orientation as a protected status in hate crime legislation. Indeed, this pattern reflects current patterns in

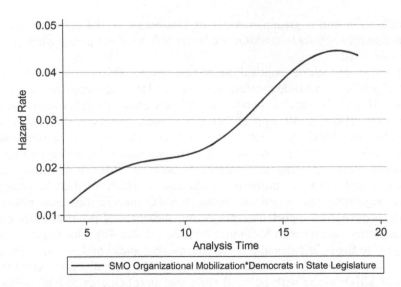

Fig. 1.   Smoothed Hazard Rate for Adoption of Sexual Orientation as a Protected
Status in State Hate Crime Legislation.

federal hate crime legislation (e.g., the Matthew Shepard and James Byrd,
Jr. Hate Crimes Prevention Act of 2009) and serves as a further testament
to the power of social movements in working within a favorable political
climate in facilitating the adoption of this policy. We discuss the implications of our findings below.

DISCUSSION

This study adds to the literature on social movement outcomes and hate
crimes by specifying how SMO mobilization and political configurations
over time affect whether states adopt anti-gay hate crime legislation.
Through the use of a unique longitudinal dataset, we build upon prior
research by examining key theoretical factors that affect movement outcomes such as SMO mobilization and political opportunities, while controlling for cultural opportunities and structural conditions. Moreover, instead
of focusing on hate crime policy broadly, we target a specific protected
category (sexual orientation) in hate crime statues across the 50 states
over time.

Our results illustrate that, SMO mobilization matters for policy passage when political allies are also present. These findings suggest that, as others have argued before us (e.g., Amenta, 2006; Amenta et al., 1992, 1994, 2005; Amenta & Young, 1999; Cress & Snow, 2000), SMOs working within a favorable political context have the potential to play an instrumental role in political change. Moreover, our specific findings regarding the interaction between SMO mobilization and the presence of Democrats in the legislature lends support to research illustrating the increasing institutionalization of LGBT SMOs (Jenness, 1995; Kane, 2003, 2007; National Gay and Lesbian Task Force, 1991; Soule & Earl, 2001). As SMOs in general become more institutionalized, their focus becomes more centered upon policy initiatives. Indeed, the LGBT movement relies heavily upon a tactical repertoire in which policy initiatives are targeted as the main goal. For instance, previous research has illustrated the importance of the LGBT movement in affecting the repeal of state sodomy laws (Kane, 2003, 2007; Soule & Earl, 2001).

Furthermore, our findings indicate that political instability and government ideology, when considered both independently and additively with SMO mobilization, both play a role in state-level policy passage. Our measure of political instability, the sameness or difference of political party between the governor and the legislative majority, suggests that hate crime policy passage is more conducive when political officials are forced to work in a bipartisan setting (Tarrow, 1998). Namely, the potential for disagreement opens avenues for societal groups that normally would not be able to influence the polity (Kane, 2003; Tarrow, 1998). In addition, the significance of our measure of political ideology, a continuum of general liberalness or conservativeness of each state's political officials, illustrates the importance of an ideologically liberal perspective in the passage of anti-gay hate crime policy passage. Future research, however, may wish to examine the directionality of the political differences between state governments and governors. For instance, Kane (2003) finds that political instability in terms of the shift to Republicans dominating the state legislature does not influence whether states decriminalize sodomy laws. It would be interesting to see whether or not the shift to Democrats dominating the legislature or a change from a Republican to a Democratic governor would play a significant role in affecting anti-gay hate crime policy as this shift would most likely be reflective of an ideological change among the citizenry.

In addition to political ideology, the presence of Democrats in the state legislature matters when SMOs also have a strong presence in the state. While Model 3 clearly illustrates that the relationship between SMO mobilization and the presence of Democrats in the state legislature is not additive, Model 4b shows that it is their interaction that significantly affects anti-gay hate crime policy passage. This multiplicative relationship suggests that, unlike political ideology, the simple presence of Democrats is insufficient for policy passage. It is, in fact, the *combination* of Democrats and SMOs that influence state-level policy passage, suggesting that political allies can influence policy outcomes when working in tandem with SMOs. Surprisingly, this was the only instance during which our political mediation hypotheses were supported. The interaction between SMO mobilization and government ideology was only marginally significant, while the interaction between SMO mobilization and political instability was not significant. Perhaps this is because events occurring between 1983 and 2008, such as the murder of Brandon Teena and Matthew Shepard, placed anti-gay hate crime legislation on the agenda for several states. These events, which were in national headlines, may have made hate crimes against members of the LGBT community more salient for state policy-makers, regardless of an unstable political context. Therefore, our study suggests that the dominance of the Democratic Party (which has historically been more supportive of LGBT issues) is important to LGBT SMO goal attainment (Rayside, 1998).

Overall, our findings indicate three main factors affecting state-level policy passage: political instability, government ideology, and the combination of a strong SMO presence with a strong presence of Democrats in the state legislature. Based on these findings, we offer suggestions for future research. In addition to examining the directionality of legislative shifts in influencing the passage of anti-gay hate crime, future endeavors should examine the political process model in other contexts, perhaps investigating different types of SMOs and/or policy initiatives. Moreover, a fruitful avenue of research may examine how state policymaking is influenced both by external (federal actions) and internal (state) forces. Allen, Pettus, and Haider-Markel (2004) argue that the national government influences state policy passage when it "sends strong, clear signals to the states concerning rewards, punishments, and the likelihood of future national government actions" (Allen et al., 2004, p. 319). Although the authors find, similar to our study, that internal state characteristics (e.g., interest group strength and competition between political parties) furthered the passage of state hate crime policies, and not the national passage of the Hate Crime Statistics Act (HCSA) of 1990, it would be interesting to note how recent federal policymaking (e.g., passage of the Matthew Shepard and James Byrd, Jr. Hate Crimes Prevention Act in

2009) would affect the incorporation of sexual orientation into state hate crime policy statutes via the response of special interest groups (Allen et al., 2004). In contrast to the HCSA, which stipulated voluntary participation by state and local law enforcement in reporting statistics to the FBI on the occurrence of hate crime (Allen et al., 2004), the Matthew Shepard Act provides the federal government with greater investigatory power if local law enforcement chooses not to pursue hate crime investigations (Woods, 2008). This piece of federal legislation, which included protections based on gender, sexual orientation, gender identity, and disability, may thus reveal to states a national preference that may foster interest group mobilization and the broadening of groups protected by state hate crime statutes (e.g., Allen et al., 2004; Dubnick & Gietlson, 1981; Haider-Markel, 2001).

Next, we do not specify the mechanisms by which these relationships operate. We simply illustrate the importance of SMO mobilization and political opportunities in hate crime legislation. Future research might investigate these mechanisms via qualitative work examining how SMOs go about attempting to affect policy change. While we have illustrated that the presence of SMOs matter in a favorable political climate, we do not quantify the specific activities in which they engage regarding policy initiatives by state over time. Perhaps some activities (e.g., ballot initiatives) affect policy passage more than others (e.g., pursuing lawsuits). Additionally, while we identify the factors that influence policy passage, future research might investigate the actual enforcement of these policies. For instance, Haider-Markel (2002) finds that law enforcement practices regarding anti-gay hate crime appear to be more strongly influenced by state law and citizen preferences than by the concerns of local-elected officials, local hate crime policies, and administrative procedures taken to investigate and prosecute these crimes. Perhaps a continuing presence of social movement organizational mobilization is necessary for law enforcement officials to continue to categorize hate crimes as such consistently.

Finally, future research might consider how the cultural context in which SMOs work affect SMO outcomes. Recent work has begun to investigate various aspects of this avenue of research, including broadly defined cultural opportunities (e.g., Borland, 2004; Faupel & Werum, 2011), as well as public opinion (e.g., Haider-Markel & Kaufman, 2006; Lax & Phillips, 2009). While we do provide a measure of percent evangelical and citizen ideology to get at the cultural context of states, our measures are somewhat limited in that we interpolated for the years 2001–2008 for percent evangelical. Given Americans' increasing acceptance of gays and lesbians (Pew

Research Center, 2013), including cultural aspects in future research endeavors may prove to be fruitful.

In sum, our findings suggest that SMO mobilization *and* political opportunities most consistently predict the rate of anti-gay hate crime policy passage. States with a stronger presence of LGBT SMOs and with a large number of Democrats in the state legislature, as well as more liberal and unstable state governments, are quicker to pass anti-gay hate crime statues than states with fewer SMOs and conservative, stable governments. These results illustrate that political systems intertwine with collective action on the part of state citizens to produce meaningful political change.

NOTES

1. See Cornwall, King, Legerski, Dahlin, and Schiffman (2007) for an exception.

2. We focus on this time period because the first state to include sexual orientation as a protected status did so in 1984, and the last in 2005. Our analysis encompasses the years from 1983 to 2008 to ensure that we capture any previous or lagged effects of social movement mobilization on the inclusion of sexual orientation as a protected status (see Kane, 2010).

3. Although this measure reflects "laws prohibiting intimidation or interference with civil rights, laws that create separate bias motivation crimes, and laws that provide penalty enhancement provisions," (Haider-Markel & Kaufman, 2006, p. 167), we concentrate on the second type. As such, eleven of our years do not coincide with Haider-Markel and Kaufman (2006). These discrepancies were, however, justified via other sources in addition to those mentioned above. Furthermore, although the District of Columbia has legislation that protects against anti-gay hate crime, we do not include it in our analyses. Including Washington D.C. would likely skew our analysis as it serves as the headquarters for special interest groups (e.g., the National Gay and Lesbian Task Force and the Human Rights Campaign) and may favor the impact of social movement factors on the passage of sexual orientation as a protected status. Moreover, several of our independent and control variables, including political stability, government ideology, and citizen ideology, do not include data for Washington D.C.

4. Due to Nebraska's unicameral state legislature, we coded this state as having an equal number of Democrats and Republicans in its upper- and lower-houses. Running the analyses with or without Nebraska does not affect our results.

5. Issues with multicollinearity may occur with a VIF as high as 10 or as low as 4 (O'Brien, 2007). Multicollinearity was not a problem in our models. Correlations between our key variables of interest are available upon request.

6. Although the General Social Survey provides a direct measure of attitudes regarding homosexuality, this measure is an aggregated national-level measure. We do not disaggregate this variable due to the potentiality of obscuring temporal effects over time within states (Lax & Phillips, 2009).

7. We consider Utah, Arizona, Colorado, and New Mexico as adjacent to one another.

8. States that have not adopted anti-gay hate crime legislation by 2008 are considered right-censored observations (Cleves, Gutierrez, Gould, & Marchenko, 2010).

9. All of our key variables did not significantly interact with time individually or collectively and therefore maintain the proportional-hazards assumption. We used log(time) in our analysis of the proportionality assumption because this function of time is most commonly used in time-dependent covariates (Survival Analysis with Stata, n.d.). Following the assumption of proportionality ensures that the effects on policy passage do not vary with time except in ways we already parameterized. Last, we used Cox-Snell residuals to assess model fit and examined outliers to identify influential points (Cleves et al., 2010).

10. The hazard ratios of government instability for the political mediation models are 2.56 (4a) and 2.25 (4b), respectively.

ACKNOWLEDGMENTS

We would like to acknowledge Melinda Kane for her generosity in sharing her data on state-level LGBT organizations over time. We appreciate her professional courtesy tremendously.

REFERENCES

Aiken, L. S., & West, S. G. (1991). *Multiple regression: Testing and interpreting interactions.* Newbury Park, CA: Sage.

Allen, M. D., Pettus, C., & Haider-Markel, D. P. (2004). Making the national local: Specifying the conditions for national government influence on state policymaking. *State Politics and Policy Quarterly, 4*(3), 318–344.

Amenta, E. (2006). *When movements matter: The Townsend plan and the rise of social security.* Princeton, NJ: Princeton University Press.

Amenta, E., & Caren, N. (2004). The legislative, organizational, and beneficiary consequences of state-oriented challengers. In D. A. Snow, S. A. Soule, & H. Kriesi (Eds.), *The Blackwell companion to social movements* (pp. 461–488). Malden, MA: Blackwell Publishing.

Amenta, E., Caren, N., Chiarello, E., & Su, Y. (2010). The political consequences of social movements. *Annual Review of Sociology, 36,* 287–307.

Amenta, E., Caren, N., Fetner, T., & Young, M. P. (2002). Challengers and states: Toward a political sociology of social movements. *Research in Political Sociology, 10,* 47–83.

Amenta, E., Caren, N., & Olasky, S. J. (2005). Age for leisure? Political mediation and the impact of the pension movement on US old-age policy. *American Sociological Review, 70*(3), 516–538.

Amenta, E., Carruthers, B. C., & Zylan, Y. (1992). A hero for the aged? The Townsend movement, the political mediation model, and the U.S. old-age policy, 1934–1950. *American Journal of Sociology, 98*(2), 308–339.

Amenta, E., Dunleavy, K., & Bernstein, M. (1994). Stolen thunder? Huey Long's 'share our wealth,' political mediation, and the second new deal. *American Sociological Review, 59*, 678–702.

Amenta, E., & Young, M. P. (1999). Making an impact: The conceptual and methodological implications of the collective benefits criterion. In M. Giugni, D. McAdam, & C. Tilly (Eds.), *How movements matter: Theoretical and comparative studies on the consequences of social movements* (pp. 22–41). Minneapolis, MN: University of Minnesota Press.

Armstrong, E. (2002). Forging gay identities: Organizing sexuality in San Francisco 1950–1994. Chicago, IL: University of Chicago Press.

Baumgartner, F. R., & Mahoney, C. (2005). Social movements, the rise of new issues, and the public agenda. In D. S. Meyer, V. Jenness, & H. Ingram (Eds.), *Routing the opposition: Social movements, public policy, and democracy* (pp. 65–86). Minneapolis, MN: University of Minnesota Press.

Becker, A. D., & Scheufele, D. A. (2011). New voters, new outlook? Predispositions, social networks, and the changing politics of gay civil rights. *Social Science Quarterly, 92*(2), 324–345.

Berrill, K. T., & Herek, G. M. (1992). Primary and secondary victimization in anti-gay hate crimes: Official response and public policy. In G. M. Herek & K. T. Berrill (Eds.), *Hate crimes: Confronting violence against lesbians and gay men* (pp. 289–305). Newbury Park, CA: Sage Publications.

Berry, W. D., Ringquist, E. J., Fording, R. C., & Hanson, R. L. (1998). Measuring citizen and government ideology in the American states, 1960–93. *American Journal of Political Science, 42*, 327–348. Retrieved from http://www.uky.edu/~rford/stateideology.html

Borland, E. (2004). Cultural opportunities and tactical choice in the Argentine and Chilean reproductive rights movement. *Mobilization: An International Journal, 9*(3), 327–339.

Box-Steffensmeier, J. M., Jones, B. S., Alvarez, M. R., Beck, N. L., & Wu, L. L. (2004). *Event history modeling: A guide for social scientists*. New York, NY: Cambridge University Press.

Burstein, P., & Sausner, S. (2005). The incidence and impact of policy-oriented collective action: Competing views. *Sociological Forum, 20*, 403–419.

Cleves, M., Gutierrez, R. G., Gould, W., & Marchenko, Y. V. (2010). *An introduction to survival analysis using Stata* (3rd ed.). College Station, TX: Stata Press.

Cornwall, M., King, B. G., Legerski, E. M., Dahlin, E. C., & Schiffman, K. S. (2007). Signals or mixed signals: Why opportunities for mobilization are not opportunities for policy reform. *Mobilization: An International Journal, 12*, 239–254.

Cress, D. M., & Snow, D. A. (2000). The outcomes of homeless mobilization: The influence of organization, disruption, political mediation, and framing. *The American Journal of Sociology, 105*(4), 1063–1104.

Dubnick, M., & Gietlson, A. (1981). Nationalizing state policies. In J. J. Hanus (Ed.), *The nationalization of state government*. Lexington, MA: Lexington Books.

Earl, J., & Soule, S. A. (2001). The differential protection of minority groups: The inclusion of sexual orientation, gender, and disability in state hate crime laws, 1976–1995. *Research in Political Sociology, 9*, 3–33.

Faupel, A., & Werum, R. (2011). Making her own way: The individualization of first-wave feminism, 1910–1930. *Mobilization: An International Journal, 16*(2), 181–200.

Ferree, M. M. (Ed.). (2002). *Shaping abortion discourse: Democracy and the public sphere in Germany and the United States*. Cambridge: Cambridge University Press.

Frank, D. J., & McEneaney, E. H. (1999). The individualization of society and the liberalization of state policies on same-sex sexual relations, 1984–1995. *Social Forces, 77*(3), 911–943.

Gamson, W. A. (1990). *The strategy of social protest* (2nd ed.). Belmont, CA: Wadsworth.

Grattet, R., Jenness, V., & Curry, T. R. (1998). The homogenization and differentiation of hate crime law in the United States, 1978 to 1995: Innovation and diffusion in the criminalization of bigotry. *American Sociological Review, 63*, 286–307.

Haider-Markel, D. P. (2000). *Appendix: State and local hate crime laws, 1979–2000*. Retrieved from http://people.ku.edu/~dhmarkel/app-hcl.html

Haider-Markel, D. P. (2001). Policy diffusion as a geographical expansion of the scope of political conflict: Same-sex marriage bans in the 1990s. *State Politics and Policy Quarterly, 1*, 5–26.

Haider-Markel, D. P. (2002). Regulating hate: State and local influences on hate crime law enforcement. *State Politics and Policy Quarterly, 2*(2), 126–160.

Haider-Markel, D. P., & Kaufman, M. S. (2006). Public opinion and policymaking in the culture wars: Is there a connection between opinion and state policy on gay and lesbian issues? In J. Cohen (Ed.), *Public opinion in state politics*. Stanford, CA: Stanford University Press.

Haider-Markel, D. P., & Meier, K. J. (1996). The politics of gay and lesbian rights: Expanding the scope of the conflict. *Journal of Politics, 58*, 332–349.

Jenness, V. (1995). Social movement growth, domain expansion, and framing processes: The gay/lesbian movement and violence against gays and lesbians as a social problem. *Social Problems, 42*(1), 145–170.

Jenness, V. (1999). Managing differences and making legislation: Social movements and the racialization, sexualization, and gendering of federal hate crime law in the US, 1985–1998. *Social Problems, 46*, 548–571.

Jenness, V., & Grattet, R. (1996). The criminalization of hate: A comparison of structural and polity influences on the passage of "bias-crime" legislation in the United States. *Sociological Perspectives, 39*, 129–154.

Kane, M. D. (2003). Social movement policy success: Decriminalizing state sodomy laws, 1969–1998. *Mobilization: An International Quarterly, 8*(3), 313–334.

Kane, M. D. (2007). Timing matters: Shifts in the causal determinants of sodomy law decriminalization, 1961–1998. *Social Problems, 54*(2), 211–239.

Kane, M. D. (2010). You've won, now what? The influence of legal change on gay and lesbian mobilization, 1974–1999. *The Sociological Quarterly, 51*(2), 255–277.

Kreft, I. G. G., & de Leeuw, J. (1998). *Introducing multilevel modeling*. London: Sage.

Lax, J. R., & Phillips, J. H. (2009). How should we estimate public opinion in the states? *American Journal of Political Science, 53*, 107–121.

McAdam, D. (1982). *Political process and the development of black insurgency, 1930–1970*. Chicago, IL: University of Chicago Press.

Minkoff, D. (1995). *Organizing for equality: The evolution of women's and racial-ethnic organizations in America, 1955–1985*. New Brunswick, NJ: Rutgers University Press.

National Gay and Lesbian Task Force (1991). *Anti-gay/lesbian violence, victimization & defamation in 1990*. Washington, DC: National Gay and Lesbian Task Force Policy Institute.

O'Brien, R. M. (2007). A caution regarding rules of thumb for variance inflation factors. *Quality and Quantity, 41*, 673–690.

Pew Research Center. (2013). *Growing support for gay marriage: Changed minds and changing demographics*. Retrieved from http://www.people-press.org/2013/03/20/growing-support-for-gay-marriage-changed-minds-and-changing-demographics/

Piven, F. F. (2006). *Challenging authority: How ordinary people change America*. Canham, MD: Rowman & Littlefield.

Piven, F. F., & Cloward, R. (1977). *Poor people's movement*. New York, NY: Vintage.

Rayside, D. (1998). *On the fringe: Gays and lesbians in politics*. Ithaca, NY: Cornell University Press.

Singer, J. D., & Willett, J. B. (2003). *Applied longitudinal data analysis: Modeling change and event occurrence*. Oxford: Oxford University Press.

Skocpol, T. (2003). *Diminished democracy: From membership to management in American civic life*. Norman, OK: University of Oklahoma Press.

Skocpol, T., & Amenta, E. (1986). States and state policies. *Annual Review of Sociology, 12*, 131–157.

Soule, S. A., & Earl, J. (2001). The enactment of state-level hate crime law in the United States: Intrastate and interstate factors. *Sociological Perspectives, 44*(3), 281–305.

Steele, F., Diamond, I., & Wang, D. (1996). The determinants of the duration of contraceptive use in China: A multilevel multinomial discrete-hazards modeling approach. *Demography, 33*(1), 12–23.

Survival analysis with Stata. (n.d.). *UCLA: Academic technology services, statistical consulting group*. Retrieved from http://www.ats.ucla.edu/stat/stata/seminars/stata_survival/default.htm

Tarrow, S. (1998). *Power in movement: Social movements and contentious politics*. Cambridge: Cambridge University Press.

Tilly, C. (1978). *From mobilization to revolution*. Reading, MA: Addison-Wesley.

United States Department of Justice. (2009). *Matthew Shepard and James Byrd, Jr. Hate crimes prevention act*. Retrieved from http://www.justice.gov/crt/about/crm/matthew-shepard.php

Williams, R. H. (2004). The cultural contexts of collective action: Constraints, opportunities, and the symbolic life of social movements. In D. A. Snow, S. A. Soule, & H. Kriesi (Eds.), *The Blackwell companion to social movements* (pp. 91–115). Malden, MA: Blackwell Publishing.

Woods, J. B. (2008). Ensuring a right of access to the courts for bias crime victims: A section 5 defense of the Matthew Shepard Act. *Chapman Law Review, 12*, 389–393.

APPENDIX: STATES THAT HAVE PASSED ANTI-GAY HATE CRIME POLICY, IN ALPHABETICAL ORDER

State(s)
Arizona
California
Colorado
Connecticut
Delaware
Florida
Hawaii
Illinois
Iowa
Kansas
Kentucky
Louisiana
Maine
Maryland
Massachusetts
Minnesota
Missouri
Nebraska
Nevada
New Hampshire
New Jersey
New Mexico
New York
Oregon
Rhode Island
Tennessee
Texas
Vermont
Washington
Wisconsin

Note: Data are drawn from Westlaw, Berrill, and Herek (1992), Haider-Markel (2000), and Haider-Markel and Kaufman (2006).

SOCIAL MOVEMENTS IN ABEYANCE IN NON-DEMOCRACIES: THE WOMEN'S MOVEMENT IN FRANCO'S SPAIN

Celia Valiente

ABSTRACT

Social movements experience periods of intense activity and periods of abeyance, when collective action is very weak because of an inhospitable political climate. Non-democracies are extreme cases of hostile political environments for social movements. Drawing on a case study of the women's movement in Franco's Spain (mid-1930s to 1975) based on an analysis of published documents and 17 interviews, this paper argues that some non-democracies force social movements that existed prior to dictatorships into a period of abeyance and shape collective organizing in terms of location, goals, and repertoire of activities. Some social movements under prolonged non-democratic rule manage to link and transmit the aims, repertoire of activities, and collective identity of

Research in Social Movements, Conflicts and Change, Volume 38, 259–290
ISSN: 0163-786X/doi:10.1108/S0163-786X20150000038009

pre-dictatorship activists to those of post-dictatorship activists. This occurs mainly through cultural activities.

Keywords: Social movements; women's movements; abeyance; non-democracies; Spain; Franco

INTRODUCTION

In many Western countries, the first and second waves of the women's movement were separated by a period of abeyance (Taylor, 1989). Although the chronology of this abeyance phase varied from country to country, the inter-war period and the decades after World War II are usually considered the abeyance stage, when feminist activism was considerably weak because of non-conducive political environments. The mobilization of women activists helped bridge the first and second wave of the women's movement, enabling continuity of some networks, goals and tactics, and transmission of collective identity across decades. However, also in the last century, in some Western and developing countries, polities experienced periods of non-democratic rule. For social movements, non-democracies constitute hostile political environments *par excellence.*[1] How (or whether or when) do women's movements under long-lasting authoritarian political regimes manage to link and transmit the aims, repertoires of tactics and collective identities of pre-dictatorship activists to those of post-dictatorship activists? The concept of abeyance was developed in reference to social movements in democratic settings. Is this concept also useful for analyzing social movement continuity in non-democratic settings?

These main questions are answered in this paper with the case study of Franco's Spain. From the mid-1930 to 1975, Spain was governed by a right-wing authoritarian regime headed by General Francisco Franco which severely curtailed women's rights and status. During this abeyance phase, the nature of the political regime shaped women's organizing in at least three regards. First, the overwhelming majority of women's organizations active in previous years disappeared because the regime intensively repressed most types of collective action. Women activists frequently pursued their demands individually instead of collectively and/or within groups created during the abeyance period. Alternatively, activists also attempted to bring about social change by mobilizing within groups of civil society permitted or tolerated by the regime, such as auxiliary organizations of the

Catholic Church or housewives' associations. Second, while some activists engaged in complicated interchanges with political authorities to bring about legal reforms, others directly mobilized underground in favor of regime change. Finally, activists resorted to unobtrusive activities to achieve their goals. Activists frequently engaged in cultural activities such as writing. Through these and other activities, women activists under Franco helped link the pre- and post-Franco waves of the women's movement.

In this paper, I proceed in five steps. First, I review the literature on social movements in abeyance and scholarship on social movements in non-democracies. Second, I present the empirical case and specify the sources used in this research. Third, I succinctly describe the first wave of the Spanish women's movement. Fourth, I analyze women's organizing in Franco's Spain. Fifth, I assess the consequences of women's organizing in Franco's time on the second wave of the Spanish women's movement, which became active starting mainly in the 1970s. This paper does not describe the evolution of the Spanish women's movement between the mid-1930s and 1975 in and of itself, but rather focuses only on the features of the movement in terms of political regime/movement interactions and waves of mobilization.

SOCIAL MOVEMENTS IN ABEYANCE AND SOCIAL MOVEMENTS IN NON-DEMOCRACIES

The concept of abeyance was first used by sociologist Taylor (1989) to name the period between 1920 and the mid-1960s in the United States, which divided the first and second waves of women's collective activism. The first wave of the American women's movement developed from the abolitionist mobilization of the 1830s, reached a peak of mass mobilization between 1900 and 1920, and deflated after the suffrage victory in 1920. The second wave of the American women's movement originated in the mid-1960s and reached a peak of mass mobilization in the 1970s (Taylor, 1989, p. 762). In Taylor's words (1989), "[t]he term 'abeyance' depicts a holding process by which movements sustain themselves in non-receptive political environments and provide continuity from one stage of mobilization to another" (p. 761). In the United States, women's collective efforts that existed between 1920 and the mid-1960s provided the second wave of feminist activism with three elements: activist networks, goals and tactical choices, and a collective identity (Taylor, 1989, pp. 770–772).

Although scholarship on movements in abeyance usually affirms that political opportunities shape the course of social movements in abeyance periods (Bagguley, 2002, p. 172; Staggenborg, 1996, p. 143; Taylor, 1989, p. 761), surprisingly, this literature is silent on political regimes. Perhaps this is due to the fact that most of the empirical cases studied in articles and books on abeyance were or are democratic polities (however imperfect some of these democracies were or are). But non-democratic regimes abound outside the contemporary post-industrial world and have constituted an important proportion of regimes worldwide in most of the last two centuries.

In non-democracies, "societies lack a mechanism for regular, legitimate transfers of power sanctioned by those subject to the state" (Osa & Corduneanu-Huci, 2003, p. 610). Basic civil and political rights are not guaranteed, and the mass media are controlled by the state. Political mobilization is confined to structures sponsored by the regime, such as a single party. The manifestation of dissent is intrinsic to democracy, but in non-democracies power holders usually interpret dissent as an attack against the regime and repress it. Thus, social movement activity is a very high cost/high risk activity (Osa & Corduneanu-Huci, 2003, pp. 606, 610–611; Osa & Schock, 2007, p. 124, 127).

Studies on social movements in dictatorships are less numerous than in democracies (Almeida, 2003, pp. 345–346; Hipsher, 1998, p. 149). Generally and with exceptions, scholarship on social movements in non-democracies is state-oriented and/or policy-oriented. Authors often study collective efforts to transform the political regime and/or oppose policies elaborated by political authorities. Numerous analyses on collective activism in repressive settings focus on specific moments: transitions to democracy and to a lesser extent, periods of liberalization of authoritarian political regimes (Almeida, 2003, p. 346; Castells, 1983, pp. 215–288; Osa & Corduneanu-Huci, 2003, p. 606). In particular, the contribution of social movements to the democratization of polities is a topic of major interest in this literature (Hipsher, 1998, pp. 151–152). Although social movement activism is a highly dangerous activity, protests at times take place, and scholars have often directed their attention to the study of protest events such as strikes, demonstrations, riots, sit-ins, or armed attacks (Almeida, 2003; Fishman, 1990; Maravall, 1978; Osa & Corduneanu-Huci, 2003).

What does scholarship on social movements in non-democratic regimes say about the main concern of abeyance studies, that is, the continuity of movements between waves of mobilization? Very little, because this is not a central topic of the literature on collective action in repressive settings.

Let us remember that the focus of most analyses on movements in non-democracies is on transitions, democratization, policies, and protest events. In some cases, dictatorships destroy the organizational infrastructure of social movements active in the past but some cultures of resistance remain alive and become the bases for later mobilization. Hipsher's work documents that through the shantytown dwellers' movement in Chile, the urban poor mobilized around housing, basic services, and economic issues from the 1950s onwards. After 1973 Pinochet's coup, the shantytown movement was deactivated and re-emerged mainly in the 1980s (still under Pinochet's rule) (Hipsher, 1998, pp. 156–157). However, Hipsher does not specify the mechanisms which enabled movement revival after demobilization. Still other studies present social movements as if these appeared *ex novo* during the liberalizing phase of non-democratic regimes or in the last years of authoritarian rule. Such is the case of Castells' study on the social movement around urban issues which developed mainly (but not exclusively) in working-class neighborhoods in Spanish cities in the 1970s (Castells, 1983, pp. 215–288). All in all, research on social movements in authoritarian settings provides non-satisfactory accounts on whether (and when, and how) social activism is maintained under non-democratic rule.

A combination of the insights of the literatures on social movements in abeyance and collective action in non-democracies may contribute to correct the biases and/or fill in the gaps of both literatures. Attention to non-democratic regimes may help rectify the democracy-inclination of scholarship on movements in abeyance. The study of continuity of social movements under authoritarian rule may help weaken the transition-bias of studies on non-democracies by analyzing periods when the political regime is not being transformed. In addition, the analysis of continuity of social activism in autocracies may mitigate the state- and policy-inclination of scholarship of social movements in authoritarian regimes by studying what happens not only in the political arena but also in society. To develop such a combination of findings from both literatures, let me present them in some detail related to the thesis that in democracies and non-democracies, the political opportunity structure influences social movements in terms of (i) location, (ii) goals, and (iii) repertoire of activities.

(i) Regarding the location of collective action, the abeyance literature on democracies makes explicit claims. Taylor (1989) focuses her research on the formal women's organizations that survived between the first and second waves of the women's movement in the United States, and studied one of them in depth: the National Woman's Party. Similarly, in his analysis of the women's movement in Britain in the 1990s and the early years of the twenty-first century, Bagguley (2002) affirms that "rather than new social movement organizations emerging, abeyance is characterized by the decline and merger of pre-existing social movement organizations" (p. 174). Taylor and Bagguley argue that inhospitable political climates make it arduous for social movements to attract new recruits. Subsequently, a considerable proportion of activists during abeyance times are long-time members of the movement who have also been active in the previous stage of mobilization. Conversely, Staggenborg (1996) states that "different types of abeyance structures operate in different local environments and political contexts" (p. 156). Staggenborg shows that in the 1980s and 1990s in a place characterized by high turnover of local population such as Bloomington, Indiana, the women's movement continued to exist in the absence of stable surviving movement organizations. The majority of activists during the abeyance times were not long-time members from the previous phase of mobilization.

Findings of studies on non-democracies lead me to suggest, in line with Staggenborg's argument, that in non-democratic regimes, it is probable that the central location of activism are not the surviving groups run by a core of long-term committed members from former decades. In some dictatorships, few (if any) of the social movement organizations (SMOs) from the previous period endure during the abeyance years because of strong-state repression. Committed members from the previous stage of the mobilization may be killed, in prison, in exile or living underground (Maravall, 1978, p. 22; Schneider, 1992, p. 268). Subsequently, most activists during the abeyance phase may be new to the movement. Social movement activity may be carried out by new groups created in the abeyance period. These new groups may not be SMOs but rather informal circles or networks, because dictatorships severely curtail the right to association (Maravall, 1978, pp. 65, 165–166; Osa & Corduneanu-Huci, 2003, pp. 613–618; Osa & Schock, 2007, p. 138). Otherwise, former and/or new activists may attempt to reach their goals by mobilizing within the few organizations permitted by the non-democratic regime, such as churches or cultural associations (Schneider, 1992, p. 260).

(ii) As for the goals of social movements, scholarship on democracies proposes that the adverse political environment that characterizes an abeyance period also affects the selection of goals by social movements. According to Taylor (1989, pp. 766–767), "purposive commitment" is a feature of movements in abeyance. In the United States, in the abeyance period between 1920 and the mid-1960s, the National Woman's Party focused on a single goal: an equal rights amendment. Given the small number of National Women's Party activists during abeyance years, its leaders rejected other versions of a feminist program and deliberately invested the energies of members in the single issue of a constitutional amendment.

In contrast, the literature on social movements in repressive settings seems to indicate that it is unlikely that in dictatorships, movements focus on a single goal. Political regime change is the goal of many movements (and not exclusively of democratization movements), because most activities of movements are severely constrained by the lack of the most basic rights (Castells, 1983, p. 222). Social movements may also pursue the goal of policy reform in order to erode the most arbitrary, repressive, or discriminatory measures enacted by policymakers. In both cases, the non-democratic nature of the political regime influences social movements making them prone to fight for various political goals. Additionally, social movements may try to achieve other goals, such as the improvement of women's status, the economic betterment of the working-class or the amelioration of living conditions in disadvantaged neighborhoods (Castells, 1983; Hipsher, 1998, p. 149; Maravall, 1978).

(iii) With respect to the repertoire of activities, the literature on democracies states that in abeyance periods, social movements often engage in activities that are less confrontational and obtrusive than the activities undertaken during insurgent phases (Bagguley, 2002, pp. 173–174; Taylor, 1989, p. 771). This scholarship also notes that movements have a tendency to focus on cultural activities at times of abeyance (Staggenborg & Taylor, 2005). Crucial to the original conception of abeyance, and how it has been used in subsequent decades, is the implication that there will be the transmission of knowledge providing continuity between waves of movement activism (Staggenborg, 1996; Taylor, 1989).

Findings of the literature on social movements in autocracies lead me to argue that in non-democratic regimes in abeyance years, SMOs and activists are especially prone to engage in unobtrusive activities, and particularly in cultural ones. In the face of state repression, social movement activists are likely to put a lot of effort into activities that can be pursued by individuals alone and partially out of the public arena because collective protest in public spaces is usually banned and

many activists are not collectively organized. Examples of this type of
activity are intellectual enterprises such as conducting research on history and sociology. Similarly, activists may engage in cultural activities
because some of these may not be prohibited by dictatorships, unlike
political activities (Maravall, 1978, pp. 9, 100–104). Through cultural
activities, committed militants may transmit knowledge between
phases of mobilization.[2]

EMPIRICAL CASE AND SOURCES

In this paper, I analyze social movements in abeyance under non-
democratic rule with the empirical case of the women's movement in
Franco's Spain. I use the definition of "women's movements" coined by
Ferree and Mueller (2004): "all organizing of women explicitly as women
to make any sort of social change." Women's organizing as women is
usually termed "feminist" when it makes "efforts to challenge and change
gender relations that subordinate women to men" (p. 577). However,
women's mobilization as women may try to tackle other social relations.

After a military coup against the democratic Second Republic
(1931–1936), a three-year bloody civil war (1936–1939) took place. It
ended with the victory of Franco's supporters. A right-wing authoritarian
regime governed the country until 1975. Unquestionably, in Franco's
Spain, the political climate was extremely unfavorable to social movements.
Freedom of expression and association was banned and a severe censorship
was imposed on mass media. The only political organizations permitted
were the single party *Falange* and its auxiliary organizations, such as the
Feminine Section of the *Falange*, which managed most women's issues in
Franco's Spain. Former members and leaders of left-wing and Republican
organizations were ferociously repressed (Linz, 1970).

In Franco's Spain, the political environment was also very hostile to the
women's movement. Gender equality policies elaborated during the Second
Republic (see below) were dismantled by Francoist policymakers.
Furthermore, Franco's dictatorship intensively pursued women's subordination. Civil law considered married women as minors. Motherhood was
defined as women's main obligation toward the state and society. The role
of mothering was perceived as incompatible with other activities, such as
waged work. The state took measures to prevent women's labor outside the
home. An example of this was the requirement that a married woman

obtain her husband's permission before signing a labor contract and engaging in trade (Ruiz, 2007).

The Catholic Church played a paramount role in society and politics. Spain was a nearly homogeneous Catholic country after the expulsion of Jews in 1492 and of Muslims in 1609. The Catholic Church significantly contributed to the anti-feminist imprint of Francoist policies for women by endlessly predicating women's subordination to men, women's confinement to home and family, and the restriction of women's sexuality to reproduction within marriage. In the area of reproductive rights and sexuality, public policies conformed to the restrictive Catholic doctrine, for example, by criminalizing abortion in all circumstances and prohibiting the selling and advertising of contraceptives (Morcillo, 2010).

Franco's Spain is an empirical case particularly useful to study women's organizing during an abeyance phase in an authoritarian setting because Franco's regime lasted four decades. Such a lengthy period meant that there was no other scenario but a dictatorship for social movement activists.[3] Moreover, the international arena was to some extent favorable to gender equality claims only at the very end of the dictatorship, with the United Nations declaration of 1975 as International Women's Year and the preparation of the First World Conference on Women to be held in Mexico in 1975. In contrast to Franco's Spain, other dictatorships such as those of some Latin American countries lasted a shorter period, and in the 1970s and 1980s existed in an international context more conducive to gender equality.

Academic works are a main source of this paper, which could not have been written in the absence of an existing (and vast) scholarship on the Franco's regime and a (not so vast) bibliography on some parts of the women's movement under the dictatorship. In Franco's Spain, some members and leaders of women's organizing were prolific authors, and subsequently scholars can study their activism partly through their publications. As shown below, part of women's organizing took place in women's auxiliary organizations of the Catholic Church, such as Women's Catholic Action. It is a strand of the women's movement less studied than other strands such as women's organizing in the underground opposition to the dictatorship. Thus, I chose to analyze published primary sources by Women's Catholic Action. It published a monthly periodical for its leaders: *Bulletin for Leaders* (*Circular para Dirigentes*). I have consulted all issues of *Bulletin for Leaders* between 1955 and 1966. Women's Catholic Action also published a magazine for a wider female readership: *Path* (*Senda*). I have consulted all issues of *Path* between

1952 and 1966. In addition, in 2009 in Madrid, I conducted 11 face-to-face semi-structured interviews with leaders of the women's movement active during the dictatorship. Interviews lasted between 35 minutes and 2 hours. The ages of the youngest and eldest interviewees were 70 and 94 years, respectively. Eight interviewees were in their 80s. In 2010 in Madrid, I also conducted six face-to-face semi-structured interviews with close relatives of activists who were dead or seriously ill and subsequently could not be interviewed. These interviews with relatives lasted between 60 and 90 minutes. All interviews were conducted in Spanish, which is my native language. I tape-recorded and transcribed all interviews in full. Due to space constraints, direct quotes are included in this paper only from interviews with activists.

In the three types of sources of data (bibliography, published primary sources, and interviews), I looked for information on women's organizing in Franco's Spain regarding location, goals, and repertoires of activities. I also searched for data on the existence (or absence) of links in women's activism before, during, and after the dictatorship. The pursuit for evidence in the sources was deduced from the literatures on movements in abeyance and movements in non-democracies, and did not require coding or the use of a qualitative research software program. I made every attempt to use information that comes from two or more unrelated sources.

In spite of the frailties of memory, interviews were particularly helpful and unique sources because these reveal what could not be made public in the dictatorship under mass media censorship. As of this writing some of the interviewees are already dead or no longer available for interviews because of health reasons. I could ask my interviewees questions that were not satisfactorily answered by studying the bibliography (and published primary sources). For instance, bibliography very often (but not always) analyzes women's activism in a specific period of the political history of the country (be it the Second Republic, the dictatorship or the transition to democracy), while I attempt to unravel continuities across political periods.

THE FIRST WAVE OF THE SPANISH WOMEN'S MOVEMENT

In the nineteenth century, individual activists such as social reformer Concepción Arenal and writer Emilia Pardo Bazán claimed that the position of Spanish women as a group was subordinate and unfair, stated that women's destiny should not be confined to marriage and maternity, and demanded among other things women's access to education, paid employment, and public areas such as social action and cultural production (Nash, 1994, p. 163). The first wave of the Spanish women's movement was composed principally (but not exclusively) of three types of SMOs: women's rights groups; left-wing associations; and female Catholic organizations. Women's rights groups were formed in the main cities of the country, and comprised upper and upper-middle class women, whose educational attainment was considerably higher than that of the average Spanish woman (in 1900, 71 percent of Spanish women were illiterate) (Nash, 1994, pp. 164–165). Most of these groups were set up in the first decades of the twentieth century, that is, later than in other Western countries. The most important women's rights group was the National Association of Spanish Women (*Asociación Nacional de Mujeres Españolas*, ANME). It demanded among other things women's access to education, equality of women and men before the law, the vote, and the prohibition of prostitution. The ANME manifesto did not include any demand that was openly anti-Catholic, such as divorce, contraception, or abortion (Nash, 1994, p. 170; Scanlon, 1976, pp. 203–209).

Since the last decades of the nineteenth century, working-class women were organized as women within left-wing political organizations, such as the Spanish Socialist Workers' Party, anarchist organizations, and later the Spanish Communist Party. These left-wing women's associations were principally interested in the improvement of working-class women's lot, and linked this goal to class struggle and the erosion or disappearance of class inequality. These left-wing women's associations also demanded among other things women's access to paid employment and education, the end of sex discrimination in the labor market, the recognition of women's reproductive rights, and sexual liberation (Scanlon, 1976, pp. 102–103, 241–245).

Female Catholic organizations were formed in the first decades of the twentieth century. For example, female Catholic unions were founded between 1909 and 1920 principally in some of the main cities. These organizations provided various types of assistance to their members, including mutual aid, religious and professional training, and recreational opportunities. Female Catholic unions argued that the improvement of working-class women's situation would not be achieved by class struggle, but through conciliation of workers' and employers' interests under the influence of Catholic social doctrine (Nash, 1994, p. 169).

An upsurge of women's organizations (of all sorts) took place during the first Spanish experiment with full democracy in the twentieth century:

the Second Republic (1931–1936). In 1931, three women were elected to the Constitutional Assembly: Clara Campoamor, Victoria Kent, and Margarita Nelken. These three had formerly defended feminist causes. On December 9, 1931, the Constitutional Assembly approved a Constitution. It declared women and men equal before the law, instituted divorce for civil marriages, established that civil law would regulate the search to establish paternity, and instituted female suffrage (Scanlon, 1976, pp. 261–290).

WOMEN'S ORGANIZING IN FRANCO'S SPAIN

In general, standard accounts on the women's movement (as a whole) in Franco's Spain are written mainly from a historical perspective and are not ingrained in sociological theory on activism. These scholarly works state that, at least during the first three decades of the dictatorship, women's organizing did not happen. This literature dates the advent of the women's movement at different points in time between the mid-1960s and the mid-1970s. At that time, women's groups advancing gender equality claims appeared in the opposition to the authoritarian regime, where they encountered illegal left-wing political parties and unions. After 1975, women's groups mushroomed in Spain. The second wave of the Spanish women's movement reached a peak of mobilization during the transition to democracy and the early 1980s, when it continued to exist in a consolidated but less public and visible way (di Febo, 1979; Martínez, Gutiérrez, & González, 2009; Salas & Comabella, 1999; Scanlon, 1976, pp. 320–356).

The analytical insights of the abeyance literature and scholarship on social movements in non-democracies enable me to elaborate a different account of women's organizing in Franco's Spain. Rather than exterminating the women's movement that existed prior to the dictatorship, the non-democratic political regime forced the women's movement into a period of abeyance and deeply influenced women's organizing regarding location, goals, and repertoire of activities.

Location

In Franco's Spain, because of state repression, hardly any important women's associations from the Second Republic remained in place. In the near absence of women's SMOs from the previous wave of mobilization, women's activism shifted to two main arenas: organizations permitted by the regime (women's groups within the Catholic Church, and housewives' associations); and new women's SMOs. Women activists tended to lack experience in the previous phase of women's collective action.

For the first wave of the Spanish women's movement, the Franco's dictatorship meant an almost fatal blow. In Francoist policymakers' view, Spanish feminism was historically associated with the left, liberalism and lay, or anti-clerical politics; these three political options were targets to be eliminated by the dictatorship. Especially in the civil war and the post-war years, when state repression was particularly ferocious, some feminists went into exile, including the first three female parliamentarians of the Second Republic. Others were dead. Some of those who remained in the country were in prison, while those outside the prison walls ended their political activities and kept silent in order to survive (di Febo, 1979).

Scholarship sporadically mentions the establishment of Spanish left-wing women's groups and networks in exile. In the 1940s in Mexico and France, some women who had been active in the Anti-fascist Women's Group (*Agrupación de Mujeres Antifascistas*, AMA) of the Second Republic were among the founders of the Spanish Women's Union (*Unión de Mujeres Españolas*, UME), and the Union of Spanish Anti-fascist women (*Unión de Mujeres Antifascistas Españolas*, UMAE) respectively. But these and other women's initiatives in exile did not result in the reconstruction in exile of the women's movement from the Second Republic. The main goals of UME and UMAE were not demands around women's issues but the fight against the dictatorship, and the support to prisoners and underground political dissidents in Franco's Spain (Domínguez, 2009, pp. 77–80). In addition, the women's (and men's) exile was geographically dispersed. For example, the three first women parliamentarians of the Second Republic, Clara Campoamor, Victoria Kent and Margarita Nelken, lived in Switzerland, the United States, and Mexico, respectively.

Secondary sources do not refer to any feminist organization from the Second Republic which continued its activities in the first years of Franco's Spain, with one partial (but important) exception: The Spanish Association of University Women (*Asociación Española de Mujeres Universitarias*, AEMU). The AEMU was legally established in 1953 and became a member of the International Federation of University Women in 1955. According to the 1953 AEMU's statutes, the purpose of the AEMU was to support female university students and women with university degrees in their professional careers. The AEMU was set up by some women linked to a women's SMO active between 1920 and 1937: the Female University

Youth (*Juventud Universitaria Femenina*, JUF). Some of the leaders of the first wave of the Spanish feminist movement had belonged to the JUF, including Clara Campoamor, who was a member of Parliament between 1931 and 1933 and also JUF president until 1933. The association created in 1953 had a different name from its predecessor (AEMU instead of JUF), and the members of the first AEMU directive teams were carefully chosen among women who were not particularly known for their connection to the JUF (Maillard, 1990).

In Franco's Spain, some of the women's efforts against the anti-feminist ideals promoted by political authorities (and the hierarchy of the Catholic Church) were advanced by female leaders and activists within auxiliary organizations of the Catholic Church mainly from the 1950s onwards. The Catholic Church also partly supported or inspired other social movements such as the labor movement (Fishman, 1990; Linz, 1970, p. 259).

Let me use the case of Women's Catholic Action established in Spain in 1919 to illustrate this surge of women's organizing. Most leaders and activists of this women's lay organization were from the upper- and upper-middle classes. The primary activities of Women's Catholic Action were religious and charitable. Some leaders of Women's Catholic Action had actively promoted the establishment of female Catholic unions (Nash, 1994, p. 169). During the Second Republic, Women's Catholic Action also engaged in political activities such as attempts to obtain women's votes for conservative political parties. During the civil war, leaders, and members of Women's Catholic Action continued to combine strictly religious initiatives with other activities supporting Franco's side in the rearguard.

After the civil war, Women's Catholic Action worked intensively on the reconstruction and expansion of the organization. Whereas in 1941, the Women's Catholic Action had 35,000 members, in 1953, it had almost five times more: 172,056 (Blasco, 1999, p. 160). However, its activists did not reconstruct female Catholic unions, because the Francoist regime banned any type of workers' unions (including Catholic unions) and only permitted the existence of the so-called "vertical unions," which were state-led organizations comprising employers and workers. Women's Catholic Action enthusiastically embraced the battle of the rechristianization of Spanish society after the (presumed) previous de-christianization, with initiatives such as preaching in various locations including women's prisons, charitable work, frequent religious ceremonies including masses, the rosary, and pilgrimages to sanctuaries, the incessant fight against immodesty in women's clothing, and the endless prudish battle for morality in public places such as movie theaters, dance halls, and beaches.

Given the pious and politically conservative trajectory of Women's Catholic Action up to the 1950s, it was unexpected that such an organization could be the home of women's activism to improve women's status. But the Catholic Church played a constraining or facilitating role regarding women's organizing in non-democratic regimes in different cases. In Spain in the 1950s, leaders of Women's Catholic Action shifted the perspective that guided the training to their female leaders and members of the organization. Training programs with an active pedagogy were routinely offered to (and imposed on) cadres and the rank-and-file. In these courses, women were taught to observe reality, think critically about this reality (from a Catholic point of view) and act to improve this reality. Time and again, women were urged to be active Catholics instead of passive and submissive pious souls.

Pilar Bellosillo was the President of Women's Catholic Action between 1952 and 1963, and in part obtained the inspiration to change the Spanish Women's Catholic Action from abroad. As in other authoritarian regimes, the fact that the elite had contact with other countries and traveled abroad to some extent limited the efforts that political elites made to control society (Linz, 1970, p. 266). Already in 1952, Pilar Bellosillo became a member of the World Union of Catholic Women's Organizations (WUCWO) Executive committee. She was WUCWO President between 1961 and 1974. The WUCWO enthusiastically supported an active role of lay women in public arenas. With other Catholic leaders, in national and international fora, Pilar Bellosillo continuously demanded that women (and lay people in general) play a more influential and autonomous role from the hierarchy within the Church, and that women's status in society improve (Moreno, 2005, p. 113, 125–128). As a member of the National Council of Women's Catholic Action María Quereizaeta explained in the interview:

> Pilar Bellosillo realized ... that within the Catholic Church women were discriminated against ... At the WUCWO, an international organization, she was demanding that women's status improved. And she wanted to bring that battle to Spain. She wanted women's conditions in Spain to change for the better and that even within marriage, women would be respected and no longer subjected to their husband's will. (Quereizaeta, interview)

The insistence of leaders of Women's Catholic Action on women's autonomy within the Church and women's critical thinking represented a clear break with the past and encountered strong resistance within part of the Church hierarchy. In the interview, President of Women's Catholic

Action between 1962 and 1968 Carmen Victory recalled the Conference of Metropolitans (the predecessor of the episcopal conference):

> That [the Conference of Metropolitans] was my battle. I visited all the bishops, one by one. And they said to me "Do not get women out of their homes!" … And I replied "But I get women out of their homes to do good!" The [bishops] wanted women in their homes … or in the parish, praying in the pews or performing the most humble services. It was impossible to change bishops' minds. They died with that [traditional] mentality. (Victory, interview)

Member of the National Council of Women's Catholic Action María Quereizaeta explained in the interview that disagreement between leaders of Women's Catholic Action and the Church hierarchy was profound:

> In general, we did not agree with what bishops published. Some bishops supported us but these were clearly a minority … Some bishops did not like that we delivered training courses in their dioceses … At times, the bishops did not attend the closing ceremony, although we always invited them (Quereizaeta, interview).

However, the type of women's emancipation predicated by Women's Catholic Action was not without limits. Issues of sexuality and reproduction were not priorities of the organization. It also set lines that women's autonomy and critical thinking should not cross: marriage, which Catholic doctrine defines as an indissoluble sacrament, and fertility control, which was (and still is) severely restricted by Catholic doctrine. In the interview with Vice-President of Women's Catholic Action Ángela de Silva, head of the training schemes that the organization delivered to rural women, she remembered that:

> Rural women worked in the fields all day. They were their husbands' slaves … Husbands treated their wives like servants … In those days, these women [in unhappy marriages] did not separate from their husbands at all. We [training instructors] told thousands of them that they had to put up with it. It is tremendous, but in those years it was like that! (de Silva, interview)

In the interview, Vice-President of Women's Catholic Action Ángela de Silva also recalled about fertility control:

> At that time, women's status was awful. We, women, had to reproduce like female rabbits! … I firmly believe that the Catholic Church has to be more open-minded. It is impossible to have as many children as they come. But we [training instructors] could not [speak about] condoms; we avoided the issue. We told rural women not to have sex. (de Silva, interview)

Especially during the last two decades of the Francoist dictatorship, activists of different social movements such as the labor movement decided to join the organizations established or permitted by the regime in order to advance claims from these legal spaces (Maravall, 1978, pp. 74–75). This was also the case of the women's movement. In the mid-1960s, housewives associations were formed. These housewives' organizations under the auspices of the regime mobilized around consumer issues and promoted the status of housewives (Radcliff, 2011). Feminist activists from a new (clandestine) communist-influenced organization created in 1965, the Democratic Women's Movement (*Movimiento Democrático de Mujeres*, MDM) (see below), decided to join these pro-Franco housewives' associations in order to benefit from their legal status and reach a large number of women. As MDM leader Mercedes Comabella explained in the interview:

> It was tremendously difficult to have access to women if our organization was underground and illegal. In other words, bear in mind that for years we knocked door by door saying: "We are a women's group concerned about the woman's question, and would like to speak to you, and this, and that." Clearly, this was very, very difficult. First of all, because the majority of times, women slammed the door in our face … I was a convinced defender of infiltration [into housewives' associations] … After knocking doors … we barely reached 10 women when we had to reach 10,000. (Comabella, interview)

MDM activists were discovered by leaders of pro-Franco housewives' associations and were expelled from them. In 1969–1970, these MDM activists pretended to found new pro-Franco housewives' associations and managed to establish five associations in Madrid neighborhoods or villages surrounding Madrid. In reality, MDM members founded housewives' associations with a progressive, feminist, and anti-Franco orientation. These anti-Franco associations attempted to open routes for women to abandon their status of housewives and participate in the labor market, demanded collective infrastructures such as child care centers, and supported a broader feminist agenda including equality of men and women before the law and access to contraception (Comabella, interview; Radcliff, 2011; Salas & Comabella, 1999, pp. 40–45).

Goals

Franco's regime influenced the goals of women's organizing in at least two regards. Some individuals and SMOs, especially in the last half of the authoritarian regime, mobilized around the goal of persuading political elites to temper some anti-feminist policies. Alternatively, also during the last two decades of Franco's rule, clandestine women's groups were formed in the illegal opposition to the authoritarian regime, where they met underground left-wing political parties and trade unions. Regime change was one of the goals of these women's groups.

Persuading political elites to lessen the discriminatory treatment to women by civil law was one of the main goals of women's efforts made individually and collectively. In 1953, female lawyer Mercedes Formica published an article in the newspaper *ABC* titled "The conjugal home" (*El domicilio conyugal*), where she criticized that in cases of legal separation of couples, legislation stated that the family home was the husband's home. For women, a marital separation usually meant the loss of everything: home, children, and assets. Denouncing a case of domestic violence, Mercedes Formica argued that Spanish legislation left women unprotected from abusive husbands, and demanded legal reform. Formica's piece initiated a series of articles in *ABC* discussing the topic. The efforts made by Mercedes Formica and others bore fruit and the Civil Code was slightly reformed in 1958. Thereafter, among other changes, the family home was no longer considered the husband's home. Judges could decide that in cases of marital separation, if the wife was considered the nonguilty partner, she stayed in the family home and kept custody of her children. Interestingly enough, Mercedes Formica belonged to the *Falange* since the 1930s, where she occupied low-level decision-making positions. Since the 1930s, she also belonged to the Feminine Section of the *Falange* although by the time of the elaboration of the 1958 reform she had already left the women's branch of the single party (Ruiz, 2007, pp. 49, 57–61, 118–127).

Although the Spanish Association of Women Lawyers (*Asociación Española de Mujeres Juristas*, AEMJ) was legally established in 1971, the gestation of this organization dated back to the late 1950s. Under the leadership of lawyer María Telo, the AEMJ's major goals were the reform of the laws regarding women and families under the principles of equality of women and men, and the professional promotion of female lawyers. María Telo managed to become one of the four female members of the General Commission of Codification. This Commission participated in the preparation of what would become Act 14/1975 of May 2. It reformed civil law in various regards, including the suppression of the requirement that married women obtained their husbands' permission to sign labor contracts and engage in trade (Ruiz, 2007, pp. 195–228; Salas & Comabella, 1999, pp. 50–52; Telo, interview). In the interview, María Telo claimed for herself the tag "feminist" while speaking retrospectively:

> I think that I was born feminist … that one was feminist could not be said in Franco's time because that meant the revolution! … If I could not say so, I did not say so. But I have always, always considered myself feminist. (Telo, interview)

In 1973, the Spanish Association of Legally Separated Women (*Asociación Española de Mujeres Separadas Legalmente*, AEMSL) was founded.[4] However, some of their first members had periodically met in the home of one of them in an informal way in the early 1970s. This women's organization demanded a less discriminatory treatment by law and authorities to women in cases of legal separation, and also provided legal and psychological support to separated women (Salas & Comabella, 1999, pp. 52–56).

Political regime change was one of the main goals of some of the clandestine women's groups which appeared during the second phase of Franco's regime in the underground opposition to the dictatorship. This was the case of the Democratic Women's Movement (*Movimiento Democrático de Mujeres*, MDM), which was established in 1965. It was linked to the main party in the illegal opposition to the Francoist regime, the Spanish Communist Party, although some MDM members did not belong to any political party. Initially, MDM's main goal was to support political prisoners' wives and female political prisoners, but it linked these goals to a feminist agenda that sought to improve women's lives through mobilization. Moreover, the MDM managed to link working women's concerns, such as housing shortages or lack of basic infrastructure in working-class neighborhoods, with broader political issues, including lack of basic rights and liberty or class inequality (Salas & Comabella, 1999, pp. 29–33).

Repertoire of Activities

Franco's regime shaped women's repertoire of activities. Because of the ban of association, activists tried to attain goals by undertaking activities that could be pursued individually. Writing was one of these activities. Cultural activities were of paramount importance for the women's movement, since purely political activities were prohibited or severely restricted. This scenario applied to social movements in general, because the dictatorship tolerated some kinds of ideological debate, especially from the 1960s onwards, while ferociously repressing any manifestation of political dissent or contestation of core structures of the political regime (Maravall, 1978, p. 9). Not surprisingly, women's actions such as signing petitions or demonstrations were very rare (di Febo, 1979, pp. 159–160; Salas & Comabella, 1999, p. 95).

In the 1940s and 1950s, some of the first public voices against gender inequality were openly raised by women writers. As early as in 1948, María Laffitte, who by marriage had become the Countess of Campo Alange, published a book titled *The secret sex war* (*La secreta guerra de los sexos*) (Campo Alange, [1948] 1950). María Campo Alange, as she was usually known, argued that throughout history, men had dominated women and subsequently humankind had been deprived of the potential contributions that women could have made. She argued that the state of ignorance in which many women lived was not a direct manifestation of women's innate mental inferiority. Rather, women had not been given the opportunity to develop their own capabilities. Since early moments in history, women and men had fought for the right to dominate the cultural sphere.

When in 1960 María Campo Alange attempted to set up a women's group, she asked Lilí Álvarez to join the group and help recruit other members. Lilí Álvarez was the author of books on religion, sports, and women's status. She was better known for her national and international multi-sport achievements most notably reaching the Wimbledon singles' finals in three consecutive years in the late 1920s. María Campo Alange wanted the other members to have both university training and paid employment. The Seminar for the Sociological Study of Women (*Seminario de Estudios Sociológicos sobre la Mujer*, SESM) was established. SESM members wanted to analyze the position of women in Spanish society and contribute to the dismantling of gender hierarchies (Salas, 2009; Salas & Comabella, 1999, pp. 27−29). The cultural character of the group was emphasized in the interview by SESM member Carmen Pérez-Seoane: "The Seminar was basically a study circle, that is, it was not like an English group which demonstrates in the streets with placards" (Pérez-Seoane, interview).

SESM members called themselves "feminist," although the word was (and still is) used in a pejorative way in Spain. As SESM member Purificación Salas stressed in the interview:

> In the Seminar, we did not care [that "feminism" was a dirty word]. We wanted to use the word "feminist", of course. No doubt, the word had negative connotations. But precisely, we wanted it not to have that pejorative nuance. (P. Salas, interview)

Feminist collective organizing was so rare at that time that SESM members highly valued the mere fact of sharing feminist concerns with other women instead of being solitary activists. As SESM member María Jiménez enthusiastically explained in the interview:

> At that time, I was already a feminist. But I had not met many feminists because there were so few! ... [The Seminar] was a wonderful experience ... because I found women

with whom to speak about my [feminist] concerns ... Everything was so perfect! (Jiménez, interview)

After 1960, the SESM published some works collectively. In addition, some SESM members continued to publish alone. The ideas on women's place in society and within the Catholic Church contained in SESM books and articles were without doubt more egalitarian than the gender doctrine proclaimed by the authoritarian regime or the Catholic Church hierarchy and gender norms in society.

The main activities undertaken by some women's groups other than the SESM in Franco's time were also cultural events. This was the case of the Spanish Association of University Women (*Asociación Española de Mujeres Universitarias*, AEMU), which organized public lectures by prominent (and mainly male) intellectuals on arts, humanities, and social issues. By an explicit decision of AEMU leaders and members, only a few of these courses and public lectures were dedicated to women's issues. AEMU courses and lectures were attended by women and men, because the AEMU wanted to expand the range of public debate in Franco's Spain for all people (Maillard, 1990, pp. 39, 58–62; Salas & Comabella, 1999, p. 39).

CONSEQUENCES FOR THE SECOND WAVE OF THE SPANISH WOMEN'S MOVEMENT

Taylor (1989, pp. 770–72) proposes that the US women's movement of the abeyance years between 1945 and the mid-1960s had at least three consequences for the next wave of collective activism: (i) activist networks, (ii) an existing repertoire of goals and tactics, and (iii) a collective identity. Similarly, women's organizing in the abeyance times of Franco's Spain left at least three legacies to the second wave of women's mobilization: activist networks, goals, and a collective identity. More concretely, in the Spanish case, "activist networks" meant organizational structures for participation and a cadre of leaders who occupied the first gender equality positions in the new Spanish democracy. In post-authoritarian Spain, "an existing repertoire of goals and tactics" meant mainly heated debates about the goals of the women's movement. After Franco's dictatorship, a "collective identity" was based partly on knowledge of the first wave of women's activism and international feminist literature.

(i) With respect to activist networks, women's organizing in Franco's Spain left organizational structures for participation. Some of the SMOs which existed in Franco's time remained active through the transition to democracy and afterwards. For instance, the SESM continued its activities until the death of its founder María Campo Alange in 1986. In 1973, Pilar de Yzaguirre created an association to improve women's situation through cultural change: the Association for Cultural Promotion and Evolution (*Asociación para la Promoción y Evolución Cultural*, APEC). It existed up to 1982 (de Yzaguirre, interview; Salas & Comabella, 1999, pp. 45–47). These and other groups formed what can be termed as the liberal or equal rights branch of the second wave of the Spanish women's movement. As liberal branches of women's movements in other Western countries, this Spanish liberal branch identified women's inequality before the law and sexist attitudes among the main causes of women's subordination. The erosion of women's subordination would be achieved through policy reform and cultural change. In contrast with the United States, in post-authoritarian Spain, this liberal branch was clearly a minority branch within the Spanish women's movement, and so was the radical branch. Many Spanish feminist groups subscribed to varieties of Marxist feminism, in part because many feminists were members of or close to left-wing political parties and unions (Martínez et al., 2009). The survival of groups such as the SESM or the APEC was especially important, because these organizations offered women who did not embrace Marxism as main ideology the few sites where they could participate.

The activist networks formed in the abeyance period of Franco's dictatorship left the second wave of the Spanish women's movement a cadre of leaders who occupied the first gender equality positions of the new democracy. Given the long duration of the dictatorship, when Franco died in 1975, leaders of the first wave of women's activism and prominent female politicians from the Second Republic were either deceased or elderly. The first two democratic elections after Franco's death took place in June 1977 and 1979, respectively. In both elections, the majority of the vote was gained by the coalition of center-right and right-parties Union of the Democratic Center (*Unión de Centro Democrático*, UCD). In September 1977, the first gender equality institution of post-Franco Spain was established within the Ministry of Culture, the General Subdirectorate of the Feminine Condition. It was staffed in part with women active in the legal women's groups of the Franco's Spain, including Pilar de Yzaguirre from the Association for

Cultural Promotion and Evolution and Mabel Pérez-Serrano from the Spanish Association of Legally Separated Women (Salas & Comabella, 1999, pp. 104, 120–125). In 1982, the Spanish Socialist Workers' Party reached power where it remained up to 1996. Since 1982, Marxist feminists staffed gender equality institutions. But between 1977 and 1982, only liberal feminists wanted (and could fruitfully) to do so, because the UCD was ideologically in the center-right or right of the political spectrum.

(ii) As for the goals of the women's movement, women's organizing in Franco's Spain left to the second wave of the women's movement an ongoing discussion about the real objectives of feminist groups and the relationship (if any) between feminist goals and political goals in general. In the 1970s, many Spanish feminists combined membership in a feminist group with another type of organization, such as a left-wing political party or trade union, in order to participate in the democratization of the country and include feminist concerns in mainstream political life. This position was called the double membership position. In contrast, champions of the single-membership position in feminist (and only-female) associations thought that the improvement of women's status could not be pursued in feminist terms within traditional "malestream" organizations, such as parties and unions because these contributed to the perpetuation of the unequal relationship between women and men. This type of debate also existed and exists in other Western and developing countries, but in Spain it took a particularly salient, divisive, and acrimonious form (Martínez et al., 2009).

(iii) Regarding collective identity, it is "the shared definition of a group that derives from its members common interests and solidarity ... The creation of a shared collective identity requires the group to revise its history and develop symbols to reinforce movement goals and strategies" (Taylor, 1989, p. 771). The transmission of knowledge between the first and second waves of Spanish women's activism was not a straightforward process because the organizations of the first wave did not survive up to the second wave (with one exception), and Francoist mass media censorship imposed severe barriers to the dissemination of information.

Part of the communication of knowledge from the first to the second wave of women's activism occurred through the writings of activists in Franco's Spain. For instance, in 1964, SESM leader María Campo Alange published an impressive study on women's condition in Spain between 1860 and 1960 (Campo Alange, 1964). In this work, Campo

Alange highlighted the contribution to Spanish society made by prominent forerunners of the first wave of women's activism such as social
reformer Concepción Arenal and writer Emilia Pardo Bazán, first
wave women's groups including the National Association of Spanish
Women, and even left-wing feminists who were in exile during
Franco's dictatorship, such as members of the Second Republic
Parliament Margarita Nelken and Victoria Kent (Campo Alange,
1964, pp. 101—106, 119—126, 200, 208). In addition, already in the
1950s, the magazine for a general female readership *Path* (*Senda*) published by Women's Catholic Action also mentioned the foremothers of
the first wave of the Spanish women's movement: Emilia Pardo Bazán
and Concepción Arenal.[5]

Part of the transmission of knowledge between the first and second
waves of women's activism also took place through personal contacts
between feminist activists in Franco's Spain and first-wave feminists who
lived in exile. For example, when future President of the Spanish
Association of Women Lawyers María Telo individually joined the
International Federation of Women in Legal Careers (IFWLC) in 1958 and
attended the 1958 IFWLC meeting in Brussels, she met Clara Campoamor.
She was one of the first three parliamentarians of the Second Republic, had
belonged to the IFWLC since its founding in 1928, and during the dictatorship lived in exile in Switzerland. Clara Campoamor encouraged María
Telo to fight for the equality of women and men before the law in Spain
(Ruiz, 2007). In the interview, María Telo related this encounter:

> And there, I met Clara Campoamor. Yes, and I was vividly impressed by her. Yes,
> because when I was a law student [during the Second Republic], Clara Campoamor was
> a role model for me. These women [feminist political leaders of the Second Republic]
> ... I wanted to imitate them. And there I was, in that conference, when I met her ... I
> was fascinated by her, and we became very close friends. (Telo, interview)

The knowledge transmitted to the next generations by activists during
Franco's dictatorship comprised information on international feminist literature. For example, in 1949, French feminist Simone de Beauvoir published
Le Deuxième Sexe (*The Second Sex*). This book was included in the list of
books prohibited by the Catholic Church. Subsequently, *Le Deuxième Sexe*
could not be published in Spain. It was translated into Spanish and published in Argentina in the 1950s and onwards. SESM founder María Campo
Alange made reference to *Le Deuxième Sexe* in her work, for instance in the
foreword to the second edition of *The Secret Sex War* (Campo Alange,
[1948] 1950). In 1965, the Spanish translation of US feminist Betty Friedan's

The Feminine Mystique was published in Spain and was preceded by a fore-word written by SESM member Lilí Álvarez. In 1974, in Madrid, Betty Friedan delivered a public lecture, which was attended by hundreds of peo-ple. The Friedan lecture was organized by the Association for Cultural Promotion and Evolution (APEC) (de Yzaguirre, interview; Salas & Comabella, 1999, pp. 45–46). In the interview, APEC founder Pilar de Yzaguirre affirmed: "I have always thought that the international dimension is the foun-dation on which to build any type of activity" (de Yzaguirre, interview). Simone de Beauvoir and Betty Friedan were two of the most widely read and debated authors by women's activists in Franco's Spain. Consequently, after 1975, when the women's movement publicly re-emerged, it was not totally disconnected to the debates prevalent in democratic countries.

Activists in different locations were aware of the existence of other acti-vists and other women's groups. In the interview, Carmen Salas, General Secretary of Women's Catholic Action, referred to the "meetings and links with other groups ... Then, there were always contacts among activists on women's issues" (Salas, interview). Activists also perceived the differences among them. As APEC founder Pilar de Yzaguirre synthesized:

> Each group had its own role to play [within the movement]. There were radical groups ... and we [APEC members and leaders] supported the radicals ... We were adult and intelligent enough to realize that radicalism was for a different type of women who needed to be radical in order to feel good. But for us, it was the opposite ... Knowledge detracts people from radicalism and leads more to the belief that everything is very complex. (de Yzaguirre, interview)

For example, the Spanish Association of Women Lawyers was often seen as the organization pursuing legal reform (de Yzaguirre, interview; Pérez-Seoane, interview; P. Salas, interview). SESM members considered them-selves and were usually viewed by activists of other SMOs as the intellectual vanguard of the movement (Jiménez, interview; Pérez-Seoane, interview). In the interview, SESM member Concepción Borreguero explained:

> We insisted on being a small group, because in small groups people can work better than in large groups ... We were determined to be very few women, but also very pro-minent women. We were completely set on being very "selective" (not in negative terms) ... We wanted a small group to be sure that the eight or nine of us said only authentic and profound things. (Borreguero, interview)

In the same line, MDM leader Mercedes Comabella remembered the impression received from SESM members when she first met them in 1970:

> My first impression was that they [SESM members] were very cultivated women because they had university training. I thought that they were very superior to me ... I

had not attended college. Do you understand? ... I continuously felt that I was without
the proper training ... And I thought "I do not know whether I would always agree
with them or not, but what they say makes sense" ... They were not women of action,
they were intellectuals. (Comabella, interview)

Activists from different groups felt that they were mobilized to bring
about social change by attempting to improve the status of women as a
group and build a better environment for the future generation of women.
As SESM member Concepción Borreguero stated: "We were doing many
things for the women to come" (Borreguero, interview). This awareness of
each other (and of the differences among each other) and the common
understanding that all activists were trying to erode gender hierarchies
conferred the sense of belonging to the women's movement.

CONCLUSION

The concept of abeyance insightfully captures the obstacles that social
movements encounter when surviving in adverse political environments.
The notion of abeyance was originally coined from and later applied to the
study of collective action in democratic (or semi-democratic) polities.
However, as the empirical case of women's organizing in Franco's Spain
shows, the concept of abeyance can be used to understand social activism
in non-democratic regimes. The notion of abeyance prevents scholars from
concluding in a rush (and wrongly) that social movements under dictatorships are dead, and lead scholars to investigate whether social movements
are rather latent. Seen from another perspective, the concept of abeyance
puts the (potential) continuity of collective action between waves of mobilization in non-democracies where it belongs: at the center of sociological
inquiry. Generally, scholarship on social movements in non-democracies
has not adequately analyzed movement continuity because this scholarship
has mainly studied transitions to democracy, policies and protests. Some
autocracies fully destroy social movements active in pre-dictatorship times.
But other times, non-democratic regimes force social movements into an
abeyance phase and deeply influence social movements with regard to location, goals, and activities.

In relation to location of social activism, part of the literature on movements in abeyance states that in these periods, the most important SMOs
are the organizations that survive from the previous wave of mobilization,
and that these SMOs are staffed by committed militants from the former

stage of mobilization. Another part of this literature defends that different varieties of abeyance structures are useful in different contexts, and that many activists may be relatively new to the movement. In line with the latter part of this literature, this paper shows that in non-democratic contexts, it is highly probable that social movement activity takes place in locations different from surviving SMOs if organizations of the previous wave of a movement are dismantled. These new SMOs are staffed mainly by new activists because most leaders and activists of the former stage of the mobilization are repressed. Activism may also emerge in spaces of civil society such as churches and cultural groups, which are permitted or tolerated by non-democratic regimes. In contrast, in democratic politics, these spaces are not the main sites of social movement activity. Because in non-democracies part of social activism may develop in churches, it is likely that religion plays an important role in fueling collective action.

With respect to goals, part of the literature of social movements in abeyance proposes that SMOs often focus on single goals, given their reduced material and human resources. In contrast, in non-democratic political regimes in abeyance times, it is unlikely that social movements pursue single goals. The non-democratic nature of the political regime makes some (or many) social movements interested in regime change or at least in reforms within the parameters of the political regime in addition to more concrete claims, be these for instance, feminism, ecology, or working-class progress. As was the case in Franco's Spain with the women's movement, in abeyance times, when activists chose their goals, the option of political goals was likely to be present in part of the movement. The unresolved question of the right relationship between movements and the mainstream political arena is probably a legacy that movements in abeyance during dictatorships pass to the next wave of mobilization.

As for activities, the literature on movements in abeyance argues that in unfavorable political climates, movement activists choose an unobtrusive repertoire of activities. While arguing in the same line, this paper specifies that in non-democratic regimes, opportunities for collective action are so restricted that it is likely that individual acts by movement activists are of paramount importance. In the first two decades of Franco's dictatorship, when state repression of any form of collective action was at its peak, individual activism on behalf of women was crucial. Examples of this type of activism include writing and publishing on women's status and women's history from a critical perspective. Scholarship on democracies notes the tendency of social movements in abeyance to focus on cultural activities. In non-democratic regimes, cultural activities may be central for movements,

because some autocracies at times tolerate a certain degree of cultural pluralism while ferociously repressing political dissent. In Franco's Spain, activists in the women's movement built (limited) spaces for public expression
on women's and other issues with their writings and other cultural activities.
These spaces were very valuable because mass media censorship banned all
political writings against the authoritarian regime, along with any work that
was against Catholic doctrine or was considered amoral by the Church.
Women's activists divulged some views on women that were clearly more
progressive than those proclaimed by political authorities and the Catholic
hierarchy. Through cultural (and other) activities, Spanish activists handed
down to the second wave of women's activists knowledge of the first wave
of women's organizing and international feminist literature. What provided
continuity between the first and the second wave of the Spanish women's
movement was in part the transmission of knowledge through movement
entrepreneurs or leaders active during the Franco's regime.

In general, some social movements under prolonged authoritarian rule
manage to link and transmit the aims, repertoires of tactics, and collective
identities of pre-dictatorship activists to those of post-dictatorship activists.
This bridging work is done mainly through cultural activities. This work of
bridging and transmitting knowledge from one activist generation to
another is a major contribution of activists working under authoritarianism
that has yet to be recognized in the social movement literature.

In Spain, in the mid-1930s, the women's movement underwent a period
of abeyance due to the inhospitable climate provoked by the authoritarian
regime headed by Franco. Franco's dictatorship was later replaced by a
democratic regime when a new wave of women's activism emerged. Future
studies should explore what happens to social movement activity when an
authoritarian regime is not followed by a democratic regime but by a sustained period of non-democratic rule. Possibly, low social movement activity would simply be part of the permanent political situation, that is,
abeyance periods are the norm under non-democratic rule.

Research on social movements in non-democratic regimes helps refine the
notion of abeyance to understand the complex nature of long-term adverse
political circumstances and mobilization in general. That social movement
activity is carried on within surviving SMOs and/or by surviving committed
militants, and/or is focused on single or multiple goals are not key criteria in
evaluating whether a movement is in abeyance or dead. The transmission of
knowledge between waves of mobilization is the crucial indicator of a movement in abeyance. In principle, this transmission of knowledge takes place
more easily in democratic than in non-democratic regimes because in the

former SMOs and activists from the previous wave are in themselves a vestige of former times of mobilization. Under non-democratic rule, former committed militants are usually not present to pass knowledge to the next generation of activists and memories are carried on mainly through the cultural activities of movements. Memories of past grievances and past battles help subordinate groups to forge a collective identity and fuel the commitment to fight against injustices in the years to come.

NOTES

1. An earlier version of this paper received the "Women and Politics Research Section of the American Political Science Association – Best Paper Award 2010." In order to avoid repetition in this paper the expressions "non-democracies," "non-democratic (political) regimes," "dictatorships," "authoritarian (political) regimes," "authoritarianism," "autocracies," and "repressive settings" are used interchangeably.

2. A point of clarification is due here. There are contrasting approaches to the study of social movements. My account is in tune with the political process perspective rather than the new social movement approach associated largely although not exclusively with Melucci. I have chosen the former approach because it pays considerable attention to the influence of the political environment on social movements since I study the impact of a type of political regime (dictatorships) on collective action. But abeyance processes can be studied using the latter perspective (e.g., Barry, Chandler, & Berg, 2007).

3. A caveat is necessary at this point. In Franco's Spain, there were differences across decades. Historians have stressed the contrast between the war and immediate post-war and later periods (Morcillo, 2010). Variations across time are also noted throughout this article. However, during its whole existence Franco's regime was a non-democracy and subsequently constituted a political environment that was hostile for social movements. In this regard, Franco's dictatorship was truly different from the two democracies that preceded and followed it.

4. Subsequently, the AEMSL adopted other names. The AEMSL is used in the remaining of the paper.

5. For instance, *Senda*: Number 124, April 1953, p. 21; Number 154, April 1956, p. 22.

ACKNOWLEDGMENTS

For priceless comments on earlier versions, the author acknowledges the editor and four anonymous reviewers of *Research in Social Movements, Conflicts and Change*, Audrey Barberet, Rosemary Barberet, Laurence

Cox, Cristina Flesher Fominaya, Roberto Garvía, Mary F. Katzenstein, Peter Stamatov, Margarita Torre, and attentive audiences of conferences and seminars where I presented previous drafts. This work was supported by the Commission of the European Communities (contract number FP6-CIT4-028746) and the Spanish Ministry of Economy and Competitiveness (grant number HA2012-32539). This paper is dedicated to my academic mentor Eduardo López-Aranguren as a sign of deep gratitude for his continuous support.

REFERENCES

Almeida, P. (2003). Opportunity organizations and threat-induced contention: Protest waves in authoritarian settings. *American Journal of Sociology, 109*(2), 345–400.

Bagguley, P. (2002). Contemporary British feminism: A social movement in abeyance? *Social Movement Studies, 1*(2), 169–185.

Barry, J., Chandler, J., & Berg, E. (2007). Women's movements: Abeyant or still on the move? *Equal Opportunities International, 26*(4), 352–369.

Blasco, I. (1999). Las mujeres de Acción Católica durante el primer franquismo [Women's Catholic Action during the first years of the Franco regime]. In IV Encuentro de Investigadores del Franquismo (Ed.), *Tiempos de Silencio: Actas del IV Encuentro de Investigadores del Franquismo [Silent times: Proceedings of the fourth research meeting on Franco's Spain]* (pp. 158–163). Alzira: 7 i Mig Edicions.

Campo Alange, M. (1950 [1948]). *La secreta guerra de los sexos [The secret war of the sexes]* (2nd ed.). Madrid: Revista de Occidente.

Campo Alange, M. (1964). *La mujer en España: Cien años de su historia [Women in Spain: One hundred years of history]*. Madrid: Aguilar.

Castells, M. (1983). *The city and the grassroots: A cross-cultural theory of urban social movements*. London: Edward Arnold.

di Febo, G. (1979). *Resistencia y movimiento de mujeres en España (1936–1976) [Resistance and women's movement in Spain (1936–1976)]*. Barcelona: Icaria.

Domínguez, P. (2009). La actividad política de las mujeres republicanas en México [Republican women's political activity in Mexico]. *Arbor, 735*, 75–85.

Ferree, M. M., & Mueller, C. M. (2004). Feminism and the women's movement: A global perspective. In D. A. Snow, S. A. Soule, & H. Kriesi (Eds.), *The Blackwell companion to social movements* (pp. 576–607). Mablen, MA: Blackwell.

Fishman, R. M. (1990). *Working-class organizations and the return to democracy in Spain*. Ithaca, NY: Cornell University Press.

Hipsher, P. L. (1998). Democratic transitions and social movement outcomes: The Chilean shantytown dwellers' movement in comparative perspective. In M. G. Giugni, D. McAdam, & D. Tilly (Eds.), *From contention to democracy* (pp. 149–167). Lanham, MD: Rowman & Littlefield.

Linz, J. J. (1970). An authoritarian regime: Spain. In E. Allardt & S. Rokkan (Eds.), *Mass politics: Studies in political sociology* (pp. 251–283). New York, NY: Free Press.

Maillard, M. L. (1990). *Asociación Española de Mujeres Universitarias, 1920–1990* [*Spanish Association of University women, 1920–1990*]. Madrid: Asociación Española de Mujeres Universitarias & Instituto de la Mujer.

Maravall, J. M. (1978). *Dictatorship and political dissent: Workers and students in Franco's Spain*. London: Tavistock.

Martínez, C., Gutiérrez, P., & González, P. (Eds.). (2009). *El movimiento feminista en España en los años 70* [*The feminist movement in Spain in the 1970s*]. Madrid: Cátedra.

Morcillo, A. G. (2010). *The seduction of modern Spain: The female body and the Francoist body politics*. Lewisburg, PA: Bucknell University Press.

Moreno, M. (2005). Mujeres, clericalismo y asociacionismo católico [Women, clericalism and Catholic associationism]. In A. L. López & J. de la Cueva (Eds.), *Clericalismo y asociacionismo católico en España: De la Restauración a la transición* [*Clericalism and Catholic associationism in Spain: From the Restoration to the transition*] (pp. 107–131). Cuenca: Universidad de Castilla-La Mancha.

Nash, M. (1994). Experiencia y aprendizaje: La formación histórica de los feminismos en España [Experience and learning: The historical formation of feminisms in Spain]. *Historia Social, 20*, 151–172.

Osa, M., & Corduneanu-Huci, C. (2003). Running uphill: Political opportunity in non-democracies. *Comparative Sociology, 2*(4), 605–629.

Osa, M., & Schock, K. (2007). A long, hard slog: Political opportunities, social networks and the mobilization of dissent in non-democracies. *Research in Social Movements, Conflicts and Change, 27*, 123–153.

Radcliff, P. B. (2011). *Making democratic citizens in Spain: Civil society and the popular origins of the transition, 1960–78*. Basingstoke: Palgrave Macmillan.

Ruiz, R. (2007). *¿Eternas menores? Las mujeres en el franquismo* [*Eternal minors? Women in Franco's Spain*]. Madrid: Biblioteca Nueva.

Salas, M., & Comabella, M. (1999). Asociaciones de mujeres y movimiento feminista [Women's associations and the feminist movement]. In Asociación "Mujeres en la transición democrática" (Ed.), *Españolas en la transición: De excluidas a protagonistas (1973–1982)* [*Spanish women in the transition: From excluded to central figures*] (pp. 25–125). Madrid: Biblioteca Nueva.

Scanlon, G. (1976). *La polémica feminista en la España contemporánea (1868–1974)* [*Feminism in contemporary Spain (1868–1974)*]. Madrid: Siglo XXI.

Schneider, C. L. (1992). Radical opposition parties and squatters' movements in Pinochet's Chile. In A. Escobar & S. E. Alvarez (Eds.), *The making of social movements in Latin American: Identity, strategy, and democracy* (pp. 260–275). Boulder, CO: Westview Press.

Staggenborg, S. (1996). The survival of the women's movement: Turnover and continuity in Bloomington, Indiana. *Mobilization, 1*(2), 143–158.

Staggenborg, S., & Taylor, V. (2005). Whatever happened to the women's movement? *Mobilization, 10*(1), 37–52.

Taylor, V. (1989). Social movement continuity: The women's movement in abeyance. *American Sociological Review, 54*(5), 761–775.

APPENDIX: INTERVIEWS WITH AUTHOR

Álvarez de Miranda, C. (2010). Daughter of Consuelo de la Gándara. *Seminar for the sociological study of women*. Madrid, March 19.

Álvarez de Miranda, P. (2010). Son of Consuelo de la Gándara. *Seminar for the sociological study of women*. Madrid, February 3.

Borreguero, C. (2009). *Seminar for the sociological study of women*. Madrid, October 1, and October 22.

Comabella, M. (2009). *Housewives' organizations*. Madrid, November 19.

de Silva, Á. R. (2009). *Women's catholic action*. Madrid, November 9.

de Yzaguirre, P. (2009). *Association for cultural promotion and evolution*. Majadahonda (Madrid), August 28.

del Amor, M. (2010). Daughter in law of María Campo Alange. *Seminar for the Sociological Study of Women*. Madrid, April 13.

Jiménez, M. (2009). *Seminar for the sociological study of women*. Madrid, August 25.

Pérez-Seoane, C. (2009). *Seminar for the sociological study of women*. Madrid, October 1.

Quereizaeta, M. (2009). *Women's catholic action*. Madrid, October 7.

Rodríguez-Ponga, J. M. (2010). Grandson of María Campo Alange. *Seminar for the sociological study of women*. Madrid, March 16.

Salamanca, S. (2010). Daughter of María Campo Alange. *Seminar for the sociological study of women*. Madrid, April 6.

Salas, C. (2009). *Women's catholic action*. Madrid, September 25.

Salas, P. (2009). *Seminar for the sociological study of women*. Madrid, September 9.

Telo, M. (2009). *Spanish association of women lawyers*. Madrid, December 14.

Victory, C. (2009). *Women's catholic action*. Madrid, September 14.

Vindel, E. (2010). Daughter of Elena Catena. *Seminar for the sociological study of women*. Madrid, February 12.

ABOUT THE AUTHORS

Soma Chaudhuri is in the Department of Sociology and School of Criminal Justice at Michigan State University. Her research focuses on social movements, violence against women, and witch hunts. She has recently published a book on witchcraft accusations in India entitled *Witches, Tea Plantations, and Lives of Migrant Laborers in India.* She is currently working on a long-term project that explores how grassroots women participants in various empowerment programs strategize individually and collectively against domestic violence in their communities. The research is located in the city of Ahmedabad, and rural areas in the district of Kutchch and Patan, in Gujarat, India.

Patrick G. Coy is Professor and Director of the Center for Applied Conflict Management at Kent State University. He was a Fulbright Scholar in Botswana in 2010–2011, working with the Research Centre on San (Bushman) Studies. His research has been funded by the National Science Foundation, the Hewlett Foundation, the Albert Einstein Institution, the American Sociological Association, and the Council for International Exchange of Scholars. Recent publications include a co-authored book, *Contesting Patriotism: Culture, Power and Strategy in the Peace Movement.* Patrick G. Coy currently serves as Vice President of the Board of Directors of the International Peace Research Association Foundation, and as Vice President of the Board of Directors of the Cleveland Mediation Center. He has served as the Series Editor of *Research in Social Movements, Conflicts and Change* since 2000.

Carol L. Glasser is an Assistant Professor of Sociology at Minnesota State University, Mankato. Her published research addresses social movements, critical animal studies, and gender inequality. She is particularly interested in the intersections between gender and species inequality and is currently examining the relationship between the sexual abuse of women, children, and nonhuman animals. She is also interested in the role of public and applied sociology for community-based and social justice initiatives. She works regularly with various nonprofits and grassroots campaigns to conduct research and utilize research-based practices to support social justice initiatives.

Katja M. Guenther is an Associate Professor of Gender and Sexuality Studies at the University of California, Riverside. She is the author of *Making Their Place: Feminism after Socialism in Eastern Germany* (Stanford University Press, 2010). Her research interests include gender, social movements, feminism, and the state.

Howard Lune is an Associate Professor of Sociology and the Director of the Graduate Social Research Program at Hunter College, City University of New York. He specializes in research on organizations and organizational fields, with a particular focus on nonprofit and voluntary organizations. The majority of his research concerns the efforts by relatively marginal groups to organize for greater political, social, and economic power. He is presently working on a historical study of the development of the American Irish collective identity, from the founding of the United States to the end of the twentieth century.

Kelly Birch Maginot is a graduate student in the Department of Sociology at Michigan State University. Her research focuses on international migration, gender, and citizenship, in addition to feminist movements. Her dissertation explores how deported Salvadorans and their loved ones understand and practice social, cultural, and political citizenship in the United States and El Salvador. Her pre-dissertation research was conducted in San Salvador, El Salvador, during Summer 2014 on a Tinker Field Research grant.

Kerry Mulligan is an Assistant Professor of Law and Society at The Sage Colleges. She holds a PhD in Sociology from the University of California, Riverside. Her research examines the intersection of law and inequality, as well as how inequality is reproduced and resisted in institutional settings.

Sharon S. Oselin is an Assistant Professor of Sociology at the University of California, Riverside. Her research areas include gender, deviance and crime, and social movements (with a particular interest in peace movements). She is the author of *Leaving Prostitution: Getting Out and Staying Out of Sex Work* (2014), recently published by New York University Press. Her work also appears in the *American Sociological Review, Mobilization, Sociological Perspectives, Sexualities*, and elsewhere.

Christie L. Parris is an Assistant Professor of Sociology at Oberlin College. Her research focuses on social inequality, social movements, and environmental sociology. Her current research considers tactical choices of the environmental justice movement, perceptions of injustice regarding environmental and ecological injustice, and social movement factors affecting state-level policy passage. Her work has appeared in *Social Justice Research* and the *International Journal of Sustainability in Higher Education*. She received a BA in Humanities from the University of Tennessee in Chattanooga and an MA and PhD in Sociology from Emory University.

Natasha Radojcic holds a PhD in Sociology from the University of California, Riverside. Her research focuses on racial, class, and gender inequality in the LGBT Rights Movement and beyond.

Belinda Robnett is a Professor of Sociology at the University of California, Irvine. Her research interests include racial and ethnic inequality, gender relations, and social movements. She seeks to understand how racial-ethnic and gender hierarchies are formed by and maintained within formal and informal societal institutions. Her book, *How Long? How Long? African-American Women in the Struggle for Civil Rights*, analyzes the formation of women's leadership roles in the civil rights movement and highlights the gendered nature of leadership in social movements. As co-editor of *Social Movements: Identity, Culture, and the State* she was concerned with how gender intersected with organizational structure to reformulate the construction of collective identity among movement participants. Her work also examines racial hierarchy in the dating market, and illustrates that racial inclusion and exclusion is gendered. She is currently working on a book tentatively titled, *Surviving Success: African-American Political Organizations in "Post-Racial" America, 1970–2008.*

Heather L. Scheuerman is an Assistant Professor in the Department of Justice Studies at James Madison University. Her research centers on how social psychological concepts and processes structure behavior, including crime. She specifically focuses on issues of justice; broadly and in terms of how conceptualizations of justice and injustice affect behavioral outcomes. Her recent work has been published in *Justice Quarterly*, the *Journal of Criminal Justice, Sociology Compass*, and *Criminal Justice Policy Review*. She has received a BA in Sociology, Psychology, and Spanish from the State University of New York College at Geneseo and an MA and PhD in Sociology from Emory University.

Mangala Subramaniam is an Associate Professor in the Department of Sociology at Purdue University. Her research is in the broad areas of gender (and its intersections with caste, race, and class) and social movements. Her projects examine the dynamics between state power and collective action by the severely disadvantaged for rights to basic needs, such as water, food, and health. She has recently authored articles in journals such as *International Sociology* and *Current Sociology*. Her current research projects focus on violence against women and the law; gender and social impacts of institutional arrangements for improved seed technologies; and institutional arrangements for HIV prevention in India.

Elizabeth Tompkins (MA) is a graduate of Uppsala University's Department of Peace and Conflict Research, home of the internationally renowned Uppsala Conflict Data Program (UCDP). She has an interdisciplinary background in Psychology and Literary & Cultural Studies, and has investigated diverse topics such as prejudice and stereotyping, resistance movements and theory of nonviolence, child soldiers, and international crime. She is Cofounder of *PAX et BELLUM Journal* and has previously conducted research at the Institute for Security and Development Policy in Stockholm. Her current fields of interest include the rights of women in conflict and development, resistance movements, and the evolving role of journalism and the media in international affairs.

Rebecca Trammell is an Assistant Professor at Metropolitan State University of Denver. She studies inmate violence and misconduct. She is the author of the book, *Enforcing the Convict Code: Violence and Prison Culture*. Her work centers on how violence is socially constructed in prison and how inmates use violence as a social control mechanism. She also focuses on gender differences in prison culture and how men and women create relationships and manage their lives while incarcerated. Her work includes a study of restorative justices practices in Yemen and how women are shut out of this legal process. This lowers the life chances of girls and women living without the protection of local mediation rituals. She is currently working with data that focus on the connection between disrespectful behavior and inmate violence.

Celia Valiente is an Associate Professor of Sociology at the Department of Social Sciences of the Universidad Carlos III de Madrid, Spain. Her main research interests are the women's movement and gender-equality policies in Spain from a comparative perspective. She has published articles in *Gender & Society, Politics & Gender, European Journal of Political Research, South European Society & Politics*, and *Social Movement Studies*.

Beth Williford is an Associate Professor of Sociology in the Department of Sociology and Anthropology at Manhattanville College. Her research interests include transnational movements, globalization, indigenous peoples, and gender. She has published articles in *International Journal of Contemporary Sociology*, *Sociology Compass*, and *Theory in Action*. She is Program Director of Women's and Gender Studies at Manhattanville College where she also teaches a variety of classes including Activism and Social Change, Indigenous Peoples, Women in Society, and Latin American Social Movements.